GREATER CINCINNATI
BICENTENNIAL HISTORY SERIES

Board of Editors

Zane L. Miller

Gene D. Lewis

BOOKS IN THE SERIES

Making Better Citizens:
Housing Reform and the Community Development
Strategy in Cincinnati, 1890–1960
Robert B. Fairbanks

Ethnic Diversity and Civic Identity:
Patterns of Conflict and Cohesion in Cincinnati since 1820
Edited by Henry D. Shapiro and Jonathan D. Sarna

ETHNIC DIVERSITY AND CIVIC IDENTITY

Ethnic Diversity and Civic Identity

*Patterns of Conflict and Cohesion in
Cincinnati since 1820*

EDITED BY

Henry D. Shapiro
and Jonathan D. Sarna

UNIVERSITY OF ILLINOIS PRESS
Urbana and Chicago

Published with the help of the Charles Phelps Taft Memorial Fund,
University of Cincinnati.

An earlier version of Jonathan D. Sarna's essay, "'A Sort of
Paradise for the Hebrews': The Lofty Vision of Cincinnati
Jews," appeared in *Jews of Cincinnati.* Copyright ©1989
by the Center for the Study of the American Jewish Exper-
ience, Hebrew Union College—Jewish Institute of Religion.
Reprinted by permission.

Library of Congress Cataloging-in-Publication Data

Ethnic diversity and civic identity: patterns of conflict and
     cohesion in Cincinnati since 1820/edited by Henry D. Shapiro and
     Jonathan D. Sarna.
          p. cm.—(Greater Cincinnati bicentennial history series)
     ISBN 0-252-01883-4 (cl: acid-free paper)
     1. Cincinnati (Ohio)—Social conditions. 2. Cincinnati (Ohio)—
Ethnic relations—History. 3. Social classes—Ohio—Cincinnati—
History. 4. Social conflict—Ohio—Cincinnati—History.
I. Shapiro, Henry D. II. Sarna, Jonathan D. III. Series.
HN80.C55E87 1992
306'.09771'78—dc20   91-27112
                                                            CIP

Contents

Foreword

This book reminds us that historians of cities, like residents of cities, inevitably confront the stunning diversity of the persons they study and meet. To render this diversity manageable we categorize these persons (and ourselves) into groups, attribute characteristics to the groups, and define the nature of the interaction of the groups. This practice may be seen as the source of our habit of dividing persons into "ethnic" groups. But as this book makes clear, "ethnicity" is an elusive concept because it has meant different things in different periods of the past. In addition, this volume raises doubts about the contemporary assumption of a necessary connection of people, place, and culture.

For these reasons and others, readers of this collection of essays, whether Cincinnatians or not, will find it useful in thinking about the past and the meaning and significance of immigration, ethnicity, and social and urban history. The Preface and Introduction illuminate themes common to the essays, including the conflicting loyalties inherent in the dual identities of people as members of both ethnic and civic communities. The essays treat ethnic diversity and consciousness in relation to the life of the city and explore in a variety of ways various issues, conflicts, and shifts of thought from the mid-nineteenth century into that recent past in which we yet live. All but two are published here for the first time.

Ethnic Diversity and Civic Identity is the second volume in the Greater Cincinnati Bicentennial History Series, which addresses a broad range of historical topics relating to the Cincinnati region. Additional volumes will be published over the next several years. The series is a joint venture of

Foreword

the Cincinnati Historical Society and the Department of History and the Center for Neighborhood and Community Studies at the University of Cincinnati.

Zane L. Miller
Gene D. Lewis

Preface

When we first announced our intention to edit a collection of essays on ethnic diversity in Cincinnati, one wag said: "Well, I guess it'll be a pretty short book."

This isn't, but that smart remark has stood as a reminder that Cincinnati, unlike other great cities, does not define itself as an ethnically diverse community. Despite the city's attractiveness to immigrants throughout the nineteenth and twentieth centuries and the presence in her population of identifiable ethnic groups, moreover, Cincinnati's ethnic diversity does not manifest itself in the expected forms, of ethnic restaurants catering primarily to ethnic populations, ethnic neighborhoods with shops serving specialized ethnic needs, ethnic festivals celebrated principally by members of ethnic groups as events in their communal calendars, or ethnic politics. To some degree, this is the result of Cincinnati's history and especially of its situation—where it was, and when it was there.

◊   ◊   ◊

In 1787, Congress granted proprietorship of a million acres in the American West to a syndicate of New Jersey and Pennsylvania investors, the Miami Purchase Association. Under the leadership of John Cleves Symmes, the proprietors initiated an active campaign to make their Ohio valley domain attractive to prospective settlers. They laid out town-lots, streets, market squares and other public spaces. They set aside a thirty-six square-mile township as the future site for a college and called it "Oxford" as proof that civilization could flourish in the West. They granted monopolies to persons who would invest in local improvements like mills, ferries, and bridges. Most of all, according to Symmes, they made the purchase of land easy for individual settlers.

The town of Cincinnati itself was established in 1788 on high ground along the Ohio River, in a natural amphitheater with a south facing conducive to the development of market-gardening and later, viticulture. The surrounding hills would soon become sites for the location of country estates and incorporated suburban villages, creating barriers to the geographic expansion of the city. At the outset they were visual barriers only, but they gave the first settlers in the basin a sense of contained space, of safety, and security. The location of Fort Washington at Cincinnati must also have contributed to this overall sense of well-being.

The hills themselves were easily bypassed, even in the days of horse travel. The north bank of the Ohio formed a series of steps, providing a broad, flat strip of land running east and west of Cincinnati, between the hills and the river. The Deer Creek Valley opened out between the hills to the northeast. The glacial outwash valley of the Mill Creek divided the hills on the northwest side of the basin and intersected with westward tending valleys whose names are now forgotten, but which once formed the principal overland routes from Cincinnati to the newer settlements in Indiana and Illinois. After 1810, with the introduction of steamboats on the Ohio, traffic on that river ran in two directions. After 1828, with the construction of the Miami and Erie Canal, traffic on the Deer Creek and Mill Creek ran in two directions. Whether on foot, on horse, on canal boat, river boat, or rail car, from Cincinnati you could get where you wanted to go. To get there, however, you had to pass through the city. Many did. Many stayed.

During its first century of existence, Cincinnati attracted immigrants from the eastern and southern states as well as from abroad (especially Ireland and the German-speaking areas of Central Europe, the dominant sources of American immigration during this period), and rapidly assimilated them into an emerging urban culture. By 1850, the population of Cincinnati exceeded one hundred thousand. By 1870 it exceeded two hundred thousand, including eighty thousand persons of foreign birth. Commerce and manufacturing flourished. So did banking, land speculating, printing, politics, and the professions, along with education, the arts, natural science, and music.

As a community, Cincinnati concerned itself with growth and the mechanisms that would encourage growth, including the growth of its population. Its special passions were internal improvements and civic improvements—the construction of canals, roads and turnpikes, railroads, bridges, wharves, streets, street railways, sewers, waterworks, gasworks (and later on, electric generating stations), market houses, hospitals, concert halls, theaters, parks, and fountains. Few questioned the desirability of such improvements, which seemed to enhance the city's economic vitality and its quality of life at the same time, and made the city even more attractive to immigrants. What *was* debated, always long and often bitterly, was the manner in which these improvements should be carried out, and once they were completed, how they should be managed and maintained. Out of these debates emerged a political culture dedicated to growth, a civic culture of business and busy-ness. In the meantime, completion of the city's grand system of infrastructure improvements created an unintended civic landscape of monumental structures—canals, waterworks, bridges, parks, a city hall, a Music Hall—which served the community and stood as emblems of community, making Cincinnati's civic culture legible to all its citizens.

In this context, Cincinnati welcomed newcomers as additional hands to do the city's work, but also because their arrival increased the city's total population and gave continued proof of Cincinnati's status as the metropolis of the West. The newcomers themselves, wherever they were from, found in Cincinnati places to work and places to walk, places for employment and places for enjoyment. But they also found a civic culture that discouraged ethnic separatism, and city-wide institutions—including organized Protestantism, organized Catholicism, and organized Judaism—that pushed the newcomers into the life of the city as a whole. What this life was "like" is not entirely clear now, after a century or more, nor was it clear to the writers of guidebooks and travel sketches during the nineteenth century. Residents and visitors did know, however, that Cincinnati was its own place. It looked like itself. It behaved like itself. It sounded like itself. It was concerned with itself. And somehow or other, sheltered by its surrounding hills, it was the product of itself, of all its people.

◊　　◊　　◊

The histories of other industrial cities in the Northeast and Midwest to which European immigrants also flocked during the nineteenth and twentieth centuries suggest that different patterns prevailed in those places. America's seaboard cities, for example, were well-established urban centers by the beginning of the nineteenth century, with resident populations living in established, if uneasy, relationship to each other when the first period of large-scale foreign immigration began. As a result, the arrival of the newcomers not only placed stresses on those cities' service delivery systems (their ability to provide housing, employment, and so forth) but also threatened to unravel the web of existing social, economic, and political relationships. Old-timers responded by closing ranks to exclude the newcomers, to which the newcomers responded by establishing separate ("ethnic") systems of social, economic, and political relationships—at the very time that Cincinnati, as a new city in the West that necessarily drew its population from somewhere else, was emerging as a place where all were immigrants together.

In the lake cities, from Buffalo to Milwaukee, similar conditions prevailed during the late nineteenth and early twentieth centuries, when a second great period of foreign immigration commenced. These cities too were western cities, with populations drawn from somewhere else, but until the late nineteenth century their populations were small and came largely from the eastern United States. As a result, they too experienced massive stresses on existing patterns of social, economic, and political relationships when toward the end of the century immigrants began arriving in great numbers from Ireland and Germany as well as from the newer emigrant areas of southern and eastern Europe. As in Boston, New York, and Philadelphia during an earlier period, here too the old-timers—including many persons who were themselves of foreign birth—responded by closing ranks against the newcomers, and the newcomers responded by establishing separate communities.

In late nineteenth-century Cincinnati, by contrast, while the absolute number of foreign immigrants remained high, the rate of immigration declined. This decline, indeed, was the problem Cincinnatians worried about, not the sudden influx of newcomers that seemed so threatening elsewhere. And while in the Great Lakes' cities, as elsewhere in America, distinctions were made between the "old" immigrants and the "new" immigrants in such a way as to imply the essential "unassimilability" of populations from southern and eastern Europe into existing communities, Cincinnatians seemed to view all immigrants as Germans, whether they were or not. So it was just more of the same old thing, which had been a pretty good thing to begin with.

◊ ◊ ◊

Especially when compared to other industrial cities, where ethnic restaurants, ethnic neighborhoods, ethnic festivals, and ethnic politics became and remain an essential characteristic of the culture of the place, Cincinnati in the late twentieth century at least *seems* to lack ethnic diversity and ethnic divisiveness both. The city's ethnic restaurants (especially its four- and five-star "French" restaurants) serve a citywide, if not a national clientele. Its ethnic festivals are a recent development and attract—are intended to attract—visitors from the entire region. From the very first they have been promoted as major events in Cincinnati's civic calendar, of public events celebrating the community of the whole. Residential segregation of ethnic or nationality groups, whether by choice or necessity, is rare in the present. But even diligent scholarship has yielded little evidence that ethnic segregation or patterns of "ethnic succession" in neighborhoods was a special characteristic of Cincinnati in the past. And in Cincinnati, ethnic politics was never dominant even during the period of boss rule in the city. Instead, throughout the city's history more conventional patterns of American politics have prevailed, of party rather than group loyalty, and of division over how best to achieve growth and development.

Local promoters of ethnic group identity and of "ethnic pride" will surely disagree with this view of Cincinnati as a city where ethnicity is largely a private fact rather than a public issue, if only because it seems to ignore their own efforts to alter this situation. And it is true that, as ethnicity has come to seem a desirable basis for self-identification in recent years, individual Cincinnatians have discovered, or chosen, an ethnic heritage to celebrate, and sometimes have formed societies or associations of persons claiming a common ethnic background. In this they are simply acting like the Americans they are, at a time when we have all discovered ethnicity as an aspect of our identities intermediate between self and species, and as a heritage intermediate between the sometimes too-personal legacy of family experience and the always impersonal legacy of national history. The fact that some Cincinnatians now express pride because their ancestors once lived somewhere else and take a new interest in their extramural roots does not make ethnic diversity, much less ethnic divisiveness, a special characteristic of Cincinnati as a whole, however. Neither does the historian's ability to find manifestations of ethnic consciousness in the city's past.

Promoters of Cincinnati as a sophisticated and cosmopolitan community may also disagree with our assessment of ethnic diversity as an apparently unimportant factor in the creation of the city's character, as suggesting that the Queen City is "merely" midwestern and boring. In recent years, chambers of commerce and convention and visitors' bureaus across the nation have taught us that ethnic diversity is proof of a city's modern, cosmopolitan character, and one of its attractions, like every city's quaint and charming "old town" of preserved historic buildings. There are ironies aplenty, here, in contemporary attempts to differentiate among places by emphasizing characteristics all those places once shared and that earlier generations viewed as obstacles to the achievement of progress and "the pleasing homogeneity" of modern life. As a result, every city now asserts its twentieth-century uniqueness by celebrating its nineteenth-century German heritage and holding an *Oktoberfest* every September, so that the common culture of the present becomes overlaid with an ersatz common culture of the past, a kind of "pioneer days" for urban areas of the nation. It may be fun, but it ain't history.

◊   ◊   ◊

The essays in this volume respond to the reality of Cincinnati's history as an ethnically diverse community, rather than to twentieth-century notions about what the meaning and consequences of ethnic diversity in the past probably were, or to the usefulness of ethnicity as a classifier of human groups or as the basis for individual identity. They do not assume that the presence in a population of persons of diverse ethnic origins will inevitably yield a society divided into distinct ethnic groups pursuing distinct and competing agendas. But they do explore some of the circumstances under which ethnic diversity seemed to threaten civic harmony if not civic unity, and to emerge as a "problem" in the life of the city. They do not assume that ethnicity was (or is, or ought to be) a more powerful basis for the formation of group identification than religion, occupation, avocation, social class, or residence, or that the shared experience of migration or the shared heritage of common ethnic or national origins yielded homogeneous ethnic or immigrant communities whose histories can be written. But they do explore some of the circumstances under which the formation of ethnic group identity or the "maintenance" of ethnic unity was urged upon particular segments of Cincinnati's population, sometimes as a politically useful strategy and sometimes because it seemed a "natural" basis for the classification of "the races and peoples" of America. Nor do these essays assume that individuals in the past or in the present felt (or ought to feel) obliged to identify themselves in terms of one and only one category of social experience—as Germans rather than chess players. But they do explore some of the circumstances under which ethnic group identity seemed in conflict with "membership" in other kinds of groups, and some of the consequences that followed from that conflict.

Thus, the essays in this volume do not attempt to do the kind of work that we have come to expect from studies in "immigration history" or "ethnic history." They do not attempt to describe the characteristics and experiences of Cincinnati's immigrants, nor to write the "histories" of Cincinnati's ethnic groups. They do not attempt to list the contributions of Cincinnati's immigrant populations to the life of the city. They do not describe the ways in which ethnic leadership or ethnic institutions facilitated the immigrants' accommodation to American life, or conversely, in the manner of more recent scholarship, the ways in which these facilitated the maintenance of ethnic group distinctiveness. And they do not pretend to describe the ways in which Cincinnati, because of the particular ethnic composition of its population, was like or unlike other American cities and does or does not display unique patterns of culture in the present.

Instead, they attempt to address ethnic diversity directly, as a fact of Cincinnati's history, by examining situations in which some of its citizens identified themselves, or were identified by others, in terms of where they were from (or where their ancestors were from), rather than exclusively in terms of where they were. Some of the essays focus on the meaning of ethnicity for members of particular ethnic groups. Others focus on the meaning of ethnic diversity for the community as a whole. All, however, treat ethnicity and ethnic diversity not as distinct phenomena to be studied, celebrated, or bemoaned, but rather as normal aspects of modern life, as familiar a part of the urban experience as streets and markets.

Thus informed, the reader is free to dive directly into the essays, or to begin the exploration of ethnic diversity and civic identity in Cincinnati in a more leisurely fashion by reading the introduction to this volume.

◊   ◊   ◊

Under a different name and with a somewhat different intention, this project was initiated by Professor Roger Daniels of the Department of History, University of Cincinnati. We wish to acknowledge the substantial contributions he made before we assumed editorial responsibilities for its completion, and his continuing personal support of our efforts. We are grateful to our authors for their patience and cooperation as the volume took shape through many revisions, and for the encouragement and good advice provided by Professors Zane L. Miller and Gene D. Lewis, the editors of the Cincinnati Bicentennial History Series, and by Richard Wentworth and his staff at the University of Illinois Press.

Generous grants in aid of publication were provided by the Fellows of the Graduate School of the University of Cincinnati and by the Charles Phelps Taft Memorial Fund, for which support we are especially grateful.

Henry D. Shapiro
Jonathan D. Sarna

HENRY D. SHAPIRO

Ethnic Diversity and Civic Identity: An Introduction to the Problem and to the Essays

Ethnicity and Individual Identity

Until quite recently, ethnicity in America was a fact that all of us recognized but few of us liked to acknowledge, either as an aspect of national diversity or an element in our individual identities. By "ethnicity" we mean the possession of cultural traits that are the result of ancestry rather than of choice. Ethnicity unites persons of common ancestry into groups whose coherence is founded on their members' possession of common traits *and* their acknowledgement of a common ancestry. Like the concept of "race" to which it is closely related, ethnicity thus describes an American population divided by characteristics that can neither be abandoned nor shared with individuals of different ancestry. Ethnicity says that even when we eat together we do not become one people. The lines between ethnic groups, like the lines between "races," thus become barriers that cannot be crossed, and ethnic group divisions appear permanent and real, the product of the irreversible fact of ancestry. One may choose one's friends but not one's parents, or one's children, or one's ethnicity.

The concept of "race" uses the inherited physical characteristics of individuals (height, hair color, etc.) to divide the American population into groups on the basis of traits that are extraneous to the operation of a social or political system. We have thus felt no loss at our late twentieth-century abandonment of race as a central concept of social theory.[1] Ethnicity, by contrast, uses the inherited cultural characteristics of individuals to divide the American population into groups on the basis of traits that are the fundamental stuff of a social or political system, including values, language preference, and behavior. When one group possesses one set of cultural characteristics and another group possesses a different set,

1

and when these characteristics are the product of inheritance, however, America looks like not one people but several—now and in the future. That is one of our problems with ethnicity. In addition, each of us as individuals seems limited by the accident of our ancestry to a single choice of values, behaviors, and language preference—our "mother tongue" whether we know it or not. The concept of ethnicity, that is, seems to require that we eat what our parents ate, speak the way our parents spoke, raise our children the way our parents raised us, believe what our parents believed, if we are to be "ourselves." So there's another problem, and either way, ethnicity presents us with a dilemma. How can we Americans be one people if we are so profoundly and permanently divided by the irreversible fact of our multiple ancestry? And how can we as individuals be our American selves if we are bound by the accident of ancestry to retain the cultural traits of the nations and peoples from whom we are descended?

◊   ◊   ◊

Nonetheless, as human beings we have a passion for classifying things, including other human beings, and for naming things according to their classes. We want a name for ourselves and for all others, and we want names for all important subdivisions of ourselves. One simple system (that may also be universal, according to the anthropologists) distinguishes between ourselves and all others. We are called "us" or "ourselves" or "the people" or "the real people." Everyone else is called "them" or "the others," and it is clear that "ourselves" is good and "the others" is not so good. (In some languages, anthropologists tell us, "the others" is actually the same as "the bad," but this is probably only among "primitive" peoples; we moderns usually try to explain *why* "the others" is bad.) Ethnicity, which is a word that comes out of anthropology to begin with, partakes to some degree in this simple we-they system, just as identity formation develops in part out of the conscious separation of the self and "the other" (which some say is actually "the Mother").

One way or another, however, ethnicity, like identity, functions not only to classify the units of reality but also to establish the reality of the self (or the group). But here we have a puzzle. The establishment of identity, the separation of the self from the other/mother, frequently seems to be frought with peril, to appear, to the actor, as a dangerous act. Psychologists and anthropologists have notions about why this is and

2

have developed a rich literature exploring the "myths" used to explain these dangers, including the reasons for keeping secret one's "own" name. At the same time, however, the self must be asserted. The resolution of the tension thus created is one of the goals of "adjustment" according to psychologists, one of the functions of "culture" according to anthropologists; and practitioners of both disciplines have much to say about how this is achieved, differently in different cultures.

To a considerable degree, ethnicity in America participates in this same pattern. On the one hand, our ethnic identities—our membership in a group comprising persons who came from, or whose ancestors came from, a particular place—is an aspect of our sense of ourselves as distinct individuals. On the other hand, for each of us personally and for each ethnic group collectively, the assertion of self, of identity, of separateness, sometimes seem fraught with danger. At the very least, it will cut us off from the other/Mother, from membership in the larger group defined (here) in terms of nationality rather than "national origins." At the very least, it will force them to see *us* as other, different, alien; to develop a certain caution when dealing with us; to establish formal mechanisms for dealing with us, structures of relationship; and to develop formal constructs for explaining our otherness in order to resolve the tension between us and them, the conflict that our presence creates. When we begin talking about ethnicity we step out onto a perilous path.

How Americans have negotiated this path is one of the issues this book explores, indirectly, however, through a series of essays examining aspects of Cincinnati's experience as an ethnically diverse community. Some of the essays focus on the actions of individuals as they attempted to achieve some balance between the assertion of their identities as members of one or another ethnic group and their identities as members of a civic community with its own history, traditions, and culture—to the making of which they also contributed. Others focus on the actions of "the community" —what in an older tradition of analysis was called the "civis" or "body politic"—as it sought to respond to the presence of newcomers in the city and newcomers *to* the city, and to integrate them into the society, the economy, and the culture of Cincinnati.

So this is also a book about Cincinnati and its people, particularly those who came from Europe in the nineteenth century or whose parents or grandparents came from Europe in the nineteenth century, and who were identified (by themselves or by others) in terms of their European origins rather than in terms of their American destination, where they were *from* rather than where they *were*. But what happened in Cincinnati can illuminate the patterns of conflict and accomodation around the matter of ethnic identity and ethnic diversity elsewhere in the nation, and in America more generally. Whatever the particularities of Cincinnati's situation, however "special" it has seemed as a place to live, work, or visit—in the nineteenth century or in the twentieth—the city has always measured itself against other American places, other American communities, and from its earliest days as a frontier outpost envisioned itself as a great *American* city. And even in the late nineteenth century, when its high proportion of German-born or German-descended citizens led at least one observer to call it "practically a foreign city,"[2] its people were active participants in all aspects of American life, and whether native-born or foreign, defined their values and themselves, in American terms.

This focus on Cincinnati is not intended to make it a "test case" for the working out of some hypothesis. No claims are made here concerning the city's "typicality" or "atypicality." Cincinnati provides us merely with a convenient window into the past and, since it is the place where all of us have lived and worked, a community of continuing interest to us in the present. The concerns of this book are with American life and thought, and particularly with the ways in which Americans, irrespective of the ethnic group with which they most closely identify themselves (or are identified by others), have dealt with the matter of ethnic diversity. That is, after all, one of the mysteries we perform every day in America. We negotiate a sense of self as members of a variety of communities at the same time—ethnic, occupational, residential, religious, civic, regional, and national—all the while attempting to preserve our individual freedoms of choice over what we consider the important questions of the day, in politics but also in dress, hairstyle, manners, morals, foodways, public behavior, private behavior, and life-style.

Ethnicity As an Issue in an Age of Nationality

One of the great inventions of the nineteenth century was the idea of "nation." Nation linked people, place, and culture into a new kind of unit reflecting the new political, social, and economic realities of that century of progress and orderliness. Nation described a world in which geopolitical boundaries were fixed and natural, the product of history more than of diplomacy, comprising the appropriate limits of a particular people's territory. Nation described a world in which populations were distinct, differentiated from each other by language and tradition, by physical traits, dress, customs, belief systems, and by their location in time and space—especially space. Nation described a world in which geography influenced history and culture (some said both were in fact the product of geography) but also, as "environment," shaped the physical characteristics of the species and "races" that inhabited a particular terrain.

Nation also described a world in which an individual's "loyalty" was more appropriately directed to his people, place, and culture than to any king or prince, and individual identity was more appropriately derived from nationality than the status of being subject to a particular "sovereign." From this perspective, emigration and immigration created problems both practical and theoretical. If national boundaries were fixed and natural, what should be the policy of the national governments toward those who wished to cross boundaries? If populations were distinct and were defined most accurately (or most appropriately) by nationality, what were the consequences of crossing from one nation's territory into another's? If culture were linked to place as the product of history and environment, did customs, language, beliefs, and behaviors learned in one place become dysfunctional when a people moved to another place? These were among the great issues dominating public debate during the last decades of the nineteenth century and the first decades of the twentieth and provided particular focus for the emerging disciplines of ethnology and anthropology, human geography ("anthropogeography"), sociology, economics, and to some degree history, political science, and philology. For Americans in particular, these issues created, and continue to create, special difficulties.

Like "the" French, "the" Germans, or "the" English, we have assumed the existence of some ineffable pattern of culture, some spirit, some characteristic civilization that makes us ourselves and makes us different from other peoples. It is our Americanness that makes us feel as strangers when we travel abroad, and which makes immigrants and visitors alike feel like the aliens they are when first they arrive within our borders. But it is this also which makes us ourselves, allows us to talk to each other, to agree upon what is important, and to recognize the issues that divide us as well as those that unite us.

Yet while the French, the Germans, and the English assume that the "sources" of their respective national cultures are the product of their own national experience, borne by a homogeneous population resident in a unified landscape since the beginning of time, Americans have traditionally assumed that the sources of *their* culture, like the sources of their population,

5

were European, brought to the New World by generations of immigrants, representatives of all the nations and all the peoples of the world. How, then, can there be *an* American culture if the Americans are so diverse; and how can these diverse peoples be *Americans* if they, and their cultures, derive from all the places in the world?[3]

In addition, because we take unity and homogeneity to be an essential characteristic of American civilization (despite the evidence of our senses, which tells us about the reality of diversity, and the evidence of our history, which tells us about the normality of change), the persistence of ethnic identifications seems to deny unity and homogeneity. This is true, moreover, even when it is alleged to be an element in the creation of unity and homogeneity through the "pluralist" combination of many trees making one forest. At the same time, however, because we assume that who we are is where we're from, we believe that our origins as individuals and as a people (or peoples) must be taken into account, and that as a people our heritage, i.e., our geographic and cultural experiences in other places, will be as significant in shaping our present as our "history," i.e., our experience of the geography and culture of the United States. And because we also assume that diversity is a real characteristic of American society and culture, in its origins if not in its current forms, and that such diversity *ought* to make national unity and homogeneity impossible while the absence of unity and homogeneity *ought* to make intergroup conflict inevitable, we wonder why we are not always at each other's throats, indeed if there is any *we* at all.

◊   ◊   ◊

Emigration and immigration were patterns of human behavior long before the idea of nation linked people, place, and culture, but the issues they raised were of a different order in that earlier period. Especially during the eighteenth century, the migration of peoples was discussed in terms of its impact on a state and sovereign rather than on a nation and its civilization. Emigration and immigration involved the loss or gain of labor and thereby the depletion or enrichment of the resources—the wealth—of a nation-state. Since the world's resources remained constant, what one sovereign lost through emigration, another gained through immigration. What disadvantaged the one gave advantage to the other.[4] The act of migrating itself, moreover, was viewed as involving simply a transfer of allegiance from one sovereign to another. But this was a normal aspect of the human experience, contemporaries believed. One did not have to migrate in order to transfer one's allegiance. Even if one stayed always in the same place, the sovereigns came and went in orderly or sometimes disorderly succession. "The King is dead, long live the King" was no paradox, even in America.

It was from this perspective that Hector St. Jean de Crevecoeur discussed the characteristics of the American population and the availability of America as a destination for emigrants, when the United States was barely an independent nation-state. And while we have generally taken his remarks to mean that American civilization would be the product of the American experience, and thus to foreshadow our later Turnerian vision of the sources of American uniqueness, in fact Crevecoeur was talking about Americans' experience as defined by eighteenth-century concerns rather than those of a later era. For Crevecoeur, becoming American had little to do with issues of national identity, with concepts of the unity and homogeneity of people, place, and culture. For him, all that was involved was for the immigrant to give up his European (or Asian, or African) identity along with his allegiance to his European (or Asian, or African) place of birth and its rulers. It was a trade, and of a sort that contemporaries, living in an age of mercantilism, could not have misunderstood. For the migrants to America, he thought, it amounted to a pretty good deal.

What then is the American, this new man? He is either an European, or the descendant of an European, hence that strange mixture of blood, which you will find in no other country.... *He* is an American, who leaving behind him all his ancient prejudices and manners, receives new ones from the new mode of life he has embraced, the new government he obeys, and the new rank he holds. He becomes an American by being received in the broad lap of our great *Alma Mater.* Here individuals of all nations are melted into a new race of men, whose labours and posterity will one day cause great changes in the world. Americans are the western pilgrims, who are carrying along with them that great mass of arts, sciences, vigour, and industry which began long since in the east; they will finish the great circle. The Americans were once scattered all over Europe; here they are incorporated into one of the finest systems of population which has ever appeared, and which will heareafter become distinct by the power of the different climates they inhabit.... The American is a new man, who acts upon new principles; he must therefore entertain new ideas, and form new opinions.[5]

Crevecoeur's eloquence tends to blind us to the conventional character of his discourse on American civilization, and especially on the creation of an "American" population. In an age of nation-states, the "Americani-zation" of the immigrant was the product of transferring allegiance, of simultaneously abandoning and accepting. And since what was to be accepted was never entirely clear, except as an alternative to (sometime the opposite of) what was being abandoned, when Americans worried about immigration they focused on the danger to America that might occur if immigrants did not completely renounce their old allegiance.

Although this issue had its origins at least in the late colonial period and was discussed as a question of public policy during the Revolutionary and Early National periods, it became a matter of special concern during the second quarter of the nineteenth century, when the first waves of Catholic immigrants arrived in the United States, first the Irish, then the Germans. For while these emigrants from the oppression of princes and emperors might be presumed to have renounced by the act of emigration their old political allegiances, were they not still in thrall to the oppression of priest and bishop, and that prince among bishops, the Pope in Rome? How then could they be freemen and republicans?[6]

The Germans presented an additional problem. As the first non-English-speaking population to arrive in the United States in significant numbers, they struck the Americans as clannish, preferring to retain their old-world identities instead of adopting new ones in their new home. They spoke German among themselves and when their numbers permitted, they established German newspapers and German schools for their children. They seemed to bring with them not only old-world patterns of politics, including rivalries between Catholics and Protestants, church members and freethinkers, political liberals and political conservatives, but also a commitment to continued participation from America as a home base, in the European forums through which these disputes were played out.[7]

Extensive immigration from the German states during the 1840s and 1850s in particular, thus raised a new question for Americans, about what would happen if the newcomers, having renounced their old allegiance, were unwilling to renounce as completely the language and culture of their native place. The terms of discussion thus began to shift, from assimilation as the product of individual choice in the matter of political allegiance, to the possibility of integrating groups of individuals into a social and cultural system with unwritten rules that the newcomers might violate without quite knowing it. The extensive German immigration of the mid-century thus provided the occasion (but certainly not the cause) of new American attempts to define the characteristics of American civilization, and of a new American concern about the ease with which "Americanization" might occur. For while Crevecoeur's observation still seemed to apply to most immigrants of this period, that "he becomes an American by being received in the broad lap of our great *Alma Mater,*" at least some of the Germans insisted on having both parents; and like all children, sometimes found their loyalties divided.

◊   ◊   ◊

It is this issue of the dilemma of divided loyalty, its implications for the formation of ethnic group identity, and its impact on the political and social life of Cincinnati that the first essays in this volume especially illuminate. To set the Cincinnati scene, we begin with a selection from Franz von Löher's *Land und Leute in der alten und neuen Welt: Reiseskizzen* (1855), translated and edited by Professor Frederick Trautmann, describing Queen City conditions in 1849–50. Löher's account—one of the numerous descriptions of Cincinnati offered to the public during the second quarter of the nineteenth century—may be read in several ways, but it is first of all a representative example of contemporary travel literature.

Journals of journeys formed a wildly popular genre during the mid-nineteenth century, interesting for their own sake but also highly esteemed during a practical age for their obvious utility to emigrants, immigrants, and recreational travelers. Like other writers in the genre, Löher begins his account with the obligatory statement of the hardship of travel, which gave the journey elevated status and social respectability as expedition, and merit to the voyager, as explorer; mixes descriptions of life and landscape with observation and speculation on the character of America and Americans—still worth wondering about at mid-century (within two decades the focus of travel literature would shift to more exotic places, the American West of miners, cowboys, and buffalo hunters, Stanley's Africa, or American places made exotic by saying so); and, more immediate to our current concerns, takes his turn at assessing the status of German culture in Cincinnati.[8] Thus Löher may also be read for the picture of Cincinnati that he paints. And here each reader must decide which of Löher's comments are the most delicious, the most interesting, or the most helpful.

My own favorites (at the moment) are these: First, I delight in his assertion of Cincinnati's uniqueness, as the place where "the contrasts of the American East and West, together with European influences, form a new American character." Did Löher read Crevecoeur, one wonders, and find Cincinnati the convenient venue for perceiving the emergence of "that new man, the American," or did he crib from one of the numerous accounts of Cincinnati's current situation and future prospects published during the period? Did he hold conversation over dinner one evening with the famous Dr. Daniel Drake, who had just completed his own analysis of the social and ethnic character of Cincinnati for the first volume of his monumental *Systematic Treatise ... on the Principal Diseases of the Interior Valley of North America* (1850) when Löher arrived in town? Or did he make it up himself out of contemporary ideas about the consequences of mixing cultures and "races" and his own observation of Cincinnati as a culturally and ethnically mixed society? Whatever the case, Löher's observation, entered here in passing, is at once characteristic of the genre and an important reminder of the degree to which America did in fact seem a new world, and Cincinnati a new kind of place—a place of possibilities, suitable for the making of new kinds of decisions, the new solution to old problems.

And I like his description immediately following, of Cincinnati's celebration of the anniversary of the landing of the Pilgrims—the toasts made with "thin coffee" and the tables laden with "half-ripe produce"—but even more his recognition of the complex loading of this anniversary with cultural meaning. For its establishment as an event in Cincinnati's civic calendar linked the city with a seminal event in *American* (rather than local) history, suggesting analogies between the founding of the nation and the founding of the city. It also celebrated America (and by implication, Cincinnati) as a place of newcomers—immigrants all, but more particularly of Pilgrims—searchers after some lost possibility or some future hope; and asserted the providential character of Cincinnati's history, like that of America itself. As Löher says, "If the Land of freedom, where milk and honey flow, home to the holy Pilgrims, is not heaven itself, it is surely the next thing to heaven."

◊   ◊   ◊

But Pilgrims are also strangers in a strange land. This doubled edge of the image also informs Löher's observations. All elements in Cincinnati society, but especially the city's Germans, seem isolated to him, separated one from the other and from the whole that the city claimed to be. "Even in the happiest company a little of the feeling remains that one is in something of a land of exile." One may speculate about the roots of such a feeling, whether it is of the essence of the human condition, or a product of the European experience of being transplanted from ancient communities to the soil of the New World, or a peculiarity of life in the American "West" when Ohio was the frontier. Surely it was not a feeling particular to Cincinnati's German-born; for the sense of loss and of the pastness of the past that was a normal accompaniment to the fact of exile, pervaded all elements of American society during the mid-nineteenth century, vying with the equally pervasive sense of promise, of America as future, which flourished during these years.

◊　　◊　　◊

In "Community Divided: German Immigrants, Social Class, and Political Conflict in Antebellum Cincinnati," Bruce Levine describes some of the ways in which Cincinnati's Americanness, its condition as a place of possibilities, exacerbated differences among German immigrants to the city, creating patterns of diversity within the German-American community based on social class and occupation, but especially on ideology. Among the most striking of those he discusses, was a special kind of intergenerational conflict, between the liberals who fled the fatherland after the failed revolution of 1830 and those who fled the fatherland after the failed revolution of 1848. At issue here, as also in the contemporary conflict between German-American liberals and German-American conservatives, was not so much the matter of how the German systems of governance should be changed, however, but how the promise of American life might be realized, and the role that German-Americans could or should play in that process.

This discussion is especially important as a counter to the often self-serving arguments of later observers (including professional historians) concerning Germania's role in American life and thought. We have been told that German immigrants were uniformly "liberal" in their political commitments and that their liberalism was really "republicanism," so that from the outset they formed part of the mainstream of American political thought. We have been told that German political attitudes were the result of a simple transfer to American soil of old-world commitments. We have been told that German-America itself comprised a uniform and homogeneous community, in but not of America. Cincinnati's German population in particular, we have been told, comprised a united community of hard-working men and women whose principal goal was to achieve economic success individually, whose pursuit of success led them to shun political controversy, and whose impact on the city consisted primarily in their ability to infuse a barren, Puritanical culture with their love of art, music, and literature, and with their easy-going sociability. (In Löher's time it had already become conventional to speak of *Gemütlichkeit* as one of the characteristics of German immigrant culture in America, but in later years it became the sole basis for understanding the role that German-Americans had played in Cincinnati's history.)[9]

Visitors like Löher, and Cincinnati's own residents, must have known better. They will have noticed what Levine's evidence makes clear. Cincinnati's Germans participated in the public debates of the day, sometimes as Germans and sometimes as Americans. As Germans they brought new issues to public attention, especially the appropriateness of American participation in the European movements for the "national liberation" of peoples from their rulers, including the princes of the Church. But as Germans and as Americans they were divided amongst themselves according to their identification with particular social classes, occupations, communal groups within German-America (the Catholic church, the *Arbeiterverein,* the *Turngemeinde*), communal groups in Cincinnati or the United States more generally (the Catholic church, labor unions, social clubs, political parties), or "attitudes" toward slavery, equal rights, and so forth. Indeed, contemporaries may well have noticed what historians have never seen, until Levine showed us in this essay, how "the particular conditions of American society—its more open political life, its far more dynamic economic development—seemed to widen the differences among the immigrants," even while, as Frederick Jackson Turner might have said, it made them all Americans.

◊　　◊　　◊

The theme of divided loyalty and of contemporary uncertainty about the meaning of ethnic identity is less explicitly the subject of James Campbell's essay, "The New Parochialism: Change and Conflict in the Archdiocese of Cincinnati, 1878–1925." Campbell's immediate focus is on the character and activities of the Catholic archbishops of Cincinnati as managers of a complex secular institution performing social and sacred functions simultaneously. But the implicit context of their work comprised, first, the question of papal control over American priests and bishops, and the status of the American church as a "missionary" or as a "national" institution; and second, the necessity to administer the Cincinnati archdiocese as a single institution comprised of effectively independent ethnic churches—not parishes but *systems* of parishes—each with its own claims on diocesan resources and each with its own vision of what constituted "correct" as well as "appropriate" activities, both sacred and secular.[10]

In Campbell's as in Levine's essay, the competing parties present themselves to us as representatives of diverging principles, and argue their case not in terms of self-interest but in terms of general interest—what will be best for the community, whether defined as the parish, the diocese, or the cause of Catholicism itself. It is thus a variety of the issue that caused contention within German-America at mid-century, of how the promise of American life might best be fulfilled, and the role of German-Americans in that process. Although Campbell's particular focus is on what happens when there is no consensus among Catholics about what is best for the community, in the absence of effective leadership to create such a consensus, the "new parochialism" he describes in fact follows from the necessity to choose when loyalties are divided.

For the German-American liberals of whom Levine writes, it was the emergence of antislavery as an issue in national politics that made a choice of sides necessary, at the same time that it disrupted the uneasy compromise-through-silence, which had allowed both Democrats and Whigs to ignore the divisive character of slavery. For the Catholics of whom Campbell writes, it was the failing leadership of the archbishops from the time of the Purcell bank failure that made a choice of sides (between parochial and diocesan interests) necessary, at the same time that it disrupted the uneasy compromise-thorugh-silence by which the archbishops had permitted the establishment of effectively independent ethnic churches within the diocese.

As in Levine's essay also, here too the passage of time brought inevitable changes, in leadership but especially in the status of the Catholic church in America and the characteristics of its congregants. Where Archbishops Fenwick and Purcell had depended on foreign sources for funds and for personnel to maintain the church as a missionary agency, Archbishops Elder and Moeller sought to assert their independence from foreign control, by the Vatican as well as the religious orders. And where Fenwick and Purcell had accepted as inevitable the separation of foreign language congregations into a distinct diocesan system under appropriate foreign-born leadership, Elder and Moeller found that ethnic separatism no longer satisfied later generations of Catholics, who were increasingly American-born and English-speaking, and that ethnic separatism appeared as an explicit challenge to the control they were attempting to exercise over the diocese as a whole. Campbell tells the story in detail, but the result was the elimination of the entire system of parish organization based on language and hence (largely) on ethnicity, and the establishment of the more "modern" system of geographic parishes for the city as a whole, by 1921.

Campbell's analysis stresses the fact that this elimination of ethnic parishes derived from the dynamic of diocesan needs as Bishop Moeller perceived them. But Moeller's decision may also be seen as symptomatic of the emergence of "the city as a whole" as a new idea. It is from this perspective, indeed, that Moeller's own "parochialism"—evidenced in his attack on the city's public university as an institution inimical to Catholic interests, his decision to move diocesan offices and the archbishop's official residence from downtown Cincinnati to the suburban city of Norwood, and his personal discomfort with non-Catholics—seems most inappropriate to Campbell. But it also marks a change from the days of Fenwick, Purcell, and Elder, when Catholics (including the archbishops) were major players in the game of civic affairs. Instead, under Moeller, and in the context of the idea of "the city as a whole," Catholics became a self-conscious minority, an ethnic group of mixed national origins bound together by ritual (rather than vernacular) language, by ritual (rather than secular, "folk," or ethnic) practices, and by a structure of limited-purpose (in this case, "religious") institutions of uncertain authority, claiming the loyalty of individuals as a matter of personal commitment to tradition rather than as a matter of right.

◊   ◊   ◊

An additional theme of the essays by Levine and Campbell is the *meaning* of those paired feelings of promise and loss, noted in connection with Löher's observations, and the manner in which contemporaries worked out their practical implications. Both essays illuminate the contemporary tendency to *use* the concepts of past and future as the basis for erecting a social taxonomy appropriate to America and consistent with American values and the American reality. In the absence of social divisions based on inheritance or on access to power as represented by "closeness" to the

14

monarch (even the head of state was called simply "Mr. President"), and conversely because of their commitment to egalitarianism, Americans lacked both an appropriate terminology to describe real patterns of diversity and a social taxonomy that could function as a technology, to describe relationships among diverse elements and integrate them into an American whole. When, as the evidence offered by Levine and Campbell demonstrate, some groups were identified as the parties of the past and some as parties of the future, the real pluralism of American life was made comprehensible through the transformation of apparently discrete and contending groups into participants in American culture, players-out of the American drama of westering pilgrims in a new world.

In addition, both essays illuminate the contemporary tendency to use the *feelings* of loss and promise as the basis for political action and the rationale for political conflict, and to embed these feelings in institutional forms that thereby became symbols as well as vehicles for the performance of tasks (decision making, self-help, the carrying out of ritual, etc.), hence the focus of loyalties. And while we may need no explanation for the "passion" with which contemporaries debated issues of slavery, the separation of church and state, the power of government, equality, the independence of America from European influence, individual rights, or the relationship of classes, castes, parties, and groups within American society, this tendency to make institutions (and "attitudes") into emblems of past and present, to view them from the perspective of feelings of loss or feelings of promise, helps explain that "ferment" which seems so characteristic of America in the mid-nineteenth century.[11]

During the later years of the century, in contrast, the retreat into what Campbell here calls "parochialism" functioned to remove certain issues and institutions from the debate, and by normalizing them as aspects of American society and culture, to cool the passions that once had swirled around them, among defenders and antagonists both. Campbell's essay in particular helps illuminate the processes by which Catholicism established its relative independence from Rome and became an "American" religion, at the same time that it abandoned its missionary fervor and visionary commitment in favor of security and status. But it was during the same period that "German America" and "Irish America," "Jewish America" and "Catholic America"—and of course "African America" —emerged as accepted, if perhaps not entirely acceptable divisions of the American population, separate at least, if not equal.

In addition, the general willingness of Americans to acknowledge that progress and evolution were ineluctable facts—as true of society as of biology, of civil history as of natural history—made possible the new identification of those institutions or peoples who "stood for" the past as primitives. Instead of being contenders in the debate over the American future, they were explicitly noncontenders, nonparticipants. They were the institutions or the people whom progress had bypassed, leaving them untouched and intact, preserved like a mammoth in ice; or those whom progress had not yet reached; or those who, for one reason or another, were throwbacks to an earlier age, repeating in their own history and in the present, the evolution of society itself. In all cases, the "new parochialism" provided for the erection of safe-places, where they were protected from the impact of the modern world until they themselves became modern, and where the modern world in turn was protected from them.[12] By marginalizing the immigrants as "foreigners," Americans gave them a place in contemporary American society, albeit at its practical fringes. By defining them in one way or another as immature, like children or savages, however, Americans promised them, and themselves, that eventually we would all together form a single, unified, and homogeneous whole.

From Parochialism to Pluralism

For immigrant Catholics in the United States, as Campbell's essay suggests, the existence of church and hierarchy provided a structure of institutional forms around which to organize independent identities, as Catholics but especially as German Catholics, Irish Catholics, Hungarian Catholics, and so forth. But church organization and denominational structure also provided foci for the assertion of distinct ethnic or ethnocultural identity among non-Catholics, immigrant and native-born alike as, during the late 1860s and 1870s, independent congregations of believers coalesced to form distinct national churches—Lutherans, German Methodists, Episcopal Methodists, African Episcopal Methodists, Episcopalians, Congregationalists, northern Presbyterians, southern Presbyterians, and so on.[13]

American Jews lacked this institutional structure of church and hierarchy and tried to create it, both to provide themselves with the forms that legitimized their independent existence in America as members of a "denomination" and to establish a focus for their identity as American Jews. In this they were like the Catholics of whom Campbell writes, but for the Jews the campaign was doubly complex, as Jonathan Sarna's essay indicates. The Jews were not only emigrants from one or another European nation with its own traditions of Jewish community life and especially of Jewish ritual practice; they were also exiles from Zion. As emigres they were divided according to their national origins. As Jews they were united in the fact of their exile. But what were they in America? Merely members of another national community, American Jews instead of German Jews or English Jews or Polish Jews or Rumanian Jews? This was one choice, and some of the story Sarna tells is of the attempt to establish an independent American Judaism and an appropriately American pattern of Jewish ritual practice and Jewish prayer, the *Minhag Amerika* of Isaac Mayer Wise.

The Jews resisted this identification as merely members of an ethnic group, and to the degree that they also saw themselves as exiles, they had to confront the meaning of America. It was already a place where Jews could achieve, if not the independent sovereignty some desired—as in the land promised to Abraham, Isaac, and Jacob—at least liberation from the restrictions characteristically placed on them as Jews and as non-Christians by European law and European custom. Was it also a new kind of Zion, an alternative homeland where modern Jews could flourish as full participants in a modern society? Some said it was "A Sort of Paradise for the Hebrews."

As Sarna makes clear, however, this vision of America in general and Cincinnati in particular emerged at a time when the immigration of millions of Jews fleeing persecution in the Russian Empire threatened to divide the community with renewed conflicts among Jews of different national origins and with different preferences in ritual practice, including those who preferred no ritual practice at all. The idea of Cincinnati as "A Sort of Paradise for the Hebrews" thus functioned mythically to assert a unified identity at a time of divisiveness. It did so first by naming the people for whom Cincinnati was "a sort of paradise" after their shared language rather than a place, or the language of a place, or a pattern of religious belief. In addition, it asserted that Jewish identity was a matter of ethnicity rather than of belief, the product of ancestry and group identity rather than of an individual's choice of one religious system among many or one ritual system among many. At the same time, as Sarna makes clear, it also functioned to legitimize Jewish separatism (what Campbell calls parochialism) in a period of increasing anti-Semitism, when Jews were in fact being treated as a separate and alien element in the community.

◊   ◊   ◊

17

Whether Cincinnati's Germans were also treated as a separate and alien element in the community at the turn of the century is not clear. As the essays by Levine, Campbell, and Sarna indicate, Cincinnati's Germans had not comprised a coherent (much less a unified) population during the mid or late ninteenth century, but had chosen to identify themselves, and seem also to have been identified by non-Germans, with all classes, groups, and organizations of contemporary society. The Germans were Protestants, Catholics, Jews, and freethinkers. They were workers, manufacturers, merchants, managers, bankers, ministers, doctors, lawyers, musicians, and teachers. They were Democrats and Republicans, conservatives, moderates, liberals, and radicals. They were residents of all wards of the city. They would have been hard to exclude. And there were lots of them. The numerical dominance of persons of German birth or German descent throughout the United States appeared as a striking characteristic of American society after the mid-nineteenth century, and as late as 1900, persons of German birth or immediate German parentage comprised 11 percent of the total population of the continental United States, 14 percent of the total white population, and 51 percent of all persons of foreign birth or immediate foreign parentage.[14] In Cincinnati the percentages were probably higher throughout this period.[15]

That numbers alone were sufficient to create acceptability is doubtful, however, especially in the context of America's late nineteenth-century revulsion against the foreigners in her midst and the "new parochialism" by which both native- and foreign-born groups formed themselves into separate communities. What is not clear, however, is whether contemporaries recognized Germans *as such* as a group, independent of their participation as Germans in city-wide activities.[16]

It is in this context that a series of attempts at creating a coherent "German" community in Cincinnati and a concomitant effort at inventing a German ethnic identity piques Zane Miller's interest. But it reminds him of the contemporary attempt by W. E. B. DuBois and other commentators on the role of African Americans in the United States, to define blacks as an ethnic group rather than as a (biological) race, thereby establishing the legitimacy of an African presence in the United States and avoiding those discussions of "racial inferiority" and "racial superiority," which had relegated blacks to the status of an underclass. Miller uses the similarities between the arguments of DuBois and the Cincinnati advocates of German self-consciousness to notice the more general phenomenon, and as an occasion for outlining a prolegomena to the study of ethnicity as an "invented" rather than "real" concept.

◊   ◊   ◊

During the last years of the nineteenth century, Cincinnati's population growth slowed and, as its commercial and manufacturing base gradually declined, other cities—most notably the Great Lakes places where mineral resources, available bulk transport facilities on the lakes, and the great trunk lines of the railroads converged—became the rapid growth areas of the nation. To these cities the so-called new immigrants of the late nineteenth century were attracted, as were emigrants from within the United States including southern whites and southern blacks, especially after the turn of the century. As a consequence, Cincinnati did not experience the massive in-migration of southern and eastern Europeans—the Italians, Greeks, Slovenians, Poles, Lithuanians, Czechs, Russians, and east-European Jews who now seem to dominate the ethnic mix of the Great Lakes cities, especially Buffalo, Cleveland, Detroit, Chicago, and Milwaukee, and whose presence in the industrializing areas of the Southern Appalachian region, from the coal fields of Pennsylvania southwards, seemed at once a sign of progress and a threat to the "native" culture of the indigenous southern mountain people.[17]

Cincinnati's own immigration crisis would occur later, when thousands of southern whites and southern blacks arrived in the city during the late 1930s and early 1940s, some of them on their way farther north but many to stay, creating new minority populations whose presence threatened the calm of the "Serene Cincinnatians."[18] But the city received its share of immigrants from abroad during the 1890s and early twentieth century, also, and in any case was never isolated from the national mood of the period. As a result, Cincinnatians like other Americans worried about the impact these "new" immigrants would have on American society—the strain their presence would place on existing social service institutions and the criminal justice system of its cities (for were they not all paupers and criminals?) as well as on the dominance of "American" culture in the metropolitan areas of the United States.[19]

Campbell and Sarna touch on the problem that the "new" immigrants posed for the Catholic and Jewish communities respectively, and on their responses, but Andrea Kornbluh's essay, "*The Bowl of Promise:* Civic Culture, Cultural Pluralism, and Social Welfare Work," explores this issue directly. What interests Kornbluh, however, is not the development of mechanisms for the delivery of social services (immigrants are "needy" by definition, having left home, family, workplace, work, and social relationships behind) or for their "Americanization," but rather the alternative visions of civic life that emerged when immigration was defined as a crisis, and in response to the actual presence of "new" immigrants in the Queen City.

Although Cincinnati did not experience an actual immigration crisis at the turn of the century (17.8 percent of its population was foreign-born in 1900; 36.8 percent in 1870),[20] its citizens were as vulnerable as other Americans to contemporary fears that an ethnically diverse population in America's cities threatened the viability of America's culture and institutions. Such concern as Cincinnatians did express about the threat posed by the "new" immigration, moreover, may have been an indirect response to declining rates of immigration to the city, as its citizens sought to demonstrate that their city, too, was a major metropolis precisely because it experienced the same problems as New York, Boston, and Chicago.[21]

At the same time the city faced real problems. Such immigration as Cincinnati experienced must have placed intolerable pressure on the already densely populated downtown wards that served as traditional "portals of entry" for newcomers to the city, and on the aging and often dilapidated housing stock of those areas. Until 1911, moreover, overcrowding in the city could not be solved through geographic expansion, for the city was ringed by incorporated suburbs that resisted annexation in order to preserve their low density residential character, and perhaps also to exclude as best they could, "foreigners" of any kind. Even without massive immigration, however, Cincinnati's character as "practically a foreign city" set in America's heartland was noticed by at least one visitor to the Queen City during the 1890s,[22] when, according to Zane Miller, "only twenty percent of the eligible voters were native-born whites of native parentage."[23] How much these "facts" bothered contemporaries, most of whom appear themselves to have been of foreign birth or foreign parentage, and how much they simply provided Cincinnatians with a sense that they, too, ought to confront ethnic diversity as the characteristic urban problem of the age is not clear. It was in the context of this national discussion, however, that Cincinnati's well-known convention facilities were made available to the Missionary Education Movement of the United States and Canada for one of its grand expositions of missionary need and missionary opportunity. "The World in Cincinnati" featured "living dioramas" depicting life among the exotic peoples of the world, including those whom the Protestant missionary establishment had long before identified as providing fruitful fields for missionary endeavor within the United States, including Esquimaux and other native Americans, Southern Mountaineers, and "foreigners" in our cities.

At earlier expositions, too, living dioramas had been staged to present glimpses of exotic peoples and unfamiliar cultures. At the World's Columbian Exposition in Chicago (1893), these functioned as much for entertainment as for education and were principally located outside the exposition grounds themselves, along the "Midway Plaisance." At the Louisiana Purchase Exposition in St. Louis (1904), greater attempts were made to integrate the living dioramas, especially those depicting life among "primitive" peoples, into the general theme of the exposition in order to demonstrate the social, as well as the technological progress made during the past century. In either case, the messages of these living dioramas were precisely those that had become the central assumptions of the new field of cultural anthropology: that all people did the same sorts of things, although in different ways; and that the cultural usages (including the theology and system of "values") of primitive peoples represented an earlier stage of development in the history of cultural usages found among so-called modern peoples.[24]

The message of the "living dioramas" at "The World in Cincinnati" was quite a different one, however. As Kornbluh explains, the exotic peoples who interested the missionaries were those "living in darkness" (the phrase is theirs; Mark Twain's famous essay satirized the words as well as their meaning) and their exotic and alien patterns of culture were not so much "interesting" as dangerous. The missionaries saw these less as historical usages persisting into the present, less as traditional patterns unchanged by the forces of modernization, than as contemporary challenges to modern American culture, unsuitable alternatives on the ethnologic menu. Their occurrence among America's resident populations threatened the possibility of achieving national unity and homogeneity. As contemporary alternatives to (modern) Christian belief systems, moreover, they also threatened the possibility of achieving the missionaries' goal, of "the world for Christ in our generation" and not incidentally, of that millennialist goal which underlay the rhetoric of "the world for Christ" —universal conversion as a condition of Christ's Second Coming.[25] No wonder, then, if the unchurched, unconverted immigrants seemed a threat. There was a lot at stake, even in Cincinnati.

Following the conclusion of the exposition a "Continuation Committee" was organized among members of local Protestant churches to maintain enthusiasm for support of home and foreign missions, and to assess Cincinnati's own "needs" for home-missionary work. Frederick Bastel carried out the study of the city's needs through one of the first systematic surveys of social conditions conducted in the city. As might be expected, however, his findings followed the line laid down earlier by Josiah Strong's apocalyptic indictment of America's current condition, *Our Country: Its Possible Future and Its Present Crisis* (1885), out of which the Missionary Education Movement's agenda had been developed in the first place.[26]

Bastel stressed the problems caused by the presence of "new" immigrants in the city, the opportunities for missionary work among them, and the need for such missionary work if American civilization were to be preserved in Cincinnati, even while acknowledging that the city had not experienced massive in-migration from southern and eastern Europe. For Kornbluh, the significance of Bastel's work lies not in his survey results but in the project itself, which defined ethnic diversity as a "problem." As a result, while its immediate consequences may have been to exacerbate contemporary tendencies toward xenophobia and parochialism, Bastel's work appears also to have helped make Cincinnatians aware of ethnic diversity as a situation as well as a problem requiring action, and thus to have prepared the city for quite different patterns of response to the reality of diversity as it was perceived during subsequent decades.

◊   ◊   ◊

Bastel's vision, like that of Josiah Strong, was of a city divided between persons of Anglo-Scottish descent and those descended from all other "races"; between native- and foreign-born; between persons whose culture and heritage derived from the "old" immigration from northern Europe and those "new" immigrants from southern and eastern Europe. It was a complex picture of insiders and outsiders; and as elsewhere in the United States, the "old" immigrants, especially the Irish and the Germans, were counted among the insiders.

By the early 1920s, the distinction between "old" and "new" immigrants seemed no longer quite so useful as it had some thirty years before, and the immigrants themselves no longer seemed so "green," so "foreign." They were in fact, most of them, Americans—by virtue of sharing in the American experience of the First World War, if not in other more formal ways, but the war itself made even foreigners seem less foreign. Thus, although debate in the U.S. Congress over immigration restriction and the publicity campaigns waged by proponents and opponents of pending legislation kept alive the old distinctions, between the "old" immigration and the "new" immigration, and in fact generated a new interest in the possibility of establishing a hierarchy of "races" or nationalities, Americans generally were quite prepared to accept ethnic diversity once again, as a normal characteristic of their cities and their social life—if perhaps not of their national culture.

In this context a second vision of civic life in Cincinnati was articulated, of the city as a "melting pot" in which each race, each nation, will play its own instrument in the symphony of America. That is not Kornbluh's image but Israel Zangwill's, whose play of 1908, *The Melting Pot,* turned Crevecoeur's old phrase into a joke on all of us by describing an ethnically diverse world, in which a Jewish artist whose muse was a French-speaking Russian countess wrote a concerto for a German to play, while the Poles and the Slovenians applauded and the Irish serving girl stood on the sidelines making bad jokes in pidgin-Yiddish.[27]

By the early 1920s, Zangwill's phrase had caught on among immigration restrictionists still doing battle for a quota system, who noticed that the "new" immigrants were not being "melted" into Americans, which they thought was a pretty good thing, since their presence in the crucible would spoil the alloy. But Zangwill's vision of a symphony with many parts and many players, a concerto with many voices blending together, had also caught on; and it is a version of this, transformed by the playground movement into people's dance and by the pageant movement into people's drama,[28] that Kornbluh describes as epitomizing a second and pluralist vision of civic life, in her discussion of Emma Backus's pageant of Cincinnati history, *The Bowl of Promise.*

Backus's vision of the city's past and of the city's future, Kornbluh explains, is pluralist. Just as all members of the civic community are able to participate in performing the pageant (so long as they are organized into "groups"), all members of the community did participate in Cincinnati's social and economic growth in the past and its triumph over adversities of all sorts. Ethnic diversity is thus not only not an obstacle to communal vitality, but appears here to be a condition of communal vitality. Indeed, whether intentionally or not, Backus presents us with a vision of a society comprised of groups rather than of individuals, and of civic history as the story of group collaboration rather than of individual achievement. She thus erects a multitiered system of individual identity as appropriate for the city, in which ethnic diversity and civic virtue can coexist without conflict. In the process, she confronts the issue raised by Bastel, of immigration as a threat, on Bastel's terms—that is, without distinguishing between the "new" and the "old" immigration (in the third segment of the pageant, the settlement of the Ohio Valley during the early nineteenth century is depicted through the performance of folk dances from Appalachia, Holland, Hungary, Italy, Serbia, and Scotland)—by normalizing ethnic diversity as a fact of life in the Queen City.

◊　　◊　　◊

From the historical perspective taken by Backus it was easy enough to deny the importance of ethnic diversity as an obstacle to the achievement of progress, and to assert, as she did, that members of all ethnic and racial groups represented in the city had been active participants in Cincinnati's life and growth. That ethnic diversity might present occasions for conflict at any given moment, however, was something Backus also knew. This was one of the themes of her Cincinnati novel, *A Place in the Sun* (1917), for example, which demonstrated that even when the conflict was engendered by misunderstanding or stupidity, it could wound, even out-rage all parties. Others will have known this also, some from personal experience, some from that large body of political commentary generated during the Progressive era, which viewed the potential for interethnic conflict as posing a threat to civic governance for the common good, and ethnic diversity as the cause of "boss rule," hence of corruption and mismanagement in city government.[29]

According to Robert Burnham, the need to address these matters gave shape to Cincinnati's debate over a new city charter during the mid-1920s. In Cincinnati's Charter Review activities he sees not only the conventional struggle between reformers and bosses to develop mechanisms of governance that will best serve their quite different interests, but also an acknowledgement that ethnic diversity was a fundamental characteristic of American society around which any effective system of city governance would have to be constructed.

Charter revision was made possible by the "home rule" amendment to the Ohio Constitution, approved by the state's voters in 1912, which suspended sections of the Ohio Municipal Code of 1851 and permitted cities to tailor their systems of governance to what they perceived to be their individual needs. Although Cleveland, Toledo, Dayton, and other

cities rapidly enacted new "progressive" charters establishing a city manager form of government, election to council "at-large" instead of by
ward, the nonpartisan ballot, mechanisms for citizens' initiative through
petition, referendum and recall, or some combination of these, the voters
of Cincinnati barely approved even the establishment of a charter review
commission, and rejected the "progressive" charter proposed for their
approval in 1914. When a new charter was enacted in 1916, moreover, it
made only slight modifications in the system of governance then in
effect.[30]

In Cleveland, as later in Cincinnati, debate over charter revision turned
in part on the impact that reform of the electoral system would have on
the city's ethnic groups. According to a recent study by Professor Kathleen
Barber, Cleveland's new charter yielded little change in the politics of that
city, as informal agreements between the city manager and local political
leaders effectively preserved existing patterns of representation (or under-
representation) on council.[31] In Cincinnati, however, as Burnham demonstrates, the question was not simply how to achieve more equitable
representation of all elements in the society, but how to maintain a sense
of the city as a whole while acknowledging ethnic diversity. Gilbert
Bettman, Robert Taft, and other opponents of charter reform feared a
return to the war of all-against-all, which, they said, had incapacitated city
government during the days of late nineteenth-century boss rule. Murray
Seasongood, speaking for the proponents of charter reform, said that this
was a specious argument, since Cincinnati was a "homogeneous city," by
which he surely meant NOT that we are all Germans (Seasongood was
himself a Jew), but that Bakus was correct: Cincinnati society made room
for ethnic diversity, acknowledged it as fact, but made it possible for
residents to be good Germans AND good citizens.

◊　　◊　　◊

As the essays by Sarna, Miller, Kornbluh, and Burnham suggest, "ethnicity"
became a major means of categorizing the American population during
the early twentieth century. Brought to public attention by the work of the
U.S. Immigration Commission after 1907 (although contemporary usage
talked about "race" and "national origins"), by the public relations efforts
of the United States government during the First World War to assure
support for the allied cause by "hyphenated" Americans, and by the
continuing debate over the use of national origins as the basis for immigra-

tion restriction during the 1920s, "ethnicity" rapidly replaced "social class" as the critical explanation for the occurrence of social problems in the systematic surveys by social workers, and formed a central concept in the development of social work's "scientific" offshoot, sociology.[32]

When votes were counted, however, it was not on the basis of ethnicity but of precinct and ward, and when social services were "delivered" it was not on the basis of ethnicity but of neighborhood or district. For these practical reasons, as a consequence, geographic units were also used in social surveys as designating *where* populations were located, and it was an easy matter to associate such districts with the characteristics of the populations inhabiting them, indeed to characterize the regions or neighborhoods of a city according to the characteristics of their resident populations, or of the kinds of activities occurring within them. Between the late nineteenth century, when informal, seat-of-the-pants categories came into use—slum, red-light district, Little Italy, Chinatown—and the 1920s, numerous attempts were made to erect more formal and "universal" schemes for describing the social and geographic structure of cities in terms of who lived where and what went on, most notably by the so-called Chicago School of sociologists, using observations of their own city as the basis for understanding how social systems worked anywhere. But it was in this period also that the new disciplines of regional planning and metropolitan planning emerged as characteristic responses to the Progressive-era problem of "disorder," and the insights of the new sociology concerning the relationship of people, place, and culture were applied to problems of land-use and the delivery of municipal services.[33]

For the planners of the 1920s and 1930s, the ethnic character of neighborhoods was as much a "given" as the local topography. Both had to be taken into account in their descriptions of "existing conditions" and in their proposals to make the city work more efficiently, now and in the future. And for the planners of this era, to all intents and purposes what you saw was what you got: cities were stable, self-contained entities inhabited by a stable population with established social characteristics, including ethnicity.[34]

By the late 1940s, however, planning practice and planning theory began to reflect the contemporary dynamism of American cities in the flush times following the Second World War, including the out-migration of urban populations to residential areas on the metropolitan fringe and the social upheavals wrought by massive internal migration patterns during the Depression years and especially the years of the war itself. In this context, new notions of "ethnic succession" and "neighborhood decline" came into vogue. The first was an attempt to describe, or at least to name the process by which one group replaced another in a given urban area while the characteristics of the area itself, including what went on in it, remained the same. (Sociologists borrowed the concept of "ecological niche" from biology to describe the same phenomenon.) The second asserted as normal what the nineteenth century, which built in brick and stone and steel for permanence and protection, would never have imagined: the "wearing-out" of the urban infrastructure, including the built environment, and the tendency of worn-out neighborhoods to attract worn-out populations (for which the remedy was replacement of the built environment and replacement of the population through "urban renewal"). But the effect was to break up of the old identification of particular places with particular peoples and particular cultural patterns or behaviors.

From the point of view of the planners, this was just fine. It enabled them to argue for the total reconstruction (or at least the reconceptualization) of cities in terms of highest and best land-use and to demonstrate that since everything was changing anyway, existing conditions—who lived where and what went on there—created no impediment to the implementation of their plans. Both as theory and as the basis for the practice of urban renewal, however, it had another consequence of particular importance. By cutting the ties that had bound particular populations with particular places, and by denying the symbolic value that "neighborhood" had possessed as a way of providing groups with coherence and a sense of identity as members of a particular civic whole, these new notions made even persons with definable social, occupational, ethnic, or "racial" characteristics into rootless, placeless people. And while some would argue that this was merely a playing out of the American drama, that we were all "uprooted," born with a metaphoric green card instead of the proverbial silver spoon, and that in this lay the American genius for individualism and democracy, many others expressed distress over our "loss of community," and some sought to create new kinds of community independent of place through the assertion of ethnic identity.[35]

◊   ◊   ◊

It is in this context that the essays by Bruce Tucker and Zane Miller, deriving from their study of the impact of planning on Cincinnati's Over-the-Rhine neighborhood, must be read. By the 1940s, Over-the-

Rhine, once the center of Cincinnati's German community and still its symbolic center in later years, had become a "declining neighborhood" characterized by "ethnic succession," hence no impediment to projected (and expected) expansion of Cincinnati's central business district, on the edge of which it lay. As a result, planners viewed Over-the-Rhine as a natural extension of the CBD, an appropriate location for a much-needed crosstown connector, for example, rather than as a neighborhood in need of "revitalization." When Cincinnati's downtown failed to expand outward (it tended to grow upward, instead), and when suburban development made the construction of radial connectors more important than the construction of a crosstown connector in the basin, Over-the-Rhine was largely forgotten. Suburbanites bypassed it on their way in and out of downtown on the interstate highways or on Central Parkway, which ran along its edge. The district itself became a location for light industry and warehouses serving the downtown area and the residence of in-migrants— many from the South—who found inexpensive (and inadequate) housing in its nineteenth-century tenements during their first years in the city, until they moved farther north, either to the suburbs or to greater economic opportunities in the industrial cities along the Great Lakes.

By the 1960s, however, in-migration had slowed (Cincinnati's population was in decline generally), while the Great Lakes industrial cities had come on hard times as America's "rust belt" and no longer made Cincinnati a convenient stopping-off place along the way. Now, Over-the-Rhine's population no longer seemed to comprise "transients" who would take care of themselves sooner or later, but instead a permanent population in need of assistance—and control.

It was in this period that Cincinnatians—first the churches, then the social service agencies, and finally the city administration—began to rediscover Over-the-Rhine, as a "pocket of poverty," however, rather than as the stable center of Cincinnati's German heritage. At about the same time, highway construction in the lower Millcreek Valley bottoms and then urban renewal in the West End displaced thousands from those areas, most of whom were black, and some of whom moved to Over-the-Rhine.[36]

In his essay, Tucker explores some of the initial responses of social service agencies to the "problem" that Over-the-Rhine now represented, and especially the role that "ethnic identity" was believed to play in the establishment of community coherence and of the achievement of "self-empowerment" by the poor. But his particular focus is on the "invention"

28

of Appalachian identity, or more properly of *urban* Appalachian identity, in the context of contemporary self-empowerment movements.

For the Appalachian advocates working in Over-the-Rhine, as Tucker demonstrates, the reality of ethnicity as an element in the identities of their client population was never questioned, nor was the notion that "who you are is where you're from." But *where* the urban Appalachians were from was never Over-the-Rhine. That was only where they lived, at the moment, hence the temporary venue for community organizing. For the Over-the-Rhine planners of whom Miller writes, however, the whole issue of ethnic identity became problematic and was redefined as a matter of individual choice in which life-style decisions rather than national or regional origins/ancestry formed the basis for group identity. Miller examines the obligatory historical introductions to a series of planning documents created for Over-the-Rhine, and finds not only a struggle between different visions of the district's past but also disputes over the "meaning" of that past—in the past itself, and as precedent for the future of the neighborhood.

Instead of abandoning historical analysis altogether, however, or treating the neighborhood's history as merely anecdotal, the authors whose work Miller examines project into the past a vision of culture, including ethnicity, as instrumental rather than determinative. According to this view, says Miller, "Individuals in the past did not 'inherit' a culture from their race or place of origin" but "had striven to define their own culture, which was best understood as impermanent, optional, and instrumental in nature." Over-the-Rhine's ethnic heritage, like Cincinnati's, was thus infinitely diverse, comprised of the individual choices of hundreds of thousands of individuals acting across two centuries of time, and changing their minds whenever they felt like it and their life-style whenever it pleased them to do so.

APPENDIX
The Problem of German Clannishness.

Although the "clannishness" of the mid-nineteenth-century German immigrants has become a convention of mid-twentieth-century historiography, it is only certain that the German immigrants sometimes *seemed* clannish to contemporary English-speaking observers, who identified their willingness to speak German among themselves as a desire to keep themselves separate from American society. And what were they talking about anyway?

During the late nineteenth and early twentieth centuries, both opponents of immigration restriction and *proponents* of immigration restric-

29

tion regularly argued that the mid-nineteenth-century German immigrants had rapidly learned English and rapidly assimilated into American society, unlike (some said) later immigrants from eastern and southern Europe, e.g., U.S. Treasury Department, Bureau of Statistics, *Special Report on Immigration,* by Edward Young [March 7, 1871] (Washington, D.C.: GPO, 1872), vi–vii; Edward Alsworthy Ross, *The Old World in the New: The Significance of Past Immigration to the American People* (New York: The Century Co., 1914), esp. 46–66. In the context of the emerging pluralism of the 1920s, by contrast, clannishness (as manifested in the formation of ethnic communities) was sometimes viewed as an essential step in the Americanization of immigrants, and desirable for its own sake as establishing the United States as a "nation of peoples," e.g., John Daniels, *America via the Neighborhood* (New York: Harper & Bros., 1920, in the series "Americanization Studies").

The normality of ethnic community formation was also argued by Edith Abbott as part of her attack on the distinction between the "old" and the "new" immigration, and as evidence for her insistence that immigration was a universal problem with a human dimension rather than an American historical problem to be solved simply through national policy, in two volumes which have given shape to our modern approach to American immigration history, *Immigration: Select Documents and Case Records,* The University of Chicago Social Service Series, [vol 1] (Chicago: University of Chicago Press, 1924), and *Historical Aspects of the Immigration Problem: Select Documents,* University of Chicago Social Service Series (Chicago: University of Chicago Press, 1926). In an effort to disprove the distinctions alleged between the "old" and the "new" immigration she published documents "demonstrating" the tendency of German immigrants toward ethnic community formation long before this "problem" was recognized as a threat to American civilization, including a 1753 letter in which Benjamin Franklin expressed concern about the increasing isolation of the Germans in Pennsylvania from that province's English-speaking citizens, and their apparent desire to retain their German heritage in the New World (*Historical Aspects,* 415–16), and a selection from an emigrant's guide of 1829, Ernst Ludwig Brauns, *Praktische Belehrungen und Rathschläge für Reisende und Auswanderer nach Amerika* (ibid., 433), asserting that "the German communities [in America] which have become English number less than fifty, while the communities that have remained German number one thousand."

Professional historians have generally adopted the pluralist position and celebrated "clannishness" and ethnic community formation, e.g.,

Carl Wittke, *We Who Built America: The Saga of the Immigrant* (New York: Prentice Hall, 1939); *Refugees of Revolution: The German Forty-Eighters in America* (Philadelphia: University of Pennsylvania Press, 1952); and "The Germans of Cincinnati," *Bulletin of the Historical and Philosophical Society of Ohio* 20, no. 1 (Jan. 1962): 1–4; Marcus Lee Hansen, *The Atlantic Migration, 1607–1860: A History of the Continuing Settlement of the United States* (Cambridge: Harvard University Press, 1940) and *The Immigrant in American History* (Cambridge: Harvard University Press, 1940).

The obligations felt by later generations of historians to respect issues well established in the literature, even when such issues are unavailable to examination by the most diligent modern scholarship, appears e.g., in Kathleen Neils Conzen's admirable essay, "Germans," in *The Harvard Encyclopedia of American Ethnic Groups,* ed. Stephan Thernstrom, Ann Orlov, and Oscar Handlin (Cambridge: Harvard University Press, 1980), where the issue of "German clannishness" is dutifully acknowledged and then successfully ignored.

NOTES

My scholarly debt to Zane Miller, which all who work on any aspect of Cincinnati's history must share, will become apparent throughout the text and notes; but I wish also to acknowledge my personal and intellectual debt to him, incurred during more than twenty years of conversation, collaboration, and companionship. What I know about local history, and much of what I know about the historian's craft, I learned from him or with him. I am grateful for both the product and the process.

Others have contributed to my understanding of the issues discussed here, sometimes directly and sometimes indirectly, and I wish to acknowledge my debt to them also: first of all, my great teacher, Warren I. Susman; then other friends and colleagues who have also been my teachers, including Willi Paul Adams, Angela Meurer Adams, Saul Benison, Hamilton Cravens, Roger Daniels, Ronald J. Grele, Oscar Handlin, Andrea Tuttle Kornbluh, Alan Marcus, Janet Smith Miller, Barbara Ramusack, Jonathan Sarna, Werner Sollors, Rudolph Vecoli, Harry Austryn Wolfson, and my wife, Genevieve Halbrook Ray. Librarians at Case-Western Reserve University, the Cleveland Public Library, and the Cleveland Heights-University Heights Public Libraries have been uniformly gracious to this newcomer to America's North Coast, and made their rich collections available for research during the period when this essay was being written. As always, they are the crucial facilitators of scholarship, and their contributions must not go unacknowledged.

1. During the nineteenth and well into the twentieth century, the word "race" was regularly used to designate any group that might be defined by its

heritage, whether biological or cultural, as when Melville (*Moby Dick,* ch. 51) spoke of the Pequod's crew of seamen as displaying "the immemorial superstition of their race."

Where we like to draw distinctions among concepts like nationality, national origins, ethnic identity, and regional identification, and have generally abandoned the concept of biological race as providing an uncertain basis for the description or classification of peoples, they were quite content to talk about the English race, the Negro race, the Jewish race, the American race, the Japanese race, etc.

2. William Goodell Frost, "The Call of Providence" (Address delivered at the Hotel Thorndike, Boston, Nov. 21, 1894), typescript in W. G. Frost Papers, Berea College Archives. In Cincinnati during the 1890s, according to Zane Miller, "only twenty percent of the eligible voters were native-born whites of native parentage," *Boss Cox's Cincinnati: Urban Politics in the Progressive Era* (New York: Oxford University Press, 1968), 289 n. 4.

3. For a classic formulation of the problem, see the essays (and references) in David F. Bowers, ed., *Foreign Influences in American Life: Essays and Critical Bibliographies* (Princeton: Princeton University Press, 1944).

4. Gilbert Chinard argues that this was the issue that precipitated the eighteenth-century debate on the habitability of North America, "Eighteenth-Century Theories of America as a Human Habitat," *American Philosophical Society Transactions* 91 (February 1947): 27–57. The availability of America as a destination for emigrants, and the usefulness of immigration to increase the "resources," of the United States continued as a subject for discussion through the late nineteenth century, e.g., U.S. Treasury Department, Bureau of Statistics, *Special Report on Immigration,* by Edward Young, [March 7, 1871] (Washington, D.C.: GPO, 1872).

During the eighteenth century, "labor" was added to the categories used in assessing a nation-state's wealth, which earlier had consisted principally of its store of specie, and sometimes of such "natural" resources as coal and timber. One result was the emergence of the new "science" of political economy out of the work of Adam Smith, Alexander Hamilton, Jeremy Bentham, and others.

5. J. Hector St. John de Crevecoeur, *Letters from an American Farmer* (London, 1782). Frederick Jackson Turner attempted to explain the mechanism by which "the American experience" made Europeans into Americans, especially in his famous essay "The Significance of the Frontier in American History" (1893), the popularity of which among twentieth-century historians has derived from the kind of answer he offered to this famous question. A less comfortable but more persuasive answer is offered in Oscar Handlin, *The Uprooted: The Epic Story of the Great Migrations that Made the American People* (Boston: Little, Brown, 1951).

6. Contemporary attempts to restrict immigration from Catholic Europe, or to deny citizenship to Catholic immigrants, is discussed in Ray Allen Billington, *The Protestant Crusade, 1800–1860: A Study of the Origins of American Nativism* (New York: Macmillan, 1938), although Billington himself, under the influence of the "history of ideas method" in vogue when his study was written, dutifully finds the origins of antebellum anti-Catholicism in the Tudor origins of America's first

settlers rather than in contemporary American concerns. See, however, David Brion Davis, "Some Themes of Counter-Subversion: Anti-Masonic, Anti-Catholic, and Anti-Mormon Literature," *Mississippi Valley Historical Review* 47 (Sept. 1960): 205–24 and "Some Ideological Functions of Prejudice in Ante-Bellum America," *American Quarterly* 15 (Summer 1963): 115–25.

7. See Appendix: The Problem of German Clannishness.

8. For a brief discussion of the characteristics of travel literature, and of its function as providing information, thereby establishing the conventional attitudes toward particular places among outsiders and insiders both, see Henry D. Shapiro, *Appalachia on Our Mind: The Southern Mountains and Mountaineers in the American Consciousness, 1870–1920* (Chapel Hill: University of North Carolina Press, 1978), esp. ch. 1.

9. E.g., Works Projects Administration, *Cincinnati: A Guide to the Queen City and Its Neighbors* (Cincinnati: The Weisen-Hart Press, 1943), 51: "German beer and cuisine, at first confined to Over-the-Rhine, soon spread to all parts of the city. German drama . . . and chorus singing [as well as other] Teutonic customs and festivals seeped across the city, became entrenched, and filled Cincinnatians with *Gemuetlichkeit.*" Carl Wittke appears to have borrowed heavily from this account for his celebratory essay, "The Germans of Cincinnati," *Bulletin of the Historical and Philosophical Society of Ohio* 20, no. 1 (Jan. 1962): 1–4.

10. In an unpublished essay ("John Baptist Purcell: An Irish Archbishop of a German Church"), M. Edmund Hussey explores the formal mechanisms developed by Purcell for the organization of distinct sub-diocesan systems for German- and English-language congregations, including the appointment of both a German and an "Irish" Vicar General as assistants to the bishop and the immediate supervisors of the two branches of the church in Cincinnati, as early as 1838. The German Vicar Generals were John Martin Henni, later Bishop of Detroit; Joseph Ferneding; and Otto Jair, whose service continued under Archbishop Elder until his death in 1885. In this connection, see also Miller, *Boss Cox's Cincinnati,* 135; Anthony H. Deye, "Archibishop John Baptist Purcell of Cincinnati: Pre–Civil War Years" (Ph.D. diss., University of Notre Dame, 1959), ch. 5.

11. My discussion of this matter is obviously derived from the seminal insights of Marvin Meyers, *The Jacksonian Persuasion: Politics and Belief* (Stanford: Stanford University Press, 1957), and before that, of Alice Felt Tyler, *Freedom's Ferment: Phases of American Social History from the Colonial Period to the Outbreak of the Civil War* (Minneapolis: University of Minnesota Press, 1944). See also in this connection Fred Somkin, *Unquiet Eagle: Memory and Desire in the Idea of American Freedom, 1815–1860* (Ithaca: Cornell University Press, 1967) and Henry D. Shapiro, "Putting the Past Under Glass: Preservation and the Idea of History in the Mid-Nineteenth Century," *Prospects: An Annual of American Cultural Studies* 10 (1985): 243–78.

12. Cf. in this connection Shapiro, *Appalachia on Our Mind.*

13. For the "organizational revolution" in the churches, yielding denominational separatism and denominational identities, see Shapiro, *Appalachia on Our Mind,* ch. 2 and references.

On the establishment of parochial schools to support distinct ethno-cultural identities during this period, see John H. Lamott, *History of the Archdiocese of Cincinnati, 1821–1921* (Cincinnati: Frederick Pustet, 1921) and such contemporary arguments as Anton H. Walburg, *The Question of Nationality in Its Relation to the Catholic Church in the United States* (Cincinnati: Herder, 1889). On the establishment and maintenance of a separate Negro School System in Cincinnati during this period, see Wendell P. Dabney, *Cincinnati's Colored Citizens: Historical, Sociological, Biographical* (Cincinnati: Dabney Publishing, 1926), 100ff.

14. U.S. Bureau of the Census, *Historical Statistics of the United States: Colonial Times to 1957* (Washington, D.C.: GPO, 1960), based on tables A4ff., A51ff., A71ff., C185ff.

15. In 1900, persons of German birth comprised 65.9 percent of Cincinnati's foreign-born population, and 11.7 percent of the total population.

I am indebted to Sally Moffitt for making available information about the ethnic characteristics of Cincinnati's population, prepared for her *Bibliography of Cincinnati's Ethnic Groups* (forthcoming).

16. Miller, *Boss Cox's Cincinnati*, 241 suggests not: "Finally, the pattern of politics suggests that residence rather than race, religion, or ethnicity provides the touchstone to the city's social and political experience. Politics mirrored the conflicts created by the process of urbanization."

17. Persons of foreign birth or immediate foreign parentage comprised three-quarters of the total populations of the Great Lakes industrial cities in 1910, according to Charles A. Beard, *American City Government: A Survey of Newer Tendencies* (New York: Century, 1912), 24. The percentages are: Buffalo, 71.3; Cleveland, 74.8; Detroit, 74; Chicago, 77.5; and Milwaukee, 78.6 (same as New York City, which was the principal focus of national concern).

18. But not in the book of the same name, Alvin F. Harlow, *The Serene Cincinnatians* (New York: E. P. Dutton, 1950), which conveniently ends with the adoption of the new city charter of 1924 and the establishment of "good government" in the city.

19. The "new" immigration from southern and eastern Europe was said to comprise persons unfamiliar with modern systems of governance and modern patterns of economic activity, especially Italians, Greeks, Slavs, Slovenes, and Jews. In response to the conventional assumption that eastern Europeans were unfamiliar with modern economic usages and modern patterns of culture, William I. Thomas and Florian Znaniecki framed their inquiry into the comparative economic, social, and cultural usages displayed by Polish "peasants" in Poland and the United States, in *The Polish Peasant in Europe and America: Monograph of An Immigrant Group* (Chicago: University of Chicago Press, 1918). No one paid any attention to their evidence of the "modernity" of contemporary peasant culture, however, and the old assumptions not only persisted but still persist in the historiography of the late twentieth century. As a result, historians continue to argue the relationship between "modernity" and (ethnic) community formation, although happily without reference to "the immigrant problem" as problematic,

e.g., Dominic A. Pacyga, *Polish Immigrants and Industrial Chicago: Workers on the South Side, 1880–1922* (Columbus: Ohio State University Press, 1991).

The distinction between the "new" and the "old" immigration was introduced into the American discourse on immigration policy and the consequences of ethnic diversity by the widely publicized hearings held before the U.S. Immigration Commission (the Dillingham Commission) beginning in 1907. For a summary and critique, cf. Maldwyn Allen Jones, *American Immigration* (Chicago: University of Chicago Press, 1960), 177ff. and references.

20. Moffitt, *Bibliography,* but cf. Cincinnati Chamber of Commerce, *The Citizens Book,* ed. Charles R. Hebble and Frank P. Goodwin (Cincinnati: Stewart & Kidd, 1916), 58: "The percentage of foreign-born has long tended to decrease, as, for instance, from 17.8 percent in 1900 to 15.6 percent in 1910, at which date the proportion of foreign-born to native was smaller than for any other large American city. The actual number also was less in 1910 than in 1900. In no other large city did the number of foreigners decrease during this decade. In 1915 it was estimated to be 14 percent.

"It can be seen, therefore, that Cincinnati is in reality an English-American community. . . . The absence of a large foreign population is a distinctive characteristic of Cincinnati, and has contributed materially to its slow growth in population."

21. *The Citizens Book* continues: "The newer immigration of Russians, Italians, Hungarians, Servians, Greeks, Rumanians, which especially needs Americanization, numbers less than a third of the total foreign-born, or about 17,000 of the new immigration to 39,000 of the old. This number of new immigrants takes no account of the numerous transients or of the many aliens living just outside of the city limits, and it is to be compared with certain estimates, varying from 25,000 to 30,000, made by men engaged in religious and social service for immigrants of Cincinnati and district." The paragraphs following then outline the dimensions of the problem that their presence poses for the city.

Urban problems (as distinct from urban accomplishments) functioned as markers of great-city status at least from the mid-nineteenth century. In the 1860s, for example, Cincinnati had "discovered" the problem of water supply and embarked on a major program for the construction of sewers and waterworks; in the 1900s, Cincinnati "discovered" the problem of street congestion and embarked on a major program for the consolidation and rationalization of street railways and the construction of a "subway." The problems were real, and had existed for years before being identified as problems and addressed by municipal agencies. The context of their identification as problems is what counts, for they were "recognized" only after other American cities, especially New York, Boston, and Chicago, had already begun dealing with them.

Cincinnati's competitiveness in "the urban sweepstakes" for economic and cultural hegemony in the west is discussed in Richard C. Wade, *The Urban Frontier: The Rise of Western Cities, 1790–1830* (Cambridge: Harvard University Press, 1959); its continuing participation in the urban sweepstakes after 1860, and its efforts to retain its big-city status even after it had lost its hegemony in its region and even in its state, is a recurring theme in the work of Zane L. Miller, esp. "Music Hall: Its Neighborhood, the City, and the Metropolis," in Zane L. Miller and George Roth, *Cincinnati's Music Hall* (Virginia Beach: Jordan, 1978) and *Clifton: Neighborhood and Community in An Urban Setting* (with Henry D. Shapiro; Cincinnati: University of Cincinnati, 1976).

22. The phrase is from William Goodell Frost, "The Call of Providence" (Address delivered at the Hotel Thorndike, Boston, Nov. 21, 1894), typescript in W. G. Frost Papers, Berea College Archives.

23. Miller, *Boss Cox's Cincinnati,* 289 n. 4. Even in 1910, despite declining immigration to the city, this group comprised only 32 percent of eligible voters. Beard, *American City Government,* 23, notes that in 1910, native whites of native parentage comprised 35.6 percent of the aggregate population of all American cities, i.e., places with a population over twenty-five thousand.

24. Cf. Henry D. Shapiro, "The Place of Culture and the Problem of Appalachian Identity," in *Appalachia and America: Autonomy and Regional Dependence,* ed. Allen Batteau (Lexington: University Press of Kentucky, 1983), 111–41. Use of the "living dioramas" as the St. Louis exposition as field work opportunities by anthropologists appears e.g., in Caroline Furness Jayne, *String Figures: A Study of Cat's Cradle in Many Lands* (New York: Charles Scribner's Sons, 1906; reprint ed., New York, Dover Publications, 1962).

Older Cincinnatians attending "The World in Cincinnati" exposition will have remembered the annual encampment of American Indians held at the Cincinnati Zoological Garden as one of its most popular attractions, about which, see Judith Spraul-Schmidt, "The Late Nineteenth-Century City and Its Cultural Institutions: The Cincinnati Zoological Garden, 1873–1898" (Master's thesis, University of Cincinnati), 1977.

25. The missionaries normally identified their "World for Christ in Our Generation" campaigns with contemporary (secular) hopefulness about the establishment of universal peace through international agreement.

26. Josiah Strong, *Our Country: Its Possible Future and Its Present Crisis* (New York: Baker & Taylor for the American Home Missionary Society, 1885, 1891). For the impact of this work on contemporary thought, see esp. Jurgen Herbst's introduction to his edition of *Our Country* (Cambridge: Harvard University Press, 1963).

27. I'm not kidding; cf. Israel Zangwill, *The Melting-Pot: Drama in Four Acts* (New York: Macmillan, 1909 [1908]). In fact the "melting" that Zangwill envisioned was a variety of that contemporary fascination with the possibility of international peace and harmony, to be achieved through international cooperation and the establishment of international organizations, to which hope Woodrow Wilson also spoke; and America was merely the dramatist's version of "utopia," i.e., no-place.

28. On the playground movement as an effort to teach the value of "cooperation" instead of "individualism" to all children, including the children of immigrants, see Dominick Cavallo, *Muscles and Morals: Organized Playgrounds and Urban Reform, 1880–1920* (Philadelphia: University of Pennsylvania Press, 1981). On dance, and especially folkdance, as an element in playground programming, see

Patricia Mooney Melvin, "Building Muscles and Civics: Folk Dancing, Ethnic Diversity and the Playground Association of America," *American Studies* 24 (Spring 1983): 89–99.

Carl C. Taylor, *The Social Survey, Its History and Methods,* University of Missouri Bulletin, 20 no. 28: Social Science Series no. 3 (Columbia: University of Missouri, 1919) viewed the pageant as "the ultimate form of the survey exhibit" because of its ability to present "the social workers and citizens of the community [with] a social situation under the microscope. A community in miniature will pass before their eyes in order that they may see the actual interwoven, living tensions, forces and factors of their common life," ibid. 62f.

29. Even among those most sympathetic to the problems faced by "outsiders" in American society, e.g., Charles A. Beard, *American City Government,* 25: "While no fair-minded American sanctions the gratifying notion that the evils of our city governments are due to the foreigners, it is no doubt true that certain evils are aggravated by the alien character of the voting population. There has been a marked tendency of many foreign groups to fall under the domination of leaders of their own nationality [while] a natural tendency among them to retain their own customs and traditions . . . prevents their taking a large and generous view of city government as a whole." How settlement workers became mistrustful of indigenous neighborhood leadership is explored in Rivka Shpak Lissak's admirable study, *Pluralism and Progressives: Hull House and the New Immigrants, 1890–191* (Chicago: University of Chicago Press, 1989).

30. Hoyt Landon Warner, *Progressivism in Ohio, 1897–1917* (Columbus: Ohio State University Press for the Ohio Historical Society, 1964), 330ff., 453ff.

31. I am indebted to Professor Barber for sharing with me the results of her investigations into this matter, from *City Elections and Proportional Representation: A New Look* (forthcoming).

32. E.g., John R. Commons's classic text, *Races and Immigrants in America* (New York: Macmillan, 1907 and subsequent editions), where "race" (i.e., national origins) was placed ahead of social class as the critical characteristic dividing the American people.

The word "ethnicity" in fact comes into use later, although in our late twentieth-century distrust of "race" and "national origins" we frequently apply it—as I have here, following in this as in so many other areas, the lead of John Higham—in discussions of American attitudes during the first half of the century. On the "idea" of ethnicity, see Werner Sollors, *Beyond Ethnicity: Consent and Descent in American Culture* (New York: Oxford University Press, 1986), esp. 20ff., and esp. Andrea Tuttle Kornbluh, "From Culture to Cuisine: Twentieth Century Views of Race and Ethnicity in the City," in *American Urbanism: A Historiographical Review,* ed. Howard Gillette, Jr., and Zane Miller (New York: Greenwood Press, 1987), 49–71.

33. On the Chicago "school," in addition to the work of Burgess, Park, Thomas, Zorbaugh, Znaniecki, and White, see esp. Robert E. L. Faris, *Chicago Sociology, 1920–1932* (Chicago: University of Chicago Press, 1967), and John Madge, *The Origins of Scientific Sociology* (New York: Free Press, 1962).

The later vogue for "regional" analysis of the United States is a direct analogue of such attempts to divide cities into "meaningful" geographic districts. On regionalism as a response to the problem of diversity when ethnicity could not be used as explanation, see Shapiro, *Appalachia on Our Mind*. On the linkage of people, place, and culture in contemporary social theory, see Shapiro, "The Place of Culture and the Problem of Appalachian Identity," in *Appalachia and America,* ed. Batteau.

34. Although her emphasis is elsewhere, see in this connection Patricia Mooney Melvin, *The Organic City: Urban Definition and Neighborhood Organization, 1880–1920* (Lexington: University Press of Kentucky, 1987).

35. On the search for community during this period, cf. Zane L. Miller, *Suburb: Neighborhood and Community in Forest Park, Ohio, 1935–1976* (Knoxville: University of Tennessee Press, 1981), and bibliography.

36. For the story, see Zane L. Miller, "Queensgate II: A History of a Neighborhood," in *The Planning Partnership: Participant's Views of Urban Renewal,* ed. Zane L. Miller and Thomas H. Jenkins (Beverly Hills: Sage Publications, 1982), 51–79.

FRANZ VON LÖHER
Translated and Edited by Frederic Trautmann

The Landscape and People of Cincinnati, 1846–47

Franz von Löher (1818–92), lawyer, historian, professor, and archivist, wrote and edited more than forty books, mostly travels. Of interest to Americans are his travels to North America. His more than rudimentary knowledge of English enabled him to converse with Americans and write with greater familiarity than many German travelers in America. German travelers, with their "professional training and characteristic thoroughness," were recognized as some of the best commentators on America; and Löher was "especially outstanding" among them.[1] From New York he set out to see and report the land and people: Niagara Falls, Canada, New England, Maryland, Pennsylvania, Ohio, Missouri, and the Mississippi and Missouri rivers. He reported in *Land und Leute in der alten und neuen Welt: Reiseskizzen*.[2] This publication established "in Germany and abroad" his reputation as an "outstanding stylist."[3]

He came to Cincinnati expecting to stay seven days. He stayed seven months. During his stay, he also traveled into southwestern Ohio, where he was much taken with what he saw and many of the people he met, especially the Shakers of Union Village. His delight and interest in what he found can be read in his detailed and spirited account of Cincinnati and southwestern Ohio. The following is a translation of that account.[4]

Cincinnati

It was December. Weeks of steady rain had set the world afloat. We passed fleets of steamboats and smaller craft [on the Ohio River, from Pittsburgh] steering merrily through masses of errant wood and uprooted trees tossing on the yellow flood. Boats came within a hairsbreadth of hitting one another.

The river's banks were very pretty—tall, steep mountains mixed with small knolls, seldom the opening of a valley, and on each bank two levels of bottom land, one above the other, both submerged. Bends in the river formed charming lakes and shadowy inlets. But this scene stayed almost the same for two days without variation except a city or a settlement now and then. Monotonous. Usually there would be a good-sized town where a tributary emptying into the Ohio had laid down bottomland right and left [to accommodate a town of that size]. Where a tributary only dented the bank there would be at least a little town. Towns looked as alike as peas in a pod, though Gallipolis was unique with its dark stone houses.

I kept below decks rather than be whipped in the face with smoke and rain borne on icy wind. One day was like the other there, cool and quiet. Passengers were bored from morning until night. There was plenty of time to read, sleep, or stare at the passing shore. Indeed, from dumb sycamores, gracefully draped with creepers bearing bunches of white berries, one got more entertainment than from one's fellows.

On the morning of the third day we arrived at Cincinnati, but I searched in vain for the "Queen of the West." What I saw lacked all royal magnificence. Piers jutted up abruptly, and then the usual wall of shops and saloons and windowless shacks, and beyond them the familiar check-erboard of houses. But streets were very pleasant: cheerful with the green of trees and almost always ending brightly with a view of the river or of hills.

Little was to be seen of palaces. Instead of the sumptuous Catholic cathedral that could be expected in massive form, there was only a stone shepherd's hut in grand proportion with large square windows in blank walls. The inside was plain, too, like a Protestant chapel. Still, in this Catholic church, music and singing were somewhat operatic; and the bishop always preached in the full array of his vestments. Even in that condition the cathedral rose, proud and substantial, above countless little sectarian churches, a picture of Catholicism's strength and unity worldwide. The Freemasons have a big hall, decorated with a little confused Gothic. The hotels are large. A number of private houses show some good taste. Something else worth seeing is the place Mrs. Trollope built to display stylish clothing to Cincinnati's women. The Englishwoman failed at trying to improve local taste and angrily wrote her book, half truth, half distortion. It earned her such a reputation in Cincinnati that she dare not show her face if she knows what's good for her.

Cincinnati has neither open squares nor parks. Nobody thought of them when the city was being built. Even now, a country house is the most anybody feels necessary to enjoy the pleasures of nature.

Encircling Cincinnati is a broad ring of bright and wooded hills whose charming depths catch and hold the eye. The sparkling Ohio River crosses the ring. Cincinnati spreads out from one bank. On the opposite bank [in Kentucky] the Licking River empties from a wide valley into the Ohio. Seen from the hills, this panorama seems carved deeply into the landscape. In another generation it will probably be home to a half-million people. Old Longworth, who still lives in Cincinnati, once exchanged a considerable part of this land for two copper whiskey alembics—land now grown very valuable. Up and down the Ohio, white country houses shine amid vegetation along the banks. On the Kentucky side are dark forests; on the Ohio side, countless vineyards.

Planting of vineyards proceeds so fast that vintners make more money selling planting stock than wine and grapes. True, temperance societies are spreading with such zeal that they threaten to stop propagation of the seductive vine. But fortunately our German countrymen have planted it on so many hillsides and in so many fields that it is not to be rooted out. I spent many a beautiful evening in front of pretty houses surrounded by grapevines, tasting cool wine, when the heat of the day was past and millions of fireflies danced amid fragrance of forests and plants. The glittering American air is hard on the nerves, and the sultry heat deeply depressing; but mornings and evenings the air is bracingly filled with delightful fragrances.

All along the Ohio side of the river, serious agriculture has already penetrated far inland. Everywhere you look you see attractive farms dotting green forests. Only pieces of virgin forest remain, which lack the charm of our [German] forests, not having flower-filled meadows, gurgling streams, and snug retreats.

Kentuckians, Pennsylvania-Dutch, Yankees, and German immigrants built Cincinnati, a very lively city. In her the contrasts of the American East and West, together with European influences, form a new American character. Even the English seem to like Cincinnati as a place to settle. New England Yankees set the tone in business, religion, and politics; the Yankees' strict and incessant attention to business at once commands and moves everyone else. Surrounded by other kinds of people, they maintain an identity founded on provenance.

During my second week in Cincinnati they celebrated the anniversary of the landing of the Pilgrims [December 21, 1620]. Sermons and songs in

41

churches in the morning, and toasts at balls in the evening, proclaimed the same idea: if the land of freedom, where milk and honey flow, home to the holy Pilgrims, is not heaven itself, it is surely the next thing to heaven. Toasts were proposed while standing beside tables intentionally loaded with half-ripe produce of forest and field, the kind that was of such value to the new settlers. The beverage of the toasts was thin coffee.

Through the courtesy of a steward of the festivities, I got an invitation for me and my wife. When I arrived alone, out of place among nothing but couples, I thought of American freedom and went to the home of a young New England woman, to whose family I had been introduced. My invitation was pleasantly accepted, her ball gown quickly readied; and her husband, whom we bumped into at the door, wished us a happy evening. I brought my lovely companion home long after midnight. Such liberty seems strange to the European, but Americans reply that in Europe women are treated as if they never come of age.

Germans may now be half the population in and around Cincinnati. Annually they move into better parts of the city and the larger businesses, though most of them still live on the other side of the canal that bisects the city. But the city's overall appearance, and its hustle and bustle, are thoroughly English-American. Germans here, like Germans everywhere abroad, are often esteemed as individuals but thought little of as a people. I once irritated an American woman when I said I had seen her in the city's German section. "No, sir," she said sharply, "I never cross the canal." The contrast between the lower-class German section and the English is especially apparent on Sunday. In the English, everything is quiet; while in the German, people crowd into beerhalls and coffeehouses on nearby hills. "Sabbath breaking," to old-guard Americans, is an annoyance of long standing. This feeling was so strong that when some of us took a Sunday ride in several wagons, boys threw stones at us. Americans are only too happy to believe that Germans have nothing and believe nothing. Yet our countrymen, especially in Cincinnati, have split into strong factions, religious and political, and in serried ranks continually menace and attack each other.

Like most American cities, Cincinnati is still nothing but a manufacturing center and commercial hub, and will always be both. The Ohio cannot be taken away, and the land on either bank is thickly settled and produces tons of raw materials. A morning's walk in the market shows an unusual abundance and variety of things from field and forest. At Christmas every respectable butchershop will even have bears for sale.

Colorful congestion at such markets, the way shops are decorated, and the bright atmosphere are vivid reminders of Italy. Small farm-wagons line up on both sides of the square already the evening before, shafts pointing into the street, horses eating there, and open rears turned toward the business. Early in the morning, Americans of English extraction are there buying; few women are among the judges, preachers, and physicians with market baskets. German women arrive about 9:00. They would rather do marketing themselves than have their husbands bring home rancid butter and rotten eggs.

Without doubt, New York, San Francisco, St. Louis, and Cincinnati are American cities of the future. But to me, Cincinnati will not merely be a commercial hub but also a seat of education and culture, a Boston of the West. Cincinnati has quite a healthy climate for an American city, the environs are attractive, and the people incline more than elsewhere to intellectual pursuits. True, right now there is little learning here. The many educated Germans aside, I believe that in the whole city not three people can be found who can read a Greek or Latin book without help.

In these western cities, groups comprise what Americans call "our best society" have just been formed of newly rich families of all educational levels. To have traveled to Europe is a big event among these rich people; and the paintings brought back, the worst trash, are admired as great art. These groups try to separate themselves from the hoi polloi, and enclose themselves in distinct boundaries. Thus, in Cincinnati, there was a club of the English variety where annual dues were set advisedly at $100. But I met many families of English-Americans here, for whom I had deep respect.

Among farmers, as well as the upper classes of the cities, one meets relatively few who are small, narrowminded, or without considerable self-respect, which has its good and bad sides. An original view of life or deep insight into the ways of the world seldom brightens their conversation; but it is always respectful, polite, full of dry humor, abundant of practical insights, and always elevated by deep concern for all people.

There are two elite circles in Cincinnati: one of selected Episcopalians, including old landowners; the other mostly ministers, lawyers, and businessmen. Leaders of the second are the pork merchants, who do business in pork as if they supplied armies. They have a whale in their escutcheon, because swine moved through green waves of prairie grass like whales through the ocean. The two circles are jealous of each other. The first prides itself on aristocratic English or Virginia origins, the second on superior education and sociability. Now and then, leading families of one throw an affair and invite leading families of the other, to put on a special show of splendor and elegance.

There are gatherings in houses nearly every evening. Older people play whist while the younger entertain themselves briskly and boldly. Then: Spanish wines and tropical fruit, a brief dance and the mandatory piano and songs; and whoever is still lucid can enjoy the best of all moments, that late evening hour when ladies are taken home.

It really stands to reason that even Cincinnati has its rich people who are in a position to load an old steamboat with sacks and barrels of sand and stones, insure them for plenty as valuable goods, and when the river is high have ship and cargo burn quite by accident, even though, unfortunately, a few German immigrants lose their lives. I found a taste for such mischief in every American city. You can't live in one without hearing weekly of a new round of humbugs worked to everyone's satisfaction. In the winter of 1847, when American grain and meat were essential to relieve famine in Europe, all Cincinnati was nothing but a hive of incredible swindles.

During the Mexican War, companies of volunteers were raised in Ohio. Some well-known man would issue his call and open a recruiting office. In three days, German-speaking companies were full, English-speaking in ten. Then the regiment moved into tents an hour from Cincinnati. I spent a night there. The German half made merry almost all night. Rules of camp were read out, but little was to be seen of military discipline. At early-morning drill, among our countrymen [Germans], farm boys were joined by young men of a higher class. Of the latter, no one would have thought they would come to this miserable fate. The other companies were mostly Irish and Pennsylvania-Dutch, their non-commissioned officers mainly former German soldiers. The Yankee doesn't take to the musket. To his businessman's eye, selling his blood and freedom for money is not merely a nasty business, it's downright unprofitable.

Nowhere was there more farcical preparation for war than among these volunteers. One would take his place in formation wearing a torn nightshirt; another, dirty underwear. This one marched, that one sauntered. A single Prussian battalion would rout several such American regiments—but only on an open battlefield, mind you! Americans are not to be beaten on their own ground, where every farmer has his old rifle. He won't miss the eye of a squirrel high in the trees one time in ten.

Cincinnati is infested with hooligans. I saw gangs of them once, at a kind of convention. For several days, flights of passenger pigeons darkened the skies. Then came word that they had landed near the Licking River in Kentucky. Hundreds of young fellows guns on their shoulders, crossed the Ohio after the pigeons, shot them out of the trees to their hearts' content. Near the city the hunt was left almost entirely to hooligans, and therefore was seen as no longer an honest pleasure. The numbers of these toughs were equaled only by their wildness. They camped in the forest around bonfires at night. Hot black coffee and countless bottles of whiskey were guzzled. Wherever I overheard laughter and conversation, they were in licentious humor and as often of terrible as of joyful escapades. I should rather have spent the night with Indians than with those people.

Now I understood how it was possible that in a single month there were so many burglaries, murders, and other crimes of violence in Cincinnati. I once walked down a street some twenty paces behind an old clergyman. He was right in front of a firehouse. Out of it, in broad daylight, burst a tough who attacked him, hit him in the mouth with a stone, knocked out some teeth and, laughing, left with the cry: "God bless you, you damned old Dutchman!" Punishment for this outrage would have been possible only had it been possible to pluck the tough out of his gang and bring him to court without his getting away.

On the other hand, I think back with true joy on German festivals and choral jubilees on Bald Hill, a height with a delightful view on the Ohio, circled by vineyards. There was honest pleasure in wine and song, nature and company. Indeed, Cincinnati has a significant number of the most honorable and well-bred Germans. But the German press has its Marats, too, and even in the happiest company a little of the feeling remains that one is in something of a land of exile.

NOTES

Franz von Löher, "The Landscape and People of Cincinnati in 1846–47," trans. and ed. Frederic Trautmann. Reprinted from *Queen City Heritage* 45, no. 2 (1987):21–26. All rights reserved.

1. Robert G. Lunde in *Travels in the Old South: A Bibliography,* ed. Thomas D. Clark (Norman: University of Oklahoma Press, 1959), 201, 265–67.

2. English title: *Land and People in the Old and New Worlds: Travel Sketches* (Göttingen, G. H. Wigand; New York, L. W. Schmidt, 1855–58).

3. *Allgemeine Deutsche Biographie,* s.v. "Franz von Löher," by P. Wittman, vol. 52, p. 59.

4. Selected from vol. 2, p. 46ff.

BRUCE LEVINE

Community Divided: German Immigrants, Social Class, and Political Conflict in Antebellum Cincinnati

The antebellum era was a turning point in American history. First, commercial and industrial development accelerated sharply, developments tied to the growth of the urban and wage-earning population. When Thomas Jefferson was elected president in 1800, by one calculation, fewer than one in five members of America's legally free labor force worked for wages; by Abraham Lincoln's election in 1860, the proportion had reached one in two. Second, the population of the western region of the country grew explosively. Fewer than one in seven U.S. residents had lived in western states or territories in 1800; by 1860 the proportion had surmounted one in three, surpassing the number resident in the Northeast. Third, the antebellum period's mounting struggle over the future of African-American slavery radically reorganized political life and party organization, ultimately exploding in civil war.

Coincident with these three changes was a fourth. In these years immigration rose to unprecedented levels. During the last two antebellum decades alone, more than four and a quarter million Europeans entered the United States, a figure equal to 30 percent of the nation's total free population in 1840. For some time the famine-era Irish composed the largest single block of these newcomers. During the 1850s, however, the German immigration overtook and outstripped all others. The *Auswanderung* of the antebellum era initiated a massive population transfer that would make Germans the most numerous single group of nineteenth-century U.S. immigrants.[1]

Commonly treated as discrete phenomena, these momentous economic, geographical, political, and ethnic changes were all intimately interrelated as various aspects of a larger process—the development of an industrial capitalist society in the distinctive North American context. Many German immigrants were centrally involved in and deeply affected by economic development, westward expansion, and the political polarization over chattel slavery.

In grappling with these novel developments, newcomers tried to adapt values, standards, expectations, and aspirations shaped by their earlier experiences in Europe. That subtle interplay between old and new, European and American, forms one of the central themes of this paper. The process of adaptation was complicated by an important characteristic of the German immigrants. They were quite heterogeneous in socioeconomic as well as intellectual-political terms (much more so, for example, than were the famine-era Irish emigrants). The particular conditions of American society, moreover, its dynamic economy and open political life, served to widen some of the distinctions among German-Americans. Those distinctions, in turn, influenced the ways in which different German-Americans responded to the challenges facing them during America's last antebellum decades. This fact forms the second principal theme of the paper, which traces the elaboration of two broad sociopolitical currents among the immigrants—entrepreneurial liberalism and plebeian radical democracy. Both had roots in Europe, both survived transplantation, adapting to the soil of North America.

Important parts of this story unfolded in the city of Cincinnati, Ohio. By 1860, the country's third-ranked industrial city, the leading manufacturing center of the West, and a hub of interregional commerce, the self-nnointed "Queen City" had also become one of the principal centers of German-American settlement. Outsiders (and ethnic brokers offering to deliver "the Germans" on election day) frequently depicted German-America as a monolith, and prominent immigrants tried repeatedly to unite their *Landsleute* on the basis of ethnic solidarity. But the Germans of Cincinnati were in fact remarkably heterogeneous, whether measured in terms of economic status, religious affinity, or political outlook. During the 1850s, explosive economic, cultural, and political conflicts typical of the era divided and redivided the Queen City. Each of these developments touched important elements of the city's German population as well, in the process illuminating powerful centripetal as well as centrifugal forces at work within that community.

I

Annointing itself "The Queen City of the West," Cincinnati did indeed reign over that region's explosive development. In 1800 fewer than one in seven U.S. residents had lived in the whole region and only 750 dwelled in Cincinnati proper. By 1860 westerners represented more than a third of the nation's population, surpassing the number resident in the Northeast. And Cincinnati's 160,000 residents now ranked it among the ten most populous cities in the country.[2] Its strategic position on the Ohio connected it to the entire Mississippi River system. By the late 1830s the Ohio and Miami canals had also linked the city to the Great Lakes, the Erie Canal, and thus to New York City and the Atlantic. Extensive railroad construction during the following decade multiplied such local, inter-regional, and international connections. From being the West's premier mart, Cincinnati developed into its industrial capital as well. Workshops multiplied and grew in size, flanked by factories employing steam-driven machinery. An English visitor to Cincinnati observed in the early 1850s that the "character of these manufacturing districts" was "making Cincinnati one of the wonders of the New World." Its dramatic industrial development had already transformed it into the *third-ranking manufacturing center* in the country.[3]

Individual Germans had played important and visible roles in Cincinnati's development almost from its founding (in 1788) and incorporation as a town (1802). The city's first mayor, Revolutionary War officer David Ziegler, for example, was a native of Heidelberg. But for a number of decades, Ziegler's countryfolk constituted only a small portion of Cincinnati's residents. In the 1820s, the German-born apparently composed only 5 percent of the total urban population. During the 1830s, however, a combination of economic decline in Germany and economic expansion in the United States encouraged a population transfer that substantially boosted the weight of the foreign-born in the Queen City. By 1840, German-born residents may have composed from 15 to 20 percent of the city's population. By mid-century, more than 40 percent of all Cincinnatians were evidently of either German birth or parentage.[4]

The newcomers included many destined to play leading roles in the life of the city and state. As Queen City entrepreneur and chronicler Charles Cist noted in 1851: "To the industry of foreigners, Cincinnati is indebted in a great degree, for its rapid growth. Their presence here has accelerated the execution of our public improvements, and given an impulse to our immense manufacturing operations, without which they could not have reached their present extent and importance."[5] Cist was apparently thinking of entrepreneurs like Martin Baum, Albert von Stein, and the manufacturing partnership of Gross and Dietrich. Between his arrival in Cincinnati in 1795 and his death in 1831, Martin Baum became one of the city's wealthiest citizens, for a time presiding over the town council, serving as board member for the local branch of the Second Bank of the United States, and launching the Miami Exporting Company, an enterprise heavily involved in both commerce and transportation. Engineer Albert von Stein arrived in 1817 and was soon promoting and building major waterworks, first in Cincinnati, later in Virginia, Louisiana, and Alabama. Immigrating a decade after Stein, Messrs. Gross and Dietrich built the railroad that linked Dayton and Toledo. The partners paid the construction cost (approximately 3 million dollars) out of their personal funds. Samuel Hecht settled in Cincinnati in the 1840s, changed his name to Pike (the English rendering of "hecht"), and soon grew wealthy in the liquor trade. By the end of the following decade, Pike had built the city the largest opera house in the country. Sebastien Myer, Jacob Kornblüth, and others prospered in Cincinnati's important ready-made clothing industry. The "grand-daddy" of Cincinnati coppersmiths, Jeremiah Kiersted was plying his trade in the city by the century's second decade. During the 1830s, his business passed into the hands of his son Hezekiah. Business thrived, bringing young Kiersted community respect and a seat on the city council. In 1860, he presided over the Democratic party's local convention, which nominated him for the post of city commissioner. Hanoverian Frederick Rammelsberg, in the meantime, was pioneering the mechanization of furniture production. Early in the 1850s, Charles Cist rhapsodized about the new six-floor factory built by Rammelsberg and partner Robert Mitchell. "Directly and indirectly" employing some 250 workers—chiefly German- and native-born, most of them skilled—the firm annually turned out nearly a quarter million dollars' worth of beds, tables, chairs, and other cabinetware.[6]

Local, ethnic, and business historians have paid considerable attention to entrepreneurs like Baum, Stein, Gross, and Dietrich, Kiersted, and Rammelsberg. But Cincinnati's economic growth and development attracted, and was made possible by, the influx of far larger numbers of Germans who worked with their hands. As the case of Mitchell and Rammelsberg indicates, many of these immigrant working people labored in the employ of fellow *Landsleute*. During the first two decades of the nineteenth century, Martin Baum strove persistently and successfully to bring to the Queen City newly landed (often indentured) German workers from the port cities of Philadelphia and Baltimore. The bigger immigration of the 1830s further altered the ethnic complexion of the city's "economically active population." By 1840, about one in five members of the Cincinnati work force had been born in Germany. The still more numerous immigration of the next decade evidently contained an even higher proportion of manual workers.[7] During the 1840s, Germans more than doubled their share of the city's total labor force, raising it above 43 percent by mid-century.[8] (See table 2.1.)

Table 2.1. The German-Born in Cincinnati's Population and Work Force, 1850–60.

	Total Population	% of Population German-born	% of Work Force German-born
1850	115,435	29	43
1860	161,044	27	41

Sources: Carl John Abbott, "The Divergent Development of Cincinnati, Indianapolis, Chicago, and Galena, 1840–1860: Economic Thought and Economic Growth" (Ph.D diss., University of Chicago, 1971), 94; J. D. B. De Bow, *Mortality Statistics of the Seventh Census of the United States, 1850* (Washington, D.C.: A. O. P. Nicholson, 1855), 41; Joseph G. Kennedy, *Population of the United States in 1860: Compiled from the Original Returns of the Eighth Census* (Washington, D.C.: GPO), 612.
Note: Percentages have been rounded off to the nearest whole number.

Cincinnatians born in Ireland were less than half as numerous as the Germans, accounting for about 12 percent of the city's population in 1850 and 1860. Visiting Englishwoman Isabella Lucy Bird contemptuously pronounced them "here, as everywhere, hewers of wood and drawers of water." In fact, Germans, too, were heavily represented among Cincinnati's unskilled laborers. It was the imposing German presence in the skilled trades that made the greatest impression on observers like Bird. As early as 1840, when Germans composed about 20 percent of the work force as a whole, they accounted for 30 percent of all tanners and curriers and almost 40 percent of all tailors, shoemakers, and hatters, taken together. Germans were disproportionately represented in the city's dynamic furniture-making industry as well. Although precise figures are not available for 1850 or 1860, the breathtaking growth of the city's German work force combined with the steeply rising average skill level among German workers living in the largely German "Over-the-Rhine" district north of the Miami Canal indicates that German representation in Cincinnati's crafts continued to grow after 1850. "The Germans almost monopolise the handicraft trades," reported Isabella Lucy Bird during her 1854 visit to the city.[9]

II

As elsewhere, the big German immigration of the 1830s (those who arrived in this period became known as *Dreissiger*) left a deep impress on the politics of German America. In Cincinnati, it included an able, sophisticated, and energetic group of liberal intelligentsia, many of them well-educated scions of prosperous German families. In the front ranks of these young *Dreissiger* stood Karl Reemelin, Heinrich Rödter, Stephan Molitor, and Johann Stallo. They and their associates soon formed the core of a new, articulate political leadership for Cincinnati's booming German community. In Germany, classical liberalism's program, representative government plus reduced government involvement in the marketplace, had found few vocal enthusiasts. Powerful, semifeudal elites and an immiserated population hostile to rapid commercial and industrial development intimidated many would-be liberals in the middle class.[10] But in North America, where liberalism thrived, foreign-born adherents rediscovered their self-confidence and their voices.

Born in Heilbronn, Württemberg, in 1814, Karl Gustav Reemelin would eventually become the most prominent immigrant politician in the antebellum Queen City. Reemelin's father was a well-to-do businessman who "read with me, or rather, made me read to him, history and geography, and conversed with me on political economy." For his part, young Karl "was but too happy to be the recipient of ... the ripe politico-economic counsels he gave me." In economics, "it was [then] that I imbibed what some would call ... free-trade ideas."

On the political plane, he learned "how much mischief is caused by false government, and incompetent administration." But Karl Reemelin yearned for a more stimulating life. That quest soon led the young man abroad, and in 1833 he settled in Cincinnati. There he managed to combine prosperity with stimulation as a merchant, real-estate investor, railroad promoter, journalist, and political leader. Attracted to the free-trade, hard-money doctrines of the Jacksonian Democracy and repelled by the nativist and sabbatarian taint of the Whigs, Reemelin helped establish the Democratic *Volksblatt* in 1836 and won election first to the state House of Representatives and then to the state Senate. Admitted to the bar in the late 1840s, Reemelin served in 1850 as a delegate to Ohio's constitutional convention.[11]

Born in 1805 in Neustadt-on-the-Hardt in the Rhenish Palatinate, Heinrich Rödter entered his father's paper mill business at an early age. Like Reemelin, however, Rödter found work in his father's enterprise dreary and stifling, and after experimenting with a military career undertook the study of law. Subsequently involved in the liberal-democratic agitation inspired in Germany by the July 1830 revolution in France, he was forced to flee the fatherland in 1832. In the United States, Rödter soon absorbed himself in civic and political life, and he too strongly identified with the Jacksonian Democracy. Between 1836 and 1840 he managed and edited the Democratic *Volksblatt*. Thereafter, he divided his time between commerce (including, perhaps ironically, an interest in a Columbus paper mill), law, politics, and journalism (returning briefly to the *Volksblatt* in 1842, and between 1850 and 1854 publishing the small *Demokratisches Tageblatt*). Rödter served on the board of education, the city council, and both houses of the state legislature. When he died in 1857, he had recently been elected justice of the peace.[12]

Stephan Molitor was born in 1806 in Chestlitz, Oberfranken, and studied law and philosophy in Germany before migrating to North America in 1830. Here he found employment first on the staff of the *New Yorker Staatszeitung* and then with Buffalo's *Weltbürger*. In 1837 Molitor moved to Cincinnati. Within a decade, he too had been elected to the state legislature. Like Heinrich Rödter, Molitor's real medium was journalism. Indeed, Molitor went into partnership with Rödter on the *Volksblatt* shortly after settling in Cincinnati, becoming sole prorietor in 1840. He retained that position for more than twenty years, earning a reputation as a skillful polemicist and an aggressive businessman.[13]

Johann Bernhard Stallo was the youngest of this group of civic leaders. Born in the Duchy of Oldenburg in 1823 to a family of Frisian schoolmasters, he acquired a secondary education at a Catholic normal school and would for some time pursue a career in Catholic academia. But he also began to develop strong liberal-democratic views early in life and left the fatherland at age sixteen. In Cincinnati he taught German and mathematics for a time at St. Xavier's college, then accepted a professorship at St. John's College in New York during the late 1840s. Thereafter, Stallo returned to Cincinnati, took up jurisprudence, and was for four years (1849–53) Heinrich Rödter's junior law partner. In 1853, Ohio's governor appointed Stallo to an uncompleted term on the Hamilton county court of common pleas. The voters then gave him a full term in that office at the next election. It was apparently in this period that Stallo finally broke with any residual Catholicism. The most reflective and scholarly of the Cincinnati *Dreissiger,* he refined and propagated his own brand of Hegelian-derived philosophical idealism in a series of published works.[14]

As their biographies indicate, these men plunged quickly, successfully, and decisively into the bustling community life of German Cincinnati. In 1834, shortly after their arrival in the city, Karl Reemelin and Heinrich Rödter helped found one of the West's early institutional expressions of German-American liberalism, the German Society. Patterned after success-ful models in New York, Philadelphia, and elsewhere in the East, the new association aimed to assure "that as citizens of the United States we can take part in the people's government which our duty and right commands." Economic difficulties would be ameliorated through the efforts of volun-tarily associated community members. At its first meeting, the German Society pledged "through reciprocal aid" to "mutually assure ourselves of a better future, to assist those in need, and to secure generally those charitable aims which are impossible to the single individual."[15]

A handful of these *Dreissiger* became Whigs. But Whig liberalism contained a strong admixture of fundamentalist, temperance, and sabbatarian zealotry, generally alien to German liberalism and the conditions under which it had developed. These attitudes, moreover, bolstered nativist inclinations that naturally repelled would-be immigrant supporters.[16] Like the great majority of their *Landsmänner* throughout the United States, most *Dreissiger* liberals initially adhered to the Democratic party, which presented itself as the champion of equal opportunity and tolerance for cultural diversity. In 1843, thus, Rödter and Molitor helped found Cincinnati's *Deutsche demokratische Verein* (the German Democratic Association). This *Verein* dedicated itself both to uniting the city's Ger-man population behind the Democratic party and to holding the latter to liberal-democratic principles—"Equal rights and complete justice for all men, irrespective of religious or political beliefs."[17]

With the aid of institutions like the German Society and the German Democratic Association, Cincinnati's prominent *Dreissiger* sought to rally the rest of their *Landsleute* behind their sociopolitical philosophy. Karl Reemelin's political career owed much to calls for ethnic solidarity. The growth of nativism in these years, moreover, lent urgency to those calls. In 1844, a committee of progressive German newspaper editors solemnly foreswore internecine polemics and threatened to brand violators of their truce as the "common enemy of the immigrant," since "to be able to conquer the common enemy, we need more than ever to be united."[18]

But it was easier to declare such a *Burgfrieden* than to enforce it, particularly since those who declared it in the first place could not speak for the community as a whole.

On the right, *Dreissiger* liberals faced a powerful foe in the Catholic hierarchy and its lay supporters. Launched in 1837 as the country's first Catholic-German newspaper, the weekly *Wahrheits-Freund* (Friend of Truth) enabled Father John M. Henni (later archbishop of Milwaukee) to present a conservative alternative to the *Volksblatt*. In 1850, reinforcements arrived when the principal of the St. Mary's parish school, Joseph Anton Hemann, began bringing out the daily *Volksfreund* (People's Friend), a conservative Democratic paper oriented toward German Catholics. Two-thirds of the city's Germans may well have been Catholics. That fact alone automatically assured neither intellectual nor political hegemony to the Catholic hierarchy. The city's German liberal and Catholic newspapers evidently circulated in roughly equivalent numbers.[19]

But Catholic conservatives found allies among powerful figures in the Cincinnati (i.e., Hamilton County) Democratic party. As German immigration mounted, leading native-born Democrats grew increasingly wary of the growing electoral might exercised by Reemelin and company. At the same time, they bridled at the growing assertiveness of free-soil Democrats occasioned by Salmon Chase's election to the U.S. Senate. In August of 1851, the party's old-line leaders, centered around the editorial staff of the *Cincinnati Enquirer,* formed a secret faction (called the "Miami Tribe") that aimed to limit the intraparty influence of both German liberals and native-born free-soilers.[20] Eight years earlier, the *Dreissiger* had conditioned their support for the Democrats on that party's rejection of ethnic discrimination and loyalty to liberal principles. The "Miami" revelations seemed to prove that these conditions had been violated. The effect was to break the bonds of party loyalty, and for the next few years Reemelin, Molitor, and company cast about for a new electoral orientation.

III

Under fire by the 1850s from the Catholic and Democratic Right, the liberal *Dreissiger* now confronted a challenge from the Left as well. The massive immigration of the late 1840s and early 1850s, the so-called

Achtundvierziger (Forty-eighter) generation, brought more than strong backs and skilled hands to Cincinnati. The new arrivals included (as one Cincinnati chronicler would recall) "many heroic spirits that had been embittered by those injustices which had provoked the rebellion of 1848."[21]

Until rather recently, the view that 1848 had been a "revolution of the intellectuals" strongly influenced students of the era's emigration.[22] Most were willing to recognize as "political exiles" only those from the intelligentsia. Other emigrants were presumed to have left Germany solely for "economic" motives, narrowly defined. Marcus Lee Hansen's seminal article of 1930, entitled "The Revolution of 1848 and the German Emigration," gave classic formulation to this perspective. Professor Hansen simply dismissed the idea "that the large German emigration of the decade of the 'fifties was in some way associated with the course and outcome of the revolutions of 1848." Observers who "saw the crowds of stolid and slow-moving peasants, labourers with calloused hands, and worried and sober artisans realized that their thoughts were not dwelling on politics or revolution."[23] Making Hansen's assumptions even more explicit, Hildegard Binder Johnson described the certifiedly "political" *Achtundvierziger* as follows: "He affected student costume or immitated the style of the romantic hero of the Revolution, Friedrich Hecker, by wearing a broad-brimmed hat, a shirt open at the neck, and a loosely tied scarf. . . . He was set off from the mass of immigrants, the peasants and the craftsmen, by delicate hands that showed no signs of physical labor."[24]

This view of the revolution, who made it, and whom it touched obscured the dramatic broadening of the social base of dissent, protest, and resistance that had taken place in Germany since the 1830s. A convergence of economic, political, and demographic changes during the prerevolutionary decades steadily undermined the conditions in which most German small producers and wage earners, urban and rural, lived and worked.[25] Hoping to save themselves from dependence and ruin—to obtain, in the words of journeyman printer and union leader Stephan Born, "social freedom and independent existence"—such plebeians gave the 1848 revolution most of its force and radical edge. In their name leaders, parties, and popular associations demanded a more thoroughly democratic form of government (including a sharper separation of church and state) than most liberals urged; and to protect them the Forty-eighter Left sought a strong state role in limiting the polarization of wealth and poverty, curbing the appetites and prerogatives of the elite, and assuring just and harmonious relations among the society's various social classes.

The principal national labor congress of 1848, the *Allgemeine deutsche Arbeiterkongress,* promulgated just such a program. Members of the democratic intelligentsia of southern and western Germany attempted to summarize the same basic principles in the phrase *Wohlstand, Freiheit, und Bildung für Alle* (prosperity, freedom, and education for all).[26]

The emigration of the earlier 1840s had already sent to America thousands of common people imbued with such values. Those who departed after the revolution's defeat included plebeian democrats in still larger numbers. As George von Skal pointed out years ago: "While prior to 1848 . . . the liberal movement was practically confined to the educated classes, it had now spread, especially in Baden, the Palatinate and Rhenish Prussia, to the body of the people. Consequently the [political] refugees were no longer almost without exception men of high attainments and superior abilities, as had been the case before. These classes still found a large percentage, but with them came small shopkeepers, artisans, farmers, and even laborers."[27]

By the middle of the 1850s, newcomers like these were reshaping the features of German Cincinnati. "Skilled, educated, and intellectual," Isabella Lucy Bird reported in 1854, they "constitute an influence of which the Americans themselves are afraid." And not only the Americans. From this milieu came German-American leaders whose vision of freedom, democracy, and justice diverged from that cherished by most *Dreissiger* liberals. "The creeds which they profess," noted Mrs. Bird, "are 'Socialism' and 'Universalism,' and at stated periods they assemble to hear political harangues, and address invocations to universal deity." If, as always, the most self-conscious activists still constituted a small minority of the new arrivals, they were able nevertheless to play leadership roles because the experiences and aspirations they invoked resonated widely.[28]

In Cincinnati, three organizations most clearly embodied the new milieu in existence by the mid-1850s. Established in November, 1850, a general *Arbeiterverein* (workers' association) based itself principally among craft workers—especially tailors, cabinetmakers, shoemakers, carpenters, masons, bakers, locksmiths, and machinists—and some day laborers. Over the next decade its leaders included tailors Kaspar Gams, Johann Hempel, and Johann Blankenheim; cabinetmakers Gottlieb F. Wiest and L. A. Maffey; baker Ludwig Ziegler; iron molder Friedrich Oberkline; and August Willich, a former Prussian army officer turned carpenter and radical labor organizer. At various times this *Arbeiterverein* published a newspaper, maintained a cooperative grocery, and offered a range of musical, theatrical, and political activities to its members. Moreover, independent groups of German cabinetmakers, tailors, cigarmakers, coopers, laborers, and others in the city created their own trade unions.[29]

Another product of the city's *Achtundvierziger* immigration was the *Turngemeinde*, the first such body to appear in the United States. Initiated in Germany during the Napoleonic era to develop the minds and bodies of Germany's youth, the Turner movement retained its early devotion to physical culture while over the decades infusing its nationalism with an increasingly radical-democratic content. Germany's Turners plunged into the struggles of 1848–49. A group of emigres in Cincinnati, galvanized by a visit from German democratic hero Friedrich Hecker, gathered in the private rooms of housepainter J. A. Eiselen, and founded a Turner chapter in the fall of 1848. Before long the new *Gemeinde* rented a lot and erected a hall that became one of the central meeting places of German democrats. By 1854, the chapter claimed some 330 paid-up members.[30]

Isabella Lucy Bird's references to "Universalism" and "invocations to universal deity" point to the religious rationalism (or "free thought") common among *Achtundvierziger* (as well as many *Dreissiger*) activists, a general outlook that identified with the Enlightenment and rejected supernaturalism. The national *Turn-Zeitung* noted that while members covered a spectrum "from adherents of orthodox Christianity to atheists of the Hegelian school," still, "the greatest number subscribe to an independent naturalist philosophy." In that last category, agnostics rubbed shoulders with various Christian "liberals" as well as nontraditionalist Jews.[31]

More contentious, and considerably larger, than Cincinnati's Turner group was the *Verein für geistige Aufklärung und sociale Reform* (Society for Spiritual Enlightenment and Social Reform). Abbreviating its name in March 1852, to the *Verein freier Männer,* or simply the *Freimänner-verein* (Freemen's Society), this association remained dedicated to radical democracy and free thought.[32] With a probable membership between five hundred and a thousand, plus a sizeable periphery of sympathizers, the Cincinnati *Freimännerverein* defiantly conducted public meetings in its hall each Sunday morning, organized its members and supporters into mutual-insurance, reading, discussion, theater, gymnastic, and women's auxiliary groups, and sponsored a variety of public lectures and other cultural events. Its most articulate and colorful representative was the youthful Friedrich Hassaurek, a self-styled *"Social Demokrat."* As a sixteen-year-old student at the University of Vienna, Hassaurek had participated actively in the Austrian revolution. The triumph of reaction sent him to America, and toward the end of 1850 he began editing the weekly Cincinnati *Hochwächter* ("Guardian"). A paper with that name had been published in the late 1840s by Württemberger George Walker, a rationalist and polemically inclined seminarian. Under Hassaurek's direction, the new *Hochwächter* became the Freemen's voice in the city, identifying itself as "an organ for spiritual enlightenment and social reform." By the fall of 1854, its increasingly secular interests broadened the paper's self-conception, and the *Hochwächter* began calling itself simply "an organ of general progress."[33] By then the *Freimännerverein* had become an important political and cultural pole in German Cincinnati, with Hassaurek supporting and exhorting the city's labor movement, repeatedly challenging *Volksblatt* editors to verbal duels, and actually drawing such prominent opponents as German Methodist patriarch Wilhelm Nast into face-to-face public debates. Before long even the whiggish and wary *Cincinnati Gazette* was acknowledging the Freemen's best-known leader to be "a young man of much intellectual ability and force as a writer" and, more significantly, "one of the principal men of influence in this city." In 1855, the largely German Tenth Ward sent Hassaurek to the city council.[34]

Who joined these organizations? A leader of the national *Turner* movement asserted proudly in 1854 that "with few exceptions, the members of the Turner Union belong to the working class."[35] This was an

Table 2.2. Occupations of Some Early Members
of the Cincinnati *Turngemeinde*.

Occupational Category	Number	% of Total
Skilled crafts	48	66
Merchants, shippers, financiers	9	12
Manufacturers	3	4
Restaurant- and Innkeepers	5	7
Professionals	2	3
White collar	3	4
Unskilled	3	4
Total	73	100

Source: Hugo Gollmer, *Namensliste der Pioniere des Nord-Amerik. Turnerbundes der Jahre 1848–1862* (St. Louis, Mo.: Henry Rauth, 1885).

exaggeration, but one containing an important kernel of truth. Decades later, Hugo Gollmer (a Stuttgart-born lithographer and cofounder of the Cincinnati *Gemeinde*) compiled occupational and other data for many early Turners. His lists, though fragmentary, illuminate the social composition of the Cincinnati chapter. (See table 2.2.)

The profile that emerges from table 2.2 highlights two important characteristics of the Turner movement and the larger immigrant democratic milieu of which it formed a part.[38] First, craft workers did indeed furnish its socioeconomic core, in the case of the Queen City Turners, providing perhaps two-thirds of the membership. Second, the doctrines, activities, and organizations that attracted these craft workers could also appeal to other members of the community. Leading *Freimänner* thus included blacksmith Michael Doberrer, tailor George Friedlien, and machinist J. P. Fisch, as well as teacher Edward Steffens and successful bookbinder Charles Meininger.[37] Even the *Arbeiterverein* included a handful of shopkeepers, teachers, and physicians.[38] Here, in short, was the transplanted social formation that Eric Hobsbawm has described in the Old World— the coalition of "discontented petty-bourgeoisie of independent artisans, shopkeepers, farmers" plus "a mass of skilled workers" that "probably formed the main corps of radicalism in Western Europe" in these years.[39]

The social composition of the milieu as a whole helps clarify its particular *Weltanschauung*. As Isabella Lucy Bird's report had noted, the characteristically *Achtundvierziger* societies—particularly the *Arbeitervereine, Turnvereine,* and *Freimännervereine*—were frequently identified (and identified themselves) with "socialism." But very few among the radical democracy's diverse constituency understood by this term an irreconcilable struggle between labor and capital, much less one destined to collectivize property in the hands of a proletarian state and eventually dissolve classes altogether. For most, on the contrary, class conflict was something to be deplored and resolved, not organized and brought to a head. The kind of program most appealing to *Achtundvierziger* activists was outlined in a series of articles that appeared in the *Turn-Zeitung* in 1851. There, "socialism" was equated with "a democratic-republican constitution that guarantees everyone prosperity, free quality education to maximize personal capabilities, and the elimination of all sources of hierarchical and privileged power."[40] The *Sozialistischer Turnerbund* later made the point more explicit when it declared: "The socialism of today, in which we Turners believe, aims to remove the pernicious antagonism between labor and capital. It endeavors to effect a reconciliation between these two and to try to establish a peace by which the rights of the former are fully protected against the encroachments of the latter."[41]

Such an outlook commonly went under the name "red republicanism" in Europe, and it was this vision that animated most *Achtundvierziger* democrats of Ohio. That much became clear in March 1854, when representatives from *Turner-, Freimänner-, Arbeitervereine,* and kindred organizations throughout the state gathered in Cincinnati to formulate a common declaration of principles. The conference met in Freemen's Hall, located on the corner of Vine and Mercer streets in the heart of the Over-the-Rhine district. Delegates attended from Toledo, Cincinnati, Dayton, Columbus, Akron, Cleveland, Norwalk, Hamilton, Rossville, Sandusky, Chillicothe, Massillon, Portsmouth, Concordia, Black River, and Wapakoneta. They bore credentials from workingmen's associations, Freemen chapters, discussion clubs, cultural groups, singing societies, reading circles, *Turnvereine* (although evidently not Cincinnati's), farmers' societies, ad hoc mass meetings, and ethnically defined affiliates of broader fraternal organizations (such as Chillicothe's Lodge No. 6 of the Order of the Sons of Liberty). Among Cincinnati's representatives were Kaspar Gams and Gottlieb Wiest for the *Arbeiterverein;* a Freemen contingent led by Hassaurek and including two trunkmakers and a cigarmaker; and (representing the German Discussion Society) William Renau, a teacher in the city's Jewish school.[42]

In two days of deliberation, the delegates fulfilled their charge and hammered out a platform, copies of which the *Vereine* distributed by the thousands, in both German and English.[43] Not surprisingly, a number of its planks emphasized the rights and interests of the foreign-born, seeking to speed their enfranchisement and protect them while traveling abroad. The United States' long-standing refusal to intervene in European affairs, a source of special frustration to political refugees, drew correspondingly withering fire.

This platform sought to do more than defend the special interests of a particular ethnic group. Its leitmotiv, instead, was the need to defend and extend republicanism in general, at least as these Forty-eighter plebeians understood that creed. To make the American political system more representative and responsive, the convention demanded direct election and recall of all public officials and the sharp reduction of their salaries. Expressing a fervent belief in the power of education, the convention declared universal, free, compulsory schooling through the age of fourteen essential to maintaining an informed citizenry. Other proposals aimed to limit the concentration of wealth and improve the condition of the working population. These included calls to reduce the working day to ten hours, pass a mechanics' lien law, and initiate a "thorough reform" of poor houses and public infirmaries.

In the same vein, delegates asserted that the then-projected Pacific Railroad, the capstone of the era's transportation revolution, should be publicly rather than privately owned. Concerning the disposition of the vast public lands of the West, the convention endorsed the central demand of the nation's radical land-reform movement. To ensure their use as homesteads rather than as speculative investments, the convention urged, these lands should be neither given nor sold to states or private corporations but instead "granted outright to actual settlers." On the issue of slavery, the Cincinnati convention took up a radical free-soil position.[44]

The conference at Freemen's Hall placed church-state relations in this social and political context. Immigrant radical-Democrats carried in their baggage strongly secularist and anticlerical traditions. In Europe, the bond between religious and sociotemporal dissent mirrored the alliance between established churches and Europe's ruling elites. As Eric Hobsbawm observes, "basically anti-clericalism was political, because the chief passion behind it was the belief that established religions were hostile to progress." In Europe, "the line between right and left became largely that between clerical and anti-clerical." A highly placed German journalist asserted at the time that "Religion now forms the axis around which everything, including politics, revolves, and this will become even truer in the near future."[45]

The inseparability of religion and politics seemed nowhere clearer than in the Roman Catholic church, which exercised its greatest influence in southern Germany. Until 1846, Pope Gregory VI administered the Roman Catholic church in the spirit of his 1832 encyclical, *Mirari vos,* opposing alike the separation of church and state; "the senseless and erroneous idea, better still, absurdity, that freedom of conscience is to be claimed and defended for all men"; "complete and unrestrained freedom of opinion which is spreading everywhere to the harm of both the Church and the State"; freedom of the press; and all forms of rebellion against "our dearest sons in Jesus Christ, the princes." His successor, Pius IX, proved loyal to Gregory's principles, eventually summarizing his reaction to the age of revolutions in the *Syllabus Errorum,* which denounced the "error" of believing that "the Roman Pontiff can and should reconcile himself to and agree with progress, liberalism, and modern civilization." Nor, by the 1840s, did official German Protestantism provide very sharp a contrast. In the years leading up to the revolution, the Prussian monarchy authorized, and leaders of the church's pietistic right spearheaded, an energetic purge of Enlightenment-inspired currents. No wonder, then, that to Cincinnati's Catholic *Wahrheits-Freund,* "those fleeing from the various unsuccessful revolutions of Europe" appeared "full of hatred toward Catholicism" and "almost all without any religion" at all.[46]

To many later writers, European anticlericalism appeared alien, anachronistic, irrelevant in the United States, which had dispensed with established churches half a century earlier. But as Tocqueville noted in the 1830s, while the organized church "in America takes no direct part in the government of society," nevertheless religion as such "must be regarded as the foremost of political institutions of that country," one which most had come to consider "indispensable to the maintenance of republican institutions."[47] The proliferation a generation later of evangelically inspired statutes prohibiting the consumption of alcoholic beverages and strictly regulating public conduct on the Sabbath demonstrated the continuing relevance of Tocqueville's observation and of the immigrant secularists' preoccupation.

The conduct of American Catholicism seemed no more reassuring. Hostile to Protestant evangelicalism, the Catholic press also repeatedly denounced forty-eighter emigres, and a national tour by Hungarian revolutionary Lajos Kossuth attracted the church's anger like a lightning rod. As Pittsburgh's Archbishop O'Connor explained in a public letter, "the Catholics of the United States generally have shown little sympathy for Mr. Kossuth," who had earned that reception by allying with "European Socialists and Red Republicans." Two weeks later, during Kossuth's enthusiastic reception in Cincinnati, a Catholic militant raged at a Queen City forum that Americans "import traitors from Europe and make heroes of them!" Some audience members hissed but were drowned out (according to a newspaper account) by the speaker's "religious friends." Another incident the following spring further inflamed these antagonisms. In March 1853, a *Freimännerverein* member of Catholic birth died and was buried in St. Peter's German Catholic Cemetery. The cemetery's trustees objected to his presence, however, and had the corpse unearthed and reburied off consecrated ground. That step caused a sensation, and a combined party of Turners and Freemen returned the coffin to its original resting place.[48]

More fundamental was the dispute over public education that erupted around the same time. Citing pervasive Protestant influence in Ohio's common-school curriculum, Cincinnati's Archbishop John B. Purcell sought state funding for Catholic parochial schools or exemption from the public school tax for families supporting the parochial system. German freethinkers bridled. As ardent champions of a secularized but strengthened system of public education, they regarded Purcell's initiative as a reactionary attack on one of their most cherished institutions. In this atmosphere, therefore, German-born radical-democrats saw little reason to abandon the militantly secular and anticlerical aspects of their worldview. "I was a Freeman in Germany," reasoned Cincinnatian Lewis Dericus, "and why should I not be in this country?"[49]

Ohio's *Achtundvierziger* placed church-state relations in this context. "The constitution guarantees freedom of thought," the delegates declared, and this included religious, or irreligious, belief. Religion ought to be a private matter, they continued. There should be no religious test for those wishing to hold office or give testimony in court, the Bible should no longer be used as a text in the public schools, and "Sunday laws" should be abolished. While thus striving to curb the temporal power of puritan and evangelical Protestantism, the delegates identified the Roman Catholic hierarchy as an even greater threat. "In the interest of the Republic," they demanded "that the Pope's exercise of power in the United States through the medium of bishops and other agents be ended, that his interference in the affairs of the nation's citizens be energetically resisted and that the Jesuit order be treated as an open enemy of the Republic."[50]

The goals and demands embodied in the platform of Ohio's German plebeian radicals by no means signified "a conscious rejection of capitalism." But they certainly did reflect distinctive "qualities of consciousness," specifically, a desire to refashion American society along lines more consistently democratic than was acceptable to the local (and national) business and political elite.[51] Like similar meetings then occurring in Wisconsin, Kentucky, Illinois, Indiana, and elsewhere, this convention and the platform it produced provoked cries of indignation from conservative-minded opponents. The Democratic *Cincinnati Enquirer* found the very "idea of men banding themselves politically together, according [to] the place of their nativity or the language which they speak" anathema, because it "exhibits a clannishness of spirit." "It should be the object of all foreigners who arrive in this country," the editor instructed, "to become American citizens as soon as possible, and not to perpetuate their nationalities by acting together as Germans, or Irish, in political matters." The Cincinnati platform seemed to the editor a natural product of so essentially un-American a meeting. The Sunday law he defended as a proper "feature of a *Christian* government." The right of recall was a "perfectly wild and visionary idea" that "would introduce anarchy into the Government at once." The convention's fundamental error, summarized the *Enquirer,* was to be remain fixated upon "an European rather than an American model" of democracy. "The European idea of Democracy," the editor explained, "has always been essentially different from the America, and has never succeeded so well in actual trial. The former carries it to a point where it borders on anarchy and unbridled license."[52]

IV

During the 1850s, three distinct but related conflicts—concerning the relationship between labor and capital in America, the democratic revolution and its enemies, and the future of chattel slavery in the United States—revealed and amplified some of the differences within German Cincinnati sketched above.

We begin with labor and capital. In this era of dramatic economic growth and development, many among the city's working people flourished, immigrant and native-born alike. Isabella Lucy Bird believed that German *Handwerker* in Cincinnati "find a fruitful field for their genius and industry." The liberal *Volksblatt* agreed. "In America," it declared, "the worker is the sovereign." "Who is it who sets the price of labor?" it asked, and replied: "It is the worker." And again: "Most millionaires became such only because they had earlier been workers."[53]

The experience of the Puchta family seemed to confirm such observations. Arriving in Cincinnati in 1856, twenty-three-year-old Lorenz Puchta began his career here as a shoemaker's apprentice. A decade later found him the proprietor of his own shop and shoestore. As his business grew, Puchta's role began to change. He still measured and cut the leather and fitted up the lasts, and his wife Barbara Katharina assisted him in running the establishment. Lorenz Puchta assigned other production tasks to his ten or more outworking employees. As the family continued to prosper, son George (born in 1860) graduated from a business college and began to sell shoemaking machinery and leather-tanning supplies. From there he moved on to manufacturing equipment in general, "gradually extended the scope of the business and surrounded himself with a corps of assistants, enabling him to develop one of the most extensive and prosperous business concerns of the city." George Puchta's election as mayor of Cincinnati in 1916–17 crowned this intergenerational success story.[54]

Not everyone fared as well. The same dynamic American economy that offered opportunity to the Puchtas also had other effects. The increasing scale and changing organization of production transformed relations between growing numbers of employees and their employers, often widening the gap that separated their actual conditions, perceived interests, and general outlooks. Increasing job competition, seasonal unemployment, a growing division and mechanization of labor, and periodic wage cuts undermined working conditions and living standards for many. In the late 1840s and early 1850s, moreover, inflation cut further into working-class incomes.[55]

In Cincinnati, the liberal German Society had hoped to solve economic problems through community-wide cooperation and charity. During the 1850s, however, some immigrant working people turned to measures of another sort. Groups of craft workers founded producer and consumer cooperatives to protect themselves against free-market forces and the expansion of the wage-labor system. Other forms of cooperation also appeared. The Cincinnati *Arbeiterverein* cohered in 1850 out of efforts to aid tailors and other workers on strike in eastern cities. In 1853, a nationwide strike wave swept through the Queen City.[56] With the active encouragement of *Achtundvierziger* leaders like Friedrich Hassaurek, German tailors, cigarmakers, bookprinters, and waiters organized for higher wages, and German cabinetmakers collaborated with their native-born counterparts to the same end. In December, a general meeting of trade societies resolved to form a General Trades' Union (GTU), since "all trades have an equal and identical interest, and ... if united, ... could better resist the encroachments of capital and secure to ourselves a more just compensation for our labor." Sixty unions ultimately affiliated.[57]

The escalation and generalization of industrial conflict rearranged patterns of loyalty and antagonism in Cincinnati as a whole and among its German residents as well. For one thing, German-American workers drew closer to one another despite differences in locale and occupation. They had, as Cincinnati tailor and labor leader Kaspar Gams explained, "learned through experience that all the workers' individual efforts to improve their conditions are fruitless." And during the 1850s the city's *Arbeiterverein* and independent *Handwerker* unions consistently supported attempts to create a durable, nationwide German-American labor league.[58]

Class unity that crossed lines of nativity was much more difficult to effect: the 1850s witnessed repeated conflicts among the various ethnic groupings of the Cincinnati population. But the steadily increasing pressure of the trade-union struggle did force recurrent efforts among workers to reach out to one another even across ethnic boundaries, and attempts by Germans to link up with English-speaking workers began early in the decade. Cincinnati's German and native-born cabinetmaker organizations collaborated closely and effectively in the strike movement of 1853 and merged into a single union in 1859. At the end of the decade, on the crest of a new organizing wave (and in reaction to a bill in the state legislature threatening the rights of strikers), German- and English-speaking trade unionists joined in a revived GTU.[59]

The growth of working-class cohesion and the sharpening of class antagonisms weakened bonds of ethnic loyalty within German Cincinnati. Few antebellum employers considered a demand for a collective wage increase backed up with the threat of a work stoppage to be business as usual. It represented a challenge by the organized wage earners to the employer's assumed right unilaterally to govern the enterprise. An even more explicit attempt to institutionalize the work force's collective power appeared in demands for a union shop, in which joining the union was mandatory. In November 1853, journeymen typographers began a bitter newspaper strike over wages, the use of apprentices, and the demand for a union shop. The Journeymen Book Binder's Union supported the typographers, declaring that "all past experience proves that where capital had the power, it has used it for the oppression of the laboring masses," and that "the laborers in any branch of business have a right and are the proper ones to set a price upon their own labor, and also to adopt such rules and regulations as will serve to protect their own interests against the encroachments of employer and capitalist." Employers replied that these were "infringements upon the rights of proprietors." Such views were not confined to native-born employers. Six years later, the same issue was posed by the city's united journeymen cabinetmakers. Striking the city's major furniture manufacturers in 1859, the multiethnic but predominantly German union coupled wage demands with calls for a union shop and the creation of *ein stehende Comité* (a permanent "standing committee") in each factory to represent the work force's interests on a day-to-day basis.[60]

Aggressive collective action in pursuit of higher incomes was alien to the traditions and values of liberal *Dreissiger* such as Karl Reemelin, who trusted the free market to judge and reward their individual abilities and efforts. As later recorded in his memoirs, Reemelin "had brought with me, from Germany," the belief that "those that get more wages than they merit, accumulate ill-will against themselves, while those who get less than they deserve, accumulate credit for merit." In 1853, striking German-born tailors challenged such beliefs and challenged the power of their *Landsleute* among Cincinnati garment manufacturers. The employers, for their part, threatened to break the local tailors' union by selling Eastern-made garments in their shops. Amid the great cabinetmaker strike of 1859, immigrant furniture manufacturer Frederick Rammelsberg and his colleagues "firmly protest[ed] against any interference in the control or management of our factories" and vowed to "resist all action of any *union* assuming to dictate rules or regulations for adoption." They counterposed to the demand for increased workers' power a reliance on the forces of free and individual exchange. Insisting that "the law of supply and demand will regulate the scale of prices [wages] and fix it on an equitable basis," they added (in classic Lockean terms) that "No wrong, much less suffering, exists except when incapability or intemperance is the cause."[61]

V

In the waning weeks of 1853, German radicals in Cincinnati demonstrated something of their strength and combativeness as well as their continued devotion to the cause of 1848. In late December, the Queen City became the scene of the largest of the many protests across the country against the visit of Gaetano Bedini and his cordial reception at the White House. A papal nuncio, Bedini was accused of complicity in the bloody suppression of the Italian revolution of 1848 and, more specifically, in the torture and execution of Garibaldi's associate and chaplain, Ugo Bassi. As already noted, this was by no means the first conflict to pit the city's Catholic church (or, for that matter, evangelical Protestants) against German critics. But the sheer size, and dénouement, of this protest set it apart and catapulted Cincinnati's immigrant radicals into local and national headlines. The late Carl Wittke, dean of historians of German America, labeled the Queen City protest "a disgraceful demonstration by German Turners," and similar attitudes have colored other accounts.[62]

Bedini's U.S. tour brought him to Cincinnati in December 1853, where he took up temporary residence with Archbishop John Baptist Purcell on Eighth Street adjoining the St. Peter in Chains Cathedral. To the radical-democratic partisans of the 1848 revolution, this act was an unbearable provocation. A meeting hastily convened at Freemen's Hall on Christmas morning, Sunday, December 25. In the mistaken belief that Bedini planned to depart the following day, Monday the 26, the Freemen decided to take action that same Christmas night. They would march in procession to the archbishop's residence, then continue down to Fifth Street, and there burn Bedini in effigy. Hurried preparations for the impending demonstration, including the manufacture of effigy, gallows, and banners, consumed Sunday afternoon and evening. Messengers circulating through the German community visited the *Arbeiterverein* and the *Turngemeinde.* The workers' association quickly met and dispatched a contingent of about twenty to join the demonstration. The Turners held no meeting but informed their members of the planned protest, some of whom joined the march as well.[63]

As it turned out, the protesters were not the only ones active that Christmas Sunday. Word of the intended action reached the ears of Cincinnati's police chief and police judge. On the grounds that the marchers planned to harm Bedini personally, these officials detailed a large body of watchmen (police) to intercept and break up the demonstration. Unaware of these developments, the protesters gathered, organized their ranks, and stepped off from Freemen's Hall at approximately 10 P.M. Estimates of the number of participants varied from six to twelve hundred, including women and children. An unusual degree of female participation in public life had distinguished Germany's mid-century freethinkers' movement, and the Cincinnati *Freimännerverein* was correspondingly proud of its *Frauenverein.*[64] The *Cincinnati Gazette,* however, could only presume that so many "ladies of intelligence" had participated in a boisterous evening street demonstration because they had been "carried away with the intense excitement of disgust and indignation of their husbands and brothers."[65]

The procession formed up along quasi-military lines, dividing itself into four divisions, each with its own captain. Participants marched four abreast, arm in arm. Bilingual banners borne aloft reflected the Jacobin-like caste of their republicanism. "Liberty, Equality, Love and Fraternity" read one. "No Priests, No Kings, no Popery," demanded another. Others read, more simple, "Down with Bedini" and "The Gallows-Bird Bedini." A stocky German carried the gallows frame on which Bedini's effigy was to be hanged. The marchers headed down to Ninth Street as planned. There, however, they ran afoul of some one hundred members of the Cincinnati police force, who suddenly charged the demonstrators, beat them with clubs, tore down their banners, fired into their ranks at point-blank range, arrested those they could hold, and pursued those who fled through the streets. "The stampede was complete," went one account, "—husbands were separated from their wives, and screams and shouts added to the confusion of the noise of firearms." Police claimed that a marcher had fired the first shot. Freemen leaders rejected that claim, adding that no one in authority had even bothered to call upon the demonstrators to disperse before signaling the police charge.[66]

All told, the police crowded more than sixty Germans into the watch house, Friedrich Hassaurek among them. Fourteen of those arrested had sustained bullet wounds, and twenty-six-year-old Palatine native Karl Eggerlin subsequently died of his injuries. At least five marchers who escaped arrest were also wounded. On the other side, one policeman was shot in the leg. Police claimed to have confiscated a total of three pistols, one dagger, three canes, one sword cane, a sheathed butcher knife, and a few other weapons.[67]

This bloody confrontation triggered a tremendous public uproar. Prominent citizens and the English-language press at first blamed the demonstrators for the violence. So did some respected German-Americans. Prosperous coppersmith and alderman Hezekiah Kiersted initially believed "that the [anti-Bedini] procession should have been intercepted before reaching the bishop's house" and had offered personally to arrest the "ringleader" (evidently meaning Hassaurek). But as the Freemen energetically presented their version of the night's events, public reaction shifted. On Monday, Freemen and others were on the streets throughout the city handing out circulars and posting placards explaining and defending their motives and conduct the previous night. When Eggerlin died, sympathizers organized a monster funeral procession in his honor, in effect a demonstration in support of the remaining sixty-three defendants. At length, in a move furiously denounced by the mayor, the prosecuting attorney himself asked the court to dismiss the case for lack of evidence of criminal misconduct; the court agreed.[68]

The whole affair had redounded against both the Catholic hierarchy and the city's officialdom. When the Freemen established a fund to aid those wounded during the so-called Weihnachts riot, Archbishop Purcell donated ten dollars, explaining that "when there is a question of relieving those who suffer and are poor, all differences of faith or opinion should be forgotten." But the Freemen would not be mollified. League president Edward Steffens replied that "the blood of a brother, barbarously murdered, stands between you and us." Freemen could not accept the archbishop's donation, moreover, "persuaded as we are, by a long train of historical facts, and by the late occurrences, that a Jesuit under the guidelines of the despotic King of Rome can never mean good, nor deal with sincerity toward men known to cherish republican opinions and sentiments of justice, and brotherly affection for mankind, as we do. We beg to return the ten dollar bill to you, which you will find herein enclosed."[69] The momentum of the anti-Bedini protest increased during the following days. After the dismissal of charges against him and his fellows, Friedrich Hassaurek turned the tables on his accusers and pressed charges of his own against 109 policemen, the police chief, and the police judge. In the meantime, the German singing societies of Cincinnati gave a concert at Freemen's Hall to raise money to defray the legal costs arising from all this litigation.[70]

VI

In the anti-Bedini campaign, Cincinnati's radical German democrats reaffirmed their dedication to causes of 1848 and their tenacious hostility to perceived enemies of liberty and republicanism as they understood those principles. Within weeks, however, the Bedini uproar would be eclipsed by a controversy of greater immediacy and broader import for German immigrants and Americans generally. At issue was the future, and possible westward expansion, of chattel slavery.

Until the 1850s, the subject of slavery had seemed to most German-Americans a matter of little direct import. Because the vast majority of the newcomers settled in states that prohibited slavery, most initially focused their attention on matters that appeared to affect them more personally. This was true even in Cincinnati, despite the proximity of the slave state of Kentucky. True, the city's German population included some abolitionists even during the 1830s. And distaste for slavery was common among *Dreissiger* generally. But in 1843, the founding document of the *Deutsche*

70

demokratische Verein evidently took no stand on either slavery or discrimination against free blacks.

Not long afterward, however, war with Mexico and the resulting acquisition of huge tracts of western land forced the issue of slavery and its westward expansion onto the nation's political agenda. Democrats generally divided. On one side stood the "free-soil" supporters of the 1846 Wilmot Proviso, which sought an outright federal ban on slavery in all lands acquired from Mexico. Ranged against them were the backers of Lewis Cass and his conciliationist doctrine of "popular sovereignty," which placed the fate of slavery in each new state in the hands of its own citizens alone.

How did the *Dreissiger* respond? Illinois *Dreissiger* Gustav Körner supplied one answer in his landmark survey of and testimonial to the pre-1848 German immigrants published in 1880. In his discussion of Ohio, Körner retrospectively ranked Heinrich Rödter among the state's more ardent foes of slavery in the late 1840s. As a member of the Illinois legislature, Körner reported, Rödter had "called for the elimination of all those oppressive laws directed in most free states against the blacks, both slave or free," and had supported Salmon P. Chase's election to the U.S. Senate "even though he well knew Chase's opposition to slavery and everything connected with it." A major work on Cincinnati history published subsequently repeated Körner's claims and added that Rödter "was the originator of the anti-slavery plank eventually introduced in the party platform" of the Ohio Democracy. In leading these attacks against slavery, it concluded, Rödter "incurred the enmity of the Democrats."[71]

The truth appears more complex and less flattering to Rödter. First of all, the views and acts attributed to Rödter and depicted as the initiatives of a courageous maverick actually constituted party policy for Ohio's Democrats. In 1849, the state Democratic party as a whole endorsed both Salmon Chase *and* repeal of discriminatory "black laws," as part of a bargain with free-soil forces who had just obtained the balance of power in the state legislature. The Democratic state convention a year earlier did call slavery "an evil, unfavorable to the full development of the spirit" and pledged its standard-bearers "at all times [to] feel it to be their duty to use all power, clearly given by the terms of the National compact, to prevent its increase, to mitigate and finally to eradicate the evil." But if Rödter was responsible for this platform plank, that fact hardly places him in the antislavery avant-garde. In the context of the times, the plank's language was (as Eugene Roseboom aptly observed) a "pleasantly indefinite" evasion. The convention adopted this language, moreover, at the behest of the Cass faction rather than endorse the much clearer and firmer Wilmot Proviso. As another Democrat instrumental in the plank's adoption later noted, it "was framed as to say something...mean nothing, [and] promote the election of Lewis Cass." Rödter's fellow Democrat Karl Reemelin bluntly professed to "care nothing" about the black laws. And while he considered the "popular sovereignty" formula a "humbug," Reemelin also regretted the growth of abolitionism. Like the Ohio party in general, he valued sectional peace more highly than he did the elimination of slavery.[72]

Priorities like Reemelin's were widespread at mid-century, and the Compromise of 1850 both reflected and reinforced them. By seeming to resolve the question of slavery's expansion, it reduced the scope and intensity of the national debate on slavery. Most Whigs and Democrats welcomed the cease-fire. Democratic President Franklin Pierce (whom most German voters had supported in the 1852 election) assured the nation in December 1853 that "this repose is to suffer no shock during my official term, if I have the power to avert it."[73]

But precisely such a shock did arrive with the New Year. On January 4, as Cincinnati debated the *Weihnachts* imbroglio, Democrat Stephen A. Douglas of Illinois presented his Kansas-Nebraska bill to the United States Senate. As finally revised, amended, passed in Congress, and signed by Pierce, the new law explicitly struck down the Missouri Compromise of 1820 and all other federal restrictions on chattel slavery's westward expansion. From that point onward, the debate over slavery's future in the United States occupied center stage in national politics. Having already crippled the Whigs, it now divided the Democrats, splintered the short-lived nativist "Know-Nothing" party, spawned the Republicans, eventually sent Lincoln to the White House, and ultimately triggered civil war.

In Cincinnati as elsewhere, Douglas's bill polarized the populace into supporters ("pro-Nebraska") and opponents ("anti-Nebraska"). The response in German Cincinnati merits attention on a number of counts. First, despite their previous support for the national Democratic party and Douglas as a prominent spokesman for it, far more Germans mobilized against the bill than in favor of it, and Germans made up a significantly larger proportion of the city's anti-Nebraska than of its pro-Nebraska movement. Second, the social composition of the German pro- and anti-Nebraska forces diverged in significant ways. German craftsmen figured far more centrally in the resistance to slavery's expansion than in attempts to uphold Douglas, his bill, and the national Democratic administration. White-collar and political office-holding Germans, on the other hand, figured more centrally among the pro-Douglas than the anti-Douglas forces. Finally, some of the state's principal *Achtundvierziger* organizations took stands on slavery and the rights of black Americans that were far more abolition-minded than those typical of the anti-Nebraska mainstream, whether native-born or immigrant.

None of this was yet evident at the beginning of 1854, and supporters of Douglas and Pierce first denied that any anti-Nebraska movement even existed. In Cincinnati, the democratic *Enquirer* assured readers in late February that no significant protest against the Douglas bill had arisen or would arise, even though certain people "seem to imagine that there is a terrible popular excitement upon the subject of Nebraska." Such a presumption, it added, "is a great delusion having its origin in the heated brain and distempered fancy of our contemporaries. Never was an opposition more signally unsuccessful in rallying popular sentiments to its aid."[74]

Pronouncements like these may have comforted journalists and some readers, but they had little to do with reality. Large public meetings were already taking place all over the North and West in opposition to the Nebraska bill. Four days before the *Enquirer* pronounced the anti-Nebraska movement stillborn, Cincinnati's first anti-Nebraska meeting occurred. It was organized and attended almost exclusively by Germans, and convened the evening of Friday, February 24, at the *Turnhalle*.[75]

The anti-Nebraska *Gazette* found the crowd assembled there "large and enthusiastic." A committee evidently composed entirely of Turners—including tailor and *Arbeiterverein* leader Kaspar Gams; the German Discussion Society's William Renau; and rationalist-Protestant minister, Forty-eighter veteran, and ubiquitous democratic activist Adolf Gerwig—brought in a series of resolutions that the assembly adopted unanimously. The resolutions shunned conciliatory language and denounced the Douglas bill as a violation of the Constitution and the Missouri Compromise of 1820 a "disgrace to America and this age," and "solemnly protest[ed] against it in the name of humanity, liberty, and justice." Stephan A. Douglas himself had "forfeited the esteem of every citizen who has the interests of liberty in his heart."[76]

On a rainy Tuesday, March 7, a nonpartisan anti-Nebraska meeting assembled at Mechanics' Hall. Apparently called, officered, and attended primarily by non-Germans, the meeting was a large one.[77] Led by "the first men of the County of Hamilton," the March 7 meeting was decidedly less sharp in tone than the one held earlier at Turner hall. The *Gazette* had promised as much beforehand, assuring readers that it would prove that "public opinion of Cincinnati is not tinctured with fanaticism or polluted with sentiments disloyal to the Union." The first speaker, an attorney named Walker, set the tone. To begin, he assured all assembled: "I am not now and never have been an Abolitionist in the common acceptation [sic] of that word. That is, I have always felt that we of the North were bound to keep our faith in the South, so far as it was pledged by the Federal Constitution, either expressly or by clear implication, and ought not, therefore, to interfere by any other than moral means, with Slavery in the States where it was already established." Because the institution of slavery now threatened to extend itself, however, Walker considered it "a sacred duty to exert all the powers I possess" to avoid that prospect. He devoted the balance of his remarks to demonstrating the legal inadmissibility of the Nebraska bill. Charles Reemelin delivered a more forceful speech, after which the meeting adopted an anti-Nebraska resolution drafted by a committee.

Parts of the resolution passed that night echoed those endorsed by the *Turnhalle* meeting. The territories were free soil, "intended by the God of Nature for free men," they said, "and we will never consent that they shall be wrested from their hands to be exhausted by slave labor, and to become the stronghold of oppression." In at least two respects, though, the Mechanics' Hall resolutions differed from those passed earlier at the *Turnhalle*. First, in condemning the Douglas bill for allowing the South "to introduce their negroes within the Territories," those gathered at Mechanic's Hall implied a hostility not simply to slavery but to blacks themselves, an attitude common among midwestern anti-Nebraska forces. Second, threats to fight the bill's passage and implementation were liberally intermixed with conciliatory overtures to the slaveholders. "It is both for the honor and interest of the South," the resolution urged, "to maintain her plighted faith with reference to the Missouri compromise" No such formulas had been considered necessary by the German anti-Nebraska meeting.[78]

The contemptuous attitude that Democratic regulars continued to display toward the anti-Nebraska movement received an even sharper jolt in late March, when the *Enquirer* itself felt obliged to print a call to a public meeting at Greenwood Hall the evening of Friday, March 24. Entitled "Nebraska: For Freedom and Free Labor" that call bore the names of nearly a thousand individuals who identified themselves as "members of the Democratic party . . . who desire that Nebraska should be reserved for free labor, and who oppose its colonization by negro slaves, and who are prepared to resist the repeal of the Missouri Compromise." Judging by the names alone, at least 70 percent of the signatories were of German ancestry, once again suggesting the strength of opposition to slavery's expansion among this part of the city's population. Unable now to deny the magnitude and breadth of anti-Nebraska sentiment, the *Enquirer* acknowledged that the call had been signed "by a considerable number of our political friends, who have always been attached to the principles and organization of the party" and that "there are many others on the list whose Democracy is of an equally unquestionable and adamantine character."[79]

By using city directories and other sources, it is possible to identify the occupations of 348 (about 37 percent) of the 951 people who signed the Democratic anti-Nebraska call.[80] Of these, 219 were (judging by their names) evidently German-Americans, while the remaining 129 were not. The occupational breakdown of identified Democratic anti-Nebraska signatories is presented in table 2.3.

The group as a whole was heavily composed of plebeians, and this was dramatically truer of its German component. More than six in ten were either craftsmen (57 percent) or unskilled laborers (9 percent); fewer than 7 percent belonged to the city's socioeconomic elite (bankers, major merchants and industrialists). If we add the category of government office-holders to the economic elite, the proportion still remains below 10 percent.

The prominent physician and Democratic congressman George Fries presided over the meeting at Greenwood Hall.[81] His introductory remarks aimed narrowly at the issue of slavery's geographical expansion. "We have met, Gentlemen," Fries emphasized, "*not* for the purpose of reopening the dangerous and exciting subject of slavery agitation, with which to disturb the peace and quiet of the community. That work has been more unfortunately done by other parties, and in other quarters, where such treason to all the Compromises for the pacification of this vexed question was least of all to be expected." The Kansas-Nebraska Act was held to be a violation of "Democratic" principles and "democratic" doctrine, especially the doctrine of free soil. "It withholds from the pioneer settlers of this vast country all those rights held sacred by freemen throughout the world, and especially sacred to the true Democracy of the United States," Fries declared. Charles Reemelin, who again delivered the evening's main address, strove primarily to prove that the Douglas bill was "not in accordance" with the 1820 and 1850 compromises. At length, however, he turned to some more general considerations. "This country has been called the asylum of the oppressed," Reemelin noted. "If this bill should pass, it might be called the home of the oppressed, for certainly, if the oppressed were at home anywhere, it would be here."[82]

Table 2.3. Occupations of Cincinnati Democratic
Anti-Nebraska Leaders.

Occupation	Total identified		German		Non-German	
	(N)	(%)	(N)	(%)	(N)	(%)
Economic elite	35	10.1	15	6.8	20	15.5
Professional	12	3.4	3	1.4	9	7.0
White-collar	33	9.5	21	9.6	12	9.3
Office-holders	11	3.2	5	2.3	6	4.7
Shopkeepers	48	13.8	30	13.7	18	14.0
Craftsmen	179	51.4	125	57.1	54	41.9
Unskilled	30	8.6	20	9.1	10	7.8
Total accounted for	348		219		129	
Not accounted for	603		472		131	

Source: *William's Cincinnati Directory,* for both 1855 and 1856.

The resolution subsequently adopted by the meeting was drafted by a committee of six individuals, including at least one German, Stephan Molitor. Like the one passed at the predominantly non-German meeting of March 7 at Mechanic's Hall, this resolution struck a balance, a compromise, between more militant and more cautious tendencies. Declaring its hatred for slavery as such, the resolution nevertheless pinpointed the question of slavery's extension as the central issue of the moment. Compromise with the South was earnestly desired, but if "the Slave states

are not satisfied with the Missouri Act, and the large additional conces-
sions we have since made, in which we have done violence to our feelings
and our principles, but are determined again to become aggressors upon
our well established rights and liberties," if "they are determined to draw
the sword upon us," that is, then "we shall not hesitate to throw the
scabbard away" either. Finally, the assembly took a bold step and resolved
that "at the ensuing October election we will vote against any candidate
for a seat in the House of Representatives of Congress, who shall not in a
public and explicit manner declare his unqualified hostility to the Nebraska
bill." The meeting endorsed the resolution and adjourned.

One important component of the German anti-Nebraska constituency
was conspicuously absent from the dissident democratic meeting and
from the list of names affixed to its call. Prominent German-American
residents such as well-to-do coppersmith Hezekiah Kiersted had helped
initiate and organize the meeting at Greenwood Hall, as had such liberal
Dreissiger professionals as Stephan Molitor, Charles Reemelin, and J. B.
Stallo. Friedrich Hassaurek, Gottlieb F. Wiest, Kaspar Gams, and other
well-known immigrant radicals, however, took no discernible part in the
meeting's organization or conduct. They were attending the statewide
conference of German radicals discussed earlier, a meeting still in session
when the Greenwood Hall gathering occurred. The radicals nontheless
made their sentiments plain on the Nebraska issue. In a resolution sent to
and read at Greenwood Hall, the immigrant radicals declared themselves
"fully in favor of the object of your meeting... as an expression of
indignation against the monstrous Nebraska fraud, and promise our hearty
cooperation against every extension of slavery."[83]
At their own convention, however, Ohio's German radicals took a
considerably more militant, uncompromising stand against slavery and in
favor of blacks' rights more generally than did the largely German Democratic anti-Nebraska meeting. "Whigs and Democrats," they declared,
"have united around slaveholding, manhunting [a reference to the 1850
Fugitive Slave Law], and the Nebraska betrayal and have consolidated this
firm alliance under the aegis of the southern slaveholders themselves." It
was time to turn away from such politicians, they added, declaring that
"we are sick of and have forever broken with the old parties." The radical
German Democrats not only opposed the extension of slavery but went
on to demand repeal of the 1850 Fugitive Slave Law, branding it a

violation of the letter and spirit of the Declaration of Independence. Even more boldly, they called for the end of slavery itself throughout the United States.

Still the convention had not finished with the general issue. It explicitly separated itself from all attempts to turn free-soil doctrine into an instrument for the exclusion of blacks per se from the states and territories. The general demand that public lands be set aside for settlement by smallholders also stipulated that these lands be distributed to all qualified applicants, "irrespective of color." In antebellum America, this was a revolutionary demand, particularly when raised on the Kentucky border. It contrasted vividly with the much narrower concept of free soil expounded by others and with the silence on the subject in the decade-old platform of the *Deutsche demokratische Verein.*[84]

If the "German reform convention" in general angered the pro-Douglas and pro-Administration Democrats, the antislavery resolutions left them frankly dumbfounded. The call for outlawing slavery throughout the United States, protested the *Enquirer,* was "an abolition one, of the most ultra character," and its implementation would violate the federal constitution. The same was true of demands to repeal the Fugitive Slave Law, a measure "guaranteed to the slave holder in that instrument by an express provision." The editor continued: "Another abolition peculiarity is a declaration in favor of giving negroes a free homestead upon the public domain as well as whites. The true policy of this country is to discourage free negroes from remaining in the Union, and to offer every inducement for them to emigrate to other climes, where they can enjoy greater social advantages."[85]

Supporters of the Kansas-Nebraska bill in Cincinnati rallied their forces the following month. The April 5 edition of the *Enquirer* featured a call for a public meeting to endorse Douglas's bill. The wording of the call, however, revealed the defensive stance into which the Administration's supporters had been forced. "We, the undersigned, Democratic citizens of Hamilton County," it announced, "considering as we do the existence of Negro Slavery to be an evil, entailed upon this country by British avarice, and deeming it our duty to resist the extension of that evil by all CONSTITUTIONAL means—do, at the same time hold the usurpation by Congress, of UNCONSTITUTIONAL power, for that or any other purpose, to be a greater EVIL than Negro Slavery itself, pernicious alike to the freedom of the people and to the preservation of this glorious Union." It was thus federal antislavery legislation that constituted the main threat to

American liberty. "Therefore," the call concluded, "all those of our fellow-citizens, who value the freedom of the people higher than the treacherous doctrines of abolitionism" should attend a "Mass Meeting of the Democracy" on the evening of Thursday, April 6, at the marketplace on Court Street, at half past seven o'clock."[86]

The list of sponsors is suggestive in a number of ways. First, it had been signed by about three hundred people, fewer than a third the number who had initiated the anti-Nebraska meeting two weeks earlier. Second, the apparent ethnic composition of the list was almost the exact opposite of the one attached to the anti-Nebraska call analyzed earlier. (See table 2.3.) Only about a third of the pro-Nebraska signatories had German names, compared with more than two-thirds on the anti-Nebraska call. True, the fact that some one hundred Germans, including well-to-do and prestigious community members, had endorsed a pro-Nebraska meeting discounted the *Gazette*'s glib assertion on February 27 that the members of this ethnic group opposed the bill "almost to a man." That no more than about a hundred had signed, on the other hand, reinforces the impression that anti-Nebraska views were much more prevalent among the city's Germans than was pro-Nebraska sentiment. Finally, occupational analysis indicates important social differences between the pro- and anti-Nebraska German coalitions.

Occupations were determined for 128 of the pro-Nebraska signatories, 96 of them apparently non-German, 32 apparently German. Compared with the anti-Nebraska list analyzed in table 2.3, table 2.4 found a considerably weaker base among skilled producers. Fewer than one in five of the identified German signatories worked in the crafts. Adding unskilled laborers only raises the proportion to one in four. The same occupational groups, in contrast, had accounted for more than half the identified anti-Nebraska German Democrats. Corresponding to the relatively weak representation of the crafts among the pro-Nebraska signatories was the relative strength of those with white-collar occupations, primarily clerks and bookkeepers (more than a fifth), and Democratic party leaders and office-holders (another tenth).[87] Once again the contrast with the anti-Nebraska Germans is marked. Among the latter, very few had been Democratic officials (2 percent), and only 10 percent had held white-collar occupations. In a letter to the *Gazette,* an opponent of the bill claimed to find in the pro-Nebraska list few "of the popular element" but many "intimately connected with the wire-pulling of the party," including those employed by the federal government. The occupational breakdown presented in table 2.4 lends credence to the writer's accusation. So did the *Enquirer*'s own account, which boasted of the prominence at the meeting of representatives of the Democratic "Old Guard," men whose "names are associated with the history of the party in this city back to its earliest days."[88]

Table 2.4. Occupations of Cincinnati Democratic Pro-Nebraska Leaders.

Occupation	Total identified (N)	(%)	German (N)	(%)	Non-German (N)	(%)
Economic elite	14	10.9	3	9.4	11	11.5
Professional	14	10.9	2	6.3	12	12.5
Office-holders	13	10.2	5	15.6	8	8.3
Govt. employees	2	1.6	1	3.1	1	1.0
White-collar	28	21.9	7	21.9	21	21.9
Shopkeepers	13	10.2	6	18.8	7	7.3
Craftsmen	37	28.9	6	18.8	31	32.3
Unskilled	7	5.5	2	6.3	5	5.2
Total accounted for	128		32		96	
Not accounted for	164		69		95	

Source: Cincinnati Daily Enquirer, April 5, 1854, and city directories.

The meeting itself heard and voted for a series of resolutions defending the Douglas bill in the name of popular sovereignty, states' rights, antiabolitionism, party loyalty, and confidence in the Pierce Administration. George Pugh, the new senator from Ohio, explained that the meeting itself "never would have been called had only the Whigs and Abolitionists [opposed] the Nebraska bill. But a meeting of the professed Democracy of Hamilton County had been held to oppose the measure of the Administration and to condemn the President of our choice." This made it necessary for the "true Democracy to assemble and express its sentiments." The *Columbian* pegged attendance at only five hundred, while the *Gazette* acknowledged the presence of seven hundred. An enthusiastic *Enquirer* found the gathering "immense," attracting upwards of three thousand people.[89] That paper made no similarly upbeat assertions, however, about the number of Germans present. The *Enquirer* approached the subject only in an oblique, but perhaps no less telling, manner. It complained that anti-Nebraska Germans had called a meeting at the *Turnhalle* for the same night as the pro-Nebraska rally. Friendly observers reported a sizeable crowd in attendance there, filling the main hall, the galleries, and the antechamber of the saloon. Instead of denying so substantial a turnout, the *Enquirer* seemed tacitly to acknowledge it and denounced the *Turnhalle* meeting as a deliberate ploy to reduce German attendance at the simultaneous pro-Nebraska rally. The anti-Nebraska German leaders, an editorial charged, "well knew that many of their falsehoods and misrepresentations about the character of the Nebraska Bill would be exposed [there], and as they did not want to have the eyes of their deluded votaries opened to the impositions practiced upon them, resorted to the expedient of keeping them away."[90]

VII

In the decades before the Civil War, hundreds of thousands of Germans migrated to North America in search of a freer and more secure existence. The booming river city of Cincinnati attracted many of these newcomers. The conditions they discovered here were in many ways very different from those in Germany. The contrast was not so sharp, however, as to strip old ideals and causes of all resonance. Nor did new conditions heal all the breaches among the immigrants themselves. Transplanted from their native soil, both German liberalism and radical democracy proved adaptable to the American climate.

During the 1850s German Cincinnati became embroiled in conflicts that evoked European themes and in which different groups of immigrants played distinct roles. Widening class divisions that accompanied the United States' matchless industrial development indicated that migration alone had not guaranteed prosperity and "independent existence" for all. The resulting labor struggles deepened economic and philosophical cleavages within the immigrant population. Connections between past and present were particularly clear in the case of the anti-Bedini protest, which attested to the persistence of democratic, anticlerical zeal among the most recent immigrants. Stephen Douglas's bill, finally, divided German Cincinnati into a "pro-Nebraska" minority and an "anti-Nebraska" majority. *Handwerker* were especially conspicuous among the latter. In the anti-Nebraska camp, liberal *Dreissiger* limited their protest to the immediate issue of slavery's further expansion. The *Achtundvierziger* radical democrats, in contrast, targeted slavery as a whole and demanded that the western lands closed to slavery be settled by free whites and blacks alike.

During the conservative 1950s, the writing of American history was dominated by the so-called consensus thesis. Its outstanding advocate was Louis Hartz, whose *Liberal Tradition in America* (1955) argued that class differences and class conflicts had signified little in an America historically characterized by "social freedom" and "social equality," and that all sectors of society had therefore subscribed to some variant of "individualistic" Lockean liberalism. Thirty years later, in another conservative decade, a similar viewpoint is gaining currency. Basically, it holds that since a majority of American workers never adopted "a conscious rejection of capitalism," the differences in outlook that did exist must be considered negligible.[91]

The evidence and interpretation presented above does not fit this increasingly fashionable thesis. Whatever outside observers may have assumed, German Cincinnati was by no means homogeneous. In some ways, indeed, the particular conditions of American society—its more open political life, its far more dynamic economic development—seemed to widen some of the differences among the immigrants. Such differences, in turn, influenced the ways in which they responded to political challenges facing their adopted city and nation during the last antebellum decades.

NOTES

The author wishes to thank the Taft Foundation of the University of Cincinnati for the grant-in-aid that made research for this essay possible. He also thanks Sigrid Adickes, Roger Daniels, Zane Miller, Steven Ross, Jonathan Sarna, and Henry Shapiro for reading and criticizing early drafts.

1. Bureau of the Census, *Historical Statistics of the United States: Colonial Times to 1970* (Washington, D.C.: Government Printing Office, 1975), 1:117. On the comparison between German and Irish immigrants in this era, see Reinhard R. Doerries, *Iren und Deutsche in der neuen Welt: Akkulturationsprozesse in der amerikanischen Gesellschaft im späten neunzehnten Jahrhundert* (Stuttgart: Franz Steiner Verlag, 1986), chap. 3.

2. Charles Cist, *Sketches and Statistics of Cincinnati in 1859* (Cincinnati: author, 1859), 164; Secretary of the Interior, *Statistics of the United States . . . in 1860* (Washington, D.C.: Government Printing Office, 1866), xviii. Here the

Northeast (with 34 percent of the nation's population in 1860) is defined to include New England plus the Middle Atlantic states of New York, New Jersey, and Pennsylvania. The West (with 38 percent) includes Illinois, Indiana, Iowa, Kansas, Kentucky, Michigan, Minnesota, Nebraska, Ohio, Tennessee, Wisconsin, California, Nevada, and Oregon. Narrowing the "West" to encompass only the Great Lakes region (Ohio, Michigan, Indiana, Illinois, Wisconsin, Minnesota) plus Iowa, Kansas, Nebraska, and Missouri yields a regional population equal to only 1 percent of the nation's total in 1800 but 29 percent in 1860. However it is sliced, in short, the regional increase was spectacular.

3. Rev. Charles Frederic Goss, *Cincinnati: The Queen City* (Chicago: S. J. Clarke Publishing, 1912), 2:333; Steven J. Ross, *Workers on the Edge: Work, Leisure, and Politics in Industrializing Cincinnati, 1788–1890* (New York: Columbia University Press, 1985), 26, 28–9; Carl John Abbott, "The Divergent Development of Cincinnati, Indianapolis, Chicago and Galena, 1840–1860: Economic Thought and Economic Growth" (Ph. D. diss., University of Chicago, 1971), 129–34; *Statistics of the United States . . . in 1860,* xviii; Thomas Senior Berry, *Western Prices before 1861: A Study of the Cincinnati Market* (Cambridge: Harvard University Press, 1943), 510.

4. The proportion of Germans in the population in 1840 and earlier represent educated guesses; hard figures for that era are not available. Some estimates of the German weight in the city's *adult male* population in 1840 range as high as 25 to 30 percent. But the visiting Berlin historian Friedrich von Raumer believed that the German-born composed about 20 percent of greater Cincinnati's population *as a whole* in 1844, by which time the proportion was probably higher than in 1840. Cf. Charles Cist, *Cincinnati in 1841: Its Early Annals* (Cincinnati: author, 1841), 38–9; Carl Wittke, "The Germans of Cincinnati," *Bulletin of the Historical and Philosophical Society of Ohio,* 20 (January 1962), 3; Goss, *Cincinnati,* 1:181; Frederick von Raumer, *America and the American People,* tr. William W. Turner (New York: J. and H. G. Langley, 1846), 360. Estimates of the size of the second-generation German-American population at mid-century are also unavoidably imprecise; only in 1870 did the census reports begin to include such data. But note parallel estimates of the size of Ohio's German stock in Eugene Roseboom, *The Civil War Era,* vol. 4 of *The History of the State of Ohio,* ed. Carl Wittke (Columbus: Ohio State Archaeological and Historical Society, 1944), 286n.

5. Charles Cist, *Sketches and Statistics of Cincinnati in 1851* (Cincinnati: Wm. H. Moore, 1851), 48. Cist repeated this point in subsequent editions.

6. Carl Vitz, "Martin Baum, Pioneer Cincinnati Entrepreneur," *Bulletin of the Historical and Philosophical Society of Ohio,* 16 (1958), 215–39; Körner, *Das deutsche Element in den Vereinigten Staaten von Nordamerika, 1818–1848* (Cincinnati: A. E. Wilde, 1880) 177–80, 215–17; Goss, *Cincinnati,* 2:9–12, 18; [Herman Julius Reutnik], *Berühmte deutsche Vorkämpfer für Fortschritt, Freiheit, und Friede in Nord-Amerika* (Cleveland: Forest City Bookbinding, 1888), 427–30; Ross, *Workers on the Edge,* 78; Roger W. Clark, "Cincinnati Coppersmiths,"

Cincinnati Historical Society Bulletin, 23 (October 1965), 257–72; *Cincinnati Daily Commercial,* March 28, 1860; Donald C. Peirce, "Mitchell and Rammelsberg: Cincinnati Furniture Makers, 1847–1881" (Ph. D. diss., University of Delaware, 1980); Cist, *Cincinnati in 1851,* 203–4; Jane E. Sikes, *The Furniture Makers of Cincinnati: 1790 to 1849* (Cincinnati?: author, 1976), 196–98; Francis P. Weisenburger, *The Passing of the Frontier, 1825–1850,* vol. 3 of *The History of the State of Ohio* (Columbus: Ohio State Archaeological and Historical Society, 1941), 85.

7. Vitz, "Martin Baum," 228; Ross, *Workers on the Edge,* 72.

8. Abbott, "Divergent Development," 94; J. D. B. De Bow, *Mortality Statistics of the Seventh Census of the United States, 1850* (Washington: A. O. P. Nicholson, 1855), 41; Joseph G. Kennedy, *Population of the United States in 1860; Compiled from the Original Returns of the Eighth Census* (Washington, D.C.: Government Printing Office, 1864), 612. Percentages have been rounded off to the nearest whole number.

9. J. D. B. De Bow, *Statistical View of the United States . . . Compendium of the Seventh Census* (Washington, D.C.: Beverley Tucker, 1854), Appendix, 399; Kennedy, *Population of the United States in 1860,* xxxi; Isabella Lucy Bird, *The Englishwoman in America* (1856; rpt. Madison: University of Wisconsin Press, 1966), 119; Ross, *Workers on the Edge,* 94–140; Peter Harsham, "A Community Portrait: Over-the-Rhine, 1860," *Bulletin of the Cincinnati Historical Society* 40 (1982), 70. Judging from newspaper reports in the late 1850s, Germans may by then have supplied as much as two-thirds of that industry's workforce. Cf. The *Cincinnati Daily Enquirer,* March 17, 23, 1859. The ninth (1870) census, which for the first time correlated nativity and occupation, also demonstrated that German strength in Cincinnati's traditional crafts continued to grow through the Civil War era. Cf. *The Ninth Census* (Washington, D.C.: Government Printing Office, 1872), 1:783.

10. Donald G. Rohr, *The Origins of Social Liberalism in Germany* (Chicago: University of Chicago Press, 1963), 78, 96, 132–35; James J. Sheehan, *German Liberalism in the Nineteenth Century* (Chicago: University of Chicago Press, 1978), 74; Mack Walker, *German Home Towns* (Ithaca: Cornell University Press, 1971), 366–67; Karl Marx, "The Bourgeoisie and the Counterrevolution" (1848), and Friedrich Engels, "Revolution and Counterrevolution in Germany" (1852), in Karl Marx and Frederick Engels, *Collected Works* (New York: International Publishers, 1977–1978), 8:154–78, 11:3–96.

11. Reemelin, *Life of Charles Reemelin, in German: Carl Gustav Rümelin, from 1814–1892* (Cincinnati: Weier and Daiker, 1892), 12–13, 49–51, 82–83, 122–26, and passim. See also Körner, *Das deutsche Element,* 186–192; Reutnik, *Berühmte deutsche Vorkämpfer,* 296–98; Goss, *Cincinnati,* 2:10, 13–4; and a recent synthesis in Victor R. Greene, *American Immigrant Leaders, 1800–1910* (Baltimore: Johns Hopkins University Press, 1987), 49–52.

12. The Henry Rödter Papers, Cincinnati Historical Society; Körner, *Das deutsche Element,* 182–86; Goss, *Cincinnati,* 2:13; Karl J. R. Arndt and May E. Olson,

German-American Newspapers and Periodicals, 1732–1955: History and Bibliography (Heidelberg: Quelle and Meyer Verlag, 1961), 454.

13. Körner, *Das deutsche Element,* 192–94, 202–3; Goss, *Cincinnati,* 1:441–42, 454; *Cincinnati Daily Enquirer,* July 13, 16, 1853.

14. Lloyd D. Easton, *Hegel's First American Followers: The Ohio Hegelians: John B. Stallo, Peter Kaufmann, Moncure Daniel Conway, and August Willich* (Athens: Ohio University Press, 1966), chap. 2; the Henry Rödter Papers; Körner, *Das deutsche Element,* 217–25; Goss, *Cincinnati,* 2:19. Dismissing the materialist view—and even the orthodox Hegelian tenet—that subjective thought corresponds to an objective reality, Stallo held that "all external things exist only in so far as they are perceived or thought." See Easton, *Hegel's First American Followers,* 54, 69, 72–76.

15. Reemelin, *Life,* 46–47; Goss, *Cincinnati,* 2:13; Körner, *Das deutsche Element,* 185.

16. Stephen E. Maizlish, *The Triumph of Sectionalism: The Transformation of Ohio Politics, 1844–1856* (Kent: Kent State University Press, 1983), 10, 117; Paul E. Johnson, *A Shopkeeper's Millenium: Society and Revivals in Rochester, New York, 1815–1837* (New York: Hill and Wang, 1978); Daniel Walker Howe, *The Political Culture of the American Whigs* (Chicago: University of Chicago Press, 1979); Jed Dannenbaum, *Drink and Disorder: Temperance Reform in Cincinnati from the Washington Revival to the WCTU* (Urbana: University of Illinois Press, 1984), chaps. 1–5; Richard P. Latner and Peter Levine, "Perspectives on Antebellum Pietistic Politics," *Reviews in American History* 4 (1976), 15–24. In Germany, a large-scale prohibition movement arose only in the 1860s. See James S. Roberts, "Drink and Industrial Work Discipline in 19th Century Germany," *Journal of Social History* 15 (Fall 1981), 25–28.

17. Reemelin, *Life,* 88; William A. Baughin, "Nativism in Cincinnati before 1860" (M. A. thesis, University of Akron, 1950), 38–39, 84–95; Weisenburger, *Passing of the Frontier,* 465–66; Körner, *Das deutsche Element,* 208–10 (quotation on p. 209: it is unclear whether these are the *Verein*'s words or Körner's paraphrase); Max Burgheim, *Cincinnati in Wort und Bild* (Cincinnati: Burgheim Publishing, 1891), pp. 86–87; Goss, *Cincinnati,* 2:15.

18. Baughin, "Nativism," 115; Körner, *Das deutsche Element,* 210.

19. Burgheim, *Cincinnati,* 131; Körner, *Das deutsche Element,* 198–201; Wittke, "Germans of Cincinnati," 12; Philip Gleason, *The Conservative Reformers: German-American Catholics and the Social Order* (Notre Dame: University of Notre Dame Press, 1968), 15. An educated guess distributes the city's Germans in 1848 as follows: 67–68 percent Catholic, 18 percent unchurched, 11 percent practising Protestants, and 3 percent Jews. *Presbyterian of the West,* March 2, 1848; Baughin, "Nativism," 78, 127; Joseph Michael White, "Religion and Community: Cincinnati Germans, 1814–1870" (Ph.D. diss., University of Notre Dame, 1980), 47–51. For newspaper circulation figures, see the exchange between Molitor and Henni in the *Cincinnati Daily Enquirer,* July 13, 16, 1854.

20. The official name of the Democratic leadership group was "Ohio Lodge

Number One (Miami Tribe) of the Improved Order of Red men." Dannenbaum, *Drink and Disorder,* 110; Baughin, "Nativism," 129, 143; Reemelin, *Life,* 103–4.

21. Goss, *Cincinnati,* 1:181.

22. On this aspect of 1848's historiography, see P. H. Noyes' observations in his *Organization and Revolution: Working-Class Associations in the German Revolutions of 1848–49* (Princeton: Princeton University Press, 1966), 2.

23. Hansen, "The Revolution of 1848 and the German Emigration," *Journal of Economic and Business History* 2 (August 1930), 630–58 (quotation on p. 631). This thesis reappeared almost verbatim in Hansen's influential posthumous summation, *The Atlantic Migration, 1607–1860,* ed. Arthur M. Schlesinger, Jr. (New York: Harper and Row, 1961), 274.

24. Hildegard Binder Johnson, "Adjustment to the United States," *The Forty-Eighters: Political Refugees of the German Revolution of 1848,* ed. A. E. Zucker (1950; rpt. New York: Russell and Russell, 1967), p. 43.

25. See Jürgen Kocka, *Lohnarbeit und Klassenbildung: Arbeiter und Arbeiterbewegung in Deutschland, 1800–1875* (Berlin: J. H. W. Dietz, 1983); Hartmut Zwahr, *Zur Konstituierung des Proletariats als Klasse: Strukturuntersuchung über das Leipziger Proletariat während der industriellen Revolution* (Berlin: Akademie-Verlag, 1978); Wolfram Fischer, *Der Staat und die Anfänge der Industrialisierung in Baden, 1800–1850* (Berlin: Duncker and Humbolt, 1962); Jürgen Schlumbohm, "Relations of Production, Productive Forces, Crises in Proto-Industrialization," in Peter Kriedtke, et al, *Industrialization before Industrialization: Rural Industry in the Genesis of Capitalism* (Cambridge: Cambridge University Press, 1981); Frederick Daniel Marquardt, "The Manual Workers in the Social Order in Berlin under the Old Regime" (Ph. D. diss., University of California, Berkeley, 1973).

26. Stephan Born, *Erinnerungen eines Achtundvierzigers* (Leipzig: Verlag von Georg Heinrich Meyer, 1898), 145; Ruth Hoppe and Jürgen Kuczynski, "Ein Berufs- bzw. auch Klassen- und Schichtenanalyse der Märzgefallenen 1848 in Berlin," *Die Konstituierung der deutschen Arbeiterklasse von den dreissiger bis den seibziger Jahren des 19. Jahrhunderts,* ed. Hartmut Zwahr (Berlin: Akademie-Verlag, 1981), 343–61; Werner Conze and Dieter Grohe, *Die Arbeiterbewegung in der nationalen Bewegung* (Stuttgart: Ernst Klett Verlag, 1966), 25–31; Wolfgang Schieder, "Die Rolle der deutschen Arbeiter in der Revolution von 1848/49," in *Die deutsche Revolution von 1848/49,* ed. Dieter Langewiesche (Darmstadt: Wissenschaftliche Buchgessellschaft, 1983), 322–40; Gustav Lüders, *Die demokratische Bewegung in Berlin im Oktober 1848* (Berlin: Walther Rothschild, 1909); P. H. Noyes, *Organization and Revolution.*

27. George von Skal, *The History of the German Immigration to the United States and Successful German-Americans and their Descendants* (New York: F. T. and J. C. Smiley, 1908), 28.

28. Bird, *Englishwoman in America,* 120; Arndt and Olson, *German-American Newspapers,* 457; *Cincinnati Daily Enquirer,* July 16, 1853.

29. *Hochwächter,* December 10, 1851, *Die Republik der Arbeiter,* June 21,

November 29, December 20, 1851; March 27, May 1, 15, July 10, 31, September 11, November 13, 1852; September 10, 1853; *Die Reform,* May 4, 1853; Carl Wittke, *The Utopian Communist: A Biography of Wilhelm Weitling, Nineteenth-Century Reformer* (Baton Rouge: Louisiana State University Press, 1950), 178–79, 200, 205, 216, 218, 231–32; *Sociale Republik,* June 19, September 11, 1858, April 2, July 2, 1859; James Matthew Morris, "The Road to Trade Unionism: Organized Labor in Cincinnati to 1893" (Ph. D. diss., University of Cincinnati, 1969), 74, 103; Ross, *Workers on the Edge,* 150, 157–60; Burgheim, *Cincinnati,* 159–60; Easton, *Hegel's First American Followers,* chap. 6.

30. The records of the Cincinnati Central Turners, Inc., 1848–1948, at the Cincinnati Historical Society include a membership roster for 1848–1861 indicating each individual's date of admission plus miscellaneous remarks. See also the *Turn-Zeitung,* April 1, 1854; Burgheim, *Cincinnati,* 153; Leonard Koester, ed., "Early Cincinnati and the Turners: From Mrs. Karl Tafel's Autobiography," *Bulletin of the Historical and Philosophical Society of Ohio* 6 (October, 1948), 18–22; Arndt and Olson, *German-American Newspapers,* 435, 449, 453, 585; Wittke, "Germans," 6; Alice Reynolds, "Friedrich Hecker," *American-German Review* 12 (April 1946), 4; Wilbur D. Jones, "Some Cincinnati Societies A Century Ago," *Bulletin of the Historical and Philosophical Society of Ohio* 20 (January 1962), 39; *Daily Cincinnati Gazette,* March 28, 1854.

31. Easton, *Hegel's First American Followers,* passim; *Turn-Zeitung,* December 1, 1851. Unitarian minister Moncure Daniel Conway found himself "invited at times to lecture for Jewish societies" in Cincinnati and "speedily discovered that the majority of Rabbi [Isaac Mayer] Wise's [reformed] synagogue were not believers in supernaturalism, but simple deists," eager to have Judaism "accord . . . with modern science and philosophy." *Autobiography, Memories and Experiences of Moncure Daniel Conway* (Boston: Houghton, Mifflin, 1904), 1:272, 275.

32. *Hochwächter,* October 13, 1851, March 10, 1852.

33. See the *Hochwächter* for January 7, 1852 and various other issues between 1851 and 1856, as well as Körner, *Memoirs,* 1:567.

34. *Cincinnati Daily Enquirer,* March 17, 1853, the *Hochwächter,* November 26, 1851; Carl Wittke, "Friedrich Hassaurek: Cincinnati's Leading Forty-Eighter," *Ohio Historical Quarterly* 68 (January 1959), 4; Wittke, *Refugees of Revolution,* 128; A. E. Zucker, "Biographical Dictionary of the Forty-Eighters in *The Forty-Eighters,* 319; "Friedrich Hassaurek," in *Der Deutsche Pionier* 17 (1885), 3–20; C. F. Huch, "Die freireligiöse Bewegung unter den Deutschamerikanern," *Mitteilungen des Deutschen Pionier-Vereins von Philadelphia* 11 (1909), 8–9; Reutnik, *Berühmte deutsche Vorkämpfer,* 327–28; Körner, *Das deutsche Element,* 203–5, 212–14; *Republik der Arbeiter,* January 1, 1853; Roseboom, *Civil War Era,* 213; *Daily Cincinnati Gazette,* December 28, 1853; *Cincinnati Daily Enquirer,* January 11, 1854; Jones, "Cincinnati Societies," 39–40; Arndt and Olson, *German-American Newspapers,* 446; Charles B. Moore, "A Tennessean Visits Cincinnati in 1853–1854," ed. Larry G. Bowman and Jack B. Scroggs, *Bulletin of the Cincinnati*

Historical Society 36 (1978), 151–174; Conway, *Autobiography,* 272, 275, 304–309; White, "Religion and Community," 335; *Cincinnati Past and Present; or, Its Industrial History as Exhibited in the Life-Labors of its Leading Men* (Cincinnati: M. Joblin, 1872), p. 307.

35. Wilhelm Rapp, quoted in William Frederic Kamman, *Socialism in German American Literature* (Philadelphia: Americana Germanica Press, 1917), 61.

36. It seems likely that these profiles inflate the proportion of the well-to-do among the original Turners. Those for whom Gollmer could not find data probably included disproportionate numbers of his humbler and less prominent *Landsleute.* Conversely, at least some of the occupational data Gollmer did obtain in the 1880s may well have reflected the impact of individual upward mobility *since* the 1840s and 1850s.

37. Papers of incorporation of the "Association of Freemen of Cincinnati (Verein freier Maenner)," April 14, 1852, Recorder's Office, Hamilton County Courthouse; *Hochwächter,* October 13, 1851; *Williams Cincinnati Directory . . . for 1853;* Burgheim, *Cincinnati,* 150. Of the identified artisan leaders of the *Freimännerverein,* the directory indicated that only Meininger owned a shop separate from his home—a common sign that the individual was an employer rather than an employed or independent, self-employed producer.

38. See, for example, *Republik der Arbeiter,* July 10, 1852.

39. E. J. Hobsbawm, *The Age of Revolution, 1789–1848* (New York: New American Library, 1962), 154, and Hobsbawm, *Age of Capital, 1848–1875* (New York: New American Library, 1975), 16–17.

40. *Turn-Zeitung,* December 1, 1861. Hermann Schlüter believed that these articles had been written by Franz Arnold, an immigrant mechanic and organizer of producer cooperatives who was at the time closely associated the German-American labor leader Wilhelm Weitling. If so, it is another indication of the appeal of this democratic vision among even some of the most radical plebeian forces. See Hermann Schlüter, *Die Anfänge der deutschen Arbeiterbewegung in Amerika* (Stuttgart: J. H. W. Dietz, 1907), 203.

41. Augustus J. Prahl, "The Turner," in Zucker, *The Forty-Eighters,* 98.

42. *Daily Cincinnati Gazette,* March 24, 1854; *Turn-Zeitung,* April 15, 1854. On Wiest's affiliation with the *Turngemeinde,* see the Central Cincinnati Central Turner membership roster at the Cincinnati Historical Society; the *Cincinnati Daily Enquirer,* January 11, 1854; and Burgheim, *Cincinnati,* 151.

43. Burgheim, *Cincinnati,* 151.

44. *Turn-Zeitung,* April 15, 1854; *Cincinnati Daily Enquirer,* March 26, 1854. On the land-reform movement, see Helen Sarah Zahler, *Eastern Workingmen and National Land Policy, 1829–1862* (New York: Columbia University Press, 1941); Sean Wilentz, *Chants Democratic: New York City and the Rise of the American Working Class, 1788–1850* (New York: Oxford University Press, 1984), 335–43; Joe L. Norris, "The Land Reform Movement," *Papers in Illinois History and Transactions for the Year 1937* (Springfield: Illinois Historical Society, 1938), 73–82.

45. Hobsbawm, *Age of Capital,* 115, 301; Hans Rosenberg, "Theologischer Rationalismus und vormärzlicher Vulgärliberalismus," *Historische Zeitschrift* 141 (1930), 497–541 (quotation on pp. 531–32).

46. H. Daniel-Rops, *The Church in an Age of Revolution, 1789–1870* (New York: E. P. Dutton, 1965), 214–15, 244–45, 250, 281–85; Joseph N. Moody, ed., *Church and Society: Catholic Social and Political Thought and Movements, 1789–1950* (New York: Arts, 1953), 230–34; Kenneth Scott Latourette, *The Nineteenth Century in Europe: Background and the Roman Catholic Phase,* vol. 1 of *A History of Christianity in the Nineteenth and Twentieth Centuries* (New York: Harper & Row, 1958), 256–60, 270–78; Jonathan Sperber, "Competing Counter-revolutions: Prussian State and Catholic Church in Westphalia during the 1850s," and Vernon Lidtke, "Catholics and Politics in Nineteenth-Century Germany: A Comment," *Central European History* 9 (March 1986), 45–52, 117–18; Robert M. Bigler, *The Politics of German Protestantism: The Rise of the Protestant Church Elite in Prussia, 1815–1848* (Berkeley: University of California Press, 1972); the *Wahrheits-Freund* quoted in Gleason, *Conservative Reformers,* 19.

47. Alexis de Tocqueville, *Democracy in America,* ed. Phillips Bradley (1835; rpt. New York: Knopf, 1945), 1:316.

48. Roseboom, *Civil War Era,* 288–89; Wittke, *Refugees of Revolution,* 97–98, 138–39; David Mead, "Brownson and Kossuth at Cincinnati," *Bulletin of the Historical and Philosophical Society of Ohio* 7 (April 1949), 92; John W. Oliver, "Louis Kossuth's Appeal to the Middle West—1852," *Mississippi Valley Historical Review* 14 (March 1928), 481–95; *Daily Pittsburgh Gazette,* February 2, 1854; Baughin "Nativism," 126n, 154–55.

49. Roseboom, *Civil War Era,* 175–78; *Cincinnati Daily Enquirer,* January 11, 1854. Archbishop Purcell was no friend of secularized education and castigated Catholics who advocated it. See Easton, *Hegel's First American Followers,* 61.

50. *Turn-Zeitung,* April 15, 1854; *Cincinnati Daily Enquirer,* March 26, 1854.

51. Cf. John Patrick Diggins, "Comrades and Citizens: New Mythologies in American Historiography," *American Historical Review* 90 (June 1985), 614–38, esp. 625, 627.

52. *Cincinnati Daily Enquirer,* March 28, 1854.

53. Ross, *Workers on the Edge,* 78–80; Bird, *Englishwoman in America,* 19; The *Volksblatt,* November 15, 1851, quoted in the *Hochwächter,* November 26, 1851.

54. "Autobiography of George Puchta," 1933, Puchta Collection, Hamilton County Public Library; Goss, *Cincinnati,* 4:918–19; *Biographical Dictionary of American Mayors, 1820–1980,* 297–97.

55. Ross, *Workers on the Edge,* 94–144, 335 n. 30; Berry, *Western Prices,* 504; the *Nonpareil,* October 19, 22, 26, 29, 1850; and the *Hochwächter,* November 19, 26, 1851.

56. *Hochwächter,* December 10, 1851; *Republik der Arbeiter,* June 21, November

29, December 20, 1851, March 27, May 1, 15, July 10, 31, September 11, November 13, 1852, September 10, 1853; *Die Reform,* May 4, 1853; Carl Wittke, *The Utopian Communist: A Biography of Wilhelm Weitling, Nineteenth-Century Reformer* (Baton Rouge: Louisiana State University Press, 1950), 178–79, 200, 205, 216, 218, 231–32; *Sociale Republik,* June 19, September 11, 1858, April 2, July 2, 1859; James Matthew Morris, "The Road to Trade Unionism: Organized Labor in Cincinnati to 1893" (Ph. D. diss., University of Cincinnati, 1969), 74, 103; Ross, *Workers on the Edge,* 150, 157–60;

57. *Republik der Arbeiter,* April 16, 23, 1853; *Cincinnati Daily Enquirer,* March 17, April 16, 17, December 11, 1853; *Die Reform,* April 23, May 4, 7, 1853; Ross, *Workers on the Edge,* 143, 151–55.

58. Burgheim, *Cincinnati,* 159. And see various issues of *Republik der Arbeiter* between 1850 and 1853, *Die Reform* in 1853 and 1854, and *Sociale Republik* between 1858 and 1860.

59. *Nonpareil,* October 29, 1850; *Cincinnati Daily Enquirer,* April 16, 17, 1853; March 17, 25, April 1, 1859; *Die Reform,* May 4, 7, 1853; *Sociale Republik,* April 2, 1859; Ross, *Workers on the Edge,* 157–59, 189; Roseboom, *Civil War Era,* 36–37.

60. In 1853, a labor boycott of the struck newspapers ultimately helped force most employers to concede these demands. *Cincinnati Daily Enquirer,* December 4, 11, 1853, March 17, 25, 1859; *Daily Cincinnati Gazette,* November 26, 28, 1853; *Sociale Republik,* June 19, 1858, April 2, 1859, June 19, 1858, April 2, 1859: Ross, *Workers on the Edge,* 151–59.

61. Kaspar Gams's letter in *Die Reform,* May 7, 1853; Reemelin, *Life,* 41–42; *Cincinnati Daily Commercial,* April 5, 1859; Morris, "Road to Trade Unionism," 106; *Cincinnati Daily Enquirer,* April 5, 1859. While wage demands were largely satisfied in the 1859 cabinetmakers' strike, the bitter resistance of the large manufacturers doomed the union-shop and standing committee demands. In March 1860, the *Volksblatt* supported (while the labor paper, the *Republikaner,* opposed) new anti-strike legislation.

62. See, for example, the *New York Criminal-Zeitung und Belletristisches Journal,* December 30, 1853, January 6 and 13, 1854; *New Yorker Staats-Zeitung,* February 11, 1854; Wittke, "Germans of Cincinnati," 11; Ray Allen Billington, *The Protestant Crusade, 1800–1860: A Study of the Origins of American Nativism* (1938; rpt., Chicago: Quadrangle Books, 1964), 302–4; Rev. Alfred G. Stitch, "Political Nativism in Cincinnati, 1830–1860," *Records of the American Catholic Historical Society,* 47 (September 1937), 268–69; William A. Baughin, "Bullets and Ballots: The Election Day Riots of 1855," *Bulletin of the Historical and Philosphical Society of Ohio* 21 (October 1963), 267–68; Rev. Emmet H. Rothan, *The German Catholic Immigrant in the United States (1830–1860)* (Washington, D.C.: Catholic University of America, 1946), 117–18.

63. The following account draws heavily upon extensive newspaper coverage of the incident and its protracted legal and political aftermath. See the *Cincinnati Daily Enquirer,* December 27, 29, 1853, January 4, 7, 10, 11, 12, 13, 14, 15, 17,

18, 19, 22, February 12, 1854; *Daily Cincinnati Gazette,* December 28, 29, 30, 31, 1853, January 2, 6, 7, 9, 10, 11, 12, 13, 14, 16, 17, 18, 19, 20, 21, February 21, 1854.

64. Catherine Magille Holden [Prelinger], "A Decade of Dissent in Germany: An Historical Study of the Society of Protestant Friends and the German-Catholic Church, 1840–48" (Ph. D. diss., Yale University, 1954), 362–63, and especially, by the same author, "Religious Dissent, Women's Rights, and the *Hamburger Hochschule für das Weibliche Geschlecht* in Mid-Nineteenth-Century Germany," *Church History* 45 (March 1976), 42–55; Jutta Schroer Sanford, "The Origins of German Feminism: German Women, 1789–1870" (Ph. D. diss., Ohio State University, 1976); Bigler, *Politics of German Protestantism,* 217, 226; Conway, *Autobiography,* 289; Roseboom, *Civil War Era,* 35, 133, 230–40; Moore, "A Tennessean Visits Cincinnati," 153, 156; Kathleen Neils Conzen, "Ethnicity as Festive Culture: Nineteenth-Century German America on Parade," in *The Invention of Ethnicity,* ed. Werner Sollors (New York: Oxford University Press, 1989), 53; *Hochwächter,* November 19, December 31, 1851; June 16, 23, 1852.

65. *Daily Cincinnati Gazette,* December 28, 1853.

66. *Daily Cincinnati Gazette,* December 28, 29, 1853; Burgheim, *Cincinnati,* 160.

67. *Cincinnati Daily Enquirer,* January 10, 11, 12, 1854; *Daily Cincinnati Gazette,* December 28, 1853.

68. *Daily Cincinnati Gazette,* December 28, 31, 1853, January 2, 6, 1854; *Cincinnati Daily Enquirer,* January 7, 1854.

69. *Cincinnati Daily Enquirer,* January 3, 6, 1853; *Daily Cincinnati Gazette,* January 3, 6, 7, 1854; Moore, "A Tennessean Visits Cincinnati," 168; *New York Criminal-Zeitung und Belletristisches Journal,* January 13, 1854.

70. Hassaurek lost his own case against city officials and the police in February. See the *Cincinnati Daily Enquirer,* February 24, 1854.

71. Körner, *Das deutsche Element,* 186; Goss, *Cincinnati,* II, 5.

72. Reemelin, *Life,* 87–88, 98, 123; Weisenburger, *Passing of the Frontier,* 471–73; Roseboom, *The Civil War Era,* p. 25; Maizlish, *Triumph of Sectionalism,* pp. 78, 124–138, 154–55. Rödter died a loyal Democrat in 1857, the year after the Republicans mounted their first presidential campaign. Molitor and Stallo, however, became staunch Republicans.

73. *Congressional Globe,* 33 Cong., 1 sess., p. 11.

74. *Cincinnati Daily Enquirer,* February 28, 1854.

75. The *Enquirer* completely ignored this event until its March 3 edition, in which it retrospectively dismissed those who had attended as "a few Whigs and Abolitionists, aided by a sprinkling of Democrats who never do anything in the party but obstruct its action." As the year wore on, the *Enquirer*'s attempts to ridicule the growing movement against slavery's extension grew increasingly labored.

76. *Daily Cincinnati Gazette,* February 25, 27, 28, 1854; *Cincinnati Daily Enquirer,* March 3, 1854.

77. The *Gazette* of March 8 estimated that more than a thousand people braved the rain to attend the meeting. The *Enquirer* entangled itself in contradictions. Its March 8 edition reported that the meeting had been "very largely attended." The next day, it dubbed the meeting "a complete fizzle," insisting that "no more than six or seven hundred persons assembled, of whom, we are assured by a reliable authority, a considerable proportion were in favor of the bill, being drawn by curiosity alone." Though the *Enquirer*'s own account of the proceedings disproved this last assertion, the editor appeared undaunted. "Thousands who were at first inclined to be opponents of the measure are wheeling into its support," he insisted, adding confidently that "the anti-Nebraskaites are taken emphatically aback by the tide of public opinion which is setting in against them." The presence at the meeting of so prominent a Democrat as Charles Reemelin was no cause for concern or second thoughts, since Reemelin acted only because of "the failure of the party to confer upon him important offices."

On the racist admixture in much anti-Nebraska protest, see Eugene H. Berwanger, *The Frontier Against Slavery: Western Anti-Negro Prejudice and the Slavery Extension Controversy* (Urbana: University of Illinois Press, 1971).

78. See the March 8, 1854, editions of both the *Gazette* and the *Enquirer*.

79. To avoid permanently alienating so many longtime Democrats, the *Enquirer* adopted an unprecedentedly diplomatic tone. "Our friends who met Friday evening," it conceded, "have undoubtedly in their judgment significant grounds, and as it is well understood that the question is in no sense to be made a test of party fidelity, no Democrat can object to their expression." The next day's edition, however, was once again denouncing the *"secret junto of wire-working politicians"* that had initiated the gathering. *Cincinnati Daily Enquirer,* March 23, 24, 1854, emphasis in original.

80. The call appeared in the *Enquirer* of March 23, 1854.

81. The *Gazette* and the *Enquirer* characteristically offered conflicting accounts of this meeting's size and tenor. The meeting was "very large," reported the *Gazette*. On the contrary, replied the *Enquirer,* it was only "very slimly attended." Greenwood Hall was "crowded" that night, said the *Gazette*. No, the *Enquirer* demurred, it "was not one-fourth filled, and the attendance at any one time did not amount to over 250 persons." For good measure, the *Enquirer* further reduced its crowd estimate the next day, asserting now that there had never been more than 200 present. Both papers were clearly biased, but the huge number of signatures affixed to the call and the declining credibility of the *Enquirer*'s coverage of anti-Nebraska events lend greater plausibility to the *Gazette*'s version.

82. *Daily Cincinnati Gazette,* March 25, 1854; *Cincinnati Daily Enquirer,* March 25, 26, 1854.

83. *Cincinnati Daily Enquirer,* March 25, 1854.

84. *Turn-Zeitung,* April 15, 1854; *Cincinnati Daily Enquirer,* March 25, 26, 1854; *Daily Cincinnati Gazette,* March 24, 25, 1854.

85. *Cincinnati Daily Enquirer,* March 28, 1854.

86. *Cincinnati Daily Enquirer,* April 5, 1854.

87. *Cincinnati Daily Enquirer,* April 5, 1854; *Williams' Cincinnati Directory,* 1855 and 1856 editions.

88. *Daily Cincinnati Gazette,* April 6, 1854.

89. *Cincinnati Daily Enquirer,* April 6, 7, 1854; *Daily Cincinnati Gazette,* April 7, 8, 1854. The *Columbian's* estimate was cited in the *Enquirer* of April 8.

90. *Daily Cincinnati Gazette,* April 7, 1854; *Cincinnati Daily Enquirer,* April 8, 1854.

91. Louis Hartz, *The Liberal Tradition in America: An Interpretation of American Political Thought since the Revolution* (New York: Harcourt, Brace, and World, 1955), 12, 63; Diggins, "Comrades and Citizens," 625.

JAMES H. CAMPBELL

New Parochialism: Change and Conflict in the Archdiocese of Cincinnati, 1878–1925

There is a real curse in many Catholic parishes throughout the United States.... It is the dry rot of parochialism and the inability or unwillingness of the pastor and people to see the needs of the Church beyond their immediate parish.
    —Joseph Schrembs, *Catholic Telegraph,* December 13, 1923

Urban historians have described in detail the chaos and disruption that accompanied the rise of the industrial city in the post–Civil War era. For example, in *Boss Cox's Cincinnati,* Zane Miller focused on one city and its unique features.[1] Yet, he also offered a classic study of urban disintegration that applied to other cites as well. In particular, historians have stressed the impact changes in transportation had on the old walking city. The omnibus, streetcar, incline, and other transportation changes scattered the population of the old city in all directions. This demographic shift in turn put a severe strain on all aspects of city life. Thanks to the research of urban historians, the general outline of the crisis of the industrial city and attempts to stabilize it have become part of the public domain.

In the meantime, historians continue to investigate and explore other facets of the emerging industrial city. In this paper I explore one aspect of the urban crisis of the new industrial city—its impact on the Catholic church. Although the Archdiocese of Cincinnati is the prime focal point, other dioceses faced similar problems. Above all, the rise of the industrial city intensified the financial worries and concern of the clergy and spurred on clerical infighting for parishioners and territory. The rise of the new city also whetted the ambitions of the nation's bishops by pitting one diocese against another for dominance.

In the late nineteenth and early twentieth centuries internal fighting and dissension in American Catholicism reached epidemic proportions. The ensuing chaos also left Rome with no choice but to appoint an apostolic delegate to the United States in 1893 to restore order to the church here. These conflicts went far beyond the account of liberal versus conservative, ethnic conflicts, and similar themes that historians have used to explain this period.

The roots of these conflicts lay in a divisive and parochial individualism that took hold of the church from the parish level to the highest echelons of American Catholicism. On the parish level Henry Meyer, pastor of St. Stephen Hungarian Church in Cincinnati, epitomized the new parochialism. In a running dispute with his superiors over financial matters, he arrogantly dismissed diocesan officials by saying that "self-preservation is the first law, and I am fully prepared to stand on my own feet."[2] Henry Moeller (1849–1925), archbishop of Cincinnati from 1904 to 1925, personified the new parochialism in the ranks of the hierarchy. While Moeller saw and denounced the parochialism of his clergy, his life and his relationship with others often exemplified a different lesson, namely, that "Bishops are human and sometimes have some vanity and selfishness in their makeup."[3] Ironically, when Moeller wrote those lines he had another bishop in mind,[4] but in retrospect he inadvertently penned his own epitaph.

Despite warnings about the new parochialism, experience taught Meyer, Moeller, and countless others that it had become part of ecclesiastical life. The new parochialism revealed and intensified the conflict of a religious leadership ideologically clinging to Jesus, but in practice measuring success in terms of secular society. With heaven on hold, material comfort, financial independence, power within church, and a dash of respect from the rest of the world became the hallmarks of a successful cleric. In short, like most people, the clergy generally heeded the first parochial commandment of economics. They looked out for their economic interest first. Then they worried about heaven and their avowed mission.

In the archdiocese of Cincinnati, three factors underscored the parochialism of the clergy. First, in 1878 a bank operated by Edward Purcell, a priest and brother of Archbishop John B. Purcell, collapsed. The failure of the bank, repudiation of the bulk of its debt, and the ouster of Archbishop Purcell from power taught the clergy a lesson in ecclesiastical economics that most priests never forgot. In financial matters the prudent priest learned to put aside the Church's teachings about charity and to look out for himself, because he knew from the bank's collapse that few of his Catholic brethren would come to his aid in hard times.

Second, the rapid breakdown of ethnic parishes added fuel to the fire. This was particularly true between German- and English-speaking pastors scrambling for the same parishioners. On the other hand, poor minorities, such as African-Americans, elicited no rivalry among the priests, and diocesan officials had a hard time finding priests willing to help them except on a quid pro quo basis.

Third, from 1878 until 1925, the archdiocese desperately needed, but failed to get strong competent leadership to put an end to the foolishness and selfishness of the new parochialism. While many priests looked upon their parishes as their little spiritual kingdoms where they were lord and master, the archbishops often looked upon their diocese in much the same light and wanted no one telling them how to run it.

Although a detailed history of American Catholicism in this period is beyond the scope and purpose of this paper, a study of the archdiocese of Cincinnati reveals parallels both in national trends in the church and the ebb and flow of the fortunes of the city that it represented. A spirit of optimism and boosterism characterized the early history of both the city of Cincinnati and the archdiocese. Founded in 1788 by approximately twenty settlers, the city was the sixth largest in the United States by 1850 and the largest west of the Allegheny Mountains.

Although Cincinnati's Catholicism was still in its infancy, Rome in 1821 made the city a see of a new diocese, covering the entire states of Ohio and Michigan. Edward Fenwick (1768–1832), a Dominican missionary, was named its first bishop. Despite his title and position, Fenwick had a hard time living on the two or three dollars that he received in his weekly collection. In 1823, with the loan of three hundred dollars from a friend, he headed for Europe in search of aid for his diocese. His visit proved successful. Stops in Italy, France, Holland, and England netted him 3200 pounds with the promise of additional funds in the future. During his travels, he also recruited three priests and a nun for his diocese.[5]

With his financial prospects improving, he constructed a new church, which also served as his cathedral on Sycamore Street between Sixth and Seventh streets, and a seminary behind it. By 1830 additional funds from Europe allowed him to purchase another lot adjoining the cathedral where he put up a building dedicated to St. Francis Xavier that doubled as a seminary and a college for Catholic laymen.[6] Next, he started a diocesan newspaper, the *Catholic Telegraph,* which made its debut on October 22, 1831.

By 1832, Fenwick could look back on his labors and boast that his "diocese in Ohio and Michigan is flourishing. It contains twenty-four priests, missionaries, twenty-two churches and several more congregations without churches . . . whereas fourteen years ago there was not a church, and I the only missionary in the State of Ohio."[7] On September 26, 1832, while on a missionary tour of his diocese, Fenwick died of cholera.[8]

In 1833, Rome named John Baptist Purcell 1800–1883), President of Mt. St. Mary's College in Emmitsburg, Maryland, Fenwick's successor. When Purcell arrived, he could find little to justify Fenwick's rosy picture of a flourishing diocese. Overwhelmed by the diocese's debts and the condition of the clergy, Purcell noted in his diary:

> I had to give . . . my note for upwards of 500 Doll. to meet the demands of Grocers, Dry Goods men . . . for values recd. by the inmates of the Coll [sic] & Sem. before my arrival. Thousands upon thousands of Dollars had been expended on buildings which are ill constructed & inconvenient, of wretched materials, half finished, leaking, mill-dewed roofs & walls; floors loose & badly laid, hydrants left insecure against external injury—property not enclosed & people stealing our wood & coal—House full of filth—Meals ill-cooked & most ungainly & uncleanly servants . . . B. O. C. [Bernard O'Cavanugh] took the young Seminarians to Whiskey shops & to the Theatre. Came home drunk at midnight . . . another Presid. of Sem. J. V. W. [Joseph Vincent Wiseman] had the boys of the street at his heels, shouting after him as he reeled drunk thro' the streets.[9]

Purcell's pessimism about the state of the church in Cincinnati proved short-lived. Thousands of German and Irish immigrants pouring into southwestern Ohio in the 1830s and 1840s played a major role in the development of the city and church alike. The immigrants offered such a fertile mission field for diocesan officials that the church had to rely heavily upon priests and religious recruited from Europe and the older, more established dioceses along the eastern seaboard.[10] Rumors that Rome might make Purcell the first American cardinal underscored the city's growing national and ecclesiastical importance.

By 1883, Ohio had a population of about 249,000 Catholics, attending 544 churches and chapels scattered throughout the state.[11] At the same time, the church ran 238 parochial schools with an enrollment of about 48,446 students, eleven orphanages taking care of 1,454 children and nine hospitals.[12] To keep pace with the diocese's rapid expansion and to streamline its organizational structure, Rome carved several filial sees out of Cincinnati's territorial holdings, including Detroit in 1833 and Cleveland in 1847.

In 1850 Rome elevated Cincinnati to the status of an archdiocese with Louisville, Detroit, Cleveland, and Vincennes serving as its suffragan sees.[13] In 1868, Cincinnati gained another satellite with the creation of a new diocese in Columbus. By 1883, despite the loss of northern Ohio to Cleveland and eastern Ohio to Columbus, the population of the Cincinnati diocese stood at approximately 150,000 Catholics served by 189 priests. In addition, the diocese had 157 churches, 32 chapels, and 2 orphanages caring for 546 children, 3 hospitals, and 88 parochial schools with an enrollment of 20,000 pupils.[14]

In the early years of his administration, Purcell, like Fenwick before him, had to rely not only on the generosity of his flock for help, but also on European missionary societies for funds. From 1823 to 1869 the diocese received $118,569 from the Society for the Propagation of the Faith in Lyons, France. From 1830 to 1885 the Leopoldine Association in Vienna donated over $50,000 to the diocese and a host of religious articles.[15] Contributions from such societies, however, abounded with uncertainties, for church officials here never knew how much help they would receive or when it would arrive. At times Purcell or one of his lieutenants went to Europe on a fund raising and personnel recruiting mission only to return frustrated, "without bringing either a priest, or ornament or a single franc."[16]

To slough off his dependency on European missionary societies, Purcell looked for a new source of capital. At the same time scores of Catholics in Cincinnati, distrustful of public banks after the panic of 1837, and taught from early childhood to look upon priests and bishops as Christ's representatives on earth, turned to Purcell as a man whom they could trust with their money. Whether by design or accident, these dual needs— Purcell's need for capital and the laity's need for a safe haven for their money—resulted in the Purcell bank.[17]

Unfortunately, Purcell had neither the personality of a bookkeeper nor even a good head for figures. He relied on his brother, Edward Purcell (1808–81), a diocesan priest, to handle the financial accounts of both the diocese and the incipient bank. To encourage depositors, Edward paid them interest. In the beginning he offered "4 percent, but very soon thereafter 6 percent, a rate as high as . . . paid by solid and well-managed Savings Banks to their depositors."[18] At times Edward boosted the rate to eight percent.[19]

The promise of a good return on their money coupled with the implicit backing of almighty God induced hundreds of maids, laborers, coachmen, and even a "sprinkling of the better class" to leave their money in Edward's hands.[20] From the late 1830s to 1878, auditors later conservatively estimated that Purcell took in over 13 million dollars.[21]

With the deposits stashed in his brother's bank, Bishop Purcell tried his hand at "speculating for religion." With money in the bank, he made plans to build a magnificent new cathedral. In 1840, with the purchase of a large lot at Eighth and Plum streets, his dreams of a new cathedral bearing his stamp began to turn into reality. With soaring spirits, Purcell boasted to a friend "Now I want a good plan . . . for it strikes me that something uncommon ought to be made out of it to put the heretics in good humor by beautifying the City. A fine steeple would command a view of ten miles down and up the river and be seen a great distance, with the bright, resplendent Cross overtopping all."[22] By 1845, thanks in part to a generous loan from the bank, Purcell had his cathedral dedicated to St. Peter in Chains.

The Civil War, however, quickly stemmed the city's rapid growth and eroded its role as the gateway to the South. Cincinnati's failure to take the lead in the development of railroad ties with the West and the postbellum South accelerated its relative decline in the urban sweepstakes.

By the late nineteenth century, decline and disorder in both church and city pushed aside the optimism and boosterism of the region's early history. In 1884 the Court House Riot racked the city and left fifty-four dead and about two hundred wounded. The May Day Strike of 1886 once again left the city on the verge of anarchy. Charges of political graft and corruption further tarnished the city's reputation.[23]

For the Archdiocese the year 1878 marked the beginning of a long nightmare of financial woes that drove Purcell from power, shattered the confidence of his priests, and left them feuding with one another for parishioners, stipends, and territory. For over forty years, diocesan officials tried without success to end this quarreling, which left nothing but bitter feelings and hostility in its wake.

In the Fall of 1878, Edward Purcell lost the confidence of his depositors and the Cincinnati banking establishment. The immediate cause for his downfall was the collapse of a bank operated by Joseph A. Hemann, a pillar of the German-Catholic community, who reportedly owed Purcell at least $70,000. Although false, the rumor that Purcell had lost heavily in the Hemann debacle proved more than enough to panic a portion of the priest's creditors.[24] The run began with a trickle of depositors coming singly or in groups of two or three, but it quickly turned into a tidal wave with the news that the city's leading bankers no longer wanted to accept Edward Purcell's notes.[25] As the run picked up momentum, it left Edward dazed and teetering on the brink of a nervous breakdown.[26] According to the *Cincinnati Enquirer*, (December 20, 1878; December 27, 1879) in November 1878 he paid out over $100,000 to stem the tide, and by mid-December he had to ask his creditors for more time as his promises of payment tomorrow stretched into next week.

On Sunday, December 22, 1878 the archbishop told the faithful that he and his brother could no longer meet immediate demands of all those pressing for their money. He assured his followers that he had not expended the money "in waste or extravagance." It had gone for "lots, churches, and asylums in which there are 400 orphans, for the seminary and its support . . . and for various necessities." He concluded by telling his flock that he had sent his resignation to Rome. He then added that if Rome chose not to relieve him from "the heavy burden of the Episcopate" he would rely upon the charity and goodness of the clergy and laity to pay off the "Diocesan debts."[27]

Although he longed for retirement, his speech was in reality a call for a vote of confidence from the laity and clergy, but most importantly from the Holy See. It worked, at least for a while. When John Ryan, one of the city's leading meat packers, heard of Purcell's impending resignation, he assured the press that the Catholics of Cincinnati would petition the Pope to keep the old prelate at his post. Patrick Poland, another prominent Catholic businessman, took a similar stance, telling reporters that "the Catholics of this diocese would rise up to a man and do their utmost to have him [Archbishop Purcell] remain at the helm." The priests serving under Purcell left no doubt how they felt about his retirement, for they cabled the Holy See not to accept his resignation.[28]

Out of cash, Edward tried to quiet the storm by offering church property as collateral. In the midst of the panic a reporter from the *New York Sun* cornered Edward and asked him straight out if he considered all the property held in the archbishop's name as subject to the auctioneer's hammer if needed to repay the debt. "Yes," he replied, because "the property is in the name of the Archbishop, and the money has been loaned to build new churches and invest in real estate for the Church and other means of this sort. We have not squandered any of it for ourselves, but have cared for it as the property of the Church. A very small fraction of the Church property in our Diocese would pay all the debts, but we will not, I think, need to call upon the Church for any.[29]

As the crisis deepened, some of the clergy from the largest parishes in the city met to draw up plans to help Edward out of his difficulties. They also asked the archbishop to make "a public statement . . . that he holds himself, responsible for all financial claims. . . . And as security pledges all the assets . . . that belong to him, all other properties that are strictly diocesan, or common to the whole diocese." They also assured the archbishop that they were "willing to share in any sacrifices that may be necessary to relieve His Grace from the present embarrassment, and lighten the burden, which no fault of his, but rather the untold circumstances of the times, have made to press so heavily upon him."[30]

On December 25, 1878, a committee of Catholic businessmen called on Purcell and asked for his consent to launch a drive to raise money for his creditors. Their concern "visibly affected" the prelate, and he readily gave them his endorsement. Within an hour the committee raised $201,000. To raise additional funds, the laity and clergy tried and considered a variety of plans including benefit concerts, bond issues, bazaars, and lotteries. Unfortunately, each of these plans only exacerbated the frenzy of the creditors who, when they learned of some new scheme to aid them, besieged Purcell's residence to get their share before others got their hands on it.[31] At times they had to be forcibly ejected from the building.

At the beginning of the panic, no one, including the Purcell brothers, had any idea of the extent of the disaster. Edward Purcell could give very little help to auditors trying to unravel his accounts. In fact, he "had no books to turn over to them, only a bundle of notes, some $325,000 worth. . . . As for claims against him they . . . [came] in the form of passbooks and memoranda held by the depositors in the most confused, entangled and almost hopeless mass imaginable." James Callaghan, the archbishop's secretary, estimated the loss at about $100,000, but as auditors sifted through the chaotic records of the bank, this sum and the line of creditors increased daily. By mid-January 1879, optimists in the archbishop's inner circle hoped that the claims against him and his brother would level off at half a million dollars, but by February many feared that the loss might go well beyond a million.[32]

Despite mounting evidence to the contrary, Purcell's advisors continued to assure the public that "not one of the depositors would be wronged out of a dollar." To bolster the confidence of his creditors, the archbishop wrote across the face of their passbooks that "the Archbishop of Cincinnati promises to pay" the amount recorded in the creditor's book. In so doing Purcell wanted the creditors to understand that the diocese was ultimately responsible for repayment of the debt. At the same time the archbishop's advisors told doubting Thomases that "they little know the resources of the Catholic Church who think that the obligation will not ultimately be paid in full. Assistance will be given to us by the entire Catholic world"[33]

Yet, by this time, efforts to collect money in Purcell's own diocese had run into serious opposition. Otto Jair, a Vicar General and one of the diocese's most prominent German priests, complained that in the past German parishes had received very little aid from Purcell. "We, have raised the money to build our churches by the sweat of our brow," and Jair added, "I have not received a cent toward the creation of these churches from the Archbishop, nor have I asked for any." As the Purcell debt mounted, support from the clergy steadily eroded. By late May 1879, when the creditors' claims finally peaked at $3,699,651.49,[34] many priests no longer supported the archbishop's view that the debt belonged to the whole diocese.[35] Instead, they argued that Edward in running the bank had done so as a private individual and not as a representative of the church.

In May 1879 John Cardinal McCloskey, the highest-ranking church official in America and a former student of Purcell at Mt. St. Mary Seminary in Emmitsburg, Maryland, launched a national campaign to help his old professor.[36] Not surprisingly, the faltering efforts of Purcell's own diocese to pay off the debt only discouraged outsiders from doing anything about it, and the national campaign quickly lost momentum. Silas Chatard, the Bishop of Vincennes, captured the mood of many outside the diocese when he complained that "a debt like that under the present circumstances . . . is simply impossible to pay. . . . I don't see anything but inevitable failure and bankruptcy. . . . We don't want to throw our money into a swamp where it will be lost entirely."[37]

While support for his cause steadily eroded, Purcell waited word from Rome about his resignation. Finally, on April 8, 1879, he received the welcome news that the Holy See had not accepted it. To help Purcell in the present crisis and in meeting the rigors of old age, the Pope also decided to appoint a "coadjutor, with the right of succession."[38]

When a reporter from *The Cincinnati Enquirer* got hold of the story, he hastened to the episcopal residence to see how the archbishop felt about Rome's handling of his resignation. In explaining the significance of Rome's decision, Purcell emphasized that the coadjutor, when appointed, would merely help him and that he would remain in charge of the diocese.

In effect, he regarded Rome's decision as a vote of confidence. With the passing of this crisis, Purcell's thoughts turned once again to liquidating the debt, and he assured the reporter that it was only a question of time until it was paid.[39] By this time, however, the patience of the creditors had worn thin and many turned to the civil courts for help.

While the civil case inched its way through the legal system, Rome finally found another prelate willing to serve as Purcell's coadjutor. On January 16, 1880, Vatican officials wired Purcell that William Elder (1819–1904), the bishop of Natchez, had accepted the post.[40]

Elder had reservations about accepting the Queen City position, but did so as an act of obedience to the Holy See and as a favor to Purcell.[41] Every bishop in the nation knew full well that Elder was walking into a hornet's nest. When James O'Connor, bishop of Omaha, learned of his friend's appointment to the see at Cincinnati, he wanted to send his colleague a note congratulating him, but, as he thought about all the troubles Elder had suddenly inherited, he "could not find it in [his] . . . heart to do so."[42] After warning Elder about the difficulties that he faced in his "hard position" in Cincinnati, Richard Gilmour, bishop of Cleveland, tried to reassure him that God would see him through."[43]

Purcell was "much affected by the action of the Pope," for instead of merely giving him an assistant the Holy See had left him archbishop in name only by placing Elder in complete charge of the temporal and spiritual welfare of the diocese.[44]

However, the relationship between Elder and Purcell began amicably enough. They attended various public functions together.[45] Elder sought out Purcell's approval before making appointments.[46] While his health held up, Purcell continued to take a relatively active part in diocesan affairs by administering the Sacraments of Confirmation and by visiting various parishes and religious institutions.[47]

In time, the issue of repaying the creditors drove a wedge between the two prelates. From the beginning of the bank's collapse, Purcell maintained that the deposits entrusted to his care played a major part in providing the capital necessary for the growth and expansion of the church in this area, and that the diocese had an obligation to repay the debt. He staunchly reaffirmed this position in May 1880 when he gave his deposition before the Hamilton County Court of Common Pleas in the suit pressed by the creditors.[48] While Elder's conscience agreed with Purcell's contention that the diocese had a moral obligation to repay the debt,[49] expediency counseled him to reject arguments stressing the diocesan nature of the debt and to go along with the advice of the priests who wanted to pay the creditors no more than ordered by the courts.

Torn between expediency and his conscience, Elder turned to some of his episcopal colleagues for counsel. Casper Borgess, bishop of Detroit, cautioned him not to allow his sympathy for the creditors to cloud his good judgment. According to Borgess, time would cure the psychological and economic trauma of the bank's failure, and only the "intemperate, the improvident, the lazy and all kinds of beggarly wretches" in the ranks of the creditors would still demand their money. Finally, Borgess warned his friend to do very little for the creditors lest they regard his actions as "an acknowledgment of the debt as belonging to the Archdiocese of Cincinnati."[50] To Joseph Dwenger, bishop of Fort Wayne, the debt belonged to Edward Purcell and to no one else. The archbishop, Dwenger argued, "had no right to acknowledge it" as a diocesan debt.[51] Dwenger went a step further and urged Elder "to use those claims [that creditors surrendered to him] in settlement for all you can get allowed for it."[52]

Richard Gilmour, bishop of Cleveland, felt that the priests of Cincinnati, who urged a repudiation of the debt, were treating Purcell shabbily. Before his promotion to the rank of bishop, Gilmour had served as a priest under Purcell and knew that many parishes had received help from the bank at one time or another. Gilmour's outspoken position on the debt earned him the enmity of the clergy, who wanted nothing more to do with the bank failure. While he assured his critics that he had no intention of causing them needless injury, he felt obliged to "induce Cincinnati and its priests to attempt something, realizing all they had received, and owe" to Purcell.[53]

While Elder wrestled with this problem, he faced another crisis. During the course of the civil trial, Purcell suffered a stroke. For almost three years Purcell fought off paralysis, old age, periods of mental disorder, and death itself. On June 29, 1883, he suffered his fourth and final stroke, which left him on the brink of death. On July 3, 1883 he died. Upon Purcell's death, Elder immediately became archbishop since his original appointment to Cincinnati entitled him to the right of succession.[54] However, Purcell's death did nothing to stem the conflict among his priests about repaying the bank's debt.

At the same time, all the bickering and quarreling in the ranks of the clergy over repudiation of the debt only compounded the anguish and confusion of the creditors. In many ways, frustration seemed to wait for them at every turn in this bizarre case.

At each step of the appellate system the courts rejected the creditors' contention that all property in the diocese held in Purcell's name as archbishop could be sold off to pay off the bank's debt. Except for the unsold lots in St. Joseph Cemetery, the courts ruled that Purcell did not own the property outright, but merely held it in trust for the faithful of the diocese, and therefore such property "did not pass to the assignee by deed of the assignment."[55] Yet, the creditors did not come away completely empty handed, for the courts also ruled that they could recover money lent to any church or institution by the Purcells and that "any such property stand as security till its debt is repaid."[56]

Eventually the creditors recovered $5,199.90 from St. Patrick's Parish in Cumminsville; $12,042.26 from the cathedral; $6,547.41 from the cathedral school; $8,994.98 from Mt. St. Mary Seminary; and $16,360.14 from the sale of lots in St. Joseph Cemetery. On November 29, 1886, after eight years of agony, the trustees paid the creditors their first dividend, amounting to a mere 1.5 percent of the sum that they had lost in the bank. From 1880 to 1903 the creditors received five additional dividends.[57] In all, those who lived long enough recovered 7.125 percent of their money.

To many creditors the money they recovered from the church was only the tip of the iceberg in relation to the sums the Purcell brothers had allegedly dispersed to the parishes and institutions under them. Besides the civil courts, the creditors also made several emotional appeals to the Holy See for help, but once again met with only disappointment. With their legal and ecclesiastical resources exhausted, some were publicly critical of Elder for not helping them.[58] Several times Elder offered the creditors a compromise. If they stopped pressing the church in the civil courts, he promised to raise as much money as he could, guaranteeing them a minimum of $220,000 to $250,000, but the creditors rejected his offer.[59]

With time the diocese weathered the storm and recaptured some of its old vigor. Old age and death quieted the creditors. Gradually the tumultuous days of angry crowds pushing and shoving to get into the cathedral residence faded into the distant past of another age and generation. In 1887 Mt. St. Mary Seminary, which had closed its doors in the wake of the bank's collapse, reopened. By the turn of the century the formation of new parishes, which had dropped off dramatically after 1878, once again picked up momentum. Nevertheless, the bank's failure and Purcell's ouster from power served notice to the clergy that they had better look after their own financial interest.

The revolutionary changes taking place in urban America in the late nineteenth and early twentieth centuries reinforced this lesson and further intensified the financial worries and the selfish attitude of the clergy. Many churches in the diocese were magnificent edifices built on a grand scale to accommodate a presumably stable Catholic community. Here, the assumption ran, one generation after another would be baptized, married, and buried within the shadow of the same church.

The incline, electric streetcar, the automobile, and other transportation inventions dramatically altered this scenario. In Cincinnati, for example, these innovations broke through the natural barriers surrounding the city's inner basin, and Catholics, who could afford to move, poured out of the inner city to new parishes on the hilltops and more distant suburbs.

The loss of many "good" parishioners who loyally supported the Church panicked the priests left behind. Every year they found it more difficult to pay off the heavy mortgages on their churches, to meet their diocesan assessments, or even to take care of the current operating costs of their parishes. To cut their losses, they bitterly opposed the creation of any additional parishes that threatened to take territory or parishioners from them. Ironically, after 1878, the formation of a new parish generated less criticism and concern from the avowed enemies of the church than from the Catholic clergy.

Priests, saddled with new parishes, also faced formidable difficulties. Members of their congregations wanted facilities comparable to those they had enjoyed in the inner city, but were reluctant to pay the price. They expected the priests to perform virtual economic miracles. Hostility from the inner-city priests added to the care and woes of pastors in the emerging hilltop neighborhoods and suburbs and created an environment ripe for strife.

The new parochialism also severely strained relations between the secular and regular clergy.[60] In the early history of the archdiocese, church officials lacked enough secular priests to care for all the faithful under their charge, and they repeatedly asked the religious orders stationed here for help. In response the regular clergy left their monasteries to serve as missionaries, chaplains, and parish priests. This arrangement not only helped the bishops but also boosted the fortunes of the religious orders, for they quickly discovered that the parishes under their charge were a good source of income and a fertile field for recruiting new members.

Parish priests recruited from the monasteries, however, had the difficult task of trying to please two masters. As parish priest, the bishop was their superior; but as religious the provincial of their order was lord and master. As long as diocesan officials needed the services of the regular clergy, they generally gave the provincials a free hand in running the parishes under their charge. As the ranks of the secular priests gradually increased, however, diocesan dependency on the regular clergy diminished and the archbishop and his advisers began to tighten the reins over the parishes run by the religious. The religious societies resisted, for they had savored freedom too long to submit to a new order of episcopal control without a fight.[61]

To make matters worse (from the perspective of the regular clergy), most of the choice, new parishes went to the secular priests, leaving the religious societies worried that next the archbishop would ask them to hand over the old established parishes where they had labored for years. The regular clergy had no intention of surrendering these posts and prepared to fight back by resisting any attempts by the secular priests to take over, dismember, or encroach upon their parishes.

Their defensive attitude aroused strong suspicions in the chancery and among the secular priests that the religious societies were more concerned with expanding their own power, wealth, and prestige than with saving souls.[62] As these suspicions intensified, border disputes or feuds over parishioners involving the regular and secular clergy escalated from petty disputes among priests into a power struggle pitting the authority of the archbishop against that of the provincials.

Shortly after Elder took over the reins of the archdiocese from Purcell, he realized that infighting among the clergy for stipends, parishioners, and territory was on the increase and he tried to stop it. In October 1880, Elder served his priests notice that "henceforth each one must avoid interfering with persons and places belonging to another Pastor's jurisdiction." To avoid future conflicts, the bishop ordered the pastors not only to settle all disputes over parish borderlines, but also to send him a detailed description of their boundaries.[63]

Many priests paid no heed to his directions and kept probing their neighbor's domain for souls and income. Their cavalier disregard for his authority let Elder know that he had little chance of ending parish raiding without a fight. But Elder, a kind man, lacked the mettle of a tough ecclesiastical boss. He recoiled at the prospects of such a test of strength and will. Instead, his instincts impelled him to avoid an open breach with his subordinates and to wait for a more auspicious time for carrying out his policies. In 1884 Elder again took up his crusade to end parish raiding by appealing to the collective goodwill and sense of his clergy, but with no more success than his earlier efforts.[64]

The archbishop's weak leadership emanated from two primary sources. First, he lacked confidence in his ability to stand up to the clergy in a major confrontation. His lack of self-confidence was most acute during the early days of his administration, when he felt that he needed time to consolidate his hold on the diocese and to heal the wounds that had ensued from the conflicts with his predecessor and the priests loyal to Purcell. Elder did not want to stir up another hornet's nest by challenging the clergy to a showdown over parish raiding. Second, the archbishop seriously questioned how much support he would receive from his superiors, if he needed their help in disciplining troublesome priests.

In accord with Canon Law, the lower clergy could appeal to Rome for relief if they felt that local church leaders had treated them unfairly. Grievances of this nature unnerved Elder and many of his episcopal colleagues. Instead of supporting the bishops, Elder charged that Vatican officials often sided with the priests to check the powers of the American hierarchy and to curb "the tendency...manifested by some bishops towards independence in regard to the Holy See."[65]

Rome's policy of containing the powers of the bishops, according to Elder, only fanned the sparks of clerical anarchy. Indeed, parish raiding constituted but one facet of the disorder prevalent in American Catholicism. "Papal concern" for the rights of priests guilty of gross insubordination, alcoholism or sexual deviation weighed so heavily on Elder's conscience that he complained to Richard Gilmour that countless souls were "destroyed by scandal which the people are afraid to testify to in any formal way: [sic] though they will talk about them freely & the Bishop sees clearly they are true. And even he can some times get such evidence as would...convince any impartial judge, but not evidence according to [the] judicial form" demanded by Rome.[66]

To Gilmour, Rome had become an impediment to clerical discipline by meddling in the affairs of his diocese. In 1889, when Vatican officials forced him to reinstate a priest that he had suspended, Gilmour poured out his frustrations to Elder, telling his old friend

> I will not be driven, even for Rome. Rome may crush the bishop, that is
> not much, & is quite in her line. Vide Chicago, Detroit, Pittsburgh, Cleveland,
> etc,—But Rome shall not crush Richard Gilmour. She may drive him as a

bishop to the wall, but he shall retain his manhood & . . . with his face to the foe. . . . Rome has no cause to rejoice in her present attitude in America . . . all because she thinks she knows better. . . . I will live through it & die a man whatever I may do as a bishop.[67]

Vatican politics also dominated much of the private correspondence between Elder and James Cardinal Gibbons, archbishop of Baltimore and a staunch champion of the rights of the hierarchy. Gibbons regarded members of the Papal court bent on curtailing the powers of the American bishops as "the strongest antagonist we have to fear."[68]

Throughout the 1880s many high-ranking churchmen—including Gibbons, Gilmour, and Elder—grew restive, fearing that Rome would extend its dominion over the American church by appointing an apostolic delegate to this country. A papal representative, according to Elder, would not only erode the autonomy of the bishops, but also "such a person . . . would be an occasion of multiplying dissatisfaction among loose priests." Elder felt strongly that "every piece of home business . . . sent to Rome" by troublesome priests only strengthened the Vatican's arguments in favor of such a nuncio.[69]

The ubiquity of parish raiding made that problem particularly resistive to the church's traditional forms of discipline. Numerous appeals to Rome awaited him, Elder reasoned, if he took a hard line on this issue. Whenever a serious skirmish arose over borders or parishioners, the archbishop usually asked his feuding priests to lay aside their rancor, to settle their disputes in an equitable and brotherly manner, and finally to remember that "it is very important both for our own peace, & for our due respect from the people, & for our influence over them—that we ecclesiastics carefully avoid all appearances of difference among ourselves: [sic] particularly when it is connected with money interests."[70] Unfortunately, the archbishop's advice often got lost in the din of battle.

In prolonged disputes Elder customarily appointed a group of impartial priests to investigate the claims of all parties and to arbitrate their differences, but even these settlements often proved short-lived.

The archbishop had another way of keeping his men in line: promotions to a prosperous urban parish or banishment to an isolated hamlet. Tired of constantly worrying about financial matters, many priests looked forward to the day when they could take charge of a diocesan plum, a large urban parish that generously supported the church. The pastors of these posts were the aristocracy of the lower clergy and the *Catholic*

Telegraph, (July 25, 1889, p. 4) complained that "almost all the priests . . . are looking for big parishes. There is no concealing this fact. It seems to be a perfect mania among them." From their ranks the archbishop recruited his vicar generals, deans, consultors, and other top advisors. These clergymen not only enjoyed greater social prestige and power in diocesan politics than the average parish priest, but they could also afford many of the nicer things of life, including a large comfortable home, domestic help, and even travel to distant parts of the world.

By the nineteenth century the extended holiday had become both a symbol of the good life awaiting the ambitious clergyman and a panacea for the real and imaginary ills afflicting the pastors of the more prosperous urban parishes. To temper any public criticism that might arise from their taking a long holiday, these priests portrayed themselves as overworked and on the verge of a physical or mental breakdown. In reality the amount of work they did was a matter of their own discretion and conscience, since they usually had one or more assistants to take care of the midnight sick call, the early morning Mass, or anything else that they did not want to do. According to one church official, the relationship between a pastor and his assistant resembled that between a master and his servant in so far as "the pastor gets everything, and the poor assistant, who often is required to do most of the work, at least the disagreeable work, gets a mere pittance."[71]

In parcelling out assignments, diocesan leaders considered a priest's time in the ministry, age, attitude, and overall abilities. Although they tried to award the most prestigious parishes to the senior clergy for years of meritorious service, critics of Elder's administration complained that merit and seniority counted for less than one's connections with "certain gentlemen of the inner circle," namely the archbishop and his friends. In the midst of a quarrel with Elder, one priest assured him that he had no intention of becoming one of the diocese's "flattering hypocrites" so that the archbishop would appoint him to an "important congregation" where he could enrich himself.[72] Another priest angrily chided Moeller, claiming that "nobody gets any recognition except a boozer or kicker. . . . Merit seems to count for nothing in this diocese. Ecclesiastical politics rule the day."[73]

Not only did diocesan officials deny such allegations, but they also felt that their critics exaggerated the appointive powers of the ordinary. The role of a bishop, in Elder's estimation, closely resembled that of a general. To be effective both needed a free hand in deploying their forces wherever they were needed. But, once again Elder charged that Rome had checked the powers of the bishops by giving the lower clergy several important safeguards in relationship to their assignments. The Holy See expected all bishops, as their diocese matured beyond the missionary stage, to make certain churches "irremovable" posts.[74] As long as a man retained the pastorate of one of these parishes, the archbishop could not arbitrarily remove him without grave cause. In effect, once a priest took charge of a "plum parish" he enjoyed a certain amount of independence vis-a-vis the archbishop and some priests felt that they could disregard directions from the archbishop that ran counter to their own economic interests.

To qualify for one of these posts, a candidate had to pass competitive oral and written examinations measuring their proficiency in such areas as church dogma, law, morals, and liturgy. According to Elder, competitive examinations, tenure, and the right to appeal to higher authorities conspired to diminish the appointive powers of the bishops and many "spiritual evils to the people [arose] . . . from the weakening of the bishop's powers to remove" any priest that he wanted.[75]

By 1896 Elder felt that he could no longer delay taking a firm stand against parish raiding. Once again he tried to establish clearly defined borders for all the congregations. As in the past, many pastors simply ignored his orders.[76]

In 1898 Elder called a diocesan synod and made parish raiding a major item on his agenda. To put teeth in his orders, the archbishop decreed that "all priests whether secular or regular, are forbidden, under grave sin, to admit into their churches the faithful of a neighboring parish, or any other parish for the purpose of receiving the sacraments, except Holy Eucharist and Penance."[77] Neither the threat of "grave sin" nor the prospects of an eternity in hell daunted the competitive spirit of the clergy, and they soon resumed their old ways.

By the turn of the century Elder had joined the ranks of the octogenarians, and each passing year seriously taxed his physical and mental capacities to handle the many problems of the diocese. In 1900 he lost the services of his chancellor and confidant, Henry Moeller, who became the bishop of Columbus. By 1902 his failing eyesight and memory served him notice that he could no longer carry out the burdens of his office single-handedly, and he asked Rome for a coadjutor archbishop to help him in his declining years and eventually to succeed him.[78] In 1903 Rome sent Moeller back to Cincinnati as Elder's assistant and heir apparent.

Unfortunately, when he returned to Cincinnati as Elder's coadjutor,

Moeller had no more success than his friend and colleague in ending the selfish attitude of the clergy. To Moeller's dismay, pettiness not only dominated the twilight of Elder's episcopacy, it followed him to the grave. Shortly after Elder died in 1904, Moeller and his advisors launched a campaign to raise at least $2,250 from the priests of the diocese to build a suitable monument for the old prelate's final resting place. The response of the clergy, however, was apathetic and netted only $1,801.90 despite the fact that "four appeals were made."[79]

While clerical arguments and conflicts such as this were most intense in areas where the diocese had carved out new parishes, they also arose frequently among the pastors of the old established parishes. From every corner of the diocese priests plagued officials with complaints that some other priest had invaded their domain to steal parishioners, or to perform a baptism, wedding, or a funeral for which he expected a generous stipend. For years Joseph Metzdorf, pastor of St. Bernard and Daniel Buckley, pastor of St. Raphael in Springfield, Ohio, fought with each other for members and stipends. When the archbishop investigated the complaints of one priest against the other, he found himself mired in a morass of charges and counter charges. Each priest could see the beam of selfishness in the eye of his clerical neighbor, but was oblivious to his own shortcomings and want of charity and good sense. On one occasion, Metzdorf learned that his arch rival had "stolen a funeral" from him, he sent a long letter of complaint to the archbishop:

> The act of Father Buckley ... preventing me of having the funeral of Miss F. ... who was never a member of his Parish, could only have happened in one of his fitts [sic] of anger or jealousy or whatever it was. ... I am sorry that the fact is known amongst the catholics [sic] in Springfield, which was expressed to me again Sunday by lay people, "Father Buckley wants to crush St. Bernards." You can see plainly that living in peace in Springfield amongst the Priest [sic] under such conditions is absolutely impossible.[80]

Dayton, like Springfield, had its share of ugly and petty clerical disputes among the pastors of the older parishes. In lodging a complaint against John Schengber, pastor of Holy Trinity, William Hickey told Moeller that his opponent "altogether ignores the very existence of the parish, and takes in our people, as if the parish were nonexistent." On another occasion, when Moeller asked Schengber if he had raided another pastor's parish to steal a funeral, Schengber freely admitted that he had performed the ceremony. But, he added, "I can nowise [sic] explain what sort of whim, prank, or perversity it was that induced my . . . neighbor to lapse into arrant triviality, when he himself does not hesitate to fish in his neighbor's fishpond."[81]

A similar state of disorder existed in Cincinnati. According to John Hickey, who had the responsibility of running Holy Name Parish in Mt. Auburn, "almost every week . . . funerals, weddings, and baptism of persons living in the boundary lines of Holy Name . . . are going to St. Paul's, St. Mary's, St. Francis's, and St. Andrew's." From Assumption Parish in West Walnut Hills, William Conway kept the archbishop busy with his complaints that Augustine Quatman, the Pastor of St. Francis de Sales in East Walnut Hills, often raided his parish for members and that "his manner has been on the order of coercion, denunciation, uttering threats against me personally, giving the people to understand that I was deceiving them. . . . He has come almost to the shadow of the church exhorting our people to attend St. Francis de Sales."[82]

In the early twentieth century the archbishop faced another major problem that compounded his difficulties in organizing the diocese. Throughout most of the nineteenth century, diocesan officials had enjoyed relatively peaceful relations between the German- and English-speaking clergy over boundary lines and parishioners. Their biggest headaches came from trying to prevent the German priests from fighting with each other, while also suppressing similar rivalries among English pastors. At the turn of the century the distinction between English and German parishes began to break down and disputes between the clergy representing these two ethnic groups rose sharply.

While many older Germans clung tenaciously to the customs and language of their land, their sons and daughters frequently did not share their parents' enthusiasm for the culture of "the old country." With each passing year the diocese found it increasingly more difficult to find candidates for the priesthood versed in German or even interested in learning it. By 1912 the rector of the local seminary warned the archbishop that "German is noticeably on the wane. It is no longer spoken in the American home, is indifferently taught in the colleges—hence the material we get is of the crudest." Many young German-Americans attended English churches, where the priests in charge received them with open arms.[83]

To stem their losses and to woo non-Germans who lived near their churches, some of the German priests conducted their services in English. Although Vatican officials permitted Germans to join an English congregation, they did not allow English-speaking Catholics to affiliate with a German parish even if the pastor conducted his services in English. The German pastors charged that Rome had treated them unfairly and that this policy would eventually decimate their parishes.[84]

English pastors fought back by barraging diocesan officials with complaints that their German neighbors had violated ecclesiastical law by accepting non-Germans as part of their congregation. By 1910 the archbishop found himself mired down in a morass of complaints and quarrels over parish raiding as the old distinction between German and English parishes broke down even further and fanned the confusion rampant in the church.[85]

To stem this chaos, Moeller wanted not only to define the borders of each parish, but also to reclassify all congregations that no longer used German as their main language as English parishes and set their territorial limits accordingly. This plan unleashed a new barrage of criticism and opposition.[86] Pastors in charge of English congregations opposed it because they would lose parishioners and territory for the sake of keeping the old semidefunct German parishes alive. Staunch German nationalists on the other hand assailed Moeller for anglicizing their parishes and warned him that the church would lose countless German youths in the process.

In response to this argument, Moeller, whose parents had come from Germany, replied "I do not believe that the Faith is bound up in the language, and that if the German language goes the Faith will go with it. I am inclined to believe and my belief is based on experience that the children of German parents are lost to the Faith because they have not learned their religion in the English language." To silence his critics, Moeller turned to the apostolic delegate and the Vatican for their approval and support in carrying out his plan. To his dismay they repeatedly refused to back him and left him for years floundering in a sea of confusion.[87]

As the congregations and revenues of the German pastors steadily fell so did their scruples about accepting non-Germans into their congregations.[88] Moeller dutifully tried to suppress this violation of church law, but with very little success. In admonishing one German priest, the archbishop told him:

> I am surprised . . . that you insist on waiting on persons of Irish extraction. I have told you repeatedly that you had no right to do so. . . . According to the ruling of the Holy See, the Pastors of German Congregations have no

right to claim jurisdiction of persons of Irish or English extraction. I hope the time is near when we can draw territorial lines for all Congregations and that will do away with all the wrangling and quarrelling which is a cause of disedification and scandal to the faithful.[89]

The priest paid no heed to the archbishop and kept up his campaign of recruiting non-Germans. With his patience at an end, Moeller complained that "it grieved me that you whom I consider one of the most exemplary priests and very friendly disposed towards me, would flatly refuse to obey my direction." To gain the man's cooperation, the archbishop reviewed his past efforts to end the chaotic state of affairs prevalent in the diocese, concluding that "I have done all I could to give relief to German Congregations in the matter. . . . If I were to sustain your contention, I am sure, any appeal from my action would not be upheld by higher authority."[90]

With the passing years Moeller's letters to his superiors bristled with complaints about the "chaotic" state of affairs in the diocese. In 1919 the archbishop warned the apostolic delegate that "it is impossible to organize the diocese properly under the existing conditions" and that the "confusion" and "wrangling" had seriously jeopardized the Church's mission of saving souls. When he learned that Vatican officials had once again turned down his request, the archbishop complained to a close friend: "As things are now it is impossible to organize the Diocese, or take proper care of souls."[91]

As Moeller expected, the wrangling and rivalry continued. Some of his priests blamed the archbishop for not acting more decisively in ending this feuding. These complaints deeply pained Moeller and he told one critic that "you leave the impression that your superiors are not doing their duty in regards to this matter. If you knew the obstacles in the way of establishing territorial boundary lines in the Archdiocese . . . you would soon realize that you are mistaken in your contentions."[92]

Despite repeated rebuffs from his superiors, Moeller felt confident that he understood conditions in his diocese better than Rome and he continued to pressure his superiors for support. Finally, in 1921, Rome conceded and allowed him to abandon the old ethnic division of the diocese into German and English parishes and to establish territorial lines for all the parishes that no longer had a separate and distinct ethnic or racial constituency.[93]

Armed with this authority, Moeller cracked down on parish raiding, and where the parties involved could not reach an amicable settlement, he appointed a special court to resolve all disputes over boundary lines. To give the court muscle, Moeller also ordered his priests to obey the court "as Ourselves, under the penalties constituted by Ecclesiastical law against the rebellious and contumacious" and that "the pastors, who appear before the Court to swear that they will conscientiously present their case having solely in view the best interest of religion."[94] The archbishop's new get-tough tactics finally suppressed the opposition of clerical die-hards and stabilized conditions to the point that Moeller could enjoy a year of peace before his death in January 1925.

It should also be noted that the problems of the new parochialism eroded the prestige that the archdiocese had enjoyed in the councils of the American hierarchy during the mid-nineteenth century and left the suffragan bishops nominally under the jurisdiction of Cincinnati anxious to break out of its orbit and to boost the fortunes of their own dioceses.

At the turn of the century the archdiocese of Cincinnati included the dioceses of Covington, Louisville, Detroit, Grand Rapids, Fort Wayne, Indianapolis, Nashville, Columbus, and Cleveland. It encompassed about two hundred thousand square miles, an area roughly equal to the size of France. Although the archbishop, as primate or metropolitan of the church in this area, enjoyed greater prestige than the suffragan bishops under him, he could not normally interfere in the affairs of their dioceses.[95] He did, however, serve as the first court of appeals whenever a serious dispute arose between a local bishop and his flock. Vatican officials and the apostolic delegate also often called upon the archbishop to investigate and remedy conditions in other dioceses if the complaints about them were numerous. The volume and nature of the complaints from other sees show that the disorder affecting the church in Cincinnati in the late nineteenth and early twentieth centuries was not unique to this diocese.

Referrals to the archbishop also revealed another facet of the new parochialism: urban or diocesan rivalry that in many ways paralleled the petty disputes taking place on the parish level. Many bishops in this country, including Elder and Moeller, believed that American Catholicism prospered in direct proportion to the amount of home rule and benign neglect from the Vatican that it enjoyed. They did not want the papal bureaucracy or any other prelate in the church's chain of command impinging upon their domain. At the provincial level, however, the arch-bishops and their suffragan bishops parted company on the question of home rule. To maintain the prestige of the archdiocese and to keep Rome out of it, both Elder and Moeller realized that they had to maintain at least the semblance of order not only in their own diocese but also in the sees nominally under their jurisdiction. This goal often collided with the aspirations of the other bishops who wanted greater freedom from Cincinnati as well as Rome.

In their relations with each other the bishops often exhibited the same petty spirit that they deplored in their clergy. Both bishop and priest alike often succumbed to a narrow view in which their diocese or parish became for them a microcosm of Catholicism and they its lord and master, ever watchful for a chance to increase their power and prestige and ready to challenge any other church official who dared to impinge upon their authority.[96] It was upon such a myopic view of the church and the world about him that Moeller built much of his episcopal career.

Although Moeller could look objectively at the petty quarrels of his priests and shake his head in disbelief at their selfishness, he had a hard time seeing the beam of pettiness in his own eye. Instead of relieving the economic pressures on the clergy, he intensified them by partially judging a priest's success as a spiritual leader by the size of his collections. Admonishing a priest whose revenue had declined, the archbishop pointed out to him that "generally you will find that those Pastors who manage the Congregation well in a financial way are also doing their duty for the spiritual welfare of the parish."[97] Other officials reinforced this point by periodically publishing in the *Catholic Telegraph* the amount each parish contributed to the various diocesan collections.[98] While Moeller expected a generous response to his appeals for help from all the congregations under his charge, he was reluctant to come to their rescue if they began to flounder and could not meet their financial obligations.

Elder had recognized the limitations of Moeller's leadership potential and had shied away from asking Rome to name his old friend and confidant as his successor in 1903. To lead the diocese out of its spiritual wilderness and to broaden its horizons, Elder selected, because of "his acquaintance & [sic] influence with men of prominence . . . in the Church and out of it"—a quality lacking in Moeller—Camillus Maes, the bishop of Covington, as his heir apparent. To assuage Moeller's feelings, Elder assured him that "if providence should overrule my judgement and the Holy Ghost through our Holy Father should send you to me, I will be happy to learn my judgement was mistaken."[99] Later that same year the Holy Father recalled Moeller from Columbus and sent him back to Cincinnati as Elder's successor. In retrospect Elder had correctly gauged Moeller's qualifications for serving as the archbishop of Cincinnati. His views were parochial, his social life limited. Although well versed in the affairs of the archdiocese, Moeller felt uncomfortable with non-Catholics and viewed them with suspicion. His relationship with the University of Cincinnati exemplified this dimension of his personality.

Throughout his priestly and episcopal career, Moeller viewed the municipal university as a citadel of atheism and infidelity, and he strongly, but privately, criticized the university for attempting to raise funds through tax levies imposed upon the citizens of Cincinnati. In 1913, when city officials wanted a new levy of $300,000 for the university, Moeller complained to a prominent Catholic layman that the levy "puts a burden . . . on the tax payers . . . for boosting of the infidel University of Cincinnati, [and] if subject to a referendum vote, [it] ought to be objected to by every Catholic congregation."[100]

For years the *Catholic Telegraph* championed Moeller's crusade against the university. Its columns bristled with hostility and depicted the university either as "a sectarian Protestant seat of learning" or as a hotbed for spreading "materialistic philosophy." The university's leaders, the paper argued, were like "the sophists in St. Paul's day, of whom the Apostle said, 'They became vain in their thoughts and their foolish heart was darkened. For professing themselves to be wise they became fools.' And yet these are the men who assume the right to dictate what shall be taught in the . . . University which Catholics are called upon in violation of law, to support by their taxes."[101]

In May 1908 Charles W. Dabney, president of the University, invited Moeller to give the benediction at the institution's spring commencement. Moeller quickly declined, telling Dabney that "I know that the invitation is prompted by the purest and best motives. It will be impossible, however, for me to accept for two reasons: first I have another engagement for that evening and secondly I do not approve of some things taught in the University and I fear I would compromise my position by attending."[102]

Despite his negative feelings about the university, Moeller had no hard evidence that either the administration or faculty opposed the church and its teachings. For that reason the archbishop did not want to "make an attack" on the university, until he had "undeniable facts." Otherwise Moeller reasoned, "I will have to beat a hasty and ignominious retreat." To ferret out bias against the church, Moeller privately encouraged Catholics attending the university to "take down verbatim the statements of those conceited and half-baked professors. The statements will be of service . . . be alert and write out accurately the unsound teachings of the professors, giving their names and the date of their utterances."[103]

Notwithstanding his misgivings about the university and other public institutions, however, the secular world had a very low priority on Moeller's list of concerns. His life revolved around the Catholic community in his diocese. Here he felt comfortable and could savor the prestige of high ecclesiastical office as no place else. But the archdiocese was more than his cocoon. It also became the field of battle where he had to fight the erosion of episcopal power, the same old nightmare that had haunted Elder. This struggle nurtured the seeds of the new parochialism planted in his consciousness during his long tenure as chancellor. At times his obsession with upholding the prerogatives of his office so clouded his judgment that he could no longer tell real foes from the windmills of his mind.

In March 1908, the Grattan Club in Cincinnati invited both Moeller and Camillus Maes, Bishop of Covington, to its annual St. Patrick's Day banquet. Moeller declined, but Maes accepted without consulting Moeller. Maes's action infuriated the archbishop who emphatically pointed out to his colleague that ecclesiastical courtesy demanded that Maes no longer "Accept invitations to be present at public functions in my Diocese without first consulting me."[104]

Moeller's criticism stung Maes, who replied that he had accepted the invitation at the request of Covington's leading Catholics who were members of the club. Maes also asked Moeller "whether it is kind or just to oblige me to consult with you, that is practically to ask your permission to assist at any public function in your Diocese, when a simple priest may do so without any such condition?"[105]

While the iron was hot, Moeller struck another blow. He no longer wanted the Good Shepherd Sisters, stationed in Newport, Kentucky, coming to Cincinnati and begging for money. According to Moeller the nuns in Cincinnati resented anyone else moving into their territory, even if they belonged to the same religious order. Too often, the archbishop continued, the Good Shepherd Sisters in Cincinnati returned home empty handed from their visits to the business community because the Newport nuns had already tapped this source of revenue.[106]

In defense of his nuns, Maes reminded Moeller that Elder had long ago given them permission to collect money in Cincinnati for the "unfortunate creatures of your Diocese" in the Newport convent. Despite the fact that the Newport nuns bought the bulk of their supplies in Cincinnati and cared for eighty children from Cincinnati, Maes promised Moeller that they would no longer solicit money in his diocese.[107]

Instead of quitting the field of battle, Moeller retorted that "if the eighty children of the Cincinnati Archdiocese with the Good Shepherd Sisters Newport are a burden to your Diocese...[you] need not turn them out on the street, as we can, and will gladly, take them in the houses of the Good Shepherd Cincinnati," which at the time provided food and lodging for fifty-nine children belonging to the Covington diocese. Maes in turn chided the archbishop for sending him a formal protest about these alleged intrusions into the territorial limits of the archdiocese instead of discussing them with him personally.[108]

Maes's rebuke reopened an old wound. While serving as diocesan chancellor, Moeller gave a Cincinnati priest permission to validate a marriage that involved a member of Maes's cathedral parish. Moeller's actions angered Maes, who felt that the chancellor should have first discussed the case with him or some other high-ranking church official in Covington. Instead of taking his complaint to Moeller, however, Maes went over his head to Elder, charging the chancellor with a serious breach of ecclesiastical etiquette.[109] The incident embarrassed Moeller, who for years nursed a grudge against Maes because of it. The Grattan Club affair gave the archbishop a chance to even the score.

As Moeller felt his authority erode, the trappings of his office and position took on an added importance in his life and he embarked on a grandiose building program that included a palatial episcopal residence, cathedral, and seminary. Over the years the congregation at St. Peter in Chains Cathedral gradually declined as more and more Catholics left the West End and moved to the hilltops or suburbs while blacks and businesses moved into the area surrounding the cathedral. In 1881 the cathedral parish had 800 families. By 1901 it numbered 600.[110]

To make up its losses, diocesan officials wanted the cathedral exempted from any formal boundary lines "to permit any person, no matter where living in the City or its vicinity, to be a member of the Cathedral." The cathedral deserved special consideration, according to Elder, "because it is the Church at which the Bishop resides." In 1904 Moeller took the cathedral's case to the Vatican and he asked officials there "whether in establishing boundary lines of the Cathedral the exception could be made by which those living outside the Cathedral limits, could be considered it member?" The Vatican's response was an emphatic "No."[111] In light of Rome's decision, the changing nature of the neighborhood, and declining revenues at St. Peter, as reported in the *Catholic Telegraph*, (August 29, 1907) "ordinary prudence" suggested to Moeller that the time had come to look for "a suitable site for the future Cathedral."

Prudence also told him that the "honor and needs of the Archdiocese" demanded a new episcopal residence. For years many prominent Catholics had urged Moeller's predecessor, Archbishop Elder, to abandon the old "miserable house" next to the cathedral for more spacious quarters elsewhere in the city. In 1896 Mrs. Bellamy Storer offered Elder a beautiful home on prestigious Grandin Road. At the time a heavy debt hung over the cathedral and Elder did not wish to abandon the congregation in its time of need and he declined the gift. In 1903, when Moeller became coadjutor archbishop, the diocese purchased a separate residence for him at 505 West Eighth Street. Although this house had many advantages over the cathedral residence, Moeller did not regard it as suitable for a man in his position or health. He needed a home "spacious enough, to offer accommodations to Bishops of the Province... meeting and reception rooms to properly transact Diocesan affairs."[112] For years he suffered from a "delicate throat" and his physicians recommended a house in the suburbs far removed from "the smoke of Cincinnati."[113]

The third major link in Moeller's building program was a new preparatory seminary. From 1904 to 1907 the diocese had leased a large home on West Seventh Street and used it as a day school to prepare students for the priesthood. From the beginning it had a host of critics and closed after the expiration of the lease.[114] Instead of a day school in the heart of the city, the faculty wanted a boarding school in a bucolic setting where they could more closely supervise the training of candidates for the priesthood. Parents living outside Cincinnati also preferred a boarding school and were reluctant to send their boys to the Seventh Street School because it lacked living accommodations. To meet these objections, Moeller decided to build a new preparatory seminary adjoining his home and cathedral.

In June 1905, the archbishop appointed a committee of priests to select a site suitable for all three projects. Within a few weeks the committee found an ideal location in Norwood Heights. The tract embraced approximately 156 acres and commanded a panoramic view of the Millcreek valley.[115] It was a magnificent site for a cathedral, perfect in every detail save one. It was in Norwood, a separate city adjoining Cincinnati. Since Canon Law required a bishop to build his cathedral within the territorial limits of the episcopal city, the project seemed doomed from the start.

While Moeller considered this problem, he kept alive his desire to build his cathedral there with the hope that Cincinnati would sooner or later annex Norwood and perhaps all Hamilton County. Then, he reasoned, Norwood Heights would be the "center of Greater Cincinnati," the ideal spot for the cathedral.[116]

These arguments strengthened his resolve to take a chance and buy the property. At least he could build his home and the seminary there, for Church law did not lay down rules about their location. In any event, he would have the land for the cathedral and time on his side until Cincinnati annexed Norwood.

The archbishop and his advisors still faced the problem of financing the project. They discussed the possibility of the diocese's buying the land, subdividing it, and using the profits from the sale of lots to pay the expenses of the project. While this proposal intrigued Moeller the businessman, the memory of the Purcell bank failure haunted Moeller the archbishop, and he recoiled at the idea of speculating in this way with diocesan funds.[117]

Instead, he and a group of close friends formed a private syndicate, the Norwood Heights Company. To raise capital they offered its stock to the priests and laity of this diocese with the assurance that the profits would become the "personal property of the shareholder." From the beginning Moeller and several prominent priests were the largest stockholders in the company. Under their leadership the company gave sixteen acres of land to the diocese for an episcopal home, seminary, and cathedral. In return Moeller promised to build these facilities in Norwood Heights within twenty years and pay the company $45,000 for laying out the streets and sewers servicing these buildings.[118]

This agreement served two purposes. First, Moeller got the land that he wanted for his building program. Second, the company hoped that these facilities would entice Catholics to flock to the area in large numbers and create a boom in the sale of lots. In its advertisements the company urged Catholics not only to "GO OUT WHERE THE CLEAR AIR IS . . . [BUT ALSO] GET OUT IN THE NEIGHBORHOOD OF YOUR CATHEDRAL—THE RESIDENCE OF YOUR ARCHBISHOP AND IN TOUCH WITH THE CATHOLIC INSTITUTIONS AT ST. PETER HEIGHTS. . . . GET A HOME . . . IN THE MIDST OF THE CHURCH PRIVILEGES YOU PRIZE SO HIGHLY."[119] The names of the streets, Cathedral, Moeller, Fenwick, Quatman, Varelman, also reflected the Catholic character of the subdivision.

The project failed to live up to the expectation of its founders. From the beginning a host of problems, including a depressed real estate market, internal dissension, and persistent rumors that its directors were speculating for their own personal gains under the guise of religion, plagued the company. Allegations of these types infuriated Moeller, who strongly denied them.[120]

As sales of their lots languished the directors grew restive that the venture might fail and tension within their ranks mounted sharply. Despite his earlier disavowals, Moeller soon charged that some lay directors were "in the concern simply to get all the money out it they can." His resentment toward them grew stronger every time they pressed him to bail the company out of its financial difficulties.[121] By 1915, Moeller regarded the company as an "Imbroglio" and regretted the day that he had joined the venture. Nevertheless, Moeller kept the promise made earlier to its directors by building his home and a new seminary in the subdivision. Samuel Hannaford designed the episcopal residence, a palatial Italian renaissance building. Moeller proved a fastidious client and he kept Hannaford and the contractors busy with a host of complaints ranging from the size of shower curtain in his secretary's room to the water softening equipment in the basement.[122]

The new seminary opened in 1923 and from the beginning had its share of critics. Instead of using it as a minor seminary, as he had originally planned, Moeller transferred the operations of Mt. St. Mary, the major seminary, from its bucolic campus in Mt. Washington to Norwood Heights, a move that invited barbs from those who felt that an institution of this type needed more than the twelve acres of land next to the episcopal residence.[123] The critics that riled him the most, however, were those questioning the quality of instruction and training at Mt. St. Mary.

When he opened his seminary Moeller had high hopes that the other bishops of the province would send their students for the priesthood to Norwood. Ferdinand Brossart, bishop of Covington, quickly dashed those hopes by sending his philosophy students to Baltimore's seminary because of its excellence in this field. Moeller felt that Brossart had betrayed him and that, if he could not persuade his colleague, whose diocese bordered Cincinnati, to support Mt. St. Mary as a provincial seminary, he had little chance of selling the idea to other bishops in the district. To prick Brossart's conscience, the archbishop told him that "there is nothing that has given me more pain as the information that you intend to discriminate against Mt. St. Mary Seminary. I all along flattered myself with the belief that the Bishop of Covington would be one of the staunch supporters of the Cincinnati Seminary." In defense of his actions Brossart replied that "I am bound to secure as good an education for the priests as possible.... Those who know the circumstances ... at St. Mary's would condemn me justly for acting otherwise."[124]

Moeller took Brossart's reply as a slap in the face and told his colleague that "it is pretty serious and hurts for you to imply that I have failed in my stewardship, and sound judgement. By these imputations, instead of pouring balm into the sore caused by your discrimination against Mt. St. Mary Seminary, you have made it smart more keenly."[125]

A year later the archbishop evened the score. In May 1922, Brossart became ill and could not ordain his deacons to the priesthood as scheduled. He asked Moeller to perform the ceremony for him, but the archbishop refused, pleading that he could not "conscientiously" ordain men that he regarded as "not prepared for the sacred ministry."[126]

Although the Catholics of Norwood Heights built a magnificent church, St. Peter and Paul, on property acquired from Moeller, Cincinnati never did annex Norwood. Therefore the archbishop had to abandon the cornerstone of his building program—a new cathedral. For the remainder of his episcopacy, St. Peter in Chains served as the diocesan cathedral. Like a jealous priest guarding his little parochial kingdom, Moeller kept a watchful eye on the cathedral parish and he resolved never "to allow neighboring congregations that are almost defunct to incroach [sic] on the Cathedral in order to keep alive."[127]

Moeller also reflected the new parochialism in his relations with the poor, blacks, and ethnic minorities. For example, until the early twentieth century, Hungarians constituted a small minority in the Catholic community of Cincinnati and lacked both the numbers and resources to form a separate parish. Some attended the German parishes, while others held services in their native tongue at the pleasure and convenience of the Polish Catholics of St. Stanislaus at Liberty and Cutter Streets.[128]

As the number of Hungarians in the city gradually increased, many wanted to form their own parish; but, by the early twentieth century Moeller felt that the days of the ethnic parish in Cincinnati were numbered and he tried to discourage the Hungarians from forming their own congregation. Instead of heeding his advice, they kept after him until he finally gave into their demands. In 1914, he persuaded Father Edmund Neurihrer to come to Cincinnati from Hungary to start a parish for his fellow countrymen.

Neurihrer and his followers purchased the Convent of the Sisters of the Good Shepherd on Baum Street and dedicated it to St. Stephen, king of

Hungary. They made plans to convert the chapel of the convent into their parish church and to remodel the rest of the building into thirty-nine flats.[129]

Neurihrer hoped that enough Hungarian families would move into this part of the city to fill up his flats and become the nucleus for a large congregation. Once again, Moeller began to have serious misgivings about the project, but Neurihrer and his advisors assured the archbishop that the parish would succeed. The bishop reluctantly went along with their plans.[130]

Unfortunately for all involved in the project, the parish failed disastrously. Hungarians neither moved to the area in large numbers nor attended the church on a regular basis and eventually Moeller disbanded the parish. Nevertheless, the imbroglio and the failure of St. Stephen's Parish once again put the clergy on notice: "Every parish is an entity by itself; it has its boundaries within which its activities take place; each parish builds its own church, school and parish house out of its own means, and is not permitted to look for assistance from other parishers [sic], nor is it compelled to furnish assistance to other parishes."[131]

At times like this, the priests needed a man of vision and magnanimity at the helm, but unfortunately Moeller could offer them little more than a caricature of a petty bookkeeper compulsively making sure that they kept their ledgers balanced and that they understood anew the economic lesson of the Purcell failure. In response to critics who wanted him to do more for the Hungarians, Moeller retorted: The "Catholics of the diocese have very little regard for the Hungarians, and hence are not disposed to help them."[132]

The orphans in St. Joseph Orphanage also could expect little help from the priests and laity of the diocese. Because of poverty, the children had to sleep "crowded two in a single bed" and eat their meals in areas "little better than . . . cellars . . . in a condition of decay." Father John Hickey, a member of the asylum's board of trustees, also reported to the archbishop that many pastors were "positively opposed to any connection whatever with us . . . [and dismissed us] with the remark that they had their own congregation and pew rent to look after."[133]

In the final analysis, the tragedy of the new parochialism was not the failure of a bank or the emergence of a new industrial city. It was a failure of the human spirit to live up to its ideals and to realize that it had missed the mark in pursuit of the dollar. Purcell succinctly portrayed the entrepreneurial side of the church, when he boasted to a friend: "We

Catholics are not much disposed to speculate in Religion, but as this is a speculating age, we might speculate for it."[134]

In a marketing society, where Kroger sold groceries and Williams sold insurance, the Purcells, Moellers, Meyers, and associates became entrepreneurs in Catholicism. Like their secular colleagues, they frequently measured success in terms of a favorable financial balance sheet and the bourgeois trappings that went along with it. Once again Purcell inadvertently caught the pulse of the new parochialism as he fought off the infirmities of old age and prepared to meet his Maker. After a reception in his honor he reportedly told his close advisors that "words are good, but shekels are better."[135]

NOTES

1. Zane L. Miller, *Boss Cox's Cincinnati* (New York: Oxford University Press, 1968).

2. Henry Meyer to Moeller, February 25, 1920, Archives of the Archdiocese of Cincinnati (hereafter cited as AAC.).

3. Moeller to William T. Russell, February 1, 1921, AAC.

4. Moeller was referring to the Bishop of Grand Rapids, Michigan, Edward D. Kelly, who, Moeller charged, was using the public press unduly to advance his own career.

5. John H. Lamott, *History of the Archdiocese of Cincinnati, 1821–1921* (Cincinnati: Frederick Pustet, 1921), 52, 54–58, 61–62.

6. Ibid., 61–62.

7. Ibid., 65.

8. V. F. O'Daniel, *The Right Rev. Edward Dominic Fenwick, O.P.* (Washington, D.C.: The Dominicana, 1921), 424.

9. "Purcell Journal," *Catholic Historical Review* 5 (July–October 1919): 241.

10. Lamott, 84–85.

11. Compiled from *Sadliers' Catholic Directory,* 1883 (New York: D & J. Sadlier, 1883). In 1883 there were three diocese in Ohio including Cincinnati listed in *Sadliers' Catholic Directory* on p. 127; and Cleveland, p. 273; and Columbus, p. 277.

12. Ibid.

13. Lamott, 102.

14. *Sadliers' Catholic Directory,* 1883, p. 127.

15. Lamott, 175, 185–86.

16. Purcell to M. Mioland, October 21, 1836, cited in Deye, 203.

17. Time and lack of adequate records have obscured much of the history of the Purcell bank. Nevertheless, scholars have traced its origin to the panic of 1837, when many lost their savings as bank after bank closed their doors. Lamott, 190;

M. Edmund Hussey, "The 1879 Financial Failure of Archbishop Purcell," *The Cincinnati Historical Society Bulletin* 36 (Spring 1978): 8–9.

18. *The Cincinnati Enquirer,* March 2, 1879, p. 4; May 12, 1880, p. 4; March 2, 1879, p. 4 (hereafter *CE*).

19. Answer and Cross-Petition of Besudin and Mann in Supreme Court of Ohio, *Church Case* printed records 1:37–40; 41–45, cited in Lamott, 206.

20. *CE,* December 22, 1878, p. 2.

21. Lamott, 206.

22. Purcell to McElroy, September 3, 1840, Woodstock Archives, Maryland, cited in Deye, 226.

23. Miller, 61, 71.

24. *CE,* March 2, 1879, p. 4. At the time of the Hemann failure, Edward Purcell owed Hemann's company eight thousand dollars. See Hussey, 14.

25. *CE,* December 22, 1879, p. 2.

26. Edward Purcell to Mother Superior, November 3, 1879, AAC.

27. *CE,* December 27, 1879, p. 8.

28. *CE,* December 24, 1878, p. 8; December 29, 1878, p. 2.

29. Quoted in *CE,* December 22, 1878, p. 2.

30. *CE,* December 27, 1878, p. 8.

31. *CE,* December 29, 1878, p. 2; May 24, 1879, p. 4; January 19, 1879, p. 4; September 23, 1879, p. 4; February 23, 1879, p. 4; October 22, 1879, p. 5.

32. *CE,* March 2, 1879, p. 4; December 31, 1878, p. 8; January 19, 1879, p. 4; February 3, 1879, p. 4.

33. *CE,* February 26, 1879, p. 4; May 12, 1880, p. 4; February 26, 1879, p. 4.

34. *CE,* Feb. 26, 1879, p. 4; May 24, 1879, p. 12.

35. *Catholic Telegraph,* May 15, 1880, p. 4 (hereafter *CT*).

36. *CT,* May 29, 1879, p. 1.

37. *CE,* September 11, 1879, p. 2.

38. Ibid., April 9, 1879, p. 4.

39. Ibid.

40. Ibid., January 17, 1880, p. 4.

41. Elder to Purcell, January 10, 1883, AAC.

42. James O'Connor to Elder, July 6, 1880, AAC.

43. Richard Gilmour to Elder, May 30, 1880, AAC.

44. *CE,* February 13, 1880, p. 8.

45. *CE,* April 26, 1880, p. 8; *CT,* August 12, 1880, p. 4.

46. Purcell to Elder, October 15, 1880, AAC.

47. *Catholic Telegraph,* April 29, 1880, p. 4; May 13, 1880, p. 4; June 10, 1880, p. 4; August 26, 1880, p. 1.

48. Ibid., August 26, 1880, p. 1.

49. Elder to James F. Wood, September 10, 1882, AAC.

50. Casper Borgess to Elder, December 17, 1882, AAC.

51. Joseph Dwenger to Elder, February 17, 1882, AAC.

52. Dwenger to Elder, December 13, 1886, AAC.

53. Gilmour to Charles Hahne, December 22, 1886, AAC.

54. Lamott, 86.

55. Decision of Judge C. J. Own, Supreme Court of Ohio, 1888-Mannix, Assignee vs. Purcell, cited in Lamott, 199.

56. Opinion of Judge Smith in Mannix vs. Purcell printed by George R. Topp, Law Printer (Cincinnati, 1883), 81; cited in Hussey, 27.

57. Lamott, 200–201.

58. Hussey, 32, 34.

59. Elder to–, August 29, 1892, AAC, cited in Lamott, 204.

60. James H. Campbell, "New Parochialism" (Ph.D. diss., University of Cincinnati, 1981), 3.

61. Ibid., 4–5.

62. Ibid. Several chapters focus extensively on the conflict between the diocesan and regular clergy, 174–277.

63. Memorandum of Some Directions Given to the Rev. Clergy of the Diocese, October, 1880, p. 3, AAC.

64. Moeller to John Bonzano, May 22, 1919, AAC.

65. Elder to Dwenger, May 6, 1885, AAC.

66. Elder to Gilmour, August 12, 1885, AAC.

67. Gilmour to Elder, September 20, 1889, AAC.

68. James Gibbons to Elder, April 22, 1885, AAC.

69. Elder to Gilmour, November 5, 1882, AAC; March 16, 1890, AAC.

70. Elder to John Cotter, September 24, 1901, AAC.

71. Campbell, 122–24; Moeller to G. F. Hauck, August 21, 1896, AAC.

72. Francis Kessing to Elder, May 10, 1898, AAC.

73. Daniel A. Buckley, to Moeller, March 19, 1911, AAC.

74. Elder to Gilmour, August 12, 1885, AAC; John Tracy Ellis, *The Life of James Cardinal Gibbons* (Milwaukee: Bruce Publishing, 1952), 1:212–13.

75. For examples of these examinations, see the test results of Louis A. Tieman and Francis M. Lamping filed under Q-1909, AAC; Elder to Gilmour, August 12, 1885, AAC.

76. Elder to Reverend Clergy of the Archdiocese of Cincinnati, October 4, 1896, AAC; Moeller to Pastor of McCartyville and St. Patrick's, November 19, 1897, AAC.

77. Statute No. 200, Synod of Cincinnati, November 9, 1898, cited in Moeller, Decree to Pastors and Parishioners of Assumption, St. Francis de Sales, St. Elizabeth, St. Mary's Hyde Park, and St. Marks, August 22, 1905, AAC.

78. Elder to Eugene Elder, March 7, 1904, AAC.

79. William D. Hickey to Moeller, December 24, 1906, AAC.

80. John H. Metzdorf to Moeller, November 26, 1915, AAC.

81. Hickey to Moeller, October 25, 1915, AAC; J. Henry Schengber to Moeller, October 25, 1920, AAC.

82. John F. Hickey to Moeller, October 8, 1918, AAC; William C. Conway to Moeller, January 12, 1909, AAC.

83. Francis J. Beckman to Moeller, May 14, 1912, AAC; Moeller to Bonzano, May 22, 1919, AAC.

84. Elder to Thomas S. Byrne, September 12, 1897, AAC; Moeller to J. H. Pohlschneider, October 30, 1916, AAC; Moeller to Bonzano, May 22, 1919, AAC.

85. Moeller to Diomede Falconio, March 10, 1910, AAC.

86. Moeller to Charles A. O'Hern, November 2, 1920, AAC; Moeller to Mary M. Fealy, October 2, 1918, AAC.

87. Moeller to Mrs. Theod. Granzeier, February 24, 1906, AAC; Moeller to Pohlschneider, December 18, 1916; Moeller to M. Neville, October 29, 1920, AAC.

88. Moeller to Bonzano, May 22, 1919, AAC.

89. Moeller to Pohlschneider, October 30, 1916, AAC.

90. Ibid., December 18, 1916, AAC.

91. Moeller to Bonzano, May 22, 1919, AAC; Moeller to Msgr. Nicola, December 30, 1919, AAC.

92. Moeller to Martin P. Neville, October 29, 1920, AAC.

93. Moeller to Nicola, December 30, 1919, AAC; Moeller to Byrne, August 12, 1921; Moeller to Mary A. Hickey, January 14, 1912, AAC.

94. Moeller to Buckley, November 24, 1922, AAC.

95. Lamott, 112; Elder to B. A. Benedict, November 29, 1895, AAC.

96. Campbell, 278–309.

97. Moeller to Ernest Windthorst, September 10, 1916, AAC.

98. *CT,* May 23, 1895, p. 4. In an account of the 1895 collection for the local seminary, the paper asked: "WHERE DOES YOUR PARISH STAND?" Each parish was then listed in rank according to the size of its collection.

99. Elder to Moeller, February 12, 1903, AAC.

100. Moeller to Joseph Berning, May 22, 1913, AAC.

101. *CT,* March 21, 1895, p. 4; November 7, 1912, p. 4; March 3, 1899, p. 4.

102. Moeller to Charles W. Dabney, May 15, 1908, AAC. In his letter to Dabney, Moeller did not explicitly define what he meant by "some things."

103. Moeller to Ignatius Ahmann, January 2, 1923, AAC.

104. Moeller to Camillus Maes, March 17, 1908, AAC.

105. Maes to Moeller, March 18, 1908, AAC.

106. Moeller to Maes, March 17, 1908, AAC.

107. Maes to Moeller, March 18, 1908, AAC.

108. Moeller to Maes, March 30, 1908, AAC; Maes to Moeller, March 18, 1908, AAC.

109. Moeller to Maes, March 30, 1908, AAC.

110. Annual Reports, 1881, AAC.

111. Elder to Gibbons, February 23, 1898, AAC; Moeller to I. F. Horstmann, August 21, 1904, AAC.

112. *CT,* August 29, 1907, p. 4.

113. William J. Egan, *A Loving and Deserved Tribute to the Revered Memory of the Most Reverend Henry Moeller, D.D.* (Norwood, Ohio: Private Printing), 10.

114. M. Edmund Hussey, *A History of the Seminaries of the Archdiocese of Cincinnati 1829–1979* (Norwood, Ohio: Mt. St. Mary's Seminary of the West, 1979), 48.

115. *CT,* August 29, 1907, p. 4.

116. Ibid.

117. Moeller to N. J. Walsh, August 15, 1906, AAC.

118. X.B. Drexelius, Secretary, Norwood Heights Company, "Minutes," September 19, 1906, AAC; F. X. Dutton, *CT,* August 2, 1906, p. 4; *CT,* August 29, 1907, p. 4. Moeller added an important provision regarding his obligation to build a cathedral in Norwood Heights. He agreed to do so only "if conditions warrant it," namely if Cincinnati annexed Norwood and if a large population settled in the subdivision.

119. Ibid., August 27, 1908, p. 8.

120. Ibid., August 29, 1907, p. 4.

121. Moeller to Dempsey, August, 1911, AAC; Moeller to Dempsey, July 14, 1913; Moeller to Dempsey, August 1, 1913, AAC.

122. Moeller to Dempsey, April 30, 1915, AAC; Moeller to Samuel Hannaford, July 17, 1911, AAC. Despite all of Moeller's efforts to make sure the building was perfect in every detail, his successor, John T. McNicholas, abandoned it in favor of another mansion in College Hill and converted Moeller's home into the diocesan Teachers' College.

123. Egan, 9.

124. Ferdinand Brossart to Moeller, September 2, 1921, AAC; Moeller to Brossart, August 31, 1921, AAC; Brossart to Moeller, September 2, 1921, AAC.

125. Moeller to Brossart, September 4, 1921, AAC.

126. Ibid., May 2, 1922, AAC.

127. Moeller to William J. Anthony, December 2, 1922, AAC.

128. *CT,* September 2, 1915, p. 5.

129. Edward J. Dempsey to M.F. Ryan, March 18, 1918, AAC; *CT,* September 2, 16, 1915, p. 5; Philipp Eiffers, Architects, Proposal for Renovating the Good Shepherd Convent, n.d., AAC.

130. Dempsey to Ryan, March 18, 1918, AAC.

131. Dempsey to Clarence S. Darrow, March 12, 1919, AAC.

132. Moeller to Cardinal De Lai, May 30, 1920, AAC.

133. Frank H. Rowe, M.D. to Elder, October 1, 1894, AAC. For more than twenty years Dr. Rowe took care of the medical needs of the orphans. John F. Hickey to Elder, July 14, 1897, AAC.

134. John B. Purcell to Hiram Powers, February 20, 1848, Cincinnati Historical Society.

135. *Cincinnati Daily Gazette,* June 30, 1882, p. 8.

JONATHAN D. SARNA

"A Sort of Paradise for the Hebrews": The Lofty Vision of Cincinnati Jews

The Cincinnati Jewish community won widespread acclaim as the nineteenth century drew to a close. Writers, Jews and Gentiles alike, outdid one another in finding words adequate to describe it. Ohio's "wandering historian," Henry Howe, called it "a sort of paradise for the Hebrews." According to a Chicago newspaper, the *Jewish Advance,* "No other Jewish community accomplished so much good in the interest of Judaism and its people." Others termed it the "center of Jewish American life," and "the pioneer [Jewish] city of the world." According to Isador Wise, son of Rabbi Isaac Mayer Wise, many of its Jewish children, even if scattered across the frontier, vowed to remember it eternally: "If ever I forget thee . . . may my right hand be withered."[1]

Such extravagant tributes, which might have been appropriate for Jerusalem or New York, come in this case as somewhat of a surprise. Why Cincinnati? Its Jewish population was generally modest in size, especially in comparison to coastal Jewish communities. Its leading Jewish families may have acquired considerable wealth, but certainly not on the level of New York's Jewish elite. Nor was it a community characterized by extraordinary piety and learning, at least not in any traditional sense. Nevertheless, as the praises sung to it demonstrate, Cincinnati Jewry, especially in the late nineteenth century, occupied a singular position in American Jewish life. It was the oldest and most cultured Jewish community west of the Alleghenies, and had, many thought, a spirit all its own.

This spirit reflects Cincinnati Jewry's own onetime self-image, an image revealed in selected (mostly elite) writings and described by onlookers. Symbolically speaking, the community had come to represent a vision of the future, a Jewish version of the American dream, a "sort of paradise," not yet fully realized, but surely moving in the right direction. This vision, if not as unique as local Jews believed, was best articulated in the nineteenth century, when the city itself was at its height and most of its Jews were of Central European descent. Yet, in some ways, it continued to exercise a powerful hold long into the twentieth century, the city's relative decline in population and status, and the immigration of East European Jews notwithstanding. Today, for most Cincinnati Jews, this vision is but a dim memory, testament to a bygone era. But if the vision itself has largely been lost, its echoes still reverberate: the legacy of past generations who shaped the Cincinnati Jewish community and left their impress upon it.

The Vision of the Founders

Jews numbered among Cincinnati's earliest settlers. While none arrived in 1788, when the first organized group of white settlers landed, individual Jews may have passed through the city by 1814, when Israel Byer's name is recorded in a newspaper advertisement. Dr. Jonas Horwitz, usually remembered for his role in preparing the Hebrew text of the 1814 Dobson Bible, the first independently printed Hebrew Bible in the United States, turned up in Cincinnati in 1816 advertising a vaccine for smallpox. He seems to have beat a hasty retreat when local doctors attacked him for fear-mongering.[2] As a result, the man generally regarded as Cincinnati's "first Jew" was Joseph Jonas. A native of Plymouth, England, he immigrated to New York in 1816, joining some of his relatives who had preceded him there, and he later set out for Cincinnati arriving on March 8, 1817. In a memoir published in 1845,[3] he reports that, as a young man, "he had read considerably concerning America, and was strongly impressed with the descriptions given of the Ohio River, and had therefore determined to settle himself on its banks, at Cincinnati." Warned by a Philadelphia acquaintance that "in the wilds of America, and entirely amongst Gentiles, you will forget your religion and your God," he "solemnly promised" to avoid both perils. He kept the promise, became a successful "mechanic" (watchmaker and silversmith) and later a state legislator, and in 1824 helped to found Cincinnati's first congregation, the forerunner of Congregation Bene Israel, now known as Rockdale Temple.

Jonas's memoir, the basis for much of what is known about the man, gives early expression to some of the central ideals that would in later years form the basis of the community's self-image and lofty vision. Even if not widely known in written form, the memoir's major motifs achieved wide currency, for this was the history of the community as told by its "founding father," a patriarch who remained in the city for fifty years. We know from other sources that the contents of the memoir circulated in oral tradition and became embedded in popular folklore.[4] As such, the document merits particularly close attention.

What strikes one first is the effort to cloak the mission of Cincinnati Jews with a divine aura. "The fiat had gone forth," Jonas reports, "that a new resting place for the scattered sons of Israel should be commenced, and that a sanctuary should be erected in the Great West, dedicated to the Lord of Hosts, to resound with praises to the ever-living God." Here was the Puritan "errand into the wilderness"—itself a biblical motif—cast anew into Jewish terms. Cincinnati Jews, Jonas implied, were following in the tradition of the patriarch Abraham, and going forth into the land that God had appointed for them. Rabbi James K. Gutheim, writing shortly after Jonas's memoir appeared, expanded on this same theme in a published sermon: "Here, where formerly the savage, under superstitious ceremonies, brought horrible sacrifices to his 'Great Spirit': arises now in a powerful chorus of many voices the sacred motto of our faith: 'Hear oh Israel, the Lord our God, the Lord is One!' "[5] Cincinnati Jews, then, believed that they had a special mission: to establish a Jewish "resting place" in a region where Jews had never penetrated before. One has the sense that being far from the center of their faith, they, like so many other pioneers, needed continual reassurance that theirs was holy and preordained work, imbued with ultimate divine meaning. Christians received similar reassurance in their churches. To be sure, even among the generation of founders, many Jews strayed far from their faith, violating traditional religious command-ments with impunity. Jonas himself once wondered what great things might happen "if only a *few* of the most able and respectable would commence *sincerely* keeping their Sabbaths and festivals." He was, by his own account, the "Solitary," the only observant member of the (Bene Israel) congregation.[6] Yet the community's larger sense of mission—its vision of Cincinnati as a "sanctuary" and a "resting place" for Jews, and as a bridgehead spreading Judaism into the "Great West"—continued to carry great power long after ritual practices had declined, and even into the twentieth century. This helps explain, among other things, why many Cincinnati Jews looked so disfavorably upon Zionism, a movement that saw only one proper "resting place" for Jews, the land of Israel.

A second theme stressed by Jonas in his memoir concerns Jewish-Christian relations in Cincinnati. Where throughout the world Jews faced hatred and bigotry, and many were treated as second class citizens, he reports that such had never been the case in the Queen City:

> From the period of the arrival of the first Israelite in Cincinnati, to this date, the Israelites have been much esteemed and highly respected by their fellow citizens, and a general interchange of civilities and friendships has taken place between them. Many persons of the Nazarene faith residing from 50 to 100 miles from the city, hearing there were Jews living in Cincinnati, came into town for the special purpose of viewing and conversing with some of "the children of Israel, the holy people of God," as they termed us. From the experience which we have derived by being the first settlers of our nation and religion in a new country, we arrive at the conclusion that the Almighty will give his people favour in the eyes of all nations, if they only conduct themselves as good citizens in a moral and religious point of view.[7]

Others agreed with Jonas, one historian describing Cincinnati of that day as a city "of mutual good will and understanding" where Jews and Christians interacted freely.[8] In 1834, we are told, "fifty-two gentlemen of the Christian faith, our fellow citizens," donated $25 each toward the building of the city's first synagogue. Christians had helped fund synagogue buildings before, notably in Philadelphia where Benjamin Franklin was one of the contributors, and the reason in both cases was probably the same. As a contemporary explained to readers of *The Western Messenger,* they "seem to have thought it better, that these children of Israel should worship God after the manner of their fathers, than not worship at all."[9]

What may be more important is the fact that Jews and Christians in early Cincinnati also interacted socially. We learn from an 1843 letter sent by Reverend Edward Winthrop, minister and writer, to his friend Harriet Boswell in Lexington, Kentucky, that they visited one another's homes and discussed religion together:

> P.S. I forgot to mention that I have become acquainted with several of the most influential Jews in Cincinnati, and that I am quite a favorite among them. Many of them attended my lectures at St. Paul's and expressed themselves much delighted. A few weeks ago I spent the evening at the house of Mr. Jonas, the most learned and intelligent Jew I have ever met with. His wife is said to be the daughter of the richest Rabbi in London.[10] She is coming to see Mrs. Winthrop. Mr. Jonas and I examined the prophecies together, and he read and sang Hebrew for me. Mrs. Jonas occasionally joined in the conversation, and afterwards regaled us with cake and chocolate. Mr. Mayer, another wealthy Jew, has also invited me to his house. He is the father of that pretty young Jewess that I saw married at the synagogue some

three months since. She and her husband attended my lecture on the signs of the times.[11]

Of course, social interaction does not necessarily imply complete social acceptance. Much of the interest in local Jews sprang from motives of curiosity; the Jew was seen as an "exotic." What's more, many of those who befriended Jews continued to hope, with the pious editor of *The Western Messenger,* that they would ultimately "see that Christian principle diffused throughout the earth, is the only power that can restore the sceptre to Judah." Still, the image drawn by Jonas, and reinforced by other early Jews, was that of a community where Jews and Christians stood "upon the most intimate terms," as if realizing (as it had not been realized in Europe) the dream so long cherished by advocates of Jewish emancipation. Jonas made the point explicitly in 1836 when he spoke at Bene Israel's consecration. He used the occasion to contrast Jews' persecution in other lands with the "safe asylum" that they found "in this free and happy country."[12]

Although Cincinnati's first Jews, including the Jonas and Moses families, David I. Johnson, Samuel Joseph, and Jonas Levy were all from England, German Jews began immigrating to the city only slightly later. According to an unverifiable nineteenth century source, "The first German Israelite family came to Cincinnati in 1817 and met with so hospitable a reception that it wrote to its co-religionists in Germany letters which were full of praise and in which it was declared that the Lord of Heavenly Hosts had prepared for its people scattered throughout the world a land of freedom and happiness in the far-off West of America. These letters powerfully stimulated the Jews of Germany to migrate."[13]

Whether or not any German Jews actually arrived in 1817, they certainly came in growing numbers during the succeeding decades, from 1820 to 1870. From letters and newspaper reports that reached them before their emigration, many envisioned America in general, and Cincinnati in particular, as a promised land where economic opportunities abounded and Jews faced none of the restrictions that had so embittered their lives in the German states. We know, thanks to Stephen Mostov's careful research, that a large proportion of Cincinnati's German Jews originated in Southern Germany, particularly from the small Bavarian province of Upper Franconia and from the Rhenish Palatinate. Individual villages in these areas witnessed a great deal of chain migration: emigrants, in other words, called on their former *Landsleute* to come and join them.

135

Thus, the small Bavarian village of Demmelsdorf, which in 1811 had a total Jewish population of only 136, saw no fewer than thirty of its Jews (twenty-eight men and two women) emigrate to Cincinnati between 1830 and 1865, including virtually every young Jewish male in the community. The Pritz family, prominent Cincinnati distillers, were among those who hailed from Demmelsdorf, and, in later years, sang praises "to the sturdy industry and pristine rectitude" of that community's natives. No community of comparable size in all of Europe, Benjamin Pritz believed, "sent forth a larger proportion of inhabitants who have as successfully fought the battle of life."[14]

Whether they were German or English, the founding fathers of Cincinnati's Jewish community shared, as we have seen, a common dream: to find a 'promised land' in the American frontier where Jews could settle as citizens, succeed economically, practice their religion freely, and coexist happily and on equal terms with their Christian neighbors. It was a dream thoroughly compatible with the aspirations of the local citizenry as a whole. The first directory of Cincinnati (1819) spoke of residents' "liberal mode of acting and thinking," their "spirit of enterprise," their "temperate, peaceable and industrious character." Jesup W. Scott, writing in Charles Cist's *Cincinnati in 1841,* predicted "that within one hundred years from this time, Cincinnati will be the greatest city in America, and by the year of our Lord two thousand, the greatest city in the world." Horace Greeley, after visiting Cincinnati in 1850, proved only slightly less effusive. Cincinnati, he declared, was destined to become "the focus and mart for the grandest circle of manufacturing thrift on this continent."[15] There was then during this period a widely shared "boom town" mentality, a spirit of boundlessness, a sense of unlimited potential for growth and development. Jews, recognized as being among the founders of the city, shared in this public mood. With their parallel vision of Jewish Cincinnati they then took it several steps further.

"Many of the Rich People of the City Are Jews"

The Jewish vision of Cincinnati, as it developed during the second half of the nineteenth century, rested on four central and interrelated premises: First, that Jews could succeed economically in the city; second, that they could interact freely and on an equal basis with their non-Jewish neighbors; third, that they had a mission, both as good citizens and as good Jews, to work for civic betterment; and finally, that they had an obligation to develop a new kind of Judaism in Cincinnati, one better suited than traditional Judaism to the new American milieu. These assumptions all deserve to be explored at considerable length, and necessarily involve a fair degree of oversimplification, since one could obviously find individual local Jews who did not share them at all. For all of their limitations, however, they do explain much about the spirit of Cincinnati Jewry. They encapsulate the outlook that made the community historically distinctive.

To begin with, the vision that the founders of the Cincinnati Jewish community advanced needed a secure financial basis on which to rest. Economic motives loomed large among the factors that first impelled Jews to immigrate to America's shores, and it was the search for opportunity, the quest for the "American dream," that subsequently induced many to make the arduous journey across to Pittsburgh and down the Ohio River. In many ways, material success was the precondition that made everything else that Jews accomplished in Cincinnati possible.

The story of Joseph Joseph, founder of a distinguished Cincinnati Jewish family, is typical. "He was born near Frankfurt, Germany, on the 12th of July, 1847 ... and at the age of seventeen years came alone to America. He had heard many reports concerning the opportunities of the new world that were attractive to him and he hoped to find better business opportunities than he felt he could secure in the fatherland."[16] As it turned out, he found what he was looking for in Cincinnati, and his company prospered. Had he been less fortunate, or had Cincinnati offered him fewer opportunities, he would undoubtedly have moved somewhere else, as in fact many did. Dreams alone, in other words, could not sustain a Jewish community. To build the kind of community that the founders envisioned required a critical mass of Jews who both cared about being Jewish, and were at the same time successful, charitable, and secure enough to help bring some of these dreams to fruition.

Thanks to nineteenth-century Cincinnati's booming local economy, Jews did ultimately succeed in Cincinnati and some achieved substantial wealth. Yet, as Maxwell Whiteman discovered, most started off extremely modestly. They began in the most typical of all Jewish immigrant occupations—peddling:

Philip Heidelbach ... arrived in New York in 1837. A fellow Bavarian helped him invest all of his eight dollars in the small merchandise that bulged in a peddlar's pack. At the end of three months the eight dollars had grown to an unencumbered capital of $150. Heartened by this splendid return Heidelbach headed for the western country, peddling overland and stopping at farm houses by night, where for the standard charge of twenty-five cents he could obtain supper, lodging and breakfast. In the spring of that year Heidelbach arrived in Cincinnati. He peddled the country within a radius of a hundred miles from the source of his supply of goods, frequently traveling through Union and Liberty counties in Indiana. Before the year was out Heidelbach accumulated a capital of two thousand dollars.

Stopping in Chillicothe to replenish his stock, Heidelbach met [Jacob] Seasongood and the two men, each twenty-five years old, formed a partnership. They pooled their resources and for the next two years labored at peddling. In the spring of 1840 they opened a dry goods store at Front and Sycamore Streets in the heart of commercial Cincinnati under the firm name of Heidelbach and Seasongood. The new firm became a center for peddlers' supplies at once, and as their business expanded they branched into the retail clothing trade. Meanwhile Philip Heidelbach was joined by his brothers, and Seasongood was followed by other relatives. Their business prospered considerably and in 1860 the erstwhile peddlers established a banking house which continued until 1868 when Jacob Seasongood resigned as a partner of the firm to pursue other interests.[17]

Most Jews, as Whiteman points out, remained peddlers for only a short time. The road that they traveled once they cast off their packs, however, was a distinctive one, different from that traveled by other newcomers to the city. Like their counterparts in Europe and in other American cities, Cincinnati Jews concentrated in well-defined sectors of the economy, notably the garment industry. They developed an informal credit system of their own to stimulate investment in these sectors. At the same time, and in contrast to other immigrants, they kept their distance from such local occupations as pork packing, candle and soap making, brewing, iron works, machine and carriage making, and steamboat production. Why Jews made the economic decisions they did is a complicated question that cannot satisfactorily be answered here. Suffice it to say that previous occupational experience, local hiring practices, peer pressure, cultural attitudes, perceived potential for success, and a desire to work alongside other Jews were all important factors. Whatever the precise reasons, by 1860, according to Mostov, "the manufacture, distribution, and sales of men's ready-made clothing and other apparel supplied at least a portion of the livelihood for well over one-half of Cincinnati's Jews." Sixty-five of seventy wholesale clothing firms in the city were Jewishly owned. Thanks to Jewish entrepreneurship, as well as the Singer sewing machine introduced in the 1850s, Cincinnati itself had become, in Mostov's words, "the ready-made clothing capital of the West." In an unguarded moment,

Jews boasted in 1858 that they "almost monopolize[d] the Clothing Trade of the entire West and South West."[18]

Not all Cincinnati Jews, of course, were involved in the clothing trades. One study, based on census data, claims that "by 1860 Cincinnati Jews were involved in over 100 occupations." They worked, among other things, as peddlers, clerks, servants, salesmen, butchers, bookkeepers, doctors, teachers, artists and even as billiard table makers. Thirteen percent of the city's working Jews made their living in the dry goods business. Another seven percent, including the Pikes, the Freibergs, and later the Fleischmanns (more famous as makers of high quality compressed yeast) worked in the liquor trade—which, before Prohibition, was one of Cincinnati's most important industries. A substantial number of Jews were also engaged in the manufacture of cigars. Overall, then, and notwithstanding the industries that they avoided, the economic situation of Cincinnati Jewry looked bright indeed. Leon Horowitz, whose Hebrew guidebook to America, published in Berlin in 1874, was designed to stimulate Rumanian Jewish emigration to the United States, recognized this. The Queen City's Jewish population, he gushed, was "multiplying by leaps and bounds. . . . They are busy negotiating in every branch of trade, and many of the rich people of the city are Jews."[19]

By 1929, when Barnett Brickner surveyed Jewish occupations in Cincinnati, important changes had taken place. Given occupational and intergenerational mobility, few Jews now worked as laborers and peddlers, while the number of Jewish lawyers, doctors, and dentists had multiplied several fold. The clothing trade still employed a disproportionate percentage of Jews, but now a large majority of them were white-collar workers: Jewish tailors and garment workers did not encourage their children to follow in their footsteps. Numerous Jews, taking advantage of their right to own property, entered the real estate business, hoping (vainly as it turned out) to benefit from a boom. In addition, "practically all" of Cincinnati's auctioneers and pawnbrokers were now Jews, and one Jew, I. M. Libson, singlehandedly owned most of the city's major motion picture houses. Jews also owned or managed four of the city's largest department stores, secured almost half of the city's insurance business, and served as directors of leading banks. Nor does this by any means exhaust the list of Jewish occupations. To take just two unusual examples, Max Senior, one of Cincinnati's most prominent Jews, earned his living from the explosives business, and Sidney Weil, who made his money in the automobile industry, became in 1929 the first Jewish president of the Cincinnati Reds.[20]

If Jews maintained a somewhat distinctive profile within Cincinnati's economy, they nevertheless sought to be integrated into the city's economic structure as a whole. Given their importance to the local economy, and the fact that they and their Gentile neighbors often came from similar German backgrounds, they were not usually disappointed. In 1895, Maurice J. Freiberg served as president of the Chamber of Commerce, an organization that took in Jewish members from the start. His father, Julius Freiberg, had been elected an honorary member of the same organization, the highest honor that the chamber bestowed, and was praised at his death for his "cosmopolitan citizenship . . . ever ready to serve the best interests of the municipality, supporting liberally every measure for the advancement and improvement of the city of his residence." This was an exceptional case, to be sure, but numerous Jews claimed membership in the Business Men's Club and other civic associations, and most seem to have carried on extensive dealings with non-Jews.[21] The Ohio Valley National Bank, formerly the banking house of Espey, Heidelbach and Company, was even a Jewish-Christian commercial partnership, a rare but by no means unique case.[22] All of this, of course, was completely in line with the Jewish vision of the city: "In Cincinnati," Max B. May, a future local judge, boasted in 1904, "the Jews play a prominent part in the commercial and professional life of the community . . . and the prominent Jews are large stockholders and officers and members of the boards of directors of the large national banks and trust companies."[23]

Social Integration—Social Discrimination

Cincinnati Jews claimed equality with their neighbors not only in the economic realm. They believed, as we have seen, that Jews should be able to interact with their non-Jewish neighbors on an equivalent social basis as well. Isador Wise's depiction of Jewish-Christian relations in the city as "always" being "peculiarly pleasant, cordial, [and] mutually forbearing" gave voice to this belief and found many an echo. As late as 1939, the Hebrew weekly *Hadoar,* mostly read by immigrant East European Jews, reported that Cincinnati was proud of "the fine mutual relationship that continuously reigned between Jews and Christians from the very beginning."[24]

We know from studying other cities that where Jews had "pioneer" status they generally fared better than where they were seen as latecomers and interlopers. We also know from John Higham's research on anti-

Semitism and from Judith Endelman's recent study of the Jewish community of Indianapolis that "the degree to which Jews were involved in the early growth of a city and had achieved a notable and respected place in public and private life ... directly influenced how later generations of Jews were received."[25] It is nevertheless remarkable that the idyllic image of Cincinnati as a community where Jews and Christians "always" coexisted harmoniously lasted long into the twentieth century, despite available evidence to the contrary. The multiple rehearsals of the same theme underscore the fact that this was an article of faith for local Jews, an integral part of their image of themselves and their community.

Evidence that Jews and Christians in Cincinnati did often interact on a remarkably harmonious basis is not difficult to find. The city's leading rabbis in the nineteenth century, Isaac Mayer Wise and Max Lilienthal, set the pace, both priding themselves on their close friendships within the Gentile community. Wise was especially close to the local Unitarians, whom he considered "our allies," and was on intimate terms with their ministers, Moncure D. Conway and Thomas F. Vickers.[26] As for Lilienthal, he is credited with being the first rabbi to preach in a Christian pulpit, and according to an appreciative account published by Lafcadio Hearn, he "won the title of 'the Broad Church Rabbi,' having particularly, on one occasion, produced a sensation by gratuitously attending to all the duties of Rev. Dr. Spaulding of the Plum-street Universalist Church during the absence of that minister." Lilienthal also made a point of cultivating friendships among leading lay gentiles in Cincinnati, and was invited into their homes. His star student and later successor as rabbi of Congregation Bene Israel, David Philipson, followed his example in this respect, participating actively in interfaith activities and interacting socially with numerous non-Jewish friends.[27]

Beyond the leadership level, one can find evidence of close Jewish-Christian interactions in clubs and discussion groups, and particularly close cooperation in German cultural activities, like the *National Saengerbunde,* forerunner of the May Festival. A select number of Jews also won recognition as members of the local elite. *The Blue Book and Family Directory* of Cincinnati (1890) and Clara Devereux's *Blue Book of Cincinnati Society* (1916–17) both included Jews in their registers of "prominent residents," and Ben LaBree's *Notable Men of Cincinnati,* published in 1903, listed no fewer than twenty-five Jews among the five hundred most important residents of the city, a ratio of 5 percent, or about the same as the ratio of Jews to the city's population as a whole. From a sociological point of view, perhaps the best indicator of close Jewish-Christian relations is the intermarriage rate, evidence that the two groups not only interacted in business and formal settings but in intimate ones as well. How Jews and Christians felt about intermarriage, and what problems such unions created is not the issue here; the revealing fact is that such intermarriages took place at all. Barnett Brickner, in a study of Cincinnati Jewish intermarriages covering 1916–18, found that 20 of 439 marriages were intermarriages, a rate of 4.5 percent. How this compared to earlier rates cannot be determined, but intermarriages certainly involved well-known members of the community. In two well-publicized late nineteenth-century cases, Rabbi Isaac Mayer Wise's daughter, Helen, eloped with James Molony (They raised their children as Jews), and Charles Fleischmann's daughter, Bettie, married Christian R. Holmes.[28]

However, another side to Jewish-Christian relations in Cincinnati exists, which does not comport to the regnant image, and has, as a result, been less frequently told. This is the story of anti-Jewish prejudice in Cincinnati, particularly manifestations of social discrimination. In 1848, for example, a Jew named Charles Kahn met with hostility when he purchased three acres of land on Ludlow Avenue to build himself a house in Clifton. According to Arthur G. King, Clifton's historian, a self-appointed committee of "gentlemen" soon visited Kahn and advised him that he would enjoy a happier life and find more congenial neighbors if he built his home elsewhere. "Very well gentlemen," Kahn is said to have replied, "if you do not care to have a Jew living near you, you cannot object to dead Jews, and shall have many of these, for many years, in no condition to offend you." Kahn then sold his lot to K. K. Ahabeth Achim ("The Holy Congregation of Brotherly Love"), which used the land for its cemetery.[29] Hatred of Jews also figures prominently in the first Jewish novel set in Cincinnati, entitled (perhaps revealingly) *Hannah; or, A Glimpse of Paradise* (1868) by H. M. Moos. Edgar Armhold, its Jewish hero, is born poor, achieves wealth, intermarries, loses his wife's love, changes his name to Clermont Harland, and dies after an unhappy life. In the interim, he faces considerable prejudice. "I only know he is a Jew, and I have a natural antipathy toward Jews," Hannah, his future wife says at one point. "I never did like to come in contact with them." Others agree with her. However stilted and unrealistic the novel as a whole may have been, the complex portrait of post–Civil War Cincinnati as a city where Jews as a class met with hate while individual Jews were loved, and where Jews could attain great financial and social success in spite of continuing prejudice, certainly rings true.[30]

In 1882, Isaac Mayer Wise, who witnessed and condemned a great deal of anti-Jewish prejudice in Cincinnati, especially during the Civil War, admitted in one of his rare negative comments about the city as a whole (written, it should be noted, in an obscure review distributed mainly to rabbis) that "there did exist a residue of that sectarian prejudice among Jews and Gentiles also in this cosmopolitan West and this enlightened city, which drew a line of demarcation, visible and tangible, in all social relations." He implied, by using the past tense, that conditions had since improved. In fact, however, anti-Semitism erupted in late nineteenth- and early twentieth-century Cincinnati too, as it did elsewhere in the country during this period, though given the status of local Jews, its effects were less severe than in some other communities. Several clubs, including the Cincinnati Country Club, the Cincinnati Woman's Club, the Commercial Club, the Junior League, and the Avondale Athletic Club refused (or in some cases ceased) to accept Jewish members, and with a handful of exceptions, "there was a general tendency to exclude German Jews from Gentile social gatherings attended by both sexes after six o'clock." The most prominent college preparatory school for girls likewise kept Jews out—even if the Jew happened to be the daughter of popular Cincinnati Symphony Orchestra maestro Fritz Reiner. Meanwhile, Jewish clubs that once had been prominently included in the community "blue book," no longer were; socialite Clara Devereux apparently decided that their existence had ceased to be a matter "of social interest." Most serious of all, Jews found themselves frozen out of positions in certain banks and law firms.[31]

These and other manifestations of social discrimination, did not seriously threaten Jews' economic well-being, much less their physical security. Old line Jewish families remained as prominent as they always had been, and Jews continued their active participation in business, the professions, civic affairs and local politics. Yet, evidence of local anti-Semitism pointed up a more general problem: a disturbing disjunction between Cincinnati as Jews envisaged it, and Cincinnati as it actually was. For a long time, Jews lived with this contradiction. They overlooked it, suppressed it, or rationalized it away. In the long run, however, it would have to be confronted. For in many ways, the Jewish vision of Cincinnati was simply too good to be true.[32]

"If It Were Not For The Support of the Jews"

The Jewish vision of Cincinnati, starry-eyed as it may have been, did not encourage communal complacency. To the contrary, in what we have listed as one of their major tenets, local Jews stressed that as good citizens and good Jews they had a mission to work for civic betterment. Education, culture, philanthropy, social work and good government stood among the leading causes that Jews embraced, often in a spirit of civic pride and noblesse oblige, or as part of the Jewish Social Justice movement, roughly equivalent to the Protestant Social Gospel. Feeling that "he must do something for the public good," Rabbi Max Lilienthal, to take just one example, "was for years member of the School Board, member of the Board of examiners, member of the University Board, president of a medical college, member of the City Relief Board and other benevolent organizations, and was . . . popular and influential in the city of Cincinnati and far beyond its confines, more so, perhaps, than any rabbi ever [previously] was in America"—at least that was the opinion of his friend, Rabbi Isaac Mayer Wise. Writing more than half a century later, in 1938, journalist Alfred Segal spoke of a "Jewish aristocracy" in Cincinnati, "whose merit was in its culture, its abundant philanthropy, and its devotion to the highest civic responsibilities." For some, indeed, these "merits" almost appear to have been religious duties. They substituted for more traditional rites and worship long since abandoned.[33]

Philanthropy was for many years the hallmark of Cincinnati Jewry, what set it apart from other Jewish communities across the United States. Boris Bogen, who wrote the standard textbook on Jewish philanthropy (based in part on his own work in Cincinnati), and who was one of the pioneers of scientific charity, considered the city's Jewish community to be nothing less than "the examplar [*sic*] of social service for the eyes of all other Jewries." Isador Wise, writing for a Gentile audience, made the same claim. Nor, as we shall see, was it an idle boast. Cincinnati introduced numerous innovations into the world of Jewish social service, and in the early decades of the twentieth century served as the training ground for Jewish communal service professionals. In 1913, community leaders even established a short-lived School of Jewish Social Service in the city. "For a number of years," its brochure read, "Cincinnati has been the home of the leading spirit in organized Jewish charity. . . . [It has] acquired a reputation for efficient[ly] training social workers and has supplied leading workers to many cities."[34]

The history of Jewish giving in Cincinnati dates all the way back to the first half of the nineteenth century. By 1850 the community boasted the first Jewish hospital in America, founded in that year, as well as several mutual aid, benevolent, and ladies' charitable societies, and even a fund to aid the needy of Palestine. Jewish charities increased in number during the second half of the century, especially with the onset of mass East European Jewish immigration in the 1880s. A particularly significant development occurred in 1896 when major Jewish charities in the city federated into the United Jewish Charities, only the second Jewish federation in the country (the first was in Boston). Among other things, the new federation encouraged administrative efficiencies, set up a combined city-wide campaign for funds, and introduced "the most progressive and far-reaching methods in its work," including preventive social work techniques, the so-called Cincinnati method of caring for tubercular patients, widows' pensions, and special efforts "to rehabilitate the family wherever possible." It also initiated the call for a National Conference of Jewish Charities, and hosted the first meeting of that organization, forerunner of the Council of Jewish Federations.[35] Thanks to their new federation, Cincinnati's twenty-eight thousand Jews also gave more money to Jewish charities than ever before. During the first year of joint solicitation by the United Jewish Charities the amount raised was "double ... the totals of all moneys previously raised by the constituent associations." In 1910, $117,372 was raised, the highest per capita rate of giving of any major Jewish community in the United States, and $15,000 more than was raised in that year by the three hundred thousand Jews of Brooklyn.[36]

Cincinnati Jews took an active role not just in their own charities; they were deeply involved in non-Jewish charities as well, realizing that they played no less important a role in improving the quality of the community. Rev. Charles Goss's history of Cincinnati, for example, portrays Charles Fleischmann as a man who contributed to practically "every charitable institution in his home city. No worthy object, public or private, was ever denied his earnest support." The same volume describes Millard Mack as "a liberal contributor to all charitable organizations." Other Jews, we know, participated in the work of the National Citizens League, the Tuberculosis League, and the Avondale Improvement Association. It was, however, in the Associated Charities of Cincinnati (founded in 1879) and the Community Chest (founded in 1915) that Jews played particularly active roles. The former published a list of bequests and endowments that includes numerous Jewish names, headed by the Hebrew Orphans Fair that made its bequest back in 1881. In 1894, Henry S. Fechheimer helped to incorporate the Charities, and two years after that Rabbi David Philipson served as one of its vice-presidents; thereafter, Jewish names were never absent from its Board of Directors. The Community Chest was actually modeled in part on the federation concept introduced by the city's United Jewish Charities. It listed Boris Bogen as one of its "pioneers," David Philipson as one of those who "stood out conspicuously in their active service," and at least twenty-four other Jews who served either as members of its Board of Directors or as leaders of its annual campaign. Perhaps for this reason, the Chest contributed some $200,000 to Jewish Foreign Relief in 1920, more that year than it contributed to any other individual cause. Indeed, the Community Chest proved so successful, and worked so closely with the Jewish community, that some leading Jews eventually abandoned "parochial" Jewish philanthropy altogether, and devoted all of their communal attention to the Chest. It became their symbol of Jewish universalism, the comfortable synthesis that permitted them to display "Jewish values" while helping the community at large.[37]

Both Jewish and general philanthropies in Cincinnati rallied in the twentieth century behind the aims of "scientific charity." No longer were donors content, as once they had been, to (in the words of the United Jewish Social Agencies) "relieve the deserving poor . . . prevent want and distress and discourage pauperism." Instead, they spoke of "prevention," "social philanthropy" and "education," and supported projects aimed at improving community (and especially the immigrant community's) health, welfare and "happiness." The Jewish Settlement (later Community House), founded in 1899 and inspired by Jane Addams's Hull House, embraced many of these goals. Among other things, it supported tenement reform, pure milk for babies, and medical inspection for school children, sponsored Americanization classes, vocational training, kindergartens, and Camp Livingston, and helped initiate the Big Brothers Association, and later the Big Sisters, to help disadvantaged youth and to fight juvenile delinquency. The social work principles of "scientific charity" also inspired such local Jewish sponsored or aided projects as the United Jewish Charities playground; the Pay-Heath clinic; the mental hygiene program; the Penny Lunch Association, which in Orthodox areas of the city served kosher lunches; the United Jewish Social Agencies bakeshop, founded in 1929 and particularly important during the Depression; and even, although the origins of the idea were far more ancient, the Hebrew Free Loan Society, organized on a self-help basis by the immigrant East European Orthodox

146

Community. All alike did their part to realize the lofty vision that Cincinnati Jews had cherished from their earliest days in the city: to make theirs a model community, a "sort of paradise."[38]

The same ultimate aim stood behind local Jews' concern for education and culture. In the case of the former, a traditional Jewish value, it was Rabbi Max Lilienthal who again took the lead: he served as a member of the board of education, promulgated educational reforms, authored a textbook, and served as a regent of McMicken University (later the University of Cincinnati). After the public schools were, with Jewish support, established on a firm and nonsectarian footing in the 1860s,[39] Cincinnati Jews abandoned the last of their Jewishly sponsored private and parochial schools, and became prime public school supporters, relegating Jewish studies to afternoon and Sunday schools (new Jewish day schools were founded in the twentieth century). Jewish students achieved exemplary public school records, and a disproportionate number went on to finish high school: for several decades beginning in the 1880s, Jews are said to have comprised between 20 and 30 percent of each year's high school graduating class. Subsequently, many Jews (how many is uncertain), including women, went on to college: some went to Harvard and other East Coast universities, others stayed closer to home in Ohio. Nor did concern for education end there. From the late nineteenth century onwards, at least one Jew usually won election to the board of education (the most notable were Board Presidents Samuel Ach and William Shroder for whom public schools were later named) and numerous Jews served as school room teachers. Indeed, what Lafcadio Hearn wrote of Cincinnati's Jews in the 1870s continued to be true long afterward: "They make the education of their children a sacred duty, and in this they patronize the Public Schools and the Public Library. They are the most firm supporters of our public educational system."[40]

Jews also firmly supported local institutions of culture. That so many first-generation Cincinnati Jews had been exposed to culture in Germany, and therefore valued music, art and theater, much as their non-Jewish German neighbors did, certainly explains much of this interest. Thanks to their new wealth, and the relative openness of Cincinnati society, even pre–Civil War Jews were known for being "sociable and . . . disposed to enjoy themselves."[41] But culture, especially to newly emancipated Jews, also meant more: It represented a commitment to western civilization and its canon, an embrace of artistic and humanistic values, and an almost religious exultation in what the human mind could create. By bringing culture to Cincinnati, then, Jews sought to raise the city to a metropolis of the highest rank, on a par with London, Paris, Vienna, and Berlin. This endeavor was all part of their overall commitment to the city and its development.

Several Cincinnati cultural institutions, including Pike's Opera House and Krohn Conservatory, have carried Jewish names. The art museum, the symphony orchestra, the public library, the theater, the May Festival, and numerous other cultural programs and institutions, to say nothing of the arts' fund, heavily depended (and still depend) on Jews for much of their support. "None of the great charities, none of the theatres, none of the societies of art, artistic development or music, could live if it were not for the support of the Jews," William Howard Taft once said, speaking of Cincinnati. However much he exaggerated for the benefit of his Jewish listeners, it nevertheless remains true that Cincinnati Jews played a central role in creating and maintaining their city's cultural institutions.[42]

For all of these efforts, Jews probably made their most important contribution to civic betterment in Cincinnati through their work in the sphere of politics. This marked a significant change, because before the Civil War Cincinnati Jews took pride in their "lack of political office-seeking," an attitude that both made a virtue out of traditional Jewish necessities and reflected widespread popular suspicions of those who declared politics their calling. We know that Henry Mack served on the city council as early as 1862, and that one year later Isaac Mayer Wise was nominated for the Ohio Senate, a nomination that, at the insistence of his congregation, he declined. By the last third of the nineteenth century, however, local Jews were serving in a full range of elective and appointive offices. A 1904 account lists some fifty different Cincinnati Jews who at one time or another engaged in "public service," and includes individuals who served as mayor, common pleas judge, county solicitor, prosecuting attorney, county clerk, state senator, member of the state house of representatives, county commissioner, appraiser of customs, city council member, school board member, police commissioner, U.S. commissioner, sinking fund trustee, and justice of the peace. In 1900, two Jews actually ran against one another for the mayor's chair: Julius Fleischmann, who won, and Alfred M. Cohen. That Jews could attain such offices was in part a tribute to the city's political machine: It made sure that Jews received their due. Jewish involvement in politics also reveals much about Jewish-Christian relations in the city: social prejudice, as it existed, did not apparently stand in the way of Jews' political advancement. What may even be more revealing, however, is the fact that Jews sought these offices in the first place. Some no doubt enjoyed the power and prestige; others, it later turned out, misused their power for personal gain. Yet for many, public office was a burden; it meant time away from business and family. They served less out of joy than out of a sense of duty and calling, the same Progressive-era feelings of paternalistic altruism that motivated elite non-Jews. At least in some cases, they used their time in office to promote their vision of what Cincinnati should become.[43]

The good government movement, culminating in the passage of a new city charter in 1924, serves as an obvious case in point. Murray Seasongood, the Jewish lawyer who spearheaded the anticorruption campaign, had a vision of how local government could work more efficiently and better, without corruption and at reduced costs. His foray into the political arena stemmed from his desire to effect the kind of changes that he advocated. He was a man with a mission, and Jews were prominent among those who flocked to his side. "From its inception," Brickner reports, "the Charter Movement received the support of the Jewish element. A good part of the funds for the campaign, as well as the leadership in the district and ward organizations, came from the Jewish groups. The Jewish women were particularly helpful in the organizational side of the campaign." In addition, Rabbi David Philipson threw his own weight and prestige behind the good government cause: urban reform appealed to his sense of justice and holiness. To be sure, some Jews did not support Seasongood. Republican Gilbert Bettman, later State Attorney General, for example, believed "that a party was better reformed from within than from changing the form of government." Still, he too acknowledged that reform and good government were fundamentally necessary. The ideals that Cincinnati's Jewish leaders cherished for their community—their sense of obligation and mission as well as their vision of what the community could become—demanded nothing less.[44]

"To Endear and Preserve Our Religion"

The vision of Cincinnati Jews that we have been tracing might be described as a kind of civil religion, independent of church, socially integrative, and reflecting "deep-seated values and commitments." While selectively derived from Judaism, the central tenets that Cincinnati Jews upheld cannot themselves be described as Judaism: essential commandments, traditional rituals, and historical consciousness were all left out.[45]

149

Traditional Judaism, however, found few exponents in Cincinnati. As we have seen, even in Joseph Jonas's days, religious laxity was the rule. The traveler I. J. Benjamin described the Jews he met as having "little interest in spiritual matters." According to Stephen Mostov's figures for 1851, over one-fifth of the community did not affiliate with any synagogue at all. Although by 1851 there were four different synagogues to choose from—Bene Israel (English and Dutch Jews), Bene Yeshurun (German Jews), Ahabeth Achim (German Jews living in the Over-the-Rhine), and the so-called Polish Congregation, the forerunner of Adath Israel—the majority of Jews who did affiliate attended only on an irregular basis. The fear, an understandable one, and one by no means unique to Cincinnati, was that Judaism would be unable to survive its encounter with the New World: Ritual laxity, assimilation, and intermarriage, many thought, would eventually bring about Judaism's demise.[46]

Religious reform, evident already in the 1840s, was an effort to stem this tide. In 1848 Bene Israel and Bene Yeshurun both revised their constitutions "to prevent disorder and impropriety." Various traditional and customary practices, such as kissing the Torah, or banging on the desk for order now fell under the ban. Such practices, in the words of one Bene Israel regulation, tended "to create irreligion and derision rather than a due respect and reverence for the precepts of our holy religion." Increasingly, the wealthy and socially conscious men who ruled Cincinnati's synagogues sought dignity and decorum in their religious life: services that both comported with their own Americanized mores and that could be proudly displayed to gentile visitors. Concerned more with aesthetic than with ideological reforms, they sought a new balance—one that would preserve Jewish identity, even as it heightened Judaism's appeal to outsiders, unaffiliated Jews, and the young.[47]

The history of Cincinnati Judaism, indeed of American Judaism as a whole, changed in 1854 with the appointment of Isaac Mayer Wise as rabbi of Bene Yeshurun. Born in Steingrub, Bohemia, in 1819 and trained in Germany, Wise immigrated to the United States in 1846 and quickly established himself as a "Reformer." In his first major pulpit, at Congregation Beth El in Albany, he stirred controversy with a series of ritual modifications aimed at improving decorum; he also organized a mixed choir. This helped precipitate his firing, led to a memorable melee on the holiday of Rosh Hashanah when the congregation's president lashed out at him and knocked off his hat, and soon resulted in the founding of a new congregation, Anshe Emeth, which he served as rabbi until being called to

Cincinnati. How much Bene Yeshurun's leaders knew of all this when they appointed him (and agreed to his demand for a life contract) is not clear, but they surely realized that, in Wise, they were getting one of the most able young men then serving in the American rabbinate: a leader who combined within himself traditional and modern learning, boundless energy and ambition, facility in both German and English, and remarkable personal charisma.[48]

In accepting the Bene Yeshurun position, Wise made clear that he shared the vision of those who hired him. He promised to elevate his new synagogue into "a model congregation for the whole West and South," and pledged "to maintain and defend the honor of our sacred faith opposite all religious sects." He was, he pointed out, "a friend of bold plans and grand schemes."[49] In a city filled with bold planners and grand schemers, one that envisaged itself becoming the greatest city in America if not the world, he found himself right at home.

Years later, Wise compared Bene Yeshurun in 1853 to "a company of brave and daring men, each longing to do some noble and heroic deed, but unable, because there was no true and capable leader." With his arrival, he wrote, the congregation "having at last found one in whom it could put implicit faith, readily submitted itself . . . and marched forward bearing the glorious banner, 'Reform.' " Bene Yeshurun's members, however, did not imagine that in following Wise they were creating a separate movement or denomination within Judaism. Instead, they and Wise saw themselves as the harbingers of *American* Judaism, a legitimate heir to the Judaism practiced by different waves of Jewish immigrants. They believed, in other words, that the Reform Judaism that they were establishing in Cincinnati—the "forms, formulas, customs and observances" that Wise modernized—would in time be recognized as the rite, or *minhag,* of *all* American Jews, displacing the Spanish-Portuguese, German, and Polish rites then practiced by different synagogues. From a Cincinnati point of view, of course, this was only fitting; it was a logical Jewish extension of the "Cincinnati dream." The city that represented the future of America as a whole, the "gateway to the west," would shape America Jewry's destiny as well. The Reform rite established at Bene Yeshurun would become the "American rite"; its prayerbook (which Wise optimistically entitled *Minhag America*) would become the prayerbook of Jews nationwide.[50]

This nexus between Cincinnati's destiny and that of Reform Judaism helps explain why, even in a city where so many Jews observed Judaism in the breach, Reform Judaism nevertheless became part and parcel of the local Jewish ethos. To help spread Reform became, if nothing else, an act of local patriotism, a means of boosting Cincinnati's nationwide status. As a result, Reform grew rapidly in Cincinnati; it also penetrated further than it did in most other American cities. As early as 1854, Congregation Bene Israel, impressed by Wise's manner and ideas and probably worried that he might lure members away from its congregation, decided that it too would elect him rabbi; they even agreed to pay half of his salary. Bene Yeshurun wouldn't hear of the idea, however, so Bene Israel hired "a reformer" of its own, Rabbi Max Lilienthal, whom they took on Wise's recommendation. The two congregations proceeded, if not always at the same pace, to introduce a series of aesthetic and liturgical reforms. Changes included shorter and more decorous services, organ music, vernacular prayers, mixed choirs, abolition of headcoverings, abandonment of the second day of Jewish holidays, and more. "We want Reform in order to endear and preserve our religion," Wise explained, "we are practical."[51]

The strategy apparently paid off, for both congregations grew in size and wealth. In 1865, Bene Yeshurun laid the cornerstone for a magnificent new Moorish-style synagogue building to be erected on Plum Street. It wanted the building to be not only a Jewish but also a Cincinnati landmark, and made sure that it was designed by one of the city's foremost architects, James Keys Wilson. Significantly, the site chosen was just opposite the city's leading Catholic and Unitarian churches, symbolic of the coequal role that Wise believed Judaism should play in the city. Bene Israel followed suit in 1869 dedicating an imposing Gothic building on Eighth and Mound streets, opposite the Quaker Meeting House. While not as impressive as the Bene Yeshurun building, it too was designed to be an architectural monument. Indeed, both buildings, in accordance with Reform Jewish ideology, were designated "temples," not synagogues. Rather than await the rebuilding of the temple in Jerusalem, Reform Jews now declared that each synagogue was to be a temple unto itself.[52]

It was, however, not just its temples that made Cincinnati the center of Reform Judaism. Far more important was the fact that the city became home to Reform's premier newspaper and to its central institutions and organizations: the *American Israelite* (the name itself is significant), founded as the *Israelite* in 1854 and renamed in 1874; the Union of American Hebrew Congregations, founded in 1873; Hebrew Union College, founded two years later; and the Central Conference of American Rabbis, founded in 1889. Cincinnati Jews, led by Rabbis Wise and Lilienthal, took the lead in creating, nurturing, staffing, and supporting all of these, willingly so, since they saw them as instruments through which both Reform Judaism's destiny and Cincinnati's might ultimately be realized. Hebrew Union College, which at the time of its founding was the only rabbinical seminary in America, became particularly important in the life of the city. It served as a magnet for attracting important Jewish scholars, drew in highly motivated students from around the country (many of whom simultaneously studied at the University of Cincinnati), brought to the city important speakers and programs, and spread Cincinnati's name throughout the entire Reform movement and across the world of Jewish scholarship. Moreover, the college demonstrated anew the sense of shared destinies that we have seen to be so characteristic of the entire Cincinnati Jewish relationship. Typically, in promoting the college to American Jews, Cincinnati Jews promoted their fair city as well:

> On account of her high culture and her love for music and art Cincinnati has come to be called the 'Paris of America.' Her public schools, her colleges and other educational institutions, together with her unequaled Public Library rank second to none in the United States. The Cincinnati Jews rank first in intelligence, culture, education and—Judaism. What more fitting place then could have been selected wherein to locate the College? Is it not perfectly natural that it should be located among such a people with such advantageous surroundings?[53]

Still, despite all of this, Reform Judaism never gained a monopoly in Cincinnati. Traditional Orthodox Judaism maintained a continuous presence in the city from Joseph Jonas's day onward, and the city directory always listed at least one Orthodox synagogue, usually more. Of the pre–Civil War synagogues, Adath Israel, known for years as the "Polische Schule" (Polish Synagogue), was founded sometime in the 1840s (possibly under a different name),[54] and maintained its Orthodox orientation into the twentieth century, when it affiliated with the Conservative movement. Congregation Ahabeth Achim, the only German synagogue in the upper west end part of the city, was founded in 1847, and maintained its orthodox orientation into the 1870s. Congregation Sherith Israel ("Remnant of Israel"), founded in 1855, consisted of the "remnant" of Bene Israel that remained Orthodox and opposed the Reforms promulgated by Max Lilienthal. Its rabbis included Bernard Illowy, one of the most learned and influential early Orthodox rabbis in the entire country. After the Civil War and particularly once East European Jewish immigration to the city increased in the 1880s, several new Orthodox synagogues were founded. In 1866, Schachne Isaacs, who had immigrated to Cincinnati from the Lithuanian province of Suwalki back in 1853, founded Congregation Bet Tefillah ("Reb Schachne's Shul"), in time the largest Orthodox synagogue in the city. Other Orthodox synagogues founded by immigrants included Beth Hamidrosh Hagodol (Lithuanian), Ohav Shalom (Russian), Anshe Shalom (Rumanian), B'nai Jacob (Polish) Yad Charutsim (artisans), Kneseth Israel, B'nai Avraham, and New Hope (Tikwoh Chadaschah), the latter founded by German emigres in 1939.[55]

At least through World War II, however, Orthodox Judaism maintained its own separate existence; it never became part of the larger Jewish community's vision of itself. In the eyes of most Jews, Cincinnati was still the "home" of Reform. Reform Jews continued to be the wealthiest, most numerous, and most visible Jewish element in the city. Furthermore, unlike in the East where the Conservative Movement grew rapidly, in Cincinnati the tide still seemed to be moving Reform's way. Two German Orthodox synagogues founded before the Civil War, Ahabeth Achim and Sherith Israel, merged in 1907 into the Reading Road Temple (not synagogue), and instituted moderate reforms. Twenty-four years later, during the Great Depression, the temple became part of Isaac M. Wise Temple (formerly Bene Yeshurun); its members "joined the crowd." Cincinnati Jews who believed in the inevitability of Reform naturally took this as confirming evidence that they had been right all along. Reform, the Judaism that they had developed and promoted for so many years, was destined to become just what they had envisioned: American Judaism. They assumed that the children of the East Europeans, as good Americans, would soon become Reform Jews too, and that Orthodoxy would eventually wither away and disappear.[56]

Paradise Lost

The Jewish vision of Cincinnati, the tenets that the community upheld and the hopes that it cherished, remained largely unrealized. The city became neither the urban center that the first immigrants foresaw nor the model community that their children strove to create. Instead, later generations, unfamiliar with past history, saw Cincinnati as just another middle-sized American Jewish community, one far less important than Cleveland or Chicago. The dreams that once made the city exceptional in Jewish eyes were, with the passage of time, forgotten.

To some extent, Jews themselves were to blame: the utopia that they wished for, the "new era" that once stood at the center of their hopes, was, in retrospect, only a pipe dream, more a testimony to post-Emancipation fantasies than to local realities. No matter how unrealistic the local Jewish vision may have been, however, the fact that Cincinnati failed to remain even a regional Jewish center must largely be attributed to the weakening of the city itself. Just as the rise of the community had been tied to Cincinnati's own destiny, so too its subsequent decline; the two went hand in hand. The numerous factors associated with that decline—the collapse of the river trade, the development of the Far West, the routing of railway lines through Chicago, the rise of competing midwestern cities, political mismanagement, and so forth—affected the city's Jews no less than their Gentile neighbors.

As Cincinnati's character changed during the twentieth century, the assumptions that formerly guided its Jewish life were increasingly called into question. For one thing, where Jews formerly depended on being able to succeed economically in the city, now they no longer could. Some of the wealthiest old-line families fell on hard times. Potential newcomers found that opportunity knocked louder for them in Chicago or in the booming cities of the two coasts. Jews did still interact with their non-Jewish neighbors in Cincinnati, more so than in many another city. But they could no longer deny that they faced blatant social and religious discrimination in the city as well. Several local employers refused to hire Jews, well-known social clubs refused to admit them, and many Christian homes were closed to them at night. The sense of belongingness that early Jews had so cherished grew more and more attenuated.

In the area of civic betterment, Jews continued to play an exceptional role, participating actively in the major educational, cultural, philanthropic and civic organizations that the city offered. But they no longer did so from a sense of mission, as if from their efforts alone a great society could be brought about. Nor did they anymore expect Jewish charities to assume a pioneering role in social and community work. Instead, support for Jewish charities markedly declined. Where once, as we have seen, the city took first place nationwide in terms of per capita Jewish giving, by the last quarter of the twentieth century it had fallen to the bottom half of the national scale, ranking below most other midwestern cities.

Finally, Cincinnati's relationship with Reform Judaism underwent a change. Once the acknowledged center of American Reform, believed by its adherents to adumbrate what American Judaism as a whole would become, the community in the twentieth century lost both its sense of Jewish mission and its certainty regarding Reform's future. Already in the 1930s, the city's leading Orthodox rabbi, Eliezer Silver (who considered himself the chief rabbi not only of the city but also of North America as a whole), consciously challenged Reform's domination, seeking to demonstrate that Orthodoxy too could flourish under American conditions. During the next three decades, he built up Cincinnati's reputation as a center of Orthodoxy, created a range of new Orthodox institutions, trained a generation of young people, and gathered around him a coterie of wealthy laymen who supported the projects that he initiated.[57]

Meanwhile, following World War II, Reform's principal lay body, the Union of American Hebrew Congregations, left Cincinnati and moved to what had clearly become the new center of American Judaism, New York. Hebrew Union College remained firmly ensconced on Clifton Avenue, despite abortive efforts to move it, but Cincinnati became a less important part of its overall identity too. No longer did the "Cincinnati School" train virtually all American Reform rabbis, as once it had. Now it shared that task with three other branches of the school: New York (formerly the Jewish Institute of Religion), Los Angeles, and Jerusalem.[58]

Yet for all that it had lost, the Cincinnati Jewish community remained distinctive, quite unlike communities of similar size like Kansas City, Rochester, Buffalo, or Providence. The legacy of the past explains why. The nature of the immigrants who settled and shaped the community, the kind of Judaism that they practiced, their lofty communal vision—all of these left an impress on the community's character that continues to be evident even today. A recent article seeking to explain "what is so special about Cincinnati Jewry" still found the answer in the history of the German Jewish community, its "ambition," "eagerness to assimilate," and "premonition of success."[59] The era of German Jewish hegemony has long since passed, and by now the city's East European Jews have prospered and come into their own. But, as Cincinnatians know, the memories linger on.

Perhaps the central surviving symbol of Cincinnati Jewry's nineteenth-century grandeur is 'historic' Plum Street Temple: magnificent, gaudy, and now considerably faded, a tourist attraction. Looking at it, one is struck anew by the vision that it represents: its boundlessness, triumphalism, and daring. Yet at the same time the vast, moorish-style edifice seems cold and remote, thoroughly out of place in Cincinnati, in jarring contrast to the image evoked by the city's Jewish community today. In fact, Plum

Street temple has also long since been superseded; Bene Yeshurun (now Wise Temple) maintains another synagogue building with a quite different and more contemporary ambience in suburban Amberley. Still, historically minded members of the community continue to preserve Plum Street, and the building remains in use for religious services, weddings and communal events. The ornate structure, now a National Historic Landmark, serves a useful purpose, standing as a monument to days gone by when Reform was young, Cincinnati was booming, and hopeful dreams abounded.

Table 4.1. Estimated Jewish Population of Cincinnati.

Year	Population
1820	16
1830	100
1840	1,000
1850	2,800
1860	7,500–10,000
1870	8,000–12,000
1880	8,000–12,000
1890	15,000
1900	16,000
1910	28,000
1920	25,000
1930	23,500
1940	21,800
1950	22,000
1960	25,000
1970	28,000
1980	21,500
1987	25,000

Source: Stephen G. Mostov, "A 'Jerusalem on the Ohio.' The Social and Economic History of Cincinnati's Jewish Community, 1840–1875." (Ph.D. diss., Brandeis University, 1981), 76; Barnett Brickner, "The Jewish Community of Cincinnati, Historical and Descriptive, 1817–1933" (Ph.D. diss., University of Cincinnati, 1933); The American Jewish Year Book; *Demographic Study of the Greater Cincinnati Jewish Community* (1987).

NOTES

1. Henry Howe, *Historical Collections of Ohio* (Norwalk, 1896), 787 (originally written in 1877); on Howe, see Larry L. Nelson, "Here's Howe: Ohio's Wandering Historian," *Timeline* 3 (December 1986):42–51; "Cincinnati Jews," undated clipping (c. 1884) pasted into the 1879–81 volume of the (Chicago) *Jewish Advance,* Klau Library, Hebrew Union College-Jewish Institute of Religion, Cincinnati, Ohio; *St. Louis Tribune* quoted in Barnett R. Brickner, "The Jewish Community of Cincinnati, Historical and Descriptive, 1817–1933," (Ph.D. diss., University of Cincinnati, 1933), 17; Isador Wise, "Judaism in Cincinnati," in *Cincinnati: The Queen City,* ed. Charles F. Goss (Chicago, 1912), II, 21.

2. Ann Deborah Michael, "The Origins of the Jewish Community of Cincinnati, 1817–1860" (M.A. thesis, University of Cincinnati, 1970), 28, 56; idem, "The Origins of the Jewish Community of Cincinnati 1817–1860," *Cincinnati Historical Society Bulletin* 30 (1972), 155; *Liberty Hall and Cincinnati Gazette,* April 8, 1816; Joseph Levine, "Economic Activity of Jews in Cincinnati Prior to the Civil War" (Prize Essay, Hebrew Union College, 1957). On Horwitz (sometimes spelled "Horowitz," he also was variously known as Jonas and Jonathan), see also M. Vaxer, "The First Hebrew Bible Printed in America," *Jewish Journal of Bibliography* 1 (1940):20–26; and Edwin Wolf 2d and Maxwell Whiteman, *The History of the Jews of Philadelphia from Colonial Times to the Age of Jackson* (Philadelphia, 1975 [1956]), 308–13.

3. Joseph Jonas, "The Jews Come to Ohio," reprinted in Jacob R. Marcus, *Memoirs of American Jews 1775–1865* (Philadelphia, 1955), 1:205–15 (hereafter *Marcus-Memoirs*); also in Morris U. Schappes, *A Documentary History of the Jews in the United States, 1654–1875* (New York, 1971), 223–35.

4. According to the most famous story, quoted by David Philipson in the name of Jonas's daughter, an old Quaker lady came to see Jonas, and said " 'art thou a Jew? Thou art one of God's chosen people. Wilt thou let me examine thee?' She turned him round and round and at last exclaimed, 'well, thou art no different to other people.' " David Philipson, "The Jewish Pioneers of the Ohio Valley," *Publications of the American Jewish Historical Society* 8 (1900):45; for other details of Jonas's life see ibid, 56.

5. James K. Gutheim, *Address Delivered At the Laying of the Corner Stone of the Congregation "Bnai Yeshurun"* . . . *14 October 1846* (Cincinnati, 1846), 1. Interestingly enough, this same theme was implied as early as 1825 in a fundraising letter sent out by Bene Israel's leaders. "We have congregated," they wrote, "where a few years before nothing was heard but the howling of wild Beasts, and the more hideous cry of savage man." See "Appeal for Congregational Assistance" (1825), reprinted in Schappes, *A Documentary History,* 178.

6. *Marcus-Memoirs* 1:215. Dr. Jacob R. Marcus suggests to me that members of the Moses family were also traditionally observant. Jonas, he says, may have been "solitary" only in terms of his own family.

7. *Marcus-Memoirs* 1:205–6.

158

8. Brickner, "Jewish Community of Cincinnati," 319 on the basis of contemporary comments.

9. *Marcus-Memoirs* 1:209; [Samuel Osgood], "First Synagogue in the West," *The Western Messenger* 2 (October 1836): 204; for Philadelphia, see Wolf & Whiteman, *History of the Jews of Philadelphia,* 143.

10. Jonas's second wife was Martha Oppenheim (London *Jewish Chronicle* [May 14, 1880]:5). She may have been the daughter of Simeon Oppenheim, secretary of London's Great Synagogue, but I have been unable to confirm this.

11. Edward Winthrop to Mrs. Harriet Boswell, February 1, 1843 (Special Collections, King Library, University of Kentucky, Lexington, Kentucky.) Harriet Boswell's interest in Jews may have been stimulated by the family's ties to the Gratz family (Benjamin Gratz's second wife was Ann Boswell). For a parallel relationship between a Christian minister and prominent Jewish laymen, see Arthur A. Chiel, "Ezra Stiles and the Jews: A Study in Ambivalence," in *A Bicentennial Festschrift for Jacob Rader Marcus,* ed. B. W. Korn (Waltham, 1976), 63–76. On Jonas's interest in theology and "the Prophecies," see Philipson, "Jewish Pioneers," 56.

12. [Osgood], "First Synagogue in the West," 205, 206; Philipson, "Jewish Pioneers," 45.

13. Armin Tenner, *Cincinnati sonst und jetzt* (Cincinnati, 1878), 47, as translated in Rudolf Glanz, *Studies in Judaica Americana* (New York, 1970), 54. The first German Jews in Cincinnati, according to Joseph Jonas, arrived in 1820; *Marcus-Memoirs* 1:206. For the names of early English Jews, see the 1825 *Cincinnati Directory* as reprinted in *Publications of the American Jewish Historical Society* 9 (1901), 155.

14. Mostov, "A 'Jerusalem' on the Ohio," 75–81; Goss, *Cincinnati: The Queen City* 4:326 (Although Goss does not directly attribute the quoted words to Pritz, subjects are known to have supplied their own biographies). See also Marc Lee Raphael, *Jews and Judaism in a Midwestern Community: Columbus, Ohio, 1840–1975* (Columbus, 1979), 17: "Almost every Bavarian Jewish family [in Columbus] was from Mittelsinn, a tiny village on the Sinn River."

15. *City Directory* (1819) quoted in Clara Longworth de Chambrun, *Cincinnati: Story of the Queen City* (New York, 1939), 137–38; J. S. Scott quoted in Mostov, "A Jerusalem on the Ohio," 54, 71; Greeley quoted in *Cincinnati: A Guide to the Queen City and Its Neighbors* (Cincinnati, 1943), 50.

16. Goss, *Cincinnati: The Queen City,* 117.

17. Maxwell Whiteman, "Notions, Dry Goods, and Clothing: An Introduction to the Study of the Cincinnati Peddler," *Jewish Quarterly Review* 53 (April 1963): 306–21, esp. 312–13.

18. Mostov, "A 'Jerusalem' on the Ohio," 110–14; Stephen G. Mostov, "Dun and Bradstreet Reports as a Source of Jewish Economic History: Cincinnati, 1840–1875," *American Jewish History* 72, no. 3 (March 1983): 351; *American Israelite* (June 18, 1858) quoted in James G. Heller, *As Yesterday When It Is Past* (Cincinnati, 1942), 21–22. On Jews in the clothing trades, see Judith Greenfeld,

"The Role of the Jews in the Development of the Clothing Industry in the United States," *YIVO Annual* 2–3 (1947/8): 180–204; Moses Rischin, *The Promised City* (New York, 1962), 61–68. The Jewish traveler I. J. Benjamin, describing his visit to Cincinnati on the eve of the Civil War, observed that an important Cincinnati business "although not engaged in by Jews—is the trade in salted pork." I. J. Benjamin, *Three Years in America,* trans. Charles Reznikoff (Philadelphia, 1956), 1:315.

19. For three somewhat divergent accounts, see Michael, "The Origins of the Jewish Community of Cincinnati," 107–26, esp. 116, 122; Brickner, "Jewish Community of Cincinnati," 254–78, 465–82; and Mostov, "A 'Jerusalem' on the Ohio," 86–141. For the quote, see Leon Horowitz *Rumaniah VeAmerika* (Berlin, 1874), 25; and Randi Musnitsky "America's Goodness: An Edited Translation of Leon Horowitz's *Tuv Artsot Habrit*" (Ordination thesis, HUC–JIR, 1983), 59.

20. Brickner, "Jewish Community of Cincinnati," 254–78, 465–82.

21. Goss, *Cincinnati The Queen City* 2:361; 3:866. See also the many biographies of local Jewish notables in volumes 3 and 4.

22. Brickner, "Jewish Community of Cincinnati," 273; cf. Mostov, "A 'Jerusalem' on the Ohio," 116: "For the entire period from 1840 to 1865 only five business firms in Cincinnati are known to have included both Jewish and non-Jewish partners." The situation changed somewhat after the Civil War.

23. Max B. May, "The Jews of Cincinnati," in ed. Charles T. Greve *Centennial History of Cincinnati and Representative Citizens* (Chicago, 1904), 1:948.

24. Wise, "Judaism in Cincinnati," 21; Samuel Cohon, "Introduction," *Hadoar* 19 (June 9, 1939): 513 (translation mine).

25. Judith E. Endelman, *The Jewish Community of Indianapolis* (Bloomington, 1984), 3; John Higham, *Send These To Me,* 2d ed. (Baltimore, 1984), 142–43; Richard L. Zweigenhaft and G. William Domhoff, *Jews in the Protestant Establishment* (New York, 1982), 87–88.

26. Benny Kraut, "Judaism Triumphant: Isaac Mayer Wise on Unitarianism and Liberal Christianity," *AJS Review* 7–8 (1982–83): 187–91.

27. Allan Tarshish, "Jew and Christian in a New Society: Some Aspects of Jewish-Christian Relationships in the United States, 1848–1881," in *A Bicentennial Festschrift for Jacob Rader Marcus* ed. B. W. Korn (Waltham, Mass. and New York, 1976), 579; Lafcadio Hearn, *Barbarous Barbers and Other Stories* (Tokyo, 1939), 264 (copy in Klau Library, Hebrew Union College); see David Philipson, *Max Lilienthal* (New York, 1915), esp. 70–75, 96–100; and Douglas Kohn, "The Dean of American Rabbis: A Critical Study of the Life, Career and Significance of David Philipson as Reflected in His Writings" (Ordination Thesis, HUC–JIR, 1987). Philipson quotes Lilienthal as claiming that "Cincinnati took the lead in fostering a brotherly sentiment between Jews and Christians (p. 73)."

28. Brickner, "Jewish Community of Cincinnati," 282, 286, 319–23, 458; Carl Wittke, "The Germans of Cincinnati," in *Festschrift German-American Tricentennial Jubilee: Cincinnati 1983,* ed. Don H. Tolzmann (Cincinnati, 1982), 8;

Susan W. Dryfoos, *Iphigene: Memoirs of Iphigene Ochs Sulzberger of The New York Times* (New York, 1981), 12–13; Goss, *Cincinnati: The Queen City* 4:324. In determining the intermarriage rate I have recalculated Brickner's figures (p. 458), and deleted the year 1919, which saw an unusual number of postwar marriages and skews the intermarriage rate downward. If the 1919 data is included, the intermarriage rate falls to 3.6 percent. *The Double Triangle News-YMHA Newsletter,* November 1921, places the intermarriage rate for 1915–1920 at 4 percent.

29. Michael, "The Origins of the Jewish Community," 43; Arthur G. King to Jacob R. Marcus (August 12, 1961), American Jewish Archives. For earlier evidence of prejudice, see Marcus, *Memoirs of American Jews* 1:359, where Henry Seesel reports that in 1844 "some ruffian from the country . . . knocked me out into the middle of the street, calling me a 'damned Jew dog.'" See also the slurs contained in local credit reports about Jews as quoted in Mostov, "Dun and Bradstreet Reports as a Source of Jewish Economic History," esp. 343–53.

30. H. M. Moos, *Hannah: Or a Glimpse of Paradise* (Cincinnati, 1868), 28. Moos's last lines (p. 351) may have been directed at Cincinnati Jews: "But where is the glimpse of Paradise? There, there, kind reader, where he sleeps in peace, beyond the reach of all earthly woes."

31. *The Hebrew Review* 2 (1881–82): 189; Brickner, "The Jewish Community of Cincinnati," 306–19, 321, 347; Zane L. Miller, *Boss Cox's Cincinnati* (Chicago, 1968), 52; David Philipson, *My Life As An American Jew* (Cincinnati, 1941), 172; Polk Laffoon IV, "Cincinnati's Jewish Community," *Cincinnati Magazine* 10 (April 1977): 47, 49; Iola O. Silberstein, "Diversity on Converging Pathways: Mary H. Doherty and Helen G. Lotspeich," *Queen City Heritage* 41 (1983): 8, 12. Cincinnati's Jewish Clubs and their members are listed in *The Blue Book and Family Directory* (Cincinnati, 1890), 87–92, but not in Clara Devereux's *Blue Book of Cincinnati Society* (Cincinnati, 1916). See also Howe, *Historical Collections of Ohio,* 787: "There is but little visiting between the families of Jews and Gentiles (1877)."

32. On the problem of myth and reality, see Jonathan D. Sarna, "The 'Mythical Jew' and the 'Jew Next Door' in Nineteenth-Century America," in *Anti-Semitism in American History* ed. David A. Gerber (Urbana, 1986), 57–78.

33. *Hebrew Review* 2 (1881–82):188–89; Alfred Segal quoted in Philipson, *My Life As An American Jew,* 497.

34. Boris Bogen, *Born A Jew* (New York, 1930), 80; Isador Wise, "Judaism in Cincinnati," 22; [*Prospectus for A*] *School of Jewish Social Service Conducted Under the Auspices of the Jewish Settlement* (Cincinnati, 1913), 4–5.

35. Heller, *As Yesterday When It Is Past,* 22–33; Brickner, "The Jewish Community of Cincinnati," 180–253; Max Senior, "Cincinnati: The Pioneer in Federation," *Jewish Charity* 4, no. 6 (March 1905): 181–82; Max Senior, "Tuberculosis Cases in Cincinnati," *Jewish Charity* 3, no. 6 (March 1904): 138–39; Harry Viteles, "Preface," *Cumulative Index of the Twenty-One Annual Reports of the United Jewish Charities of Cincinnati, Ohio* (Cincinnati, [1918]), 2–6.

36. Senior, "Cincinnati: The Pioneer in Federation," 182; Boris Bogen, *Jewish Philanthropy* (New York, 1917), 52.

37. Goss, *Cincinnati The Queen City* 4:325, 776, 716, 301, 690; James Albert Green, *History of the Associated Charities of Cincinnati 1879–1937* (Cincinnati, 1937), 27–29, 33, 70–71, 82–84; The Community Chest of Cincinnati and Hamilton County, *The First Twenty Years 1915–1935* (Cincinnati, 1935), 1, 20, 32, 135–41, and attached table; Brickner, "Jewish Community of Cincinnati," 236–38.

38. Brickner, "Jewish Community of Cincinnati," 180–253; Viteles, "Preface," 2–6.

39. Emblematic of Jews' insistence on nonsectarian public school education was their firm opposition to Bible reading in the public schools. In a celebrated court case (1869–72) that included Jewish depositions (*Minor v. Board of Education of Cincinnati*), the Ohio Supreme Court upheld the right of Cincinnati's Board of Education to dispense with Bible reading in the public schools; see *The Bible in the Public Schools* (New York, 1967); Robert Michaelsen, "Common Schools, Common Religion?" *Church History* 38 (1969): 201–17; F. Michael Perko, "The Building Up of Zion: Religion and Education in Nineteenth-Century Cincinnati," *Cincinnati Historical Society Bulletin* 38 (Summer 1980): 97–114; Philipson, *Max Lilienthal,* 474–87.

40. Hearn, *Barbarous Barbers,* 132, 264; Brickner, "Jewish Community of Cincinnati," 340–49; cf. Lloyd P. Gartner, "Temples of Liberty Unpolluted: American Jews and Public Schools, 1840–1875," in *A Bicentennial Festschrift for J. R. Marcus,* ed. Korn 157–89. In an 1883 visit to Cincinnati, Henrietta Szold found that at the University of Cincinnati, "most of the lady students are Jewesses;" quoted in Alexandra L. Levin, *The Szolds of Lombard Street* (Philadelphia, 1960), 162.

41. Benjamin, *Three Years in America* 1:312.

42. Brickner, "Jewish Community of Cincinnati," 279–85, see p. 279 for the Taft quote; see also Laffoon, "Cincinnati's Jewish Community," 46.

43. May, "Jews of Cincinnati," 948; Brickner, "Jewish Community of Cincinnati," 15, 324–32; Miller, *Boss Cox's Cincinnati,* 173–241.

44. Brickner, "Jewish Community of Cincinnati," 332–36; Miller, *Boss Cox's Cincinnati,* 133, 185; for Bettman, see Iphigene Molony Bettman file, American Jewish Archives, Cincinnati, Ohio.

45. Robert Bellah, "Civil Religion in America," in *American Civil Religion,* eds. Russell E. Richey and Donald G. Jones (New York, 1974), 23, 28; see also John F. Wilson, *Public Religion in American Culture* (Philadelphia, 1979); and Jonathan Woocher, *Sacred Survival: The Civil Religion of American Jews* (Bloomington, Ind., 1986).

46. On Jonas, see text at note 6 above; for other evidence of laxity, see Benjamin, *Three Years in America,* 2:278; Mostov, "A 'Jerusalem' on the Ohio," 150, 162.

47. Mostov, "A 'Jerusalem' on the Ohio," 164–68 (quoting original syna-

gogue minutes). For the emphasis on preserving Judaism into the next generation as a motive for Reform, see the 1824 petition to the Charleston Congregation Beth Elohim reprinted in Joseph L. Blau and Salo W. Baron, *The Jews of the United States 1790–1840: A Documentary History* (New York, 1963), 554; and Jonathan D. Sarna, "The Debate Over Mixed Seating in the American Synagogue," in *The American Synagogue: A Sanctuary Transformed,* ed. Jack Wertheimer (Cambridge, 1987), 375.

48. Isaac M. Wise, *Reminiscences* (1901; 2d ed., New York, 1945); James G. Heller, *Isaac M. Wise: His Life, Work and Thought* (New York, 1965), 124–83; Naphtali J. Rubinger, "Dismissal in Albany," *American Jewish Archives* 24 (November 1972): 161–62; Leon A. Jick, *The Americanization of the Synagogue 1820–1870* (Hanover, N.H., 1976), 115, 121–29, 154–55.

49. Quoted in Mostov, "A 'Jerusalem' on the Ohio," 170.

50. I. M. Wise, *The History of K. K. Bene Yeshurun . . . Published In Commemoration of the Fiftieth Anniversary of its Incorporation.* (Cincinnati, 1892), 1, 19; cf. Kraut, "Judaism Triumphant," 183–85.

51. Heller, *As Yesterday When It Is Past* and Philipson, *The Oldest Jewish Congregation in the West* trace the histories of Bene Yeshurun and Bene Israel; see also Alan I Marcus, "Am I My Brother's Keeper: Reform Judaism in the American West, Cincinnati, 1840–1870," *Queen City Heritage* 44 (Spring 1986): 3–19. Wise's quote is from the *American Israelite,* August 14, 1863, as quoted in Brickner, "Jewish Community of Cincinnati," 59. According to David Philipson, Lilienthal came to Bene Israel on the recommendation of "prominent Jewish families" whose sons attended his New York boarding school, *Max Lilienthal,* 59.

52. Rachel Wischnitzer, *Synagogue Architecture in the United States* (Philadelphia, 1955), 70–73, 76.

53. *The Sabbath Visitor* 16 (August 1886): 1; Steven A. Fox, "On the Road to Unity: The Union of American Hebrew Congregations and American Jewry, 1873–1903," *American Jewish Archives* 32 (November 1980): 145–93; Michael A. Meyer, "A Centennial History," in *Hebrew Union College-Jewish Institute of Religion at One Hundred Years,* ed. Samuel E. Karff (Cincinnati, 1976), 7–283.

54. The founding date of Adath Israel presents something of a puzzle. Charles Cist, *Sketches and Statistics of Cincinnati in 1851* (Cincinnati, 1851), 82–83 and *Sketches and Statistics of Cincinnati in 1859* (Cincinnati, 1859), 198 refers to a "Holy Congregation, Gate of Heaven" (Shaar Hashomayim), which Mostov, "A 'Jerusalem' on the Ohio," p. 155, takes to be the forerunner of Adath Israel. He claims that it was founded in 1850, dissolved in 1852, and reestablished as Adath Israel in 1853. Isador Wise, "Judaism in Cincinnati," p. 41, claims that the congregation was actually founded "somewhere around 1846." When cited by Ann Deborah Michael, "The Origins of the Jewish Community of Cincinnati," p. 45, this becomes "in 1846." Barnett Brickner, "Jewish Community of Cincinnati," p. 103, argues that the congregation was actually founded earlier in the 1840s. In 1847, according to his account, the congregation split up, and in 1854 Adath Israel received its charter. On the other hand, Louis Feinberg, Adath Israel's

longtime rabbi, claimed in an article in *Hadoar* (19, no. 29 [June 9, 1939]:520) that the congregation was actually founded in 1847. Until better sources are located, the question remains open, but it is worth noting that Isaac Leeser found *two* Polish congregations in existence when he visited Cincinnati in 1851, one of which he names as "Gates of Heaven," while the other he does not name at all. Subsequently, he reports, the two congregations merged; see *Occident* 10 (1852): 47.

55. Louis Feinberg, "The Orthodox Community," *Hadoar* 19 (June 9, 1939): 520–21; Brickner, "Jewish Community of Cincinnati," 106–11; Elcanan Isaacs, "Nathan Isaacs," in *Men of the Spirit,* ed. Leo Jung (New York, 1964), 575–77. On New Hope congregation, see Benny Kraut, *German-Jewish Orthodoxy in an Immigrant Synagogue: Cincinnati's New Hope Congregation and the Ambiguities of Ethnic Religion* (New York, 1988).

56. On the assumed inevitability of Reform, see Brickner's discussion of the Reading Road Temple, "Jewish Community of Cincinnati," 93; and David Philipson's private thoughts on the dedication of Adath Israel in 1927: "I have no fear for the future of liberal Judaism in the United States. This is the only form that can appeal to American-born and American-reared youth! [*My Life As An American Jew* (Cincinnati, 1941), 378]."

57. Aaron Rakeffet-Rothkoff, *The Silver Era in American Jewish Orthodoxy* (Jerusalem and New York, 1981), esp. 77–92, 166. ("Here in the ... home of Reform Judaism, Silver wanted to raise the [Orthodox] Agudah's banner."); see also the special Cincinnati section of the New York *Morning Journal* (April 14, 1948) dedicated to Silver. I am indebted to Prof. Jacob R. Marcus for this item.

58. The UAHC's move to New York engendered a revealing debate. See *American Israelite* 95 (October 25, 1948 to November 25, 1948) especially the letter by Isaac M. Wise's son and namesake in the issue of November 25, 1948, p. 3: "Cincinnati will not allow herself to be deprived of her position as the center of American Israel."

59. Polk Laffoon IV, "Cincinnati's Jewish Community," *Cincinnati Magazine* 10 (April 1977): 46.

ZANE L. MILLER

Cincinnati Germans and the Invention of an Ethnic Group

So far as I know, no Cincinnatian in the mid-nineteenth century, during the heyday of German migration to this city, talked about the need for or the utility of constructing in Cincinnati a German community, that is, an organized group or groups dedicated to enlisting as many Germans as possible in the preservation of German ideals or customs or the genius of the race. Yet in the late nineteenth and early twentieth centuries many people talked and acted as if such a community existed, or might exist, or should be brought into existence. Some of the people who talked and acted this way, whom we now label nativists, looked upon this as a dread prospect. Some of this talk and action occurred among German-speaking Cincinnatians who regarded it as a good idea, despite the acknowledged difficulties of creating and sustaining such a community. And the way they talked and acted suggested that the Germans and Cincinnati were not unique.[1]

There was, of course, no lack of German organizations in the city at the turn of the century. Besides the ubiquitous *Bauvereinen,* (lit., "building societies," later "Savings and Loan Associations") there were German-speaking trade unions among the brewery workers, bakers, and typographers; a maze of singing societies, rifle clubs, Turner societies, mutual aid associations, charity organizations; and groups dedicated to German language or literature. In 1915, according to August B. Gorbach, former secretary and president of Typographia No. Two, and a "prominently-known . . . advocate of the rights of the people," there were 114 of these special interest groups. He thought they were valuable institutions and he wanted "to set aside the opinion . . . that German societies exist only to promote social sessions" by emphasizing "the real work done . . . in bettering the conditions of members, not only socially, but financially as well," by

165

providing helpful and understanding friends and assistance in making a living or during hard times.[2]

Yet some hoped that certain German organizations would perform a third service by creating and sustaining a sense of German community among Cincinnati's diverse German-speaking individuals. At least two potential candidates for such service had been in existence for some time. One, the *Pionier Verein,* established in 1869, required forty years of residence in the United States of all candidates for membership. Another was the German Literary Society, established in 1877. Although most of their members lived outside the Basin, they, like most other German societies, met in the Over-the-Rhine district or along Central Avenue to the west, the principle German residential districts during the mid-nineteenth century. In 1914, the *Pionier Verein,* which aimed to "renew and affirm old ties of friendship" and "to preserve the history and experiences of German pioneers in Cincinnati," had nine hundred members, most of them artisans, clerks, and shopkeepers, people too busy making a living to spend much time defining and building a German community. The Literary Society in 1910 listed one hundred members, who represented "the nobility of the mind of Cincinnati's German population." Its membership consisted largely of professionals, and their objective was to "cultivate and further German literature." Also by 1910, according to its president, the organization had lost its spark. Only 30 percent of the members turned out for meetings, only eighteen papers were read, and the discussions, he said, were "boring."[3]

Thus, neither the *Pionier Verein* nor the Literary Society seemed satisfactory solutions to the problem of building a German community. Hence, and increasingly after 1880 in the context of rising American nativism and fear of continuing assimilation, advocates of a Cincinnati German community emphasized the notion of preserving German culture, and of establishing a united and organized German base and institutional structure as a prerequisite to attaining that goal. In the 1880s and 1890s, the Reverend Anton Walburg, a native American of German descent, stoutly defended the maintenance of German Catholic parishes in German neighborhoods as the best means of preserving the German community from contamination by the American nationality, which he described as a "hotbed of fanaticism, intolerance, and radical ultraviews on matters of politics and religion," and as a sink in which "all the vagaries of spiritualism, mormonism, free-lovism, prohibition, infidelity, and materialism generally breed."[4] In 1900, the *Volksblatt,* a German language daily newspaper, hailed a public *Pionier* celebration as "a true German family reunion . . . where one was able to see together again the true pillars of our city's Germandom . . . who, although having . . . years ago found a new home in this country, still hold firmly to the ways and tongue of the motherland." Four years later, addressing himself to the threat of Sunday closing laws and prohibition, a *Pionier* warned that, "since the German no longer emigrates to Cincinnati and since we are down to our last reserves, so to speak," it was praiseworthy but no longer enough for individuals merely to "foster German customs and mores, to sing the beautiful German songs, and to preserve the noble German speech for their descendants." Germans, he maintained, must be more aggressive as an organized political bloc, "for if there is trampling to be done" by nativist Americans through attempts to enact Sunday closing and prohibition laws, only Germans could be counted on to "take care of the trampling." In 1909, according to the *Enquirer,* the Reverend Dr. Carl August Voss "stirred [a German] audience to a frenzy of enthusiasm" by shaming "those who were not proud of their forbearers, [who] Americanize their names, and shrink from being known as Germans for fear it will jeopardize their social position."[5]

At the turn of the century, this concern to fabricate a German community, to secure a "respectable future" for Germans and their descendants, as the *Volksfreund* put it, yielded two new kinds of German societies, the *Taggellschaft* and the *Stadtverband,* both of which were federations. The *Taggellschaft,* the German Day Society, tried to bolster the waning sense of Germanness among Germans by holding elaborate public celebrations of German national holidays and of conspicuous dates in the history of German immigration. The *Stadtverband* focused its efforts on politics and preserving "personal liberty," especially the right to drink and to enjoy an open Sunday, German language instruction in the public schools, and nonrestrictive immigration laws.

Most of the leaders in these two organizations, like the members of their constituent societies, were newspaper editors, teachers, part- or full-time politicians, physicians or lawyers, and trade unionists in German unions—people with a vested interest in cultivating a German clientele. The active membership of both organizations came to some 8,396 in 1910, about one-fourth of the city's adult males of German stock, and had a predominantly Protestant and Republican orientation.[6]

They faced a frustrating task. It was difficult to find a common denominator among the various socioeconomic classes, socialists, Lutherans,

Catholics, and Methodists who comprised the German-speaking population. There existed, moreover, barriers of dialect and provincial origins, and throughout the early twentieth century, as before, Germans scattered geographically across the face of the metropolis, assimilating as they went. In 1905, one discouraged enthusiast pronounced the Day Society a failure. No organization yet founded, he explained, could persuade Germans "may they be businessmen or academicians, artisans or farmers, churchmen or freethinkers, to set aside all petty prejudices which in private life divide man from man" and inspire them, despite differences in "places of birth or rank and standing in society . . . to think about . . . the language, the customs, their 2,000 year-old history, the great men who have made their race famous and who belong [in] common to them all." In 1909, the *Volksblatt* protested that "to this day petty state regionalism still maintains itself on American soil in the societies and popular festivals."[7] And in 1915, Gorbach, the new president of the Day Society, hopefully noted that "with the victories of the German nation estimation and respect for everything German will increase."[8]

We know now, of course, that the reaction to World War I in Cincinnati produced neither estimation and respect for everything German nor the unity and coherence among Germans around German ideals and customs and the genius of the race for which Gorbach and others so ardently yearned. We also know that organized efforts to preserve and sustain German ideals and customs, but not the genius of the race, continued in Cincinnati during the 1920s and 1930s, and indeed continue to this very day.[9] What we don't know, or at least what I don't know, is what these efforts mean, or how they may be interpreted. But I do have some notions about aspects of the contexts within which such efforts proceeded. These may be useful in attempts to formulate an agenda for the study of ethnicity in the United States, and more immediately in Cincinnati.

This kind of work might begin about 1870 when the notion caught on that America was, was becoming, or ought to become a unified and homogeneous entity characterized by a uniform and homogeneous culture. This concept caused trouble when people noticed a conflict between this notion and what they perceived as reality, especially the apparent heterogeneity of America.[10] People used various techniques to handle this problem of diversity. Some, like the compilers of the federal census bureau's *Social Statistics of Cities* in the 1880s, argued that history would eventually mold a modernizing country comprised of diverse races, religions, and cities into a uniform and coherent entity.[11] Others, however, remained skeptical of the probability that history or other forces would resolve "naturally" the problem of diversity. Some of these people sought by one means or another to alter the nature of reality to align it more closely with the concept of homogeneity.

During the late 1890s, for example, W. E. B. DuBois published *The Philadelphia Negro* and other related works.[12] A close examination of DuBois's work suggests that he was interested first in the inherent identifying characteristics of races, their geniuses, and in the development (and preservation) of those geniuses. DuBois was also interested in the internal identifying characteristics of territorial units, including neighborhoods, cities, regions, and nations. This interest included both the physical and social environment but especially the patterns of behavior and interaction among the peoples within such territories, and particularly the way in which social processes inhibited or facilitated the development of racial geniuses and the social and economic modernization of races. In this work DuBois concentrated on the black race in the United States, which he depicted as a backward, lamentably fragmented, and more imperfectly realized as a community than even the Cincinnati German community. Although he offered no definite conclusions about the ultimate status and role of African-Americans in the developing modern American nation, he rejected several turn-of-the-century racial policies proposed by whites. He rejected the notion of blacks as a race so inferior and inflexible that it would soon die out in modern society, or so inferior and inflexible that it should be ejected from a modernizing nation and deported to some territory more suitable to its race traits and tendencies. And he also rejected the notion of the black as a race so inferior and inflexible that it should be eliminated and improved by genetic and social amalgamation into the dominant white race in a modernizing American nation.

Instead, DuBois depicted the black race as containing the potential and adaptability for successful participation in the competition of modern life in a modernizing nation, a competition in which the as yet unmanifest genius of the black race might reveal itself first among African-Americans in America. He projected a possible future in which blacks might become and function (under the terms of equal opportunity among races) as a separate, cohesive, and interdependent race somewhere among the lower ranks of the hierarchy of unequally modernized races in a modernizing America. He thought that blacks might become more coherent as a race if their leaders developed programs to bring backward blacks of all classes up to the minimum social, educational, and occupational standards of modernity. He thought American society might be held together by the guarantee of equal opportunity to all the races in the competition for places in the modernizing racial hierarchy, and by an appropriate distribution of understanding and respect for races lagging behind those more advanced in the process of modernization.

His immediate concern however, was with a crisis, a fear that the direction of racial policy within the United States might fall irrevocably into the hands of those who would deny the African-American this opportunity to compete. If so, they would both destroy the potential for the development of the black in America as a modern race and disrupt the peaceful development of a modern and modernizing society in the United States, one which itself might benefit from the preservation and utilization of some of the products of the conservation of the genius of the black race.

This analysis of *The Philadelphia Negro* is not intended to suggest that Cincinnati Germandom in the late nineteenth or early twentieth centuries contained a Teutonic counterpoint to W. E. B. DuBois, although it may well have. It is intended to suggest, however, a certain similarity of motive, vision, and strategy that links DuBois and Cincinnati's German advocates of the preservation and sustenance of German ideals and customs and the genius of the race. Both began their analysis by articulating a sense of crisis—the potential for the disappearance of group identity and the values and institutions that supported it, and the consequent emergence of patterns of disunity and violence. Both shared a conception of the race as possessing a genius and the capacity for modernization. Both proposed a strategy for survival and development through federated organizations designed to function as unifying elements for the integration of the German and black communities around the preservation and perpetuation of the ideals and customs and genius of the race. Both exhibited a tendency to create a viable racial neighborhood, either in the Over-the-Rhine or the Seventh Ward of Philadelphia, and to call for the assistance of those members of the race who lived elsewhere to sustain and improve the neighborhood. And both displayed a concern for the adaptation of the German and the black races within the city conceived as a larger pluralistic racial-territorial unit in a racially pluralistic and modernizing nation.

My account, of course, is merely a suggestive silhouette. A thorough and detailed analysis of this aspect of Cincinnati's Germans in this period remains to be attempted. If done, however, it might be subtitled "The

Invention of a Race-Based Ethnic Group and Its Consequences."[13] It would look for the structure of the ideas promulgated by German community advocates by examining what they said and did not say. It would also examine what they did and did not do to illuminate the consequences of ideas and to explore reactions to them. Such a study of the advocacy in Cincinnati for establishing, preserving, or reestablishing a German community should be knowledgeable about the ideas, activities, and problems of similar persons here and elsewhere in the same period (like DuBois), in order to avoid a distorted picture of American civilization at the turn of the century.

It should be stressed, however, that DuBois and Cincinnati's turn-of-the-century advocates of a German community looked to the past, but not to recreate it. Rather they looked backward to identify the characteristics, traditions, and "genius" of the race, factors that could be used to guide its development and the pace of that development into something new. For them, the past was neither a potential alternative to the present or future nor the source of the culture (way of life) of a group. Instead, for them the past was the seedbed and germ and a source of inspiration (see what we have achieved) for the emergence and nurture of something new and different within a larger and ultimately homogeneous society. For DuBois certainly, and probably for Cincinnati's advocates of a German community, that process would yield ultimately a society of equal races identical in their modernity. That future society would be characterized by a common heritage of racial modernization and appreciation of the fully realized geniuses of all the races. Perhaps then would emerge the golden age of true brotherhood through the amalgamation (intermarriage) of the races themselves and of their geniuses.[14]

This study of the invention of an ethnic group and its consequences might also cover in a separate section the period from 1920 to the 1950's. The section might focus on attempts to develop and sustain a separate German heritage in a nation conceived as consisting of *permanently* separate groups with separate heritages. Don H. Tolzmann has told us, for example, that despite the so-called anti-German legacy of World War I, some German ethnic and German organizations continued to strive in the 1920s and 1930s for the preservation and perpetuation of German culture.[15]

But this was not an exclusively German or German-American endeavor. Many Cincinnatians in this period boasted of "our" German musical heritage.[16] At the same time Germanistics flourished at the University of Cincinnati,[17] encouraged by a new identification of German literature both as an expression of the culture of a particular place (rather than a race) and as a "classical," hence universal literature, a designation designed to rank it as the first among equals. In addition, the comprehensive city plan of 1925 listed the city's legacy of skilled German workmanship and its pool of German immigrants as advantages for the Queen City in its economic competition with other cities.[18] Some went further than that. Lewis Alexander's history of *Greater Cincinnati and Its People*, published in 1927, named the Germans "in their numbers and nationality . . . the most important ingredients in the community."[19] He also claimed, in a section on "The German People," that "no class . . . have contributed more in brains, sinews, labor, and money, toward building up Cincinnati and making it what it is today, than the Germans. And no class deserves greater credit."[20]

As that last sentence suggests, Cincinnatians in this period celebrated more than merely their German legacy. In the 1920's, for instance, the American House, allegedly the first community center in the United States devoted exclusively to the foreign-born, welcomed Germans as well as other immigrants and urged Cincinnatians to accept and treat foreign-born groups with respect. In addition, the celebrants of the golden jubilee of the Music Hall in the 1920's apotheosized Theodor Thomas, a former Cincinnati conductor, as a champion of "classical" European music, including that composed by Germans, and Stephen Foster as a composer of authentically American types of music. Indeed, as part of that same celebration Music Hall itself was refurbished to accommodate not only classical music from European nations but also a ballroom called the Topper Club, where people in the late 1920s and 1930s danced and watched each other dance to another authentically American music, black jazz and its variants.[21]

What I have not seen, however, is a history of the context, motive, vision, strategy, events, and processes that comprised this concern for the preservation of heritages, though I have a hunch about an outline for such a story. Its subject might be cultural pluralism in the context of the catching on of an idea that America was, was becoming, or ought to be a culturally pluralistic nation. In this period we no longer confront the race thinking of the turn of the century, with its tendency toward the vertical and hierarchical arrangement of superior and inferior races, its assumption of the ultimate and necessary subordination of each race in a modern nation to modernization, its disposition to attack separately the separate problems of each group, and its anticipation of an eventual golden age of uniformity and homogenization through the merging of the geniuses of the races.

Instead, the new taxonomy contained a horizontal bias. It exhibited a tendency to *separate* notions and problems of race and ethnicity and to emphasize place over race as a cultural determinant and as a source of subcultures among all races. In addition, each of these place-based cultural units seemed to carry with it a potential for an entire way of life rather than a particular genius that it might contribute to the nation, and each seemed equal or potentially equivalent in value. In the new taxonomy each place-based ethnic group seemed appropriately separate and equal, or potentially equal, in instances, for example, where a group had lost, forgotten, or been deprived of its culture, a situation to be overcome by cultural tutelage, often in a physical and social environment specially designed or selected for the purpose of inculcating and perpetuating the group's culture.[22]

This context cast familiar turn-of-the-century issues in a different light, suggesting a different range of potential solutions and a different approach to solving problems, a bias toward a tangled bank or ecological notion of interdependence that encouraged attempts at comprehensive solutions to whole constellations of problems. To some, this view made even temporary subordinate status for particular groups seem outrageous and unjust, and prompted demands for intergroup understanding and equality of treatment of groups as groups, sometimes by the reservation of a particular place for a particular group but also sometimes by efforts to reduce the intensity of pluralism within a particular polity or institution to prevent the whole from being riven by misunderstanding and conflict.

These efforts to provide particular and appropriate places and/or quotas for particular groups took several forms. They include the invention and adoption of a comprehensive metropolitan plan with a comprehensive zoning ordinance that segregated the city residentially by socioeconomic classes. That plan also included recommendations for the creation of a variety of homogeneous and separated subcommunities as building blocks for the larger community, the pluralistic metropolitan region, and the construction of racially segregated public housing projects designed on the homogeneous community principle and equipped with institutions to develop a sense of community.[23] This same view encouraged some to advocate the adoption by the United States of comprehensive quotas for immigration restriction, and similar quotas for the admission of certain peoples to certain institutions. It encouraged, too, the proposal and adoption of comprehensive and horizontal administrative-political schemes, such as that embedded in Cincinnati's 1925 city charter. That document established a weak mayor-small council elected at large under a proportional representation system of voting to protect minorities. It also provided for a city manager armed with civil service and administrative autonomy to carry out council policy through department heads representing equal, or potentially equal, departments (equal to one another and to the city manager, as experts protected by civil service).

Finally, such a study might contain a third and separate section dealing with the ethnic revival of our own times, which might begin in the 1950's. Its subject might be the revolt against racial or cultural determinism of any sort in the context of the catching on of an idea that America was, or was becoming, or ought to become an individually pluralistic society. In such a society, individuals in pursuit of themselves, rather than race-based or place-based groups with inherent characteristics and tendencies, formed the basic elements of action and analysis. And such individuals by definition possessed the capacity and right to define and redefine themselves and their culture, to do their own thing, to pursue and display their chosen and often temporary "life-styles" by changing and multiplying their organizational affiliations and commitments to causes and groups as changing circumstances and private predilection or whimsy might suggest.[24] Such a study might include references to David Riesman's *The Lonely Crowd* (1950) and William White's *The Organization Man* (1956), which worried about the problem of conformity, as well as to Ken Kesey's *One Flew Over the Cuckoo's Nest* (1962) and Tom Robbin's *Still Life with Woodpecker* (1980), which offered solutions to the problem of conformity.

Such a study might also include references to a simultaneous impulse to do historical "community" and/or ethnic studies. These works sought to legitimize individual pluralism in the present by projecting it into the past as a dynamic factor in history. They argued that in the past autonomous or liberated individuals made independent decisions about their life styles, that those decisions yielded patterns of behavior and action that established cultures or communities created and sustained as a matter of choice by individuals and that such cultures or communities could be modified in the course of time by individual decisions while enduring in their fundamental structural and behavioral elements over long periods of time. According to these studies, such cultures or communities might (but need not) manifest themselves territorially, and might be influenced by but were definitely not "determined" by racial, social, economic, or political factors or systems, or by a "given" way of life.[25]

Such a study might take a variety of ethnic phenomena in Cincinnati as subjects of concern. It would surely note the virtual disappearance here of German-born people and a German-speaking population, as well as the rapid decline after 1960 of migration to Cincinnati by Southern blacks and Appalachians. In this context such a study might seriously and fruitfully examine the black power movement and the new politics of ethnic conflict and the neighborhood organization revolution;[26] the definition of the Over-the-Rhine district as a particular inner-city problem and the assignment to it of an historic function as a port of entry for immigrants, Appalachians, and blacks. It might explore the revival and patronage in Cincinnati of the St. Patrick's Day Parade, as well as the creation and patronage of the Appalachian Arts Festival, the West End Arts and Humanities Consortium for the preservation of black culture in a devastated and dying black ghetto, the Miami Purchase Association for Historic Preservation (and especially its concern for the preservation of the architecture of the Over-the-Rhine district), the International Folk Fair, and the recent Clifton-Fest in a decidedly unteutonic neighborhood as well as the invention and patronage of Cincinnati's Oktoberfest.

Such a study might suggest that in our recent past people have chosen to define culture in any way that seems to fit their personal situations at the moment, a definition that yields necessarily only short-term commitments. It might suggest that people used those definitions as vehicles through which to affiliate temporarily with groups (sometimes more than one at a time) and/or to participate in events to satisfy their individual pursuit of autonomy and self-fulfillment, not to forward the welfare of the group or the larger society. This tendency may explain both the contemporary popularity of ethnicity and historic preservation and help us to differentiate the present from the past, and thus to think and act more clearly about both in a society of individual pluralism.[27]

NOTES

1. On the question of a Cincinnati German community in the late nineteenth and early twentieth centuries see Guido A. Dobbert, "The Disintegration of an Immigrant Community: The Cincinnati Germans, 1870–1920" (Ph.D. diss., University of Chicago, 1965); and Don H. Tolzmann, "The Survival of an Ethnic Community: The Cincinnati Germans, 1918 through 1932" (Ph.D. diss., Univer-

sity of Cincinnati, 1983). For my initial examination of this issue, see Zane L. Miller, "Boss Cox and the Municipal Reformers: Cincinnati Progressivism, 1880–1914" (Ph.D. diss, University of Chicago, 1966), especially 1:78–80, 101–6, and, for nativism, 198–216, 210–13. For a briefer account, see Zane L. Miller, *Boss Cox's Cincinnati: Urban Politics in the Progressive Era* (New York, 1968), 29, 35, 63–66. A most useful analysis of the nature of German community in an urban setting during the mid-nineteenth century is Kathleen Neils Conzen, *Immigrant Milwaukee, 1836–1860: Accommodation and Community in a Frontier City* (Cambridge, Mass., 1976). See also her "German-Americans and the Invention of Ethnicity," in *America and the Germans,* eds. Frank Tremmler and Joseph McVeigh (Philadelphia, 1985), 1:13ff., and her "Ethnicity as Festive Culture: Nineteenth-Century German America on Parade," in *The Invention of Ethnicity,* ed. Werner Sollers (New York, 1985), 44–76.

2. August H. Gorbach, *Deutscher Vereins-Wegweise von Cincinnati, Ohio* (Cincinnati: Stadtverbandes von Cincinnati, 1915), 5–6.

3. Dobbert, "Immigrant Community," 102–8.

4. For the quote, and commentary from a different perspective, see Robert D. Cross, *The Emergence of Liberal Catholicism in America* (Cambridge, Mass., 1958), 22, 26, 98–99, 174. On Walburg's views, see also (Cincinnati) *Catholic Telegraph,* March 5, 1891, p. 4.

5. Dobbert, "Immigrant Community," 110–11.

6. Ibid., chap. 4.

7. Ibid., 148–94.

8. Gorbach, *Vereins-Wegweise,* 13.

9. Tolzmann, "Survival of an Ethnic Community," 13.

10. Henry D. Shapiro, *Appalachia on Our Mind: The Southern Mountains and Mountaineers in the American Consciousness, 1870–1920* (Chapel Hill, N.C., 1978), ix–xix.

11. Zane L. Miller, "The Rise of the City," *Hayes Historical Journal,* 3, nos. 1–2 (Spring and Fall 1980): 73–83.

12. Zane L. Miller, " 'Race-ism' and the City: The Young DuBois and the Role of Place in Social Theory, 1893–1901," *American Studies* 30, no. 2 (Fall 1989), 89–102. See also W. E. B. DuBois, *The Philadelphia Negro: A Social Study* (New York, 1967, orig. ed., 1899), and his related works: "Strivings of the Negro People," *Atlantic Monthly* 80, (July 1897): 194–98; *The Conservation of Races* (New York, 1969, orig. ed., 1897); *The Study of the Negro Problems* (Philadelphia, 1898); *The Negroes of Farmville, Va.: A Social Study* (Washington, D.C., 1898).

13. Cincinnati women participated also in the process of redefining themselves as a group. See Carol Jean Blum, "Women and the City: Cincinnati, 1840–1900" (Ph.D. diss., University of Cincinnati, 1987). I do not mean by this paragraph to suggest that the advocates of a Cincinnati German community and DuBois were unique. I suspect similar studies of other groups in other places during this period would yield similar results.

14. It seems to me that in this work DuBois is not advocating cultural

pluralism but racial pluralism as a temporary strategy. He wanted blacks to become equal to other social units by becoming identical to them in their modernity. At that moment, "perhaps a century from today," and only then, would the issue of racial intermarriage become a serious social policy question. See DuBois, *The Philadelphia Negro,* 393–94. For a contrary view see Elliot M. Rudwick, *W. E. B. DuBois: Propagandist of the Negro Protest* (New York, 1969).

15. Tolzmann, "Survival of an Ethnic Community," 283–363.

16. Cincinnati Music Hall Association, *Golden Jubilee Souvenir, 1878–1928* (Cincinnati, 1928), 44–48.

17. Tolzmann, "Survival of an Ethnic Community," 307–13. I am indebted to my friend Henry D. Shapiro for the explanation of "classical" literature as universal.

18. Cincinnati City Planning Commission, *The Official City Plan of Cincinnati, Ohio* (Cincinnati, 1925), 14.

19. Lewis Alexander Leonard, ed., *Greater Cincinnati and Its People: A History* (New York, Chicago, and Cincinnati, 1926), 1:581–82.

20. Ibid., 104, 2:577.

21. Zane L. Miller, "Music Hall: Its Neighborhood, the City and the Metropolis," in *Cincinnati's Music Hall* (Virginia Beach, Va., 1978), 44–47.

22. Warren I. Susman, "The Thirties," in *The Development of an American Culture,* eds. Stanley Coben and Lorman Ratner (Englewood Cliffs, N.J., 1970), 179–82; Shapiro, *Appalachia,* 244–65; Thomas Jackson Woofter, Jr., *Races and Ethnic Groups in American Life* (New York and London, 1935). It should be noted as another characteristic of this period that the past now seemed worth preserving as a source of the authentic culture of the nation and its various subcultures. From this view stemmed the impulse to attempt recreations of the whole way of life of the nation or one of its units in one period or another, as in the restoration of Colonial Williamsburg or in *A History of American Life* series, edited by Arthur M. Schlesinger and Dixon Ryan Fox. See also Zane L. Miller, "Pluralizing America: Walter Prescott Webb, Chicago School Sociology, and Cultural Regionalism," in *Essays on Sunbelt Cities and Recent Urban America,* eds. Robert B. Fairbanks and Kathleen Underwood (College Station, 1990), 151–76.

23. Cincinnati City Planning Commission, *Metropolitan Master Plan 1948* (Cincinnati, 1948); Cincinnati City Planning Commission, *Residential Areas* (Cincinnati, 1946); Cincinnati City Planning Commission, *Communities* (Cincinnati, 1947); Robert B. Fairbanks and Zane L. Miller, "Race, Planning and Housing in Cincinnati, 1925–1954," in *The Martial Metropolis: U. S. Cities in War and Peace,* ed. Roger W. Lotchin (New York, 1984), 191–222; Robert B. Fairbanks, *Making Better Citizens: Housing Reform and the Community Development Strategy in Cincinnati, 1890–1960* (Urbana, 1988).

24. Geoffrey Giglierano and Zane L. Miller, "Downtown Housing: Changing Plans and Perspectives, 1948–1980," *The Cincinnati Historical Society Bulletin* 40, no. 3 (Fall 1982): 167–90; Zane L. Miller, "The Politics of Community Change in Cincinnati," *The Public Historian* 5, no. 4 (Fall 1983): 17–35; Zane L.

Miller, *Suburb: Neighborhood and Community in Forest Park, Ohio, 1935–1976* (Knoxville, Tenn., 1981), xxiv–xxvi, 28ff.

25. I refer here to the vogue (since the mid-1950s) for the "new" urban, political, social, labor, ethnic, women's and community history, all of which share a concern for the autonomous or potentially autonomous (and occasionally liberated) individual as the fundamental unit of analysis, sometimes but not always by concentrating on the geographic and socioeconomic mobility of individuals or on individual voting behavior. For convenient introductions to this literature see Michael Kammen, ed., *The Past Before Us: Contemporary Historical Writing in the United States* (Ithaca, 1980), and James B. Gardner and George Rollie Adams, eds., *Ordinary People and Everyday Life* (Nashville, Tenn., 1983). The concern to snap the "giveness" of culture was not, apparently, an exclusively American phenomenon. See, for example, Raymond Williams, *Culture and Society, 1780–1950* (New York, 1983, orig. ed., 1958). Williams talks about the rejection of culture (p. 317), but makes a plea for the creation of a common English culture, a democratic and dynamic one shaped by the participation of all classes of individuals in the making and remaking of the culture. He seemed to seek a community of experience in the process of culture building. Finally, this perspective suggests a reconsideration of the so-called consensus school of American historians. Some, such as Louis Hartz, concluded in despair that the traditional American consensus had left Americans so ideologically naive as to render them incapable of defending the tradition of individual autonomy. Louis Hartz, *The Liberal Tradition in America: An Interpretation of American Liberal Thought Since the Revolution* (New York, 1955). Others, however, such as Daniel J. Boorstin, celebrated consensus, by attempting to show that Americans, *because* of their traditional ideological naivete, had been by definition autonomous individuals, and thus inventively free of the constraints of culture and resistant to conformity, determinism and authoritarianism. Daniel J. Boorstin, *The Genius of American Politics* (New York, 1958); *The Image: A Guide to Pseudo-Events in America* (New York, 1964). What defined these historians as a school, however, was their concern with a central problem: how Americans had escaped totalitarianisms of the right and left, and how (or whether) it might escape such a fate and/or a deadening conformity in the future. For an introduction to the argument about consensus in American history see Allen F. Davis and Harold D. Woodman, eds., *Conflict and Consensus in Modern American History* 6th ed. (Lexington, Mass., 1984). I am indebted to E. Bruce Tucker for pointing out the despair in Hartz.

26. For a history of recent politics in Cincinnati, see Zane L. Miller and Bruce Tucker, "The Revolt Against Cultural Determinism and the New Urban Politics: Planning and Development in Cincinnati, 1948–1987," in *Snowbelt Cities,* ed. Richard Bernard (Bloomington, Ind., 1990).

27. Working with several people has shaped my understanding and periodization of the history of ethnicity and the city. Henry D. Shapiro has been most important, but for the construction and revision of this essay see especially his "The Place of Culture and the Problem of Identity," in *Appalachia and America: Autonomy and*

Regional Independence, ed. Allen Batteau (Lexington, Ky., 1983), 111–141. See also Patricia Mooney Melvin, *The Organic City: Urban Definition and Neighborhood Organization, 1880–1920* (Lexington, Ky., 1987); Alan I Marcus, "Back to the Present: Historians' Treatment of the City as a Social System During the Reign of the Idea of Community," in *American Urbanism: A Historiographical Review,* eds. Howard Gillette, Jr. and Zane L. Miller (New York, 1987), 7–26; Andrea Tuttle Kornbluh, "From Culture to Cuisine: Twentieth-Century Views of Race and Ethnicity in the City," ibid., 49–72; Blum, "Women and the City"; Fairbanks, *Making Better Citizens;* Alan I Marcus and Howard P. Segal, *Technology in America: A Brief History* (San Diego, 1989), 88–362; Robert A. Burnham, "Urban Politics, Municipal Government, and Urban Development in Cincinnati, 1925–1960" (Ph.D. diss., University of Cincinnati, 1991).

ANDREA TUTTLE KORNBLUH

The Bowl of Promise:
Civic Culture, Cultural Pluralism, and Social Welfare Work

What is the relationship between ethnicity and citizenship? How can an ethnically diverse community define a shared past and a common future? What communal needs and desires can be discovered among citizens of such a community? This essay examines two distinct answers developed by Cincinnati social welfare advocates in the first half of this century. In these years social welfare advocates sought to improve the living conditions of less fortunate members of society. By the 1910s and 1920s "social welfare" included not only such traditional concerns as the provision of adequate housing and employment, but new attempts to promote participation in the civic life of the community as well. Social welfare advocates of these years developed new techniques for selling their programs to a popular audience. Such publicity, or public relations work, by the early twentieth century had become an integral part of social welfare fund-raising. Designed to attract financial support from a wide range of city residents and to build enthusiasm for a broad and inclusive definition of public welfare, such Cincinnati projects as a 1912 survey of immigrants and a 1923 Community Chest pageant provide us with a mainstream perspective on the changing relationship among ethnicity, citizenship, and social welfare in the first half of the twentieth century.

These visions, which follow one another chronologically, do not both agree that ethnicity is a "problem"; but both define ethnicity as a key issue for the identity of Cincinnati as a place and for relationships among the city's inhabitants. Frederick T. Bastel, (author of the 1912 study, "Report on the Survey of the Foreign Population of Cincinnati,") and Emma Backus, (creator of the 1923 pageant, *The Bowl of Promise,*) grappled with the ways in which the concept of ethnic identity shaped concerns about social welfare and citizenship and they helped to popularize ways of thinking about these issues. Bastel suggested that ethnicity is a problem that needs to be remediated through Americanization. Backus, on the other hand, portrayed ethnic identity as a force that holds the larger community together.

Frederick T. Bastel worried in 1912 that Cincinnati might be developing distinct geographically based ethnic cultures. Such diversity, defined in cultural and not racial terms, seemed to him to threaten community cohesion in large American cities. Without a shared American culture, Bastel and his contemporaries feared, community life might well fragment into small, unconnected worlds. When he investigated the city's foreign population in 1912 he warned his Cincinnati readers that they should try to prevent the dangerous cultural patterns that had developed in cities like New York and Chicago. In those places, he reported, there were "solid colonies of foreigners" who formed cities within a city and thus slowed "the process of Americanization."[1] He warned that uncontrolled ethnic culture threatened to engulf the American way of life.

Bastel's demand for a monolithic American culture, however, gave way to a more pluralistic vision among Cincinnati social welfare advocates of the 1920s, a vision that celebrated ethnic culture rather than worrying about it. In the twenties the existence of ethnic cultures offered the promise of providing the glue with which American cities and their institutions might be held together.[2] With this outlook, using ethnic communities and agency federation as basic organizing units, Cincinnati's social welfare service network defined itself as a comprehensive system in the years after World War I. Supported by this ideological framework of cultural pluralism, in the 1920s, 1930s, and 1940s Cincinnatians built and sustained a social welfare system that offered services to citizens on the basis of their ethnic, racial, or religious group identity.

These shifting ideas about the nature of ethnic culture are embedded in the changing institutional responses Cincinnatians developed to meet what they defined as the social welfare needs of the city's citizens. In the nineteenth century, private social service had been an area of religious concern. By the early twentieth century social service had been taken over by secular forces who replaced the unifying model of religious Orthodoxy with a new theoretical model. This model suggested that a federation of organizations serving different ethnic, racial, and religious groups in the city could utilize such difference to help unite rather than divide the community.[3]

Frederick T. Bastel's 1912 survey of Cincinnati's immigrants had its roots in a missionary exhibition, *The World in Cincinnati,* held in Music Hall for three weeks in the spring of 1912. Based on similar exhibitions in London and Boston, the exposition promoters promised to bring "the life and problems of the world" to Cincinnati.[4] Exhibits modeled on foreign cities featured characteristic institutions, architecture and street life. Men, women and children from Cincinnati's Protestant churches, attired in native costumes, attempted to give visitors an authentic experience. The exposition was a great success; exposition officials estimated that 250,000 people attended it. Those Cincinnatians who did not personally view the exposition had the opportunity to read about it in local newspaper articles. The April 4, 1912, issue of the *Commercial Tribune,* for example, announced in large headlines, "Several Hundred Turned Away from Music Hall: Yesterday's Attendance at World in Cincinnati Largest in the History of the Exposition."[5]

The World in Cincinnati sought to present "strange life, both at home and abroad . . . in the most interesting and real manner." The goal of the exposition was not primarily to educate the public about foreign cultures, but rather to present the work of missionaries. "To most people," the exposition newspaper noted, "the work of the missionary is vague and unreal." Through tableau and motion pictures of "heathen lands," exposition organizers hoped to prove the necessity for missionary work. Visitors who might come to satisfy their curiousity would "go away with a new conception of the missionary enterprise." The organizers realized that not all visitors would be Christians, and that some would be "either opposed or entirely indifferent to missions." But they hoped that the "exhibition of the power of the Gospel over heathen life" would impress the visitors and that some, at least, would be "led into the Christian life by their experience." Thus the missionary exposition had a two-pronged aim to win financial support and recognition for the work of missionaries abroad and to make religious converts at home. Organizers thought that they had presented the Christian people of Cincinnati with a unique opportunity to "advance the Kingdom of God." "The redemption of the whole world for Christ can become a real task to hundreds of thousands," they declared, "and the whole church can be lifted to a high level of consecration if we do our part."[6]

The World in Cincinnati spanned three floors of Music Hall and included tableaux from China, Japan, India, Burma, Korea, Africa, "the Mohammedan World," the Phillippine Islands, Hawaii, Puerto Rico, Alaska, as well as North American groups and regions receiving missionary services. Into this latter category fell immigrants. Under the leadership of Frederick T. Bastel, missionary of the Slavic Department of the Congregational Home Missionary Society, the exhibit on immigrants to the United States focused on the task of making these newcomers into American citizens.

The immigrant exhibit, located in the Hall of the Home Land, shared the first floor of Music Hall with the displays on Hawaii, Mountaineers, the Frontier, American Indians and Alaska, Puerto Rico, the Phillipines, and Rural Districts and City Missions. The guide book, which described each of the exhibits in detail, offered an overview of immigration explaining that twenty-nine million foreigners had entered the United States since 1820. "This peaceful invasion of America by Europeans," it gushed, "is one of the marvels of the twentieth century." Viewing immigration positively it declared with "the rapid expansion of our industries we need the aliens.... If we are to continue our material prosperity," it concluded, we must have sufficient laborers."[7]

Yet the guide book proceeded to explain that immigrants did not automatically become "Americanized" just by coming to the United States. Indeed, owing to what it called a "decided change in the character of the immigration," this problem had become more pronounced: Until 1902, 82 percent of the aliens had come from Britain, Germany, Norway, Sweden, and Canada. But now 80 percent were coming from southern Europe. These earlier immigrants, which it labeled "Baltic immigrants," had not disrupted American life since they had been "related to the founders of the Republic by language, customs, and religion, and familiar with our established ideals of liberty and fraternity." Now, however, problems arose since the new Mediterrean immigrants threatened to introduce "a new element into our civilization, alien in more ways than language." According to the guide book, these new immigrants "rush into the largest cities where they can form national colonies." It understood that immigrants might desire to live "among the people who speak their own tongue," but such congregation, such self-segregation, brought with it a danger that they might fail to become integrated into American life. America's largest cities thus stood in peril of becoming foreign capitals. Immigrants' desire to hold on to old ways, the guide book warned, placed "a strain upon the civil and political institutions of our country." It cited statistics suggesting that crime and pauperism were greater among immigrants than native-born Americans, burdening the urban social welfare system.[8]

The guide book argued that while American industry needed immigrant labor, to become "real Americans" immigrants needed more than employment. They needed to be welcomed into American life—they needed to be shown "Christian hospitality." "We can assume an attitude which calls them 'Dago,' 'Sheeny,' and similar names," it cautioned, "but such a spirit will never make them good American citizens." To ensure that newcomers become good citizens, native American Christians were exhorted to treat them "as brothers and share our advantages with them." "If we do not Americanize them," the guide book warned, "they will foreignize us."9

The public schools successfully Americanized immigrant children, but reaching the adults remained a task for Christian mission boards. "To win the aliens to pure Christianity," the guide book argued, "is the work of specialists and one mission board has established a department of immigration." It reported approvingly that "many splendid examples of aliens who have become good American Christian citizens can be found in nearly every part of our country." In effect, the writers of the guide book linked Americanization and Christianization: Both strategies, they thought, would lead to the development of good citizens.10

The immigration exhibit at *The World in Cincinnati* displayed photographs, providing "vivid glimpses of scenes among immigrants on shipboard and on shore." At the exhibit's center stood a partial reproduction of the inspection room at Ellis Island equipped with stereoptican images in color illustrating immigration scenes. A tableau featured the "peaceful invasion" of the country by immigrants. From "all quarters of the earth" immigrants surged through the portals of Ellis Island. "They will pass before you," the guide book promised, "with their strange costumes, and their still stranger tongues. They will be examined by doctors and by inspectors, and you will see them as they pass out to become in time one of the small but powerful units in the building up of a mighty nation." As a grand finale, the exhibit demonstration portrayed the "absorption of the people into this nation, ending with the saluting of the star-spangled banner by the immigrants in their costumes." Echoing the melting pot vision of American life, the guide book concluded on a high note: "Perhaps America is to be the crucible of God to amalgamate the races of the earth."11

This massive public relations effort for Christian missions was judged a success by its organizers, for they accomplished their main educational goals. They had illustrated "the conditions of life that characterize the non-Christian peoples of various lands preliminary to the advent of the Gospel," had shown the means used by missionaries to propagate the Christian faith, and had demonstrated "the results of this evangelization in the lives of peoples of every land and clime." In spite of these achievements, the organizers of the missionary exposition thought that true success would only come when Cincinnati churches developed new programs with more "passion for the world's evangelization." If that awakening of spirit did not take place, they warned, "we say without hesitation it would be better that the Exposition had not been held."[12]

Inspired by *The World in Cincinnati,* the city's Protestant religious leaders organized a "continuation Committee" to launch a new local program of missionary endeavor. More personal prayers for missions, a greater study of the missionary enterprise, a larger financial commitment for every church, a "quickened spirit of service," as well as a "program of helpfulness and service to the local community," headed the list of new undertakings. At the final mass meeting of the exposition one area was targeted in particular, Protestant work "in behalf of the foreigners in our city."[13]

The Continuation Committee began its interdenominational work among the city's immigrants by hiring Frederick T. Bastel to survey the city to ascertain "just what nationalities were located in Cincinnati, where they resided and what were their church affiliations." Bastel, already in town for the exposition, stayed in Cincinnati during May and June 1912 to make his survey. His conclusion was the same as that presented at the exposition: The continuation of American industrial expansion mandated a flow of immigrant laborers, but to protect the nation such immigrants needed to be adjusted to "Christian ideals." This adjustment called for the abandonment of immigrant culture and language.[14]

"Cincinnati," Bastel reported, was "composed of Germans, Americans, Irish, Jews and Negroes, freely interspersed with Italians, Roumanians, Hungarians, Hollanders, Syrians, Greeks, Poles, Bulgarians, Servians, Croatians, Turks and peoples of three or four other nationalities." "A more variegated and motley crowd," he wrote, "can hardly be imagined." Although this ethnic diversity demonstrated Cincinnati's kinship with New York and Chicago, he thought the ethnic living patterns in those cities differed from Cincinnati. New York and Chicago, he noted, had "their solid colonies of foreigners side by side, forming cities within a city." In Cincinnati, by contrast, the "foreign populations intermingle very freely." On one single block he found native-born Americans, Germans,

Hungarians, Greeks, Italians, and Irish, and on another block Negroes, Jews, Americans, Hungarians, Germans and Irish—"all living in perfect peace and unity."[15]

Bastel counted "this intermingling of the races" in Cincinnati "a redeeming feature in the great foreign problem." In large cities where immigrants formed their own colonies, he lamented that, "the process of Americanization ... is very slow. ... But where they are mingled together," he said, "the English language becomes the common medium of inter-course for them all, and they break away more easily from their old-country customs and habits." His solution, then, was to encourage immigrants to abandon old-world customs, languages, and habits. If they abandoned their old customs and adopted American ways, they would cease to be foreign, and there would cease to be a "foreign problem." Bastel thus assumed that culture, not biology or race, characterized different nationalities. People from different racial groups could become American by trading their cultures and customs for American ways—which to him included both using the English language and the Protestant religion.

Although Bastel sought to overcome the cultural uniqueness of differ-ent ethnic groups through Americanization, his plan for work actually utilized ethnic and religious groups as organizing units for social welfare work. "I divided the city into fifteen sections or blocks," he said, "drawing a map of each section on a separate sheet of paper, with names of streets and alleys." On foot he surveyed every block and alley, ascertaining "what nationalities principally live in each block" and tabulating the results.[16] He discovered the population of Cincinnati to divide into the following categories with varying percentages: Americans, 42¾ percent; Germans, 22½ percent; British (English, Irish, Scotch, Welsh, and Canadians), 12½ percent; Jews (German, Russian, Polish, and Hungarian), 7½ percent; Negroes, 7 percent; Italians, 2½ percent; Roumanians, 2 percent; Hungarians, Belgians, Chinese, Fins, French, Hollanders, Portuguese, Scandinavians, and Turks, all 1½ percent each. Croatians, Servians, Macedonians, Bulgarians, Syrians and Greeks together totaled less than 1 percent of the population of the city.[17]

Bastel also made a census of the immigrant outreach programs of the city's Protestant, Roman Catholic and Greek Orthodox churches and missions. He arranged this information on a table that listed along one side religious denominations (Baptist, Christian, Congregational, Episco-palian, Evangelical, Evangelical Protestant, Greek Orthodox, Lutheran,

Methodist, Methodist Protestant, Presbyterian, Reformed, Reformed Presbyterian, Roman Catholic, United Brethern, and United Presbyterian) and along the other the ethnic groups served by these churches (American, Colored, German, Italian, Roumanian, Hungarian, "Holland," and Greek). As a result of his study he determined that three ethnic groups did not need any additional special missions. The Americans, who already had 212 churches, the Germans who had forty-seven, and "the Colored," who had thirty churches.[18]

The majority of the immigrants were of the Roman Catholic faith, but most of these people were without any individual church affiliation. Those who did not have a church of their own nationality worshiped in the nearest Catholic church. "In this the Romish Church has a distinct advantage over us Protestants," he declared, "for she can take in all the races under heaven, for they do not understand what is going on anyway— the mass spoken in Latin is all Greek to them." He concluded that those without their own ethnic churches and unchurched Roman Catholics presented "a great opportunity to our Protestant churches."[19]

Using his survey he constructed a plan to divide up immigration work among the various Protestant denominations. Each Protestant denomination would take on ministerial work with a particular nationality, helping to Protestantize and Americanize the immigrant population. Bastel recommended that the Presbyterians, who had already established a church in the West End for Italians with an Italian pastor, should "make the people of this nationality their entire care and do aggressive work with them." The Baptists, with both a Hungarian and a Roumanian church, should "devote themselves especially to these races." Or, if the Baptists so desired, one of those ethnic groups could be surrendered to the Methodists who had not yet claimed ethnic territory of their own. The Congregationalists could cover the Bulgarians and the Armenians, he continued, "the Christians or Episcopalians among the Syrians, and so on."[20]

Bastel did not limit his concerns about the immigrants to their religious lives. He also drew a strong connection between their spiritual well-being and their general social condition. Dismayed by the housing conditions in the basin area of the city where most immigrants lived, he labeled these residences "for the most part poor, sometimes wretched." In tenement houses, he lamented, two or three rooms constituted a flat for a family. Sanitation was a problem as well. Often the only breathing space in the crowded tenements was a foul-smelling central court lined with outhouses. "These conditions," Bastel declared indignantly, "should be remedied by the civic authorities, tenement houses should be razed to the ground and modern apartment houses such as you have in your suburbs built in their stead." Bastel noted approvingly that social organizations like the Associated Charities were at work bettering the conditions of the poor and the working man. He reported enthusiastically that a "prominent Jew recently requested the mayor to appoint an 'Immigrant Commission,' to investigate the condition of the foreigners with a view of doing social work among them." Such a commission, Bastel noted, would have nothing to do with religion. Although, he continued, "if it does its work right, it will go a long way toward helping to solve the religious problem." Clearly, for Bastel, religious salvation had a strong social justice component.[21]

Even as Bastel published his survey and plan for action, Cincinnati social welfare work was moving in a similar direction, a direction that began with the ethnic community, not the individual, as the basic organizing unit. Since 1879, Protestant social work had been conducted through the Associated Charities, a group initiated by the Women's Christian Association. But by the second decade of the twentieth century social workers sought to develop a new type of social welfare organization. After several years of study and discussion local social welfare advocates organized the Council of Social Agencies (CSA) in 1913. Originally composed of delegates from sixty-five social service agencies, the council sought to coordinate all the social service work in the city. By 1918, ninety-seven public, civic, and social agencies belonged to the council, which included the three major denominational social service coordinating bodies—the Associated Charities, the Bureau of Catholic Charities, and the United Jewish Agencies. The CSA also formed a new organization to coordinate, in a way similar to the work of the denominational groups, social welfare work in the city's African-American community.[22] This vision of a comprehensive, representative, social service system—a federation of organizations that sought to meet the needs of every racial, ethnic, and religious group in Cincinnati life—became part of the CSA's self-definition and community mission.

The CSA's fundraising arm, the Community Chest, claimed that the council's work had "afforded a common platform upon which everyone may stand, regardless of race, color, creed or nationality." The work of the CSA, the chest boasted in 1921, had become "one of the great unifying forces in the life of the city."[23] Addressing the National Conference of Social Work in June 1922 about his plan for developing "communal responsibility," Clarence M. Bookman, Executive Secretary of the Council, explained how the CSA helped to unify the diverse residents of Cincinnati. It concerned itself with community wide problems; the planning of social programs for particular groups, meanwhile, was left to those directly interested. "Communal responsibility" encouraged agency autonomy, or self-determination, among the members of the federation and led to cooperation between all the racial and ethnic elements of the metropolitan community. "In bringing about its results," Bookman declared, "Catholic, Jew, and Protestant, white and black, play their part in a co-operative way." Two slogans summed up Bookman's program for social welfare work: "close coordination of all existing social forces" and "unity in diversity."[24] In the 1920s Cincinnati social welfare advocates like Bookman explicitly described their community as a pluralistic community. They accepted as normal the fact that the city was diverse religiously, ethnically, and racially; they no longer defined diversity as Frederich T. Bastel had done in 1912, as a problem to be overcome.

In much the same manner that *The World in Cincinnati* of 1912 had attempted to educate the public about the worthy accomplishments of missionaries and to appeal for funds while offering mass entertainment, the Community Chest designed dramatic fundraising campaigns to educate the public about the city's social welfare agencies and to raise funds for them. And just as the missionary exposition promoters hoped to win souls for Christianity through their exposition, so the social welfare fund-raisers sought to convert citizens to the new gospel of cultural pluralism. Social Welfare advocates of the 1920s, eager to build a comprehensive fund-raising and social service system, promoted a pluralistic outlook that viewed all the city's racial, ethnic, and religious groups as worthy members of society. Both the practical program to coordinate the city's social welfare agencies and the accompanying ideology stressed the equality, or potential equality, of the city's diverse racial, ethnic, and religious groups.

This popularization of cultural pluralism can be seen most clearly in a Council of Social Agencies/Community Chest fund-raising pageant entitled *The Bowl of Promise*. To Emma Backus, the author of the 1923 pageant, Cincinnati's racial and ethnic cultures represented "a golden bowl of promise"—not a barrier to be surmounted, as Bastel had suggested, but a positive hope. The golden bowl, an inclusive image, could hold together everything placed inside it. It served as an instrument for display, not as a "melting pot" designed to transform the contents placed within it. Where *The World in Cincinnati* had suggested that "America is to be the crucible of God to amalgamate the races of the earth,"[25] Emma Backus disagreed. For her, ethnicity was not just a question of the past, not just a set of old-fashioned ideas and lifestyles to be traded in for new ones, but rather a continuing source of identity. She considered it a positive asset.

The Bowl of Promise celebrated the contributions made by the city's diverse racial, ethnic and religious groups to the historical development of the city's social services. A cast of five hundred Cincinnatians performed the pageant in Eden Park's natural amphitheater, inaugurating the 1923 fund-raising drive of the Council of Social Agencies and Community Chest. The performers, representing organizations belonging to the Council of Social Agencies and the major racial, ethnic, and religious groups in the city, chronicled the progress of social service in Cincinnati through a series of historic and symbolic vignettes. The organization for the pageant required that the various social agencies help different racial and ethnic groups master their own folk dances and songs. This promoted the development by each racial/ethnic group of its own culture. At the same time, by placing all groups in the same performance as part of a common history, the pageant suggested that all these individual cultures collectively made up the larger community, united both by its past and by its concern for the social welfare of all citizens.[26]

Emma Schiermeyer Backus, born in Cincinnati in 1876 to German immigrants, advocated social reform and respect for ethnic heritage. Her father operated a grocery store in Cincinnati's leading immigrant neighborhood, the West End. She married Henry W. Backus, a lawyer with the firm of Cobb, Howard and Bailey, and in 1902 settled into family life in Mt. Auburn, a hill-top neighborhood overlooking the basin area of the city where the central business district and the West End were located. Emma and Henry belonged to a circle of social workers and reformers centered on the Peoples Church, an institution located in the central business district, headed by Herbert S. Bigelow, and attended by a cadre of Cincinnati's self-styled progressives, including Edward and Edith Alexander, influential in the charter reform movement; Mary D. Brite, unsuccessful candidate for vice-mayor on the Farmer Labor ticket in 1921; and Walter J. Millard, a leader of the Socialist party. As early as 1904, Emma Backus began serving as a trustee of the Peoples Church. By 1914 the Peoples Church had become the nucleus for a group called the "Peoples Power League," which soon described itself as dedicated to "the securing of municipal ownership of Public Utilities, Old Age Pensions and other measures of Social Justice."[27]

In addition to being active members of the Peoples Church, Emma and Henry Backus devoted considerable efforts to various reform movements. Henry, for example, served as president of the Anti-Tuberculosis League and on the Board of Directors of the Council of Social Agencies. Emma's reform work took a different route. She was active in such organizations as the Woman's City Club. Organized in 1915 to bring together women of diverse political, religious, and ethnic backgrounds, the club encouraged women to work, as women, for the reform of all aspects of city life. As part of her work, she also published novels examining different social problems and in the twenties she wrote and produced many pageants and cultural performances examining Cincinnati history and the work of different social agencies.[28]

The interest Emma Backus had in ethnic culture became obvious with the publication of her third novel, *A Place in the Sun: The Story of the Making of An American* (1917). Set in Cincinnati, it is the story of Gunda, a young Hungarian orphan and factory worker, who unwittingly assumes an "American" identity and goes to work as a governess for the wealthy and socially prominent Langhorne family at their Skyland on the Knobs estate. The protagonist is a young woman from the basin area of the city, the immigrant and working class neighborhood where Bastel located the city's "foreigners" and where Emma Backus herself grew up. Gunda's story contains three main themes: (1) class conflicts that result from the upper classes' misunderstanding of the needs of the working class; (2) the issues of love, romance and sexuality; and (3) the question of nationality or ethnicity.

Gunda is Hungarian. She is proud of her ethnic heritage, so proud, in fact, that she rises to a fiery defense of Hungary and loses her job in the act. Her employer is having a dinner party, and the discussion turns to a Hungarian musician who has been passing himself off as Viennese. Mrs. Langhorne, the lady of the house, responds to the shocking news: " 'I don't believe it,' she insisted stubbornly. 'In the first place, his manners are too lovely. Max Arany is a polished gentleman. Every one knows the Hungarians are a half barbaric people in a low state of civilization. One has but to look at the specimens who come over here—a stupid, thick-headed, immoral lot, only fit for the servant class. We can never hope to make good citizens of them; they don't comprehend American ideals.' " Unable to contain herself at this overheard slander, "her pride quivering under the attack," Gunda thinks to herself: "*Not understand American ideals!* How dared they say that! Had not Hungary loved liberty better than her life when, again and again, she had sought to throw off the hated hand of Austria? Had she not fought and bled for a constitution, whereby she hoped to realize the dream of a free and united republic under her last brave leader?" When the other Hungarian, a guest at the dinner, fails to respond to the attack, Gunda finds herself stepping forward: "Why do you say that?" she demanded. "Have you not read history? *Have you never heard of Louis Kossuth?*" In *A Place in the Sun,* Hungarian heritage, far from interfering with American citizenship, thus actually enhances it. American ideals, in turn, are not the restricted property of native Americans, but of all those who love liberty and "dream of a free and united republic."[29]

In addition to using her novels as a forum for public education, Emma Backus also promoted community theater. Seeking theater that was democratic, participatory and educational, and interested in pageants, she created the Woman's City Club's Workshop Theater. The idea of providing community members with a chance to participate in drama was part of a general postwar expansion of social welfare to include recreational activities. Pageantry became popular secular entertainment in the early 1920s and gained a reputation as an appropriate teaching tool for democratic values. Text books on community drama and pageantry offered advice on how they should be written, acted, costumed, sung, and organized.

Pageantry, Mary Porter Beegle and Jack Randall Crawford claimed in one such text, began with a "conscious attempt to restore to the people a share in the creation and development of the dramatic art; in other words, to make drama truly democratic." Beegle and Crawford viewed pageants as a form of organized recreation, and they felt that such recreation would strengthen democracy. The industrial system, with its "competition, efficiency systems and labor unions had taught men to work co-operatively," they wrote, but the people had not yet learned how to "play together." Pageants that chronicled the history of a community could provide a basis for uniting all the diverse members of the community. Characteristically held outdoors, the pageants employed large casts of community residents and attracted large audiences who paid no admission fee. Proponents promoted pageants as the ultimate in democracy—in Percey Mackaye's words they were "the ritual of democratic religion."[30]

Emma Backus wrote and produced pageants for a variety of civic, educational, and social welfare agencies. Her first pageant, sponsored by the Civic and Vocational League, commemorated the one-hundredth anniversary of Cincinnati as a municipality. Several successful years of pageant production followed. She usually wrote her pageants at the request of a social or municipal agency. Irwin M. Krohn of the Park Board, for example, asked her to produce a pageant to premiere at Burnet Woods Park in August 1919. Children from twenty-six school playgrounds took part in this pageant with each playground group taking responsibility for one part of the whole and mother's clubs from the playground neighborhoods providing the costumes. This decentralized organizing principle based on discrete geographical units, playgrounds, allowed maximum participation from a large number of groups, and was particularly well suited to the pageant format. Another large-scale production in the spring of 1921 commemorated the three-hundredth anniversary of the landing of the Pilgrims at Plymouth Rock. In conjunction with the Park Board, the Board of Education, and the Playgrounds Mothers' League, the workshop theater presented a Fourth of July celebration in five of the city's parks in 1922. For these performances Emma Backus wrote *The Magic Stones: A City-Planning Pageant."* In 1922, the committee produced another Backus pageant, *Civilization,* performed once again by the children of the playgrounds.[31]

This kind of playground pageantry, of course, was not simply a local development. An article in *The American City Magazine* for August 1924, for example, declared that pageantry had found "a decided place in park playground activities." Pageantry, announced Karl B. Raymond, Director of Recreation for the Minneapolis Board of Park Commissioners, was "one of the greatest factors in developing community spirit." For the previous seven years Minneapolis park playgrounds had presented annual outdoor spectacles that attracted fifty thousand people each year. Unlike the Backus pageants, however, those produced in Minneapolis were not historical in content. Children, warned Raymond, were "too young to have an understanding of the events portrayed" in historical dramas and he feared such productions failed to interest the adult population "no longer in school and . . . unfamiliar with the subject featured." In Minneapolis the pageants consisted of such programs as *Mother Goose, The Pied Piper of Hamlin, Wedding of the Fairies,* and *Lost in Toyland.* Other contemporary chroniclers also downplayed the content of the pageants, preferring to discuss the setting, the costumes, the dance and the music.[32]

Emma Backus's call for pageants that both offered democratic participation to community members and taught democratic civics lessons attracted national as well as local attention. The December 1920 issue of *Drama* magazine, the national publication of the Drama League, reported on her

Workshop Theater, describing it as being devoted to the development of "the civic theater idea" and the furtherance of "community drama." Members of the Workshop Theater included local writers, and play producers, as well as actors, both amateur and professional. The Workshop Theater, *Drama* noted, provided "original pageants of local interest for community celebrations," which characteristically followed "the idea of educational dramatics" and discouraged the star performer for the benefit of the group. Caution had been taken in Cincinnati to avoid the unfortunate situation that occurred when playground performances introduced semiprofessionals into the cast. Semiprofessionals "may improve the performance from an exhibition standpoint," *Drama* reported, but their use "defeats the aims of the playground director, whose first concern is to produce a spirit of team play in the group." Democratic community theater like that in Cincinnati had no stars.[33]

Although busy with writing, producing, and organizing for the local dramatic community, Emma Backus also studied national and international methods of theater organization and the role of theater in democratic culture. In February 1923, she wrote an article about a recent announcement by Augustus Thomas, executive chairman of the Producing Managers' Association, that the United States would soon have a National Theater and a National Conservatory of Arts. She applauded Thomas for his realization that earlier movements for a national theater had failed because of the assumption that New York was the sole home for theater in America. Backus thought the theater belonged everywhere, and a national theater should therefore be spread throughout the nation.[34]

In addition to being geographically dispersed, Backus thought the theater should play a new role. The stage should be seen as "a sort of continuation school for the adult citizen." This educational approach, she thought, existed in France and Germany, and there it helped to build public interest in theater. The French, for example, viewed the theater as a branch of public education under the control of the national department of education. There, theaters received regular funding, "just as," she said, "agricultural schools receive in America." Cincinnati had a well-established symphony orchestra, Backus declared, "Then why not a . . . civic theater center as well." This civic theater would be an aid in encouraging playwrights to "dramatize America." American theater, she continued, would focus on what she called the country's "great movements and heroic past, its mountains and rivers, its cities made up of all sorts and conditions of men. . . . The Miami Valley alone," she declared, "would furnish a wealth of dramatic material for plays of this kind to inspire the youth of America."[35]

This picture of the American city as made up of "all sorts and conditions of men" formed the heart of Backus's *Bowl of Promise*. The pageant provided a kind of mass advertisement for the chest's 1923 fundraising drive. Emma Backus invited all the organizations in the chest to participate in the performance and after two months of preparations *The Bowl of Promise* premiered to an enthusiastic public. An estimated fifteen thousand citizens came to Eden Park on April 22, 1923, to see the final performance. The pageant had a cast of more than five hundred active participants, not counting the two hundred Boy Scouts who kept order on the pageant grounds.[36]

Staged outside, in the natural amphitheater where Seasongood Pavillion now stands, the play consisted of five episodes, divided into twenty-nine separate sections. It began in 1788 with an Indian Episode. Benjamin Stites discovered the Miami Valley, the Indians attacked Ft. Washington, and Anthony Wayne and his "gallant legion" arrived to protect the settlers. In a joint meeting seven tribes met with the settlers in making a treaty of peace, the Treaty of Greenville. In this episode, the program proclaimed, "the fires of race hatred are burned to ashes in the bowl of the pipe of peace." Young men from the Central YMCA performed the war dance that marked the attack on Ft. Washington, the Boy Scouts played Anthony Wayne and his men, and the Girl Scouts portrayed Indian women bringing the pipe of peace. The conflict between the Indians and the white settlers was transformed through this vignette into a lesson about good race relations and the different roles of men and women in waging war and peace-making.[37]

The next scene took place in 1819 as Dr. Daniel Drake assembled his friends to promote Cincinnati's first hospital. This episode, devoted to the roots of Cincinnati social service, also included John Cleves Symmes and his son-in-law, William Henry Harrison, ninth president of the United States. Judge William McMillan, "an exponent of early justice," and John Reily, the city's first schoolmaster, illustrated the pioneer roots of Cincinnati social service. Health care, government, the legal system, and education all formed components of the social service system. For Emma Backus, social service and the public welfare related to the civic health of the whole community.[38]

The third episode, titled *The Cup Runneth Over,* recreated the nineteenth-century settlement of Ohio during which "a great population flows into the city from the East and the West" and the "North and the South Clasp hands across the border." These new Cincinnatians come "from the far corners of the earth . . . until the valley fills to the rim with the homes of the workers." To illustrate this great immigration, social service agencies serving different ethnic groups performed folk dances from different cultures. Children from the Union Bethel, a settlement house specializing in serving Appalachian newcomers to the city, began the episode with a dance titled "Gateway to the South." Children from American House, a settlement house for the non-English-speaking population of the city, performed Hungarian and Serbian dances. Walnut Hills children from Hoffman Community Center performed an Italian Tarantelle and children from the Parks and Playgrounds Committee danced a Dutch Dance. The Playground Mother's League organized children to put on a Highland Schottische, and the National Catholic Community House portrayed "Italian street singers."[39]

The fourth episode described the city's role in the abolition of slavery and the Civil War. The Federation of Churches produced this scene featuring champions of abolition Lyman Beecher of Lane Seminary, Salmon P. Chase, and Harriet Beecher Stowe, author of *Uncle Tom's Cabin*. In the pageant these abolitionists appear both noble and successful and through their actions "an infamous social wrong is righted." Here, as in the earlier episodes, Backus and the community groups involved searched for a "usable past." To depict life under slavery, the Negro Civic Welfare Association, an umbrella group coordinating social work in the African-American community, performed the "plantation songs" such as "Couldn't Hear Nobody Pray," "March On," and "Rise, Shine." For the Civil War scene, Sister Anthony, "The Angel of the Battlefield," and her nurses care for wounded soldiers at the Battle of Shiloh. Representatives from the Bureau of Catholic Charities and St. Joseph's Orphan Asylum, a Catholic institution, performed this scene.[40]

The final episode of the pageant covered the period from the Civil War to 1923. Cincinnati, proclaimed by Longfellow the "Queen of the West in her Garlands Dressed," is at its prime. The Woman's City Club's Zita Fallon played the queen; gifts of fame, honor, and power were lavished upon her by players from the United City Planning Committee. But "lulled by ease and pride" the queen fell asleep on the throne. The Clinton Street Community House, serving Jewish immigrants in the city's basin, and the United Jewish Social Agencies, an umbrella group of agencies, enacted the dangers that befell the sleeping queen. Indifference, sloth and greed overtake her, stealing the symbols of her fame, honor, and power. In the end, the Council of Social Agencies, the sponsor of the pageant, rallied to the queen's rescue, and the future of the city was secured. Agencies devoted to children's health and welfare—including as the Babies Milk Fund, Hospital Social Service, the Maternity Society, the Anti-Tuberculosis League, the Bureau of Vocational Training, the Cincinnati Kindergarten Association, the Juvenile Protective Association, the Humane Society and the Social Hygiene Society—provided players who enacted the future, aptly symbolized by the city's children.[41]

Although Emma Backus told a historical story, her pageant ended with the future, Cincinnati's "promise." Backus projected that future as one in which the welfare of the city's inhabitants would become the most important concern of all. All Cincinnatians would then enjoy good will, physical and mental health, adequate housing and recreational facilities, a properly planned city, educational opportunities, and vocational training. In the pageant, the Cincinnati novelist and dramatist optimistically described her hometown as a vessel filled to the brim with concern for the future social welfare of all its inhabitants. She also conjured up a vision of a culturally pluralist city, one composed of a collection of different racial, ethnic, and religious groups, each one equal to all of the others.

The CSA, sponsor of *The Bowl of Promise,* sought to include in one representative body agencies serving all sectors of the Cincinnati community. Catholics, Jews, and Protestants, African-Americans, Italians, Hungarians, Serbs, Appalachians were all served by social work agencies included on the Council. In turn, the CSA, through the Community Chest, sought a new style of funding for social welfare. No longer would reliance on a few philanthropists meet the needs of the community. Instead fundraisers developed a campaign for democratic giving and all the people of the community, from factory workers to factory owners, were asked to contribute. Mass spectacles like *The Bowl of Promise* both advertised the work of social agencies, and popularized a new, more inclusive way of looking at the city's history and future.

The Americanization campaign endorsed by Bastel in 1912 is to us today familiar as an attempt to resolve a conflict that many twentieth-century social welfare advocates feared existed between ethnicity and civic unity. Less acknowledged today, but perhaps equally significant, was the approach taken by the Council of Social Agencies and Emma Backus. They accepted as natural the division of society into a series of self-contained units, and believed that through organization, the parts would cohere into a federated whole. This model on of social service, based on cultural and ethnic federation, would help institute a democratic and pluralistic community. That community rather than seeking to overcome diversity would celebrate it, reconciling ethnicity and citizenship in a common Bowl of Promise.

NOTES

1. Frederick T. Bastel, *Report on the Survey of the Foreign Population of Cincinnati.* (Cincinnati: Continuation Committee of the World in Cincinnati, 1912), 5, 6.

2. This characterization of the 1920s is, of course, at odds with the work of such historians as John Higham, *Strangers in the Land: Patterns of American Nativism 1860–1925* (1955; repr., New York: Atheneum, 1979). Higham centered his work on an examination of nationalism and ethnic prejudice. He notes he "passed over the whole record of inter-group cooperation except where it bore directly on the story of conflict." In his preface to the second edition of his book he writes that "Cooperation is also an impressive part of American experience." Although Higham does not say so, just as the nativism he studied varied in form over time, so did cooperation, and the views toward ethnic culture. Higham, given his orientation, tends to dismiss cultural pluralism, saying it "made little impression outside of Zionist circles" (p. 304). This article suggests the contrary, that cultural pluralism found a cosy niche in the world of social welfare and helped provide a model for the development of comprehensive social welfare programs.

3. Alan I Marcus, "Back to the Present: Historians' Treatment of the City as a Social System During the Reign of the Idea of Community," in *American Urbanism: A Historiographical Review,* eds. Howard Gillette, Jr. and Zane L. Miller (Wesport, Conn.: Greenwood Press, 1987), 16–17, makes a similar argument on the shifting ideas about urban diversity and the distinction between the late nineteenth century, the early twentieth century, and the post-1920s. Looking at American cities, Marcus suggests that a popular solution to the problem of ethnic diversity in the earlier period was a call for a hierarchical ordering of society. After 1920, he notes cities still seemed to be places of diverse peoples and enterprises but now rather than hierarchy, social forces such as culture and economics seemed to hold cities together.

4. A growing body of scholarly literature examines international exhibitions and fairs beginning with the 1851 Crystal Palace and continuing through the 1939 New York World's Fair. Such works include Paul Greenhalgh, *Ephemeral vistas: The Expositions Universelles, Great Exhibitions and World's Fairs, 1851–1939* (Manchester, U.K.: Manchester University Press, 1988); John Allwood, *The Great Exhibitions* (London: Studio Vista, 1977); E. G. Holt, *The Art of All Nations: The*

Emerging Role of Exhibitions and Critics 1850–73 (New York: Anchor Press, 1981).

5. Newspaper articles covering *The World in Cincinnati* included the following: Cincinnati *Commercial Tribune,* March 10, 1912, 1:1; April 4, 1912, 9:3; April 7, 1912, 8:1; Cincinnati *Enquirer,* April 2, 1912, 5:2.

6. *The World in Cincinnati Herald* 1 (December 1911): 8–9. Rare Books Room, Public Library of Cincinnati and Hamilton County. Three issues of *The World in Cincinnati Herald* were published. The magazine was designed to create "an exposition consciousness in Cincinnati and the surrounding cities." Such consciousness was necessary, for the exposition depended on labor from area churches. Five thousand people were recruited as stewards, costumed interpreters of missionary work, and another several thousand performed the pageant twice daily. The *Herald* provided these volunteers with instructions and gave to thousands of other Protestant church goers "a clear idea of what the exposition is to be and how they can participate in it (p. 7)." *The World in Cincinnati Herald* 1 (December 1911): 9.

7. *Guide Book of The World in Cincinnati* (Cincinnati: The World in Cincinnati, 1912), 60. Public Library of Cincinnati and Hamilton County.

8. *Guide Book,* 58–60.

9. *The World in Cincinnati,* 60–61.

10. *Guide Book,* 61.

11. Ibid., 60–62.

12. *The World in Cincinnati Herald* 3:27.

13. Ibid. 1, no. 3, 27–28. Bastel, "Prefatory Note," np.

14. Bastel, "Prefatory Note," np. *The World in Cincinnati Guidebook,* pp. 60–61.

15. Bastel, 5.

16. Ibid., 6.

17. Ibid., 6, 10.

18. Ibid., 12. Although he did not include synagogues in his table, Bastel noted that there were eleven in the city, one of which was Polish.

19. Ibid., 9.

20. Ibid., 21–22, 9.

21. Ibid., 7, 8, 9–10.

22. *The Cincinnati Social Service Directory 1918–1919* (Cincinnati: Council of Social Agencies, 1918). Cincinnati Historical Society (hereafter cited as CHS).

23. "Our Community Chest," Woman's City Club *Bulletin* (April 1921): 7. Woman's City Club Papers, CHS.

24. C. M. Bookman, "Functions of Public and Private Agencies in the Social work of the Future," *Proceedings of the National Conference of Social Work, 49th Annual Session, June 22–29, 1922,* 89–90.

25. *Guide Book,* 61.

26. *The Bowl of Promise,* printed program, *The Bowl of Promise* Scrapbook, Community Chest Collection, CHS.

27. Interview with Harry L. Backus in Cincinnati, February 1987. Minutes of the Vine Street Congregational Church and Society, Cincinnati. "Annual Meeting of the Society held Wednesday Evening December 7, 1904," p. 94. "Annual Meeting of the Society of the Peoples church, Wednesday, December 19, 1913 at Eimer's Hall, Sixth & Walnut Streets," p. 125. People's Temple Collection, CHS. Edward F. Alexander, "An Epic in City Government," Edward F. Alexander Papers, folder 11, p.5. *The People's Press,* 25 March 1918. Edward F. Alexander Papers, folder 16, CHS.

28. Interview with Harry L. Backus. "Council of Social Agencies," *Social Service News: A Magazine of Human Helpfulness.* September–October 1918, back page. Unbound periodicals, CHS. The published works of Emma Henriette Schiermeyer Backus (Mrs. Henry) include the following: *The Career of Doctor Weaver* (Boston: L. C. Page, 1913), which sold over ten thousand copies and brought Backus advance contracts from two more novels, *The Rose of Roses* (Boston: L. C. Page and Company, 1914) and *A Place in the Sun: The Story of the Making of An American* (Boston: L. C. Page and Company, 1917); *The Singing Soul: A Chinese Play in One Act* (New York: Samuel French, 1920); "Cornelius Sedam and his friends in Washington's time," *Ohio Archeological and Historical Quarterly* 41 (1932): 28–50; *Twilight Alley,* an operetta with music by Paul Bliss written for the Better Housing League, (Cincinnati: Willis Music, nd).

No text could be located for the following works attributed to Emma Backus: *The Border Line,* a full-length play featured in a radio program during the Philadelphia Susquicentennial based on George Rogers Clark and the Northwest Territory; *The Princess of the Pool,* written for a committee of Kentucky tobacco growers; *The Magic Stones: A City Planning Pageant,* produced by the Playground Theater of the Park Commission and the Board of Education on July 4, 1921; *Land of Lollypop,* performed by school children for the Anti-Tuberculosis League; *Earth Magic,* a health allegory for the Anti-Tuberculosis League; A Pictorial Map of the Northwest Territory with Henry Ogden, New York artist; *The Toast,* a play in two scenes set in Washington's first term as president, performed in 1932 by the Cincinnati Woman's Club; and *The Great White Way: A Modern Morality Play with a Prologue,* written for an annual meeting of the Associated Charities.

29. *A Place in the Sun,* 229, 230, 248.

30. Mary Porter Beegle and Jack Randall Crawford, *Community Drama and Pageantry* (New Haven: Yale University Press, 1916), 7, 16. Percy Mackaye, *Community Drama: Its Motive and Method of Neighborliness* (Boston: Houghton Mifflin Company, 1917), 11.

31. "The Pageant at the Zoo," Woman's City Club *Bulletin* (April 1919): 11. "Report on the Civic Festival May 27 and 28," Woman's City Club *Bulletin* (May 1919): 11. "Live Memories," Woman's City Club *Bulletin,* (September 1919): 6. Emma S. Backus, "A New Pageant," Woman's City Club *Bulletin* (August 1919): 10. Emma S. Backus, "Workshop Theater Committee," Woman's City Club *Bulletin* (June 1920): 15. Woman's City Club *Bulletin,* (September 1922): 13–14.

32. Karl B. Raymond, "Pageantry in the Parks," *The American City Magazine* 31 (August 1924): 95–6. H. Louise Cottrell, "Pageantry on the Playgrounds of East Orange," *Playground* 17 (September 1923): 339–41, stressed that "the three fundamentals of any production are sound, light and movement."

33. "The Work Shop Theater of Cincinnati," Woman's City Club *Bulletin* (February 1921): 8. Part of the development of the community theater movement in Cincinnati involved organizing other drama groups to cooperate. In the winter of 1921, the Workshop Theater organized a city-wide union of dramatic groups including the Rockdale Center Workshop Theater, the Wise Center, the Drama League, Community Service, the Poetry Society, the Woman's Art Club, School Social Centers, University Drama Center, the Community Players, and the Workshop Theater itself. The Drama League established a Community Drama Council with which the now united groups affiliated. Emma S. Backus, "Workshop Theater Committee," Woman's City Club *Bulletin* (June 1921): 24. The outcome of this movement was the formation of the Cincinnati Civic Theater in 1927. Under the slogan "The theater to produce plays Of the People, written For the People, performed By the People," the Civic Theater promised to give "young and old, rich and poor" the opportunity to study and produce, under spendid professional leadership, all the arts of the theater, without cost to the individual." The Theater did not have a playhouse, instead it used local auditoriums for its productions of plays by Eugene O'Neill and others. "The Cincinnati Civic Theater" (Cincinnati: The Cincinnati Civic Theater, 1927), pamphlet, CHS.

34. Emma Backus, "Toward a National Theater," Woman's City Club *Bulletin* (February 1923): 11–13.

35. Ibid.

36. "Our Community Chest Pageant," Woman's City Club *Bulletin* (March 1923): 9. Mrs. Henry W. Backus, Mrs. James Ridgeley, Mrs. Irene Carnwell, "Workshop Theater,' Woman's City Club *Bulletin* (September 1923): 15–16.

37. "The Community Chest," Woman's City Club *Bulletin* (April 1923): 8. *The Bowl of Promise,* printed program, *The Bowl of Promise* Scrapbook, Community Chest Collection, CHS.

38. "Scenes of City's Early Days to Be Portrayed in Pageant," Cincinnati *Enquirer* 16 April 1923. CHS Scrapbook "Charities and Community Chest," CHS.

39. *The Bowl of Promise,* program.

40. Ibid.

41. Ibid.

ROBERT A. BURNHAM

The Cincinnati Charter Revolt of 1924: Creating City Government for a Pluralistic Society

> Proportional representation is a plan for the co-operation of all the diverse interests of modern society.... Co-operation is to be the great sign of the twentieth century, just as democracy was the great sign of the nineteenth century ... Proportional representation is the governmental instrument through which a cooperative democracy can realize its ideals and accomplish its purposes.
> —Charles A. Beard

In the summer of 1924, reform-minded Republicans, Democrats, and Independents in Cincinnati joined together to form the City Charter Committee, a citizen's committee organized to conduct a campaign to amend the city's charter in order to provide for the city manager form of government and a small council elected at large under proportional representation.[1] In addition, the amendment called for nomination by petition, as opposed to party primaries, and a nonpartisan ballot.[2] By amending the city charter the City Charter Committee hoped to rid the city of Boss rule and thereby improve the quality of city government, dominated since the late nineteenth century by the local Republican "machine," first under the leadership of Boss George B. Cox and then his successor, Rudolph Hynicka.[3] The City Charter Committee argued that the "machine" had placed the maintenance of its corrupt patronage system above the needs of the community, resulting in waste, inefficiency, and a low level of city services.[4]

The reformers proposed to replace the existing form of city government and electoral system on the grounds that they contained certain defects that had helped give rise to Boss rule. The reformers criticized the existing form of government for decentralizing authority and responsibility, charging that neither the mayor, the executive head of the city, nor the city council, the city's policy making body, was accountable to the other. This decentralization of authority and responsibility reputedly led to governmental deadlocks and "buck-passing," making it "necessary that there be some power," the party Boss, "above" the mayor and the council "to settle their disputes and determine what they shall do."[5] In other words, in the absence of a single central authority, the Boss emerged as an extra legal figure who made policy and in effect managed the administrative affairs of the city.[6] The reformers also attributed the rise and, more importantly, the perpetuation of Boss rule to the existing electoral system, which made it possible for the majority party to elect all or almost all of the members of city council, thus leaving the minority party or parties unrepresented or under represented. Since most Cincinnatians were Republicans, this system enabled the local Republican organization and its Boss to maintain almost complete control over city council.[7]

The proposed charter amendment's city manager plan and proportional representation provisions were designed to solve the problems that, according to the reformers, had led to Boss rule. The plan sought to alleviate the need for a Boss by centralizing authority and responsibility in city council. Under the city manager plan, the executive (the city manager) was appointed by and accountable to the city council, thus eliminating the kind of division of authority that had existed between the mayor and the council.[8] The city manager plan, asserted its advocates, also took the administration of the city government out of the hands of the mayor, a "professional politician" who followed the orders of the Boss, and turned it over to the city manager, a nonpartisan "expert" who would supposedly act in the best interest of the city as a whole and insure that governmental functions were performed efficiently and economically.[9] The proponents of the proportional representation feature of the charter amendment intended it to put an end to single-party domination in Cincinnati.[10] Proportional representation, they argued, would provide for majority rule but also give organized political minorities representation in proportion to their voting strength.[11]

Under the proportional representation provision of the charter amendment, the voter *ranked* the candidates listed on the ballot in descending order according to preference. The voter would place the number "1" beside the name of the candidate whom the voter most preferred, the number "2" beside the name of the next most preferred candidate, and so on. After the balloting had been completed, the ballots were counted and sorted according to the first choice votes marked on them. Once the total number of ballots cast had been ascertained, that number was then divided by ten, or one number greater than the total number of city council seats (nine). The resulting quotient plus one determined the "quota," which was the number of votes each candidate needed to win election. If the number of first choice votes received by a candidate met or exceeded the quota, then that candidate was declared elected. If the first choice votes for a candidate exceeded the quota, the surplus votes, the votes not needed to elect that candidate, were transferred to the candidates who had been marked second on the ballots. At the same time, the candidates with the fewest number of votes were eliminated and their votes were transferred to other candidates. This process continued until nine candidates had received enough votes to meet the quota and thus win election. Under this system, any political minority able to muster one-tenth plus one of the total vote could place a representative on city council.[12]

The form of government and electoral system proposed by the City Charter Committee represented the latest advance in city charter reform as it had evolved during the first twenty years of the twentieth century. The city manager plan, which came into vogue in the 1910s, aimed to remove politics from administration with the intent of eradicating political corruption and improving administrative efficiency, and, as originally conceived, called for a small council elected at large without proportional representation.[13] The at-large election feature was directed against the ward system of representation, which had become standard in American cities. The "Progressive-era" reformers who opposed ward representation argued that it allowed political machines to control the outcome of municipal elections and that it made for large and unwieldy city councils whose members represented narrowly defined ward interests.[14] Believing that the city ought to be viewed as a "unit," not a "conglomeration of disjointed and unrelated heterogeneous parts," the opponents of ward representation advocated at-large elections on the grounds that they would free elected officials to promote the welfare of the city as a whole.[15]

By 1913, however, both at-large elections and the ward system came under fire from proportional representation advocates, who argued that both systems failed to provide for minority representation by permitting any party or "group" to elect all the members of a city council merely by securing a majority or plurality of the total vote. Proportional representation advocates saw this as a problem because they felt that a city council should represent "not the wisdom of a single group" but the "composite wisdom of the whole city."[16] Moreover, they argued that a representative city council was especially needed under the city manager plan to prevent the council from "making a partisan selection in choosing a city manager."[17] Using these kinds of arguments, proportional representation advocates persuaded the National Municipal League, the foremost municipal reform organization in the United States, to include proportional representation as part of its model city manager charter in 1915.[18] In that same year, the city of Ashtabula, Ohio, became the first American city to adopt proportional representation, and in 1921, Cleveland, Cincinnati's northern neighbor, became the first major American city to adopt proportional representation.[19]

Although proportional representation emerged as a "real issue" in the United States in the mid 1910s, it was neither new nor untried.[20] Indeed, the idea originated in the mid-nineteenth century and had been put into practice in Denmark (1855), Switzerland (1891), Tasmania, Australia (1896), Finland (1906), Sweden (1909), and South Africa (1909). Proportional representation also had American advocates during the nineteenth century.[21]

In the 1910s and 1920s, however, proportional representation began to be viewed differently, at least in the United States, than it had in the past. Late nineteenth-century American proponents of proportional representation saw it primarily as a means of providing working people with political clout so they could better defend their own interests against wealthy capitalists.[22] But by the 1910s and 1920s, this class-based view gave way to one that saw proportional representation as a mechanism for securing representation for various political, racial, religious, and ethnic groups and classes.[23] For instance, the Clevelanders who campaigned for proportional representation in 1921 argued that it would "safeguard against racial and religious prejudices" by insuring fair representation for all.[24]

The shift in the way people viewed proportional representation, however, reflected a much broader change in contemporary thought. During the late nineteenth century and into the early twentieth century contemporaries tended to think that American society ought to be homogeneous and sought to organize their world accordingly.[25] With respect to municipal reform, the quest for homogeneity manifested itself in attempts to erase lines of division, as exemplified by the movement to abandon ward representation for election at large. By the 1910s and 1920s, however, contemporaries began to view American society in a new way, as pluralistic rather than homogeneous.[26] This new pluralistic mode of thought envisioned a society divided into various political, racial, religious, ethnic, and vocational groups and classes, each possessing "its own culture," which supposedly imposed "patterns upon the natural man" and gave "him that particular individuality" that characterized that group or class.[27] According to this concept of "culture," as it was expressed by the eminent University of Chicago Sociologist Robert E. Park, every "trade, every profession, every religious sect, has a language and a body of ideas and practices not always and not wholly intelligible to the rest of the world."[28]

Applied to the question of city government, the pluralistic vision posed the problem of how to make policies for the city as a whole when it consisted of diverse "cultural" groups with different interests.[29] As indicated by the writings of the secretary of the American Proportional Representation League, Clarence Hoag, those who pushed for proportional representation in the 1910s considered it a solution to the problem of this kind of diversity. Reflecting the new pluralistic mode of thought, Hoag chided "certain municipal reformers" for their "strange belief" that "by the simple device of electing the commission or council at large by the block [plurality] vote we eliminate, as by a stroke of an enchanter's wand, all lines of division between the voters except the line between 'those who want good government and those who don't.' " Hoag too felt that "all 'ought to get together for the good of the city,' " but he did not think that everyone should be "forced to accept, without even an official voice in the deliberations, the view of one group as to *what is* for the good of the city [emphasis in the original]." To Hoag, the "way to foster mutual understanding and co-operation for the common welfare is to provide that all shades of opinion shall be represented in the council" through proportional representation.[30]

In Cincinnati, the problem of diversity emerged as a dominant issue during the second half of 1924 as representatives of the local Republican organization and the City Charter Committee engaged in a series of lively and instructive debates over the proposed amendment to the city charter.[31] Though republican spokesmen objected to virtually every aspect of the amendment, they reserved their harshest criticism for the provisions that would change the process of electing councilmen. Republican opposition, of course, stemmed from political self-interest, since the introduction of proportional representation would prevent the GOP from dominating as it had in the past. But while the debate reflected a desire to maintain or, in the case of those supporting the amendment, gain political power, it also indicated great concern over what kind of governmental system best suited a pluralistic society.

Of all the provisions of the proposed charter amendment, Gilbert

Bettman, a prominent Jewish lawyer and member of the Executive and Advisory Committee of the local Republican organization, considered proportional representation as the most "dangerous" because he saw it as an "assault upon Americanism," which, he said, should deemphasize "religious and racial distinctions." Bettman asserted that proportional representation would "split" the electorate into "groups" by encouraging people to vote along "religious or racial" lines rather than "political lines." The members of city council, maintained Bettman, would sit "not as Republicans or Democrats, nor as adherents of this or that policy, but as Catholics, Protestants or Jews, or as white men or negroes."[32]

Bettman also argued that proportional representation subverted the "American" tradition of "government by majority," which required a successful candidate for office to "get a majority of the electorate behind him." Under the proportional representation provision, however, any candidate who could garner one-tenth plus one of the total vote would be elected. Instead of "government by representatives of a majority of the people," claimed Bettman, such a system would lead to "government by some little group of people who temporarily by reason of coalition with some other group have gained for themselves the balance of power." All this, he believed, would exacerbate racial and religious differences, which the two party system and majority rule had been "designed to obliterate and soften."[33]

Republican State Representative Robert A. Taft opposed proportional representation on similar grounds. He argued that proportional representation was "contrary to the whole political history of American government" as identified with the two-party system. According to Taft, proportional representation rested on the "theory that each bloc [group] should have a representative" in city council, thus encouraging the electorate to vote along racial, religious, ethnic, and class lines. This posed a serious problem, claimed Taft, because "each bloc [group] is organized with its selfish and particular interest in view, and puts that selfish and particular interest ahead of the general welfare, and ahead of every principle of American government." In his opinion, the two-party system served as a remedy for this problem. In contrast to the theory behind proportional representation, asserted Taft, the "theory of party government is that different groups who agree on fundamental principles of government will make those principles effective by uniting in a party, and sacrificing to some extent the selfish interests of each group."[34]

Taft, then, saw the two-party system as a mechanism that helped facilitate government in a diverse society. In his view, the two major parties filtered the special interests of the various societal groups, thereby making it possible to govern in the interest of the "general welfare" as defined by each of the two parties. At the same time, the two-party system attempted to accommodate diversity by giving the different social groups representation through one of the two parties.

Murray Seasongood, the main public spokesman of the charter movement, claimed that proportional representation would not produce the divisive results the Republican organization feared. He argued that the adoption of proportional representation would neither destroy the major political parties nor put an end to majority rule but merely prevent a single party from completely dominating the city government by insuring political minorities representation proportionate to their voting strength.[35] According to Seasongood, proportional representation would allow for majority rule but also provide for "critical opposition in council."[36] By "permitting [the expression of] all shades of opinion," asserted Seasongood, proportional representation created a "better feeling in government" because political minorities could not be shut out of the policy-making process. He also thought that proportional representation would give Cincinnati "better government" because "the friction of diverse minds in argument and public discussion" yielded "the great flame of truth."[37] In other words, a city council which represented various interests and conducted its business through open discussions would make policies that served the best interest of the city as a whole. Under machine rule, claimed Seasongood, the Executive Committee of the local Republican organization, not the *elected* representatives who sat on city council, had decided what policies the city should follow.[38]

While Seasongood favored the idea of allowing political minorities representation on city council in proportion to their voting strength, he tried to quell the fear that proportional representation would foster factionalism in government by asserting that Cincinnati was essentially a "homogeneous city." By "homogeneous" he meant that Cincinnati, unlike other American cities, had "no groups of nationalities," a claim he supported by noting that over 85 percent of the population was native-born.[39] The largest foreign-born group, Germans, constituted only about 4 percent of the total population of Cincinnati. Thus, Seasongood told his audiences that they need not worry about group division along national lines.[40]

While he emphasized nationality, Seasongood ignored race and religion, the two types of group division that Gilbert Bettman had stressed. The vast majority of Cincinnatians, as Seasongood noted, were native-born, but the city contained significant racial and religious minorities. In 1920, blacks comprised 7.5 percent of the city's population. By the end of the decade, 10.5 percent of the population was black. In 1926, about 23 percent of the population of Cincinnati was Catholic and approximately 5.8 percent was Jewish.[41]

Though Seasongood described Cincinnati as a "homogeneous" city, his actions indicated that he too tended to view society as pluralistic and that he felt some concern about group division. For example, it was Seasongood who recommended changing the original draft of the charter amendment to provide for a nine-member council elected at large under proportional representation. The original draft of the charter amendment, which had been modeled after the charter adopted by Cleveland in 1921, provided for a twenty-five-member council elected by district under proportional representation.[42] By proposing a smaller council, Seasongood sought to limit the number of groups that could be represented in hopes of minimizing the potential for division within city council along group lines. Indeed, he felt that the revised charter amendment "avoided [the] objectional features of the Cleveland charter, which ... made racial, geographical, religious, and other blocks possible."[43] Thus, while Seasongood championed proportional representation as a means of putting an end to single party rule, he tried to lessen any likelihood that it would result in factional government.

While Seasongood showed some concern about factionalism, he and other advocates of proportional representation tended to emphasize its utility as a mechanism for solving the problems associated with government in a pluralistic society.[44] The staunchest proponent of this view in Cincinnati was Henry Bentley, a local lawyer who became the chairman of the City Charter Committee in the summer of 1924.[45] Bentley considered proportional representation a means of achieving some sense of unity in a pluralistic society. He argued that, in the interest of making policies for the city as a whole and insuring broad support for those policies, city council should "represent the entire citizenship," not just the majority. Through proportional representation, Bentley wanted to give all groups the chance to participate as a way of encouraging them to work together, to cooperate, in the interest of securing the welfare of the city as a whole.[46] Because proportional representation guaranteed any group that could muster one-tenth plus one of the total vote representation on city council, "the various minority groups," asserted Bentley, "would feel assured that they could not be discriminated against and forget their differences and vote as citizens instead of as groups."[47]

In essence, proportional representation sought to create, indeed, to guarantee, a kind of balance of power by using an objective mathematical formula to calculate the vote. This feature, according to the advocates of proportional representation, would help promote "tolerance" among groups by giving each group the power to "protect" itself against "attack" from another group or groups, thereby making it "impossible to discriminate against a group politically on the ground[s] of race, religion or economic status." Thus, proportional representation would supposedly induce the various groups within the city to respect and appreciate each other.[48]

Bentley's ideas concerning proportional representation and the proper function and composition of city council derived from his understanding of the principles underlying the new and pluralistic organizational structure of civic and social welfare organizations, most notably in Cincinnati the Council of Social Agencies, an organization created in 1913 for the dual purpose of facilitating "coordination" and "cooperation" among the various social welfare agencies in the Cincinnati area.[49] (C. M. Bookman, the executive secretary of the Council of Social Agencies, described the agency as "like a cameo" because "its parts" were "united yet distinct.")[50] Bentley, who sat on the board of directors of the Cincinnati Community Chest,[51] the fund-raising arm of the Council of Social Agencies, argued that "any kind" of "civic welfare" organization should represent the "different interests in the community" so that the "support of all groups" could be "enlisted." In his opinion, the Council of Social Agencies had succeeded primarily because its board of directors represented "not one class or creed, but all the different groups in Cincinnati," including "Republican and Democrat, rich and poor, Jew and Gentile, Catholic and Protestant, banker and labor leader, [and] doctor and lawyer." Despite such diversity, claimed Bentley, the board members forgot their "factional differences" and worked together in the "formulation and planning of a real community project."[52] Similarly, Bentley noted that "Catholic, Protestant and Jew, Democrat, Republican and Socialist, black and white, American-born and foreign-born, capitalist and laborer," had "submerged their differences" and "united their efforts on behalf of a better city" by working to raise funds for the Cincinnati Community Chest.[53] To Bentley, proportional representation provided a neat mechanism for making "this same power for unified action available in the political field."[54]

Bentley, much like Seasongood, believed that the best form of city government in a pluralistic society acknowledged the existence of various political, racial, religious, and ethnic groups and classes and attempted to accommodate them by giving them the opportunity to win representation on city council through proportional representation. But, according to Bentley, the institution of a city council elected by proportional representation would not only acknowledge and accommodate the various groups within the city, but also bring them together in one body and thereby help facilitate cooperation among them in the interest of securing the welfare of the city as a whole. Such notions concerning the composition and organization of city council derived from the ideas associated with its function. Since city council determined policy for the city as a whole, Bentley thought that it should represent the interests of the various groups that together made up the city.

Bentley's strong conviction that city council should make policy in the best interest of the entire city led him to support at-large elections. Under the existing city charter, which provided for a thirty-two-member city council, twenty-six council members were elected by ward and six were elected at large. Bentley opposed ward representation on the grounds that it encouraged "log rolling," the practice of council members joining together to win passage for each others pet projects. As an example of this, Bentley cited a bond issue that contained thirty-four different projects "with apparently the most important part of the plan being to give some portion of the money taken from the public to each ward represented by Council."[55] This kind of action by city council, claimed Bentley, promoted governmental inefficiency and unnecessary spending.[56] He saw at-large elections as a solution to these problems because the members of council would be "elected by all the voters in the city and would each represent the choice of the entire electorate . . . instead of . . . certain definite sections."[57] Hence, a city council elected at large would supposedly "regard the interests of the city as a whole" and "not be particularly interested in log-rolling and transferring votes for special interests."[58]

Looking back on the charter movement in 1928, Bentley argued that it became necessary to do away with the system of ward representation because the ward had "ceased to have meaning" as a "unit of government" due to technological advances and changes in the complexion of urban problems. Before the advent of modern methods of transportation and rapid communication, asserted Bentley, ward representation had served a useful purpose because Cincinnati neighborhoods remained rather isolated, which meant that "local problems" could "only be known at City Hall" through the "medium of Ward Councilmen." In addition, Bentley claimed that the problems of "government were entirely local" during the late nineteenth century, thus making ward representation "absolutely essential." But, by at least the 1920s, almost all "local problems," according to Bentley, were "inextricably" linked with "city wide" problems. For example, he noted that local sewers "empty into great trunk lines" and that highways and viaducts "must be planned with reference to access and egress of whole communities." Such changes made the ward obsolete as a political subdivision and the "ward councilman" became, in Bentley's opinion, a useless figure "from a past age."[59]

By emphasizing the need to find comprehensive solutions to urban problems, Bentley echoed the sentiments expressed by city planners during the period. But Bentley was more interested in applying such notions to city government. He wanted to establish a city council that would take a comprehensive approach to policy making in order to secure the welfare of the city as a whole.[60] In Bentley's view, such an approach stood in contrast to the kind that had yielded a bond issue containing thirty-four different projects to placate each individual ward. Hence, as a means of providing for comprehensive policy making, he supported the idea of abandoning election by ward for election at large.[61]

In answer to those who opposed at-large elections on the grounds that the voters in each ward would lose their "right to select councilmen representing" their "political views irrespective of the political complexion of the entire city," Bentley argued that the charter amendment overcame that objection through proportional representation. "Instead of each councilman representing a geographical division of the city as is the case with ward councilmen," asserted Bentley, under proportional representation "each councilman represents a constituency of similar thinking persons equal to one more than $1/10$ of the voters." "These voters," he added, "may live in different sections of the city but they agree upon their choice of a candidate to represent their views." Because Bentley placed primacy on "similar thinking" as opposed to living in the same ward, he thought that council members elected under proportional representation would represent their constituents "much more accurately" than would council members elected by ward. By "assuring minority representation," proportional representation, in Bentley's opinion, preserved the "advantages" of ward representation while obviating its "disadvantages."[62]

In his debates with Bentley in 1924, Republican Vice-Mayor Froome

Morris had offered a rather different point of view. He argued that the citizens of each ward should have the privilege of electing their own representative to city council in the interest of insuring "local representation."[63] In accordance with such thinking, Morris defended the practice of "log rolling" by claiming that it enabled council members to protect the interests of their constituents. He maintained that every council member who sat as the representative of a ward had a duty to make sure that ward did not get slighted when council decided how to use public money.[64] Morris charged those who wished to substitute at-large elections and proportional representation for election by ward with seeking to destroy "local representation" and establish "group or factional representation."[65] Such criticism, ironically, paralleled that leveled against ward representation by Bentley. While Morris claimed that proportional representation appealed to special interests along racial, religious, and ethnic lines, Bentley asserted that ward representation appealed to special interests along geographic lines.

The citizens of Cincinnati helped settle, at least temporarily, the debate over what constituted the proper form of city government in a pluralistic society by voting 92,510 to 41,105 in favor of the charter amendment at the November elections. In a landslide victory for the City Charter Committee, the charter amendment passed by a margin of more than two to one in seventeen of the city's twenty-six wards and, with the exception of blacks, won general support among the various groups and classes within the city. Over 75 percent of the electorate in ward thirteen, which contained the upper-income Jewish neighborhood of Avondale, voted for the amendment. Similarly, the amendment passed by a healthy four to one margin in ward twenty, which contained Price Hill, a neighborhood with a substantial Catholic population. In those wards where the percentage of foreign born whites equalled or exceeded that for the city as a whole, the charter amendment passed by more than a two to one margin.[66]

In contrast, the charter amendment received rather mixed support within the black community. Of the four wards that voted against the amendment, three (wards fifteen, seventeen, and eighteen)[67] were located in the West End, a poor neighborhood where a majority of the city's black population lived.[68] The amendment lost in these three wards by a vote of 5,693 to 3,878. Clearly, the citizens in these wards failed to heed the advice offered by the *Cincinnati Journal*, a Cincinnati black newspaper that had encouraged "intelligent" blacks to support political reform on the grounds that black voters had been the "tools" of white politicians and the "Underworld Negro, . . . whose greatest zenith is to get protection at the courts and run immoral 'dens' to debauch our race."[69] But unlike wards fifteen, seventeen, and eighteen, the Sixteenth Ward, another predominantly black West End ward, voted 1,363 to 1,020 in favor of the charter amendment.[70] Moreover, in those wards outside the West End, but where the percentage of blacks equaled or exceeded that for the city as a whole, the charter amendment won by a two to one margin.[71] Nonetheless, the evidence suggested that blacks on the whole did not support the charter amendment as strongly as other groups.[72]

Besides the rather limited extent of black support, the only other discernible division among the electorate was that low income and lower middle-income neighborhoods located in or near the inner-city tended to pass the amendment by smaller margins than middle- and upper-middle income neighborhoods located nearer to the periphery of the city. This distinction, however, should not be overemphasized considering the overwhelming support for the amendment in the city as a whole and the significant exceptions to the center-periphery, and perhaps income-based, pattern of voting. For instance, the electors in ward ten, a predominantly white low-income ward located just north of the basin and which included part of Over-the-Rhine and Mt. Auburn, voted 2,545 to 868, or almost three to one, in favor of the charter amendment. In addition, in the predominantly white and low-income to lower middle-income wards that contained the neighborhoods of Lower Price Hill, Sedamsville, Saylor Park, Anderson Ferry, California, East End, and Mt. Lookout, the charter amendment passed by a vote of 7,375 to 2,208. The amendment also passed by large margins in the wards that contained the working-class neighborhoods of Mohawk, Brighton, Oakley, Madisonville, South Cumminsville, and South Fairmount.[73]

Party affiliation also seemed to mean little in the charter amendment vote. Considering that most Cincinnatians were Republicans, a substantial number of voters must have broken with their party in order to account for the large plurality in favor of the charter amendment. Indeed, at the same election, republican presidential candidate Calvin Coolidge carried Cincinnati with ease as did all the candidates on the Hamilton County Republican ticket.[74]

Thus, while the debate over the charter amendment had indicated concern about city government in a pluralistic society, the electorate did not, for the most part, vote for the amendment along political, racial, religious, ethnic, or class lines. Moreover, charter leaders believed that most voters probably did not vote for the charter amendment out of support for one kind of governmental structure and voting system over another. Instead, they felt that voters adopted the amendment because they were simply fed up with the local Republican organization and the poor quality of city service it had given them for their money.[75]

If most voters cared little for one system of government over another, however, they institutionalized a form of government designed to put an end to single-party rule by providing for pluralism through proportional representation. Moreover, the charter revolt of 1924 sparked an effort to create a broadly based citizens movement that acknowledged the legitimacy and inevitability of pluralism yet sought to mitigate political conflict arising from political, racial, religious, ethnic, and class divisions by promoting "civic responsibility," a concept used to denote an altruistic devotion to the welfare of the city as a whole.[76] As the harbinger of that movement, the City Charter Committee became a local political party in 1925 with the intent of attracting all those, regardless of political or group affiliation, who wished to serve the city not for political patronage but as a matter of civic duty.[77]

NOTES

1. The executive committee of the City Charter Committee consisted of Murray Seasongood, a Republican, prominent Jewish attorney, and most outspoken critic of the local Republican organization; Henry Bentley, an attorney and Republican, who had been the leader of a movement to institute a nonpartisan ballot in Cincinnati; Edward F. Alexander, a Democrat and self proclaimed "single-taxer," who was the primary architect of the proposed charter amendment; Agnes Hilton, a Republican and "pioneer suffragette," who was a prominent figure in the local League of Women Voters; Marietta Tawney, a Republican and President of the Woman's City Club, an organization concerned with all aspects of local civic life; and Guy Mallon, a Democrat and local attorney, who was active in a variety of civic activities. See *Cincinnati Post,* July 2, 1924, p. 1; *Cincinnati Commercial Tribune,* July 3, 1924, p. 5; *Cincinnati Enquirer,* July 3, 1914, p. 20; Charles P. Taft, *City Management: The Cincinnati Experiment* (New York: Farrar and Rinehart, 1933), 55–56; William A. Baughin, "Murray Seasongood: Twentieth-Century Urban Reformer" (Ph.D. diss., University of Cincinnati, 1972), 2:880; Daniel Hurley, *Cincinnati: The Queen City* (Cincinnati: Cincinnati Historical Society, 1982), 116–117.

2. "Proposed Amendment," n.d., but ca. 1924, Henry Bentley Papers, hereafter cited as HBP (Cincinnati Historical Society, Manuscripts Collection), box 2, folder 8. Under the existing city charter, only those nominated in a party primary

could become city council candidates, a stipulation that prevented Independents from running. See Henry Bentley, "Why Cincinnati Voted for P. R. and a City Manager and What She Intends to Do About It," *National Municipal Review* 14 (February 1925): 69; Henry Bentley to Lent D. Upson, May 5, 1924, HBP, box 2, folder 3.

3. For the best account of urban politics in Cincinnati during the late nineteenth century and early twentieth century, see Zane L. Miller, *Boss Cox's Cincinnati: Urban Politics in the Progressive Era* (New York: Oxford University Press, 1968).

4. Baughin, "Murray Seasongood" 2:808–10, 815–16, 828; Walter J. Millard, "Why a New Government Was Proposed for Cincinnati," *National Municipal Review* 13 (November, 1924): 602.

5. Newspaper clipping, "Change in Charter is Debated," n.d., but ca. 1924, n. p., HBP, box 2, folder 3; Newspaper clipping, "Council Acts in Public Behalf," n.d., but ca. 1924, n. p., HBP, box 2, folder 3; Henry Bentley, "Proposed Amendment to City Charter Insures Efficient Management of City Affairs," July 18, 1924, p. 2, HBP, box 2, folder 4.

6. This theory on why the city Boss rose to prominence seems to have been widely accepted among contemporaries. For example, the political scientist Ernest S. Bradford asserted that the "diffusion of municipal authority among the mayor, councilmen, and various elective officials and boards enables an expert in practical politics [the Boss] to gather up these loose ends of power and wield them for his own advantage. To a considerable degree, he unifies the city government, often determining upon a policy for the municipality and carrying through the necessary measures by means of his control of all the separated divisions of official authority. He thus frequently performs a real function, supplying missing cogs in the machinery, and making otherwise disconnected wheels and springs work together in a single compact mechanism. But he builds up a political machine, operated for private profit. If the boss actually renders a useful service to the city, he exacts an exorbitant compensation in the way of waste and graft." See Ernest S. Bradford, *Commission Government in American Cities* (New York: Macmillian, 1911), 212. For other expressions of this view see, Frank J. Goodnow and Frank G. Bates, *Municipal Government* (New York: Century, 1919), 109–10; Thomas Harrison Reed, *Municipal Government in the United States* (New York: Century, 1926), 98, 101, 107; Austin F. Macdonald, *American City Government and Administration* (New York: Thomas Y. Crowell, 1929), 157–58.

7. For example, the sitting city council in 1924 consisted of thirty-one Republicans and only one Democrat.

8. While the city manager placed ultimate authority in city council, it also provided for *functional* separation between the city manager and the city council by giving the manager control over the administrative affairs of the city. The proposed charter amendment stipulated that, except "for the purpose of inquiry," the council had to go "through the manager" in its dealings with the administra-

tive departments of the city. Furthermore, the amendment prohibited the council from interfering "with the appointment or removal of any of the officers and employees in the administrative service." See "Proposed Amendment," n.d., but ca. 1924, p. 1, HBP, box 2, folder 8.

9. "Talk by Murray Seasongood at the Horace Mann Welfare Association," October 9, 1924, p. 7, Murray Seasongood Papers, hereafter cited as MSP (Cincinnati Historical Society, Manuscripts Collection), box 33, folder 9; "Murray Seasongood Speaking at the Hoffman School Before the North Walnut Hills Improvement Association," n.d., but ca. 1924, p. 2, MSP, box 33, folder 9.

10. Edward F. Alexander to Murray Seasongood, October 12, 1923, p. 1, Ed F. Alexander Papers (Cincinnati Historical Society, Manuscripts Collection), box 2, folder 9; Newspaper clipping, "Council Acts in Public Behalf," n.d., but ca. 1924, HBP, box 2, folder 3.

11. Newspaper clipping, "Claim P. R. Promotes Religious and Racial Toleration," n.d., but ca. 1925, HBP, box 4, folder 4.

12. "Proposed Amendment," n.d., but ca. 1924, pp. 2–3, HBP, box 2, folder 8.

13. Bradley Robert Rice, *Progressive Cities: The Commission Government Movement in America, 1901–1920* (Austin: University of Texas Press, 1977), 100–109; Martin J. Schiesl, *The Politics of Efficiency: Municipal Administration and Reform in America, 1800–1920* (Berkeley: University of California Press, 1977), 173; Harold A. Stone, Don K. Price, Kathryn H. Stone, *City Manager Government in the United States* (Chicago: Public Administration Service, 1940), 33.

14. C. G. Hoag, "The 'Representative Council Plan' of City Charter," *Equity* 15 (January, 1913): 80, Citizens Forum on Self Government Collection (University of Cincinnati Libraries, Archives and Rare Books), box 4; Harry Aubrey Toulmin, *The City Manager: A New Profession* (New York: D. Appleton, 1915), 42–43; John H. Humphreys, "Proportional Representation," *National Municipal Review* 5 (July 1916), 370–71. See also Rice, *Progressive Cities,* 77–78.

15. Toulmin, *The City Manager,* 42–43. See also John J. Hamilton, *The Dethronement of the City Boss* (New York: Funk and Wagnalls, 1910), 40–42, 46–47: Bradford, *Commission Government in American Cities,* 164.

16. Clarence G. Hoag, "Proportional Representation, Preferential Voting, and Direct Primaries," *National Municipal Review* 3 (January 1914): 54.

17. Augustus R. Hatton, "The Ashtabula Plan—The Latest Step in Municipal Organization," *National Municipal Review* 5 (January 1916): 58.

18. "Twenty-First Annual Meeting of the National Municipal League," *National Municipal Review* 5 (January, 1916): 189.

19. William E. Boynton, "The Proportional Manager," *Independent* 92 (October 20, 1917): 135; Lamar T. Beman, comp., "Proportional Representation," *The Reference Shelf* v. 3 (New York: H. W. Wilson, 1925), 74, 113, 115; George H. Hallett, Jr., *Proportional Representation—The Key to Democracy* (Washington, D.C.: National Home Library Foundation, 1937), 134.

20. Herman G. James, "Proportional Representation: A Fundamental or a Fad?" *National Municipal Review* 5 (April 1916): 273.

21. John R. Commons, *Proportional Representation* (New York: P. Y. Crowell, 1896), 237–38, 243–45; J. Fischer Williams, *Proportional Representation and British Politics* (New York: Duffield, 1914), 78–82.

22. In 1883, for instance, one proportional representation advocate argued that it would assist the "anti-monopoly" movement by giving "the people liberty to assail a party that is about to enslave them." See Simon Stetson, *The People's Power: How to Wield the Ballot* (San Francisco: W. H. Hinton, 1883), 31. In 1894, the American Proportional Representation League, which had been founded the previous year, promoted proportional representation on the grounds that it would give "those considerable classes of voters, like farmers, mechanics and laboring men" a greater voice in politics. See, *Proportional Representation Review,* 1 (June 1894): 105. Similarly, John R. Commons, the eminent labor economist, supported proportional representation as a means of improving the condition of farmers and laborers. See Commons, *Proportional Representation,* 185, 223–25, 230. And, according to the *New Encyclopedia of Social Reform,* the promotion of proportional representation in the United States prior to 1910 focused primarily on the concerns of labor. See *The New Encyclopedia of Social Reform,* 3d ed. (New York: Funk and Wagnalls, 1910; reprint ed., Arno Press, 1970), s.v. "Proportional Representation."

23. Augustus R. Hatton, "Making Minorities Count," *New Republic* 5 (November 27, 1915), 96–98; Harry H. Freeman, "First Proportional Representation Election in Kalamazoo," *American City* 18 (May 1918): 455; "The 'Melting Pot' in the Cleveland City Council," *World's Work* 47 (January 1924): 250–51.

24. As quoted in, Beman, "Proportional Representation," 117. See also J. L. Conger, "Justice to Both Minority and Majority Through Proportional Representation," *American City* 23 (July 1920): 59.

25. Henry D. Shapiro, *Appalachia on Our Mind: The Southern Mountains and Mountaineers in the American Consciousness, 1870–1920* (Chapel Hill: University of North Carolina Press, 1978), x–xi, 15–16, 31, 57–58, 61, 114, 243; John Higham, *Send These to Me: Jews and Other Immigrants in Urban America* (New York: Atheneum, 1975), 199.

26. It is difficult to say precisely when this shift occurred. It is my impression that the homogeneous and pluralistic modes of thought coexisted as alternative visions during the 1910s but that the pluralistic vision became dominant in the 1920s. It should also be noted that the discovery of this shift in thought leads me to shy away from treating the years from roughly 1895 to 1920 as one distinct *unit* called the "Progressive era." In his study of the commission form of government, which came into vogue among municipal reformers around 1900 only to be supplanted by the city manager plan in the 1910s, Bradley Robert Rice criticizes historians, most notably Samuel P. Hays and James Weinstein, for treating the so-called Progressive era as static. In particular, Rice claims that Hays and Wein-

stein tend to "blur the commission and manager plans together," when in fact "the manager concept was clearly a successor to the commission idea." Without telling us why, Rice contends that "commission government was much more a product of the 'Progressive Era' than its successor." See Rice, *Progressive Cities,* xvi–xvii.

27. Robert E. Park and Ernest W. Burgess, eds., *Introduction to the Science of Sociology* (Chicago: University of Chicago Press, 1924), 46, 50, 722.

28. *Encyclopedia of the Social Sciences* (New York: Macmillian, 1933), v. 2, s.v. "Assimilation," by Robert Park. William B. Munro, professor of municipal government at Harvard University, expressed a similar kind of view. Munro claimed that "Men and women, whether old or young, prefer to think in groups rather than as individuals." As a consequence, "every community," argued Munro, had "a group mind" or several "group minds," each with its "own opinion forming processes." According to Munro, individuals were "impelled" to "gravitate into one or another of these groups" by "inheritance, environment or some other factor, and thereafter their individual opinions on public questions" were "in some cases wholly determined, in other cases modified, by virtue of their group affiliations." Munro also asserted that these groupings, which he identified as "party divisions," developed, especially in "large cities," not only from "differences of political belief but to some extent from community of race, religion, occupation, or geographic propinquity." Individuals "bound together by any of these non-political ties," he noted, displayed a "tendency towards solidarity in their partisan allegiance." See William Bennett Munro, *Municipal Government and Administration,* 2 vols. (New York: Macmillian, 1923), 1:289.

29. It should be noted that factionalism in government was not a new concern in the United States. For example, James Madison addressed the issue in 1787 in *Federalist* number 10. Madison, however, did not identify the problem of factionalism with "cultural" group diversity. Instead, he worried about factionalism resulting from the "division of the society into different interests and parties" based on the "possession of different degrees and kinds of property." See Alexander Hamilton, John Jay, and James Madison, *The Federalist,* Modern Library College Editions (New York: Random, n.d.), 55–56.

30. Hoag, "The 'Representative Council Plan' of City Charter," 80–81.

31. Charles P. Taft considered these debates the "high spots" of the charter campaign. See, Taft, *City Management,* 68.

32. Gilbert Bettman, "Reasons Why the Proposed Changes in Cincinnati's Government to a City-Manager-Proportional Voting Government Should be Rejected," November, 1924, pp. 8–9, 11–12, Gilbert Bettman Papers (University of Cincinnati Libraries, Archives and Rare Books), box 23.

33. Ibid., 8, 10; See also *Cincinnati Commercial Tribune,* November 3, 1924, pp. 1, 4.

34. *Cincinnati Times Star,* October 21, 1924, p. 26.

35. "Murray Seasongood Speaking Over the Radio," November 3, 1924, p. 2, MSP, box 33, folder 9.

36. "Murray Seasongood Speaking at the Hoffman School Before the North Walnut Hills Improvement Association," n. d., but ca. 1924, MSP, box 33, folder 9.

37. "Murray Seasongood Speaking Before the League of Women Voters," October 21, 1924, p. 3, MSP, box 33, folder 9.

38. "Murray Seasongood Speaking at the Clifton Improvement Association," October 24, 1924, p. 1, MSP, box 33, folder 9.

39. "Murray Seasongood's Talk Before the People's Church," October 12, 1924, p. 5, MSP, box 33, folder 9.

40. "Murray Seasongood Speaking Before the League of Women Voters," October 21, 1924, p. 2, MSP, box 33, folder 9.

41. See, U.S. Department of Commerce, Bureau of the Census, *Fourteenth Census of the United States, 1920: Population,* v. 3, table 11, p. 41; U.S. Department of Commerce, Bureau of the Census, *Fifteenth Census of the United States, 1930: Population,* v. 3, part 2, table 23, p. 535; U.S. Department of Commerce, Bureau of the Census, *Religious Bodies: 1926,* v. 1, table 31, pp. 392–93. Regardless of the actual composition of the population, contemporaries tended to view the city as divided into various groups. For example, when Cincinnati Shriners presented a satirical play in 1924 that, among other things, considered the possible effect of proportional representation, they envisioned the election of a city council "consisting of a colored gentleman with a chrysanthemum representing the 18th Ward, a Jewish gentleman, representing Avondale, a little Dutchman representing the Mohawk District, etc." See Unsigned letter to Emily R. Kneubuhl, December 16, 1924, p. 2, HBP, box 2, folder 8.

42. Ed Alexander, "An Epic in City Government," April 18, 1949, p. 6, Ed F. Alexander Papers, box 2, folder 11. See also Philip W. Porter, *Cleveland: Confused City on a Seesaw* (Columbus: Ohio State University Press, 1976), 19, 46; James F. Richardson, "Political Reform in Cleveland," in *Cleveland: A Tradition of Reform* eds. David D. Van Tassel and John J. Grabowski (Cleveland: Kent State University Press, 1986), 162–64.

43. Murray Seasongood, *Local Government in the United States: A Challenge and an Opportunity* (Cambridge: Harvard University Press, 1933), 25.

44. "Murray Seasongood's Talk Before the People's Church," October 12, 1924, p. 3, MSP, box 33, folder 9; Newspaper clipping, "Claim P. R. Promotes Religious and Racial Tolerance," n. d., but ca. 1925, HBP, box 4, folder 4.

45. Baughin, "Murray Seasongood" 2:882.

46. Henry Bentley, "How Council of Nine Would Be Elected Under Proposed Charter Amendment: Plan Used in Private Corporations," reprint from the *Cincinnati Commercial Tribune,* July 20, 1924, n. p., HBP, box 2, folder 8.

47. Henry Bentley's response to the critics of the proposed charter, untitled document, n. d., but ca. 1924, p. 2, HBP, box 3, folder 5. See also Cincinnatus Association, *Minutes,* October 8, 1924, n. p., Cincinnatus Association Papers (Cincinnati Historical Society, Manuscripts Collection), ser. 2, box 1.

48. Newspaper clipping, "Claim P. R. Promotes Religious and Racial Tolerance," n. d., but ca. 1925, HBP, box 4, folder 4.

49. Bentley, "How a Council of Nine Would be Elected Under the Proposed Charter; Plan Used in Private Corporations," reprint from the *Cincinnati Commercial Tribune,* July 20, 1924, n. p., HBP, box 2, folder 8; Andrea Tuttle Kornbluh, " 'The Bowl of Promise,': Social Welfare Planners, Cultural Pluralism, and the Metropolitan Community, 1911–1953," (Ph.D. diss., University of Cincinnati, 1988), 160. See also Frank J. Bruno, *Trends in Social Work, 1874–1956* (New York: Columbia University Press, 1957), 194, 200–201, 205.

50. Woman's City Club, *Bulletin* 9 (February, 1924): 17, Woman's City Club Records (Cincinnati Historical Society, Manuscripts Collection), box 49.

51. "Publicity Release," n. d., HBP, box 2, folder 5.

52. Bentley, "How Council of Nine Would be Elected Under Proposed Charter Amendment; Plan Used in Private Corporations," reprint from the *Cincinnati Commercial Tribune,* July 20, 1924, n. p., HBP, box 2, folder 8.

53. "Excerpts From Talk of [sic] Henry Bentley before the Optimist Club," April 23, 1925, p. 1, HBP, box 3, folder 6.

54. Bentley, "How Council of Nine Would be Elected Under Proposed Charter Amendment; Plan Used in Private Corporations," reprint from the *Cincinnati Commercial Tribune,* July 20, 1924, n. p., HBP, box 2, folder 8.

55. Newspaper clipping, report of a debate between Henry Bentley and Froome Morris, n. d., but ca. 1924, HBP, box 2, folder 3.

56. Ibid. See also Henry Bentley, "Proposed Amendment to City Charter Insures Efficient Management of City Affairs," July 18, 1924, p. 1, HBP, box 2, folder 4.

57. "Stevens," untitled paper outlining the views of Henry Bentley, n. d., but ca. 1924, p. 1, HBP, box 3, folder 4.

58. Newspaper clipping, "Charter Amendment Assailed by Morris," n. d., but ca. 1924, HBP, box 2, folder 3.

59. Henry Bentley, "Address Before the Building Owners & Managers Ass'n," May 15, 1928, pp. 4–5, HBP, box 6, folder 3.

60. Similary, the U.S. Children's Bureau, as Clarke Chambers has told us, began to take a comprehensive approach toward child welfare work in the 1920s. According to Chambers, the Children's Bureau in the 1920s viewed the "welfare of the child" not as "something to be treated in separate compartments by separate agencies using separate and special techniques. The child was one, and unless the organic unity of the child was kept constantly in mind, welfare work would surely falter or go astray. The doctor and dentist, the teacher, the recreation supervisor, the judge, the social worker, the psychologist and psychiatrist all had special roles to play; none could perform his special function effectively and humanely without an awareness of all areas of the child's life. In this spirit the Children's Bureau, together with many other agencies and associations both public and private, sought in the several states the compilation of all laws bearing upon the child into comprehensive codes." See Clarke A. Chambers, *Seedtime of*

Reform, American Social Service and Social Action, 1918–1933 (Minneapolis: University of Minnesota Press, 1963), 55.

61. Henry Bentley, "Address Before the Building Owners & Managers Ass'n," May 15, 1928, p. 5, HBP, box 6, folder 3.

62. Ibid., 6–7. See also Henry Bentley, "Proposed Amendment to City Charter Insures Efficient Management of City Affairs," July 18, 1924, p. 1, HBP, box 2, folder 4.

63. Newspaper clipping, "Charter Amendment Assailed by Morris," n. d., but ca. 1924, HBP, box 2, folder 3.

64. Newspaper clipping, "Change in Charter Debates," n. d., but ca. 1924, HBP, box 2, folder 3.

65. Newspaper clipping, "Charter Amendment Assailed by Morris," n. d., but ca. 1924, HBP, box 2, folder 3.

66. See *Cincinnati Post,* November 14, 1924, p. 21; Ward Map of Cincinnati, 1920, (University of Cincinnati, Langsam Library, Government Documents Department); Ward Map of Cincinnati, 1930, (University of Cincinnati, Langsam Library, Government Documents Department); "Table Showing the Computed 'Combined Median Rental' and 'Derived Representative Income' Together with [the] Total Number of Families and Computed "Total Income," for Cincinnati: 1930, pp. 1–4, Census Tract Data Center Collection (University of Cincinnati Libraries, Archives and Rare Books), box 24, folder 10; Department of Sociology of the University of Cincinnati, "Cincinnati Census Tracts contained in Wards— 1930," Census Tract Data Collection, box 5, folder 4; James A. Quinn, Earle Eubank, and Lois Elliot, *Cincinnati Population Characteristics by Census Tracts, 1930–1935* (Columbus: Ohio State University, 1940), x; U.S. Department of Commerce, Bureau of the Census, *Fourteenth Census of the United States, 1920: Population,* v. 3, table 13, pp. 799–800; U.S. Department of Commerce, Bureau of the Census, *Fifteenth Census of the United States, 1930: Population,* v. 3, part 2, table 23, p. 535.

67. The only other ward that failed to pass the amendment was ward six, which was located in the inner city and populated mostly by poor whites. The local press suggested that the amendment failed in this area because ward six was the home ward of "Republican Boss" Rudolph K. Hynicka, who had taken over the reigns of the Republican "machine" after the retirement of George B. Cox. See, *Cincinnati Post,* November 8, 1924, p. 8; Newspaper clipping, "Plurality," *Cincinnati Enquirer,* n. p., November 14, 1924, HBP, box 3, folder 2; Taft, *City Management,* 10–11, 17–18; Miller, *Boss Cox's Cincinnati,* 207–8, 227–28.

68. In 1920, about 57 percent of the city's black population lived in the West End. By 1930 about 61 percent of all Cincinnati blacks lived in the West End. See U.S. Department of Commerce, Bureau of the Census, *Fourteenth Census of the United States, 1920: Population,* v. 3, table 13, pp. 799–800; U.S. Department of Commerce, Bureau of the Census, *Fifteenth Census of the United States, 1930: Population,* v. 3, part 2, table 23, p. 535.

69. Newspaper clipping, "Birdless Ballot and the Negroes' Vote," *Cincinnati Journal,* January 26, 1924, p. 4, HBP, box 2, folder 6.

70. The *Cincinnati Post* took special notice of the election results from the Sixteenth Ward because it was considered a "Republican stronghold." See *Cincinnati Post,* November 14, 1924, p. 21.

71. U.S. Department of Commerce, Bureau of the Census, *Fourteenth Census of the United States, 1920: Population,* v. 3, table 13, pp. 799–800; U.S. Department of Commerce, Bureau of the Census, *Fifteenth Census of the United States, 1930: Population,* v. 3, part 2, table 23, p. 535; *Cincinnati Post,* November 14, 1924, p. 21.

72. Other than to note that American blacks traditionally voted republican and that Cincinnati blacks tended to align themselves with the local Republican party, it is difficult to ascertain why blacks did not support the charter amendment as strongly as other segments of the population. During the campaign, the City Charter Committee attempted to "reach" the black community through contacts with Republican Wendell P. Dabney, the owner and editor of the *Union,* a weekly black newspaper, and Reverend Edmund H. Oxley of St. Andrew Episcopal Church, a black church located in the West End. See Miller, *Boss Cox's Cincinnati,* 36–37, 77–78, 86, 166–67, 179; City Charter Committee, "Report on the Executive Committee Meeting," October 13, 1924, p. 2, Charter Committee of Greater Cincinnati Records (Cincinnati Historical Society, Manuscripts Collection), box 81, folder 7; Newspaper clipping, "Wendell P. Dabney, Black Publisher," *Cincinnati Herald,* February 17, 1973, n. p. (Cincinnati Historical Society, Princeton File); Newspaper clipping, "Dr. E. H. Oxley to Retire," *Cincinnati Enquirer,* December 24, 1956, n. p. (Cincinnati Historical Society, Princeton File); Newspaper clipping, "Death Claims Father Oxley," *Cincinnati Herald,* April 21, 1973, n. p. (Cincinnati Historical Society, Princeton File).

73. See *Cincinnati Post,* November 14, 1924, p. 21; Ward Map of Cincinnati, 1920 (University of Cincinnati, Langsam Library, Government Documents Department); Ward Map of Cincinnati, 1930 (University of Cincinnati, Langsam Library, Government Documents Department); U.S. Department of Commerce, Bureau of the Census, *Fourteenth Census of the United States, 1920: Population,* v. 3, table 13, pp. 799–800; U.S. Department of Commerce, Bureau of the Census, *Fifteenth Census of the United States, 1930: Population,* v. 3, part 2, table 23, p. 535; Department of Sociology of the University of Cincinnati, "Cincinnati Census Tracts contained in Wards–1930," Census Tract Data Collection, box 5, folder 4; Quinn, *Cincinnati Population Characteristics by Census Tracts, 1930 and 1935,* x; "Table Showing the Computed 'Combined Median Rental' and 'Derived Representative Income' Together with [the] Total Number of Families and Computed 'Total Income,' For Cincinnati: 1930," Census Tract Data Collection, box 24, folder 10. In addition to the source cited above, my assessment of income levels is based on the character of the housing stock within particular neighborhoods.

74. Henry Bentley, untitled manuscript, n. d., but ca. 1924–1925, HBP, box 2, folder 4.

75. Bentley, "Why Cincinnati Voted for P. R. and a City Manager," 69; Millard, "Why a New Government Was Proposed for Cincinnati," 605.

76. "Community of Interests," n. d., but ca. 1927, n. p., HBP, box 5, folder 5; Henry Bentley, "City Government, Speech delivered at [the] 3rd Civic Dinner of the Charter Committee," January, 1928, p. 5, HBP, box 3, folder 2. Speaking before a group of West End blacks on February 22, 1925, Henry Bentley called on blacks "as citizens" to become "members" of the City Charter Committee and "unite with all the other good citizens of Cincinnati and forget little factional differences and little personal objections" and "stand with other good citizens for good government," which, in part, meant providing the West End with the same quality of service as "any other part of the city." See *Cincinnati Enquirer,* February 23, 1925, p. 10.

77. Henry Bentley, speech delivered after third successful charter election, n. d., but ca. January, 1930, pp. 3–6, HBP, box 7, folder 2; *New York Times,* February 28, 1932, sec. 3, p. 6.

BRUCE TUCKER

Toward a New Ethnicity: Urban Appalachian Ethnic Consciousness in Cincinnati, 1950–87

> While I was growing up in Over-the-Rhine [during the 1950s], I didn't know
> that I was an Appalachian. Alright. I really didn't realize that I was an Appala-
> chian until I was about twenty-one years old.... Since we were born in Cin-
> cinnati, second generation Appalachians ... we considered ourselves Buckeye
> [native Ohioan]. When somebody would talk about white trash or hillbilly, I
> always thought of somebody else.
> —Larry Redden, February 18, 1986

The discovery of an Appalachian identity by a contemporary Appalachian
advocate marked an important stage in his own career, and this is how it
was presented in a recent oral-history interview. It also suggests that a new
ethnic consciousness took shape among the city's Appalachians in the
1960s and 1970s. During his childhood, the speaker acquired a sense of
himself as an inner-city resident with no ties to a region or culture beyond
his neighborhood. In 1969, at the age of twenty-one, however, he claimed
an Appalachian ethnic heritage and decided to become an activist in
Cincinnati's Appalachian ethnic movement.

One way of understanding the speaker's comment is as a biographical
event that transformed his sense of self from inner-city resident to urban
ethnic. It follows that if a sufficient number of similar biographical events
occurred among people with common characteristics in Cincinnati at this
time, then urban Appalachians warrant designation as a distinct urban
ethnic group. This approach assumes that ethnicity is a fixed category of
social organization determined by measurable criteria, and it affords us
only the opportunity to ascertain whether Cincinnati's Appalachians did
indeed constitute a legitimate ethnic group.

The conventions of our discipline, however, require that we go beyond
assessing the validity of our subjects' ideas to comprehend why their ideas
made sense to them. To achieve this level of analysis, it may be more

225

fruitful to think of ethnicity as a process of identification, the act of inventing a perception of ethnic status to convince others. Identities are fictions contingent upon time and place, stories invented to resolve the problem of discontinuity in self-definition. If we wish to know how some Cincinnatians with an Appalachian background (our speaker among them) came in the 1960s and 1970s to claim an ethnic consciousness that they had not claimed previously, then we will need to investigate the origins and consequences of their initiative to reconstitute their relationship to American society.[1] That is, we need to learn why it seemed that an ethnic identity made sense as the solution to the problem of who they were at this particular time. In this context, the rhetoric of urban Appalachian ethnic identification in Cincinnati was an exercize in self-definition that sought to establish the possibility of both individual and group ethnic identity for mountaineers who had moved to the city.

The consequences of defining ethnicity as a process rather than a fixed condition are significant because the language of ethnicization among Cincinnati's Appalachians could be interpreted simply as a political strategy by an urban interest group seeking its fair share of public resources. This interpretation emphasizes the "practical" reasons for ethnic identification and relegates the matter to one of local and merely peripheral significance. Seen in the context of similar expressions of ethnic consciousness in the 1960s and 1970s throughout the United States and elsewhere, the invention of Appalachian ethnic identity in Cincinnati has wider and enduring implications for the study of American civilization.[2] This essay will attempt to explain the development of an Appalachian ethnic consciousness in Cincinnati as part of a more generalized reconceptualization of the place of ethnicity in American culture during those decades.

A rejection of the conventional explanation of the relationship of immigrant groups to American society and the construction of a new definition of ethnicity that persists in our own time was at the heart of the ethnic revival. Since the 1920s, American social theorists had explained the problem of diversity in American culture by defining ethnicity as a group identification based on place of origin. In other words, ethnicity remained fixed and immutable, and migrants did not lose their cultural identity when they moved away from their place of origin.[3] Culturally specific characteristics persisted, they argued, particularly among groups of urban immigrants that clustered in ethnic enclaves, and the coherence of American civilization was derived from cultural group diversity. Thus cultural identity persisted within a place-based conceptualization of American pluralism.[4]

In the 1950s, however, social scientists began to abandon the deterministic implications of place-based culturalism and to posit instead a definition of culture as an identification freely chosen by autonomous individuals. A classic form of the argument appears in Oscar Handlin's *The Uprooted* (1952). Handlin sought to understand the experience of immigrants in terms of its impact on individual migrants. Migration, he suggested, disrupted the peasant world of face to face relationships embodied in church, village, and family, which gave coherence and stability to the migrants' lives, and it left traditional institutions, ideas, and behavior in disarray. According to Handlin, immigrants reorganized themselves in America into groups according to their national origins, and through voluntary associations they created a sense of communal solidarity that enabled them to cope with the loneliness and alienation they experienced in American cities.[5] In addition, they clustered together in urban neighborhoods, seeking communal solidarity in a country that made no place for peasant ways.

In this analysis, Handlin redefined American pluralism, proposing individual choice as the essential determinant in the adaptation of peasant immigrants to American life. Bewildered by the fluidity of American society, by transformations in which their own institutions—churches, neighborhoods, and the press—were continually reconstituted in American forms, immigrants abandoned their reliance on group associations and learned to negotiate their way as unattached individuals in American society. Thus immigrants discovered "what it was to be an individual, a man apart from place or station," and in the process they came to know "what was essential in the situation of Americans."[6]

Historians have disputed the usefulness of Handlin's argument in understanding American immigration history, but for the purposes of this essay *The Uprooted* is significant because it exemplifies a new attempt among social scientists in the 1950s to come to terms with diversity in American culture. Handlin's designation of self-definition as the critical ingredient in the reconstitution of ethnic identity in the United States meant that newcomers were no longer constrained by the culture of their place of origin, or indeed by any culture at all. The essence of American civilization in this new vision of pluralism was the ability to chose one's identity according to individual preference, a possibility that for Handlin precluded the persistence of ethnic characteristics.[7]

In Cincinnati the revolt against place-based culturalism took shape in the 1950s as Cincinnatians discovered mountain people in their midst, defined them as a social problem, and proposed solutions. Earlier evidence of a growing awareness of an Appalachian presence in Cincinnati, of the identification of that presence as a problem for the community, and of the special character of Cincinnati's population is sporadic but clear. In 1941, for example a report from the Public Library of Cincinnati and Hamilton County suggested that the migration of southern whites (and blacks) into some of Cincinnati's established neighborhoods had resulted both in decreased use of library services in those neighborhoods and in excessive book loss. Another commentator worried in 1943 about the problems posed for race relations in Cincinnati by recent arrivals from the mountains. The next year, six pastors from the West End issued a joint statement calling on parishioners to practice a "Christ-like neighborliness toward both the mountaineer and Negro neighbors who are moving into our part of the West End."[7]

During the next several years, concern over the presence of mountaineers in the city intensified, and in 1954 social workers, clergy, teachers, and other public officials came together at a conference called especially to consider how to work effectively with mountaineers in Cincinnati. The conference was organized by the Mayor's Friendly Relations Committee, a volunteer organization established in 1943 to promote harmonious race relations, and the Social Service Association of Greater Cincinnati. As reported in the *Cincinnati Enquirer* (April 30, 1954), in the opening address sociologist Roscoe Giffin of Berea College, Kentucky described Cincinnati's mountaineers as temporary victims of an archaic culture who would eventually become modern urban citizens. This point of view rested on an understanding of the migration from the mountains as simply a domestic variant of the process that had brought millions of European immigrants to America's cities and therefore subject to the prevailing idea that migrants typically progressed from traditional peasant culture to urban modernity.[8]

Giffin argued that mountain culture burdened migrants with several liabilities, leaving them ill-prepared to cope with the exigencies of urban living. He contended, for example, that life in the mountains had isolated mountaineers from modern economic and social developments. Whereas the basis of the nation's wealth now rested on manufacturing, mountaineers depended on subsistence farming. Whereas modern Americans relied on the school system to transmit "important knowledge and behavior patterns," he continued, mountain people "were carriers of a tradition which considers a little "readin' and writin' the goal of formal education." In contrast to urban dwellers, who were accustomed to modern medical facilities and methods of health care, mountaineers were indifferent and often suspicious of modern medical practices. Mountain culture did not impart an inclination towards thriftiness and the modern habit of financial planning, a liability that resulted in constant debt and poverty for mountaineers in cities. Further, Giffin described mountaineers as "familist" or kin-centered, implying that their culture furnished neither the impetus nor the means to create institutional networks for urban survival. Giffin offered contrasting images of the mountaineer, the vigorous Indian fighter of the past and the rejected military service candidate of the present, to highlight his argument that contemporary mountaineers were bearers of a failed culture.[9]

Perhaps the most distinguishing liability of mountain culture that hindered the smooth adjustment of mountaineers to the city, according to Giffin, was the orientation of the region to fundamentalist religion. Fundamentalism, he argued, encouraged its adherents to accept poverty as "evidence of virtue and assurance of eternal salvation," discounted the importance of achievement in the present life, and did not support initiatives for overcoming poverty, ignorance or disease. The chief difference between modern urban dwellers and mountaineers, Giffin concluded, was the inclination among the latter "to take things easy, to adjust to life's demands rather than to strive for mastery over the environment with innovation and organization."[10]

In the same way that Handlin believed that the decision to migrate was the first step in the abandonment of peasant culture, Giffin argued that the choice of modern mountaineers to leave an agricultural and rurally based culture augured well for their future adoption of urban ways. Further, he suggested that although Cincinnatians might perceive mountaineers as a "peculiar people" whose mountain habits of speech, dress, and deportment rendered them out of place in the city, this condition was only temporary. The local press echoed this view, suggesting that although family disruption, sporadic school attendance, excessive credit-buying and violence often characterized the adjustment of mountain families to urban living, their problems were akin to those of any migrant group. The implication was that mountaineers, like Cincinnati's Germans before them, would eventually adopt an appropriately urban culture.[11]

Giffin's address to the 1954 workshop, along with a summary of the proceedings, was printed in pamphlet form and circulated among the city's social workers and clergy, and it became the basis for much of the commentary by professionals on the presence of mountaineers in Cincinnati. Using the pamphlet from the conference, social workers, social welfare planners, and other public officials by the early 1960s developed a common definition of the "problem" of mountaineers in the city, and they agreed on an appropriate solution. Since most argued that urban mountaineers, contrary to earlier predictions, were not making the expected transition from peasant migrant to modern American urban dweller, much of the commentary centered on how to *make* the transition happen.[12] The preferred solution was to modernize the mountaineer by offering alternative behaviors and attitudes that individuals could choose to follow. Giffin, for example, advised social workers to "implant the motivations and behavior which go with formal education, dependable work habits, maintenance and improvement of housing conditions, more realistic use of cash income and sharing in community responsibilities which accompany urban living."[13] Others suggested that enlightened social work, understanding the culture of mountain folk and avoiding judgmentalism, would generate the desired behavior.[14]

Significantly, the city's social workers and public officials did not doubt that the transition of the mountaineer to modern city dweller would eventually take place. Because they interpreted the experience of migrants from the mountains within a general theory of the adaptation of immigrants to American life, they anticipated that mountaineers, like all other immigrants, would eventually assimilate and become as adept as other white Americans in the city. Viewed through this theory, Appalachians were caught up in the typical immigrant experience. In 1963, for example, the director of the Mayor's Friendly Relations Committee, Marshall Bragdon, compared urban mountaineers (now called Southern Appalachian Migrants or SAMs) with other immigrants in the country's past, asserting that Americans had attributed "strangeness" to "every newcomer group to America since the beginning. . . . So each group has been reluctant to move over, but each group by and large in our history has gotten to be known on a personal basis, thus giving a person a chance to fail or win or be accepted on his own merits or demerits."[15] In Bragdon's view, culturally specific characteristics, which isolated mountaineers, would give way to individual identities and a sense of belonging.

Similarly, Jack Hansan, Executive Director of Seven Hills Neighborhood Houses, a nonprofit organization that ran neighborhood centers in the inner city, addressed the problem of the clustering of mountaineers in low-income neighborhoods of the city. He suggested that the clustering of mountaineers in neighborhoods like Cincinnati's Over-the-Rhine was characteristic of all immigrant groups in the process of making the transition from traditional culture. "The history of the American city," he said, "is one of slums, characterized by the ghetto type of congregation of racial, ethnic or nationality groups, and I would suspect that this is probably the primary motivation for them clinging together.... So while it is characteristic of the Southern Mountaineer at this particular time, in view of other immigrant or migrant groups in our city, I would say that it was not a characteristic of the mountaineer." According to Hansan, the concentration of mountain people in one particular area of the city was a normal and temporary phase of the process by which migrant groups had traditionally established themselves in American cities and that such clustering would not persist beyond assimilation.[16]

The belief in the 1950s and early 1960s that the transition from peasant migrant to urban citizen would ultimately occur among Cincinnati's mountaineers left little need for systemic intervention by city planners, social workers, or clergy. In specific cases, it was thought, social workers could help to educate Appalachians by encouraging the substitution of modern values for outmoded ones, but the situation did not call for the development of a policy on mountaineers or on the delivery of services to them. They believed that if professionals understood Appalachian culture they could more effectively help urban migrants to abandon its liabilities, to adjust to urban life, and to move out of the inner city to more prosperous environments where native Cincinnatians would recognize them simply as suburban whites.[17]

Cincinnati's social workers believed, moreover, that the transition to urban modernity would be somewhat easier for mountaineers than European migrants because mountaineers were of "Old American" stock. That is, because they were white, largely Protestant and of British or northwestern European origins, Appalachians did not "come weighted down by the handicaps of so many of the migrant groups of American history." Adjustment would therefore require Appalachians to part with less of their cultural inheritance than other migrant groups. This prediction followed from the assumption that because culture was chosen rather than inherited, cultural liabilities were easily relinquished. Put another way, what Appalachians had learned they could choose to abandon, and in the process they would become modern, American urban dwellers.[18]

By the mid 1960s, however, the discussion of Cincinnati's mountaineers assumed a new sense of urgency. The perception that the problem of the city's mountaineers had become more acute derived in part from their growing numbers in the city and the expectation that the migration would continue.[19] More importantly, however, the discussion proceeded in the context of a wider discovery of poverty in the United States in the early 1960s and the rediscovery of Appalachia itself as a region set apart from the rest of the country by its particularly desperate poverty.[20] The renewed national awareness of Appalachia yielded a new definition of the region as an American tragedy, a symbol of the failure of the forces of modernization, and as a region in need of systemic intervention, planning, and massive federal spending.[21]

In the context of the rediscovery of poverty in the nation and in Appalachia in particular, Cincinnati's public officials began to discuss the presence of mountaineers in the city in new ways. They began to worry about the intractability of the problem they had defined in the 1950s—the seeming persistence of poverty among people they called Southern Appalachian Migrants, their poor health, and low levels of achievement and attendance in the city's schools. What distinguished the discussion from the 1950s was a new analysis of the origins of poverty and new proposals for solutions. Before this time, social welfare planners believed that the character of a people determined the condition of the city's neighborhoods and that the poverty of any particular group was attributable to the defectiveness of its culture. Now they believed that the origins of poverty were social in nature; that is, poverty stemmed from a defective environment and particularly from the lack of opportunities in education, employment, and recreation.[22] Whereas the discussion of the adjustment of mountaineers to urban living in the 1950s had focused on the liabilities of mountain culture and had not resulted in systemic social welfare programs, social welfare planners in the mid-1960s began to focus on changing the environments of poor neighborhoods to facilitate the rehabilitation of these areas and their residents.

Before the 1950s, city and social welfare planning had been conducted by professionals whose job it was to formulate and oversee the implementation of plans to combat poverty and urban blight. Now, the principal method for providing opportunities was to be achieved through community action and the maximum feasible participation of local residents in the design and implementation of rehabilitation programs for their neighborhood. The process itself was assumed to have the therapeutic value of training neighborhood residents in the conventions of urban citizenship. The new principle of community action suggested that only the residents of a given neighborhood could legitimately decide what physical design and social services could best serve their needs. Planners also believed that residents would have to be organized to develop plans to rehabilitate their neighborhoods and to create structures and a process for implementing their plans.[23]

The programmatic consequences of this diagnosis of the origins of poverty and its resolution became clear as the city's social welfare planners and social workers began to design new programs for Southern Appalachian Migrants in the inner city. They believed that the isolated residential patterns of the mountains had contributed to the making of a culture that stressed self-reliance and individualism, both of which made Appalachians in the city reluctant to seek out the services they needed. This assessment suggested that urban social welfare programs would have to address the unwillingness of Appalachian residents to involve themselves in bureaucratic urban institutions and the conventional services offered by social welfare agencies.[24] The new agenda for social welfare planners, then, became the delivery of social services to meet the culturally specific needs of SAMS.

The first effort to develop programs for Appalachians in the inner city developed in the early 1960s in Cincinnati's Over-the-Rhine neighborhood. Ernie Mynatt, a former teacher and union organizer from the mountains in Kentucky, was the central figure in this development. Mynatt first came to Cincinnati in 1955, doing factory work intermittently until 1960 when he took a position as a school teacher. In 1962, he began to function as a social worker among inner-city mountaineers in Cincinnati's Over-the-Rhine neighborhood.[25] Working first out of Emanual Community Center, in 1964 he joined with Roman Catholic students from Mount Saint Mary's Seminary of the West in nearby Norwood, Ohio, who in the summer of that year opened a storefront called the Main Street Bible Center in Over-the-Rhine. Under Mynatt's supervision, seminarians conducted a block-by-block home visitation program to discern and attempt to meet the needs of area residents.[26] The center also employed a social worker to assist Over-the-Rhine residents in obtaining social services.[27] Students organized recreational programs for children and teenagers, and eventually the center established a summer camp program for inner-city youth. Staff from the center also worked with juvenile offenders in a rehabilitation program.[28]

In 1965, Appalachian and black leaders established a second organization using the principle of community action to involve residents in the rehabilitation of Over-the-Rhine. Called the Uptown Basin Council, this group participated in health care planning for Over-the-Rhine, organized trash removal and rat control programs, established a blood bank, and lobbied for improved recreational facilities.[29] Council members assisted individual residents to obtain social welfare services from both public and private agencies. The council also sponsored an interdenominational, interracial program that brought college students from five states into the neighborhood for three-week periods both to learn firsthand about the plight of inner-city residents and to contribute to the rehabilitation of the neighborhood.[30]

A third community action program tailored to the perceived needs of Appalachians in Over-the-Rhine evolved in the fall of 1966. A group of local organizers, residents, and social workers devised an agency called the Hub to coordinate the work of various agencies in the neighborhood and to expedite the delivery of services. The organizing committee made Hub an agency of the Community Action Commission[31] and established for it an advisory committee with representation from every community council, block club and service agency in the target area.[32] Hub hired Over-the-Rhine residents as outreach workers to canvass the neighborhood for clients, to bring them to the center for assessment, and to provide follow-up assistance. In addition to its role as a social service agency, Hub served a community-organizing function. Organizers assisted residents to form block clubs that lobbied city hall for better recreational facilities, more effective law enforcement, and improved trash collection, and which assisted tenants in disputes with landlords.[33]

The experience of neighborhood residents and activists in community action programs in the inner city had the effect of raising new questions among Appalachian activists about the situation of Appalachians in the city. Faced with an increasingly militant civil rights movement gaining the attention of both local and federal authorities, Appalachian activists began to compare their progress with that of blacks. They began by defining their problems and advancing solutions separately from blacks, claimed the special minority status of urban Appalachians and ultimately proceeded toward a definition of themselves as an urban ethnic group.

The first formal urban Appalachian institution was established in 1968 when Mynatt; Michael Maloney, a former seminarian who had worked as a volunteer at the Main Street Bible Center and who was now employed as a community organizer at Hub; and other activists founded United Appalachian Cincinnati. These activists claimed a public identity for urban Appalachians and the power to tell other Cincinnatians who they were and what they needed as a consequence of who they were. The organization's bylaws committed members to "promote self-awareness and self-activity of the Appalachian people in Cincinnati, to encourage our urban institutions to respond to the needs and interests of Appalachians, and to show the community at large the power and beauty of our culture." United Appalachian Cincinnati met monthly between 1968 and 1970 to discuss such issues as the purpose and objectives of the organization, state welfare policy, and the representation of Appalachians on planning committees for the inner city.[34] Thus, the founders of United Appalachian Cincinnati intended to create a political and social infrastructure to facilitate the development of a group identity among urban Appalachians and to bring the "fact" of their existence to the attention of other Cincinnatians.[35]

During the next couple of years, Appalachian activists continued to assert the principle of Appalachian self-determination in the process of diagnosing and prescribing for the problems of Appalachians in the city which they had initiated in the formation of United Appalachian Cincinnati. Of particular concern was the situation of Appalachian youth in the inner city. Activists cited high school drop-out rates, turf wars between inner-city blacks and Appalachians, and high rates of unemployment and delinquency as evidence of a growing crisis among young Appalachians. In seeking to explain the roots of the crisis, advocates suggested that Appalachian youth were alienated both from urban society and their own culture, and that they had no experience or cultural basis for relating positively with blacks or urban institutions. The solution, then, was to recover a sense of cultural identification among Appalachian young people. To this end, they proposed to open a drop-in center that would offer programs to affirm a sense of cultural identity among the youth of the Over-the-Rhine neighborhood. The founders of the Appalachian Identity Center, as it was called, suggested that Appalachian youth had to "first be affirmed in their own identity, then moved toward meaningful contact with blacks, and with institutions in the community." The purpose of the program was to provide a space in which Appalachian youths could be reunited with their culture and empowered to live freely as "urban individuals."[36]

By 1970, the ethnic revival among Cincinnati's Appalachians was alive on several fronts. These included the opening of the Appalachian Identity Center, the formation of an Appalachian Committee within the Cincinnati Human Relations Commission (the successor to the Mayor's Friendly Relations Committee) to facilitate advocacy on behalf of Appalachians by both Appalachian activists and non-Appalachian allies, and the beginning of a project by the Junior League of Cincinnati to educate the public about Appalachian culture through the promotion of an annual crafts festival. Each of these undertakings was premised on a sense of the "differentness" of Appalachian culture and the need to promote "Appalachian-ness" as a group identity.[37]

These initiatives promoted the uniqueness of Appalachian culture and the design of culturally specific social service programs. The process of planning and implementing programs, moreover, led to a systematic attempt to understand the origins and persistence of poverty among inner-city Appalachians, an exercise that ultimately yielded a definition of urban Appalachians as a distinct ethnic group. In the summer of 1971, Michael Maloney, a graduate student in community and regional planning at the University of North Carolina at Chapel Hill, wrote a course paper entitled "Cincinnati's Appalachian Community: Action Proposals for the Seventies" to influence the formation of social policy in Cincinnati.[38] This document was circulated in Cincinnati after Maloney's return in 1972, and it became the basis for much of the discussion of the future of the city's Appalachians.

Maloney began by documenting the migration of mountaineers to mid-western American cities since 1940 and addressed, as had other commentators, the problem of the adjustment of the migrants to urban society. Maloney contended that despite current theory, which held that migrants to the city lived only temporarily in "port of entry" neighborhoods before moving to more prosperous neighborhoods elsewhere, one-third of Appalachian migrants remained in poverty in the inner city. This experience also defied the logic of contemporary antipoverty theory, according to Maloney, which held that as urban poor, inner-city Appalachians ought to be targets of programs providing opportunities in education, job training, and recreation, to assist them in moving from poverty and dependence to self-sustaining employment. In explaining the persistence of poverty among Appalachians in the inner city, Maloney articulated a theory that defined urban Appalachians as a distinct urban minority group.

The invisibility and silence of urban Appalachians, Maloney argued, prevented them from taking advantage of antipoverty programs and that prevented social welfare planners from effectively addressing their needs. Because urban Appalachians did not exist in the minds of social welfare planners, antipoverty programs could not counter the persistence of poverty. Maloney accepted the definition of Appalachian personality characteristics first postulated by John C. Campbell in 1921 that Appalachian culture fostered self-reliance, traditionalism, fatalism, and religious fundamentalism, all of which rendered Appalachians reluctant to seek out the social services they needed to make the transition to urban living.[39] In addition, existing programs were designed for urban dwellers who already accepted the values of Cincinnati's middle-class, professional culture and therefore failed to take account of the barriers to upward mobility inherent in the Appalachian personality. Consequently social workers tended to "write off" urban Appalachian clients when traditional casework methods did not result in changed behavior. Effective social work among Appalachians, he wrote, was contingent on the identification and acceptance by social workers of the "differentness" of Appalachians' family structure, psychology, and value system.[40]

Maloney proceeded with a reading of the history of social work among Appalachians in Cincinnati since the early 1950s in which he sought to explain a history of failure, of promising paths not taken. Although conferences, newspaper coverage, and the Berea workshop, a training program at Berea College (Kentucky) for social workers who worked with urban mountaineers, had all brought the special needs of Appalachian migrants to public attention in the 1950s, these efforts were overshadowed by the crisis of discrimination and poverty among blacks, a crisis that soon absorbed the interest of policy makers and public resources. Appalachians became the victims, not of their culture, as commentators a decade earlier had argued, but of their environment and invisibility.[41]

The solution to the problem of invisibility and silence, Maloney suggested, was to establish an identity for urban Appalachians as Cincinnati's second minority group and to begin community-organizing efforts among them. He suggested that Cincinnati apply for inclusion in Appalachia to qualify for funds and planning assistance from the Appalachian Regional Commission, a federal planning and funding agency created in 1965 to facilitate the "modernization" of Appalachia. In addition, the definition of urban Appalachians as a minority group would enable the city to receive funding and other resources in education and job training from the federal government. With increased resources, the city could expand its redevelopment programs in poor neighborhoods and expand its social service programs. Such strategies, he argued, would have the effect of defusing racial tensions between two groups now competing for funds and attention.[42]

Maloney based his assertion of minority group status on a definition of Appalachian culture as a subculture of American society, and he offered a reading of Appalachian history to substantiate the claim. Like other ethnic groups, he argued, Appalachians had a history that distinguished their culture from the dominant American culture. In this interpretation, Appalachia had existed as a distinct region and in isolation from American culture for almost three hundred years, and even as late as 1950, large parts of the region had remained untouched by the twentieth century. Appalachian culture with its distinctive personality traits, Maloney contended, had developed as a variant of "the value system of the American frontier as it was developed and changed in the environment of the Appalachian highlands." Consequently, when Appalachians moved to the city, "they moved across generations of time and vast psychic and cultural differences."[43] The recognition of the differentness of the Appalachian subculture and acceptance of minority status, particularly in the analysis of the roots of urban poverty and in the design and implementation of public policy, he argued, was the key to resolving Appalachian poverty and alienation in the city.

It was but a short step from this assertion of the relationship between urban Appalachians and American culture to a theory of urban Appalachian ethnicity. The notion that Appalachians constituted a distinct ethnic group took shape in part as a conversation between Appalachian activists and social scientists, a dialogue in which the activists themselves assumed the authority to name and define their own sense of identity.[44] Whether in the organization of social welfare programs in the inner city, the promotion of Appalachian culture in festivals, or in the writings of Appalachian activists, by 1972 a process in which Cincinnati's Appalachians were claiming distance from previous definitions of "Appalachianness" was underway. In 1972, Maloney attempted to define Appalachian culture as one of several subcultures within American society, and he suggested that the distinctiveness of his subculture seemed clearest to him with reference to discrimination by the dominant classes in America.

Maloney's notion of Appalachians as a distinct ethnic group stemmed in part from a critique of the existing sociological and historical literature on mountain people. Much of the literature, he argued, described Appalachian culture as a deficient variant of American culture and therefore the source of poverty and alienation among Appalachians. Maloney countered with the argument that culture "is determined by (and determines) material historical relationships," and he cautioned Appalachians not to indulge in nostalgia about their cultural heritage. "Maybe it is more important to stress . . . that much of our way of life, for example our senseless division along class lines, has been imposed on us as necessary social relationships in a class society. And it is important to stress that our problems have not been caused by our culture, but that to a great degree our culture has been determined by our oppression."[45]

Further, he advised Appalachians that "it is vain to worry about any cultural barriers to economic change and worry about economic and political barriers to cultural change." In this statement, Maloney articulated his vision of a potential movement among Appalachians based on an analysis that took oppression and discrimination as a cause of poverty and distress among Appalachians wherever they lived and took cultural solidarity among Appalachians and pluralistic social relations among the subgroups of American society as the solution.[46]

The consequences of thinking of Appalachians as an ethnic group became apparent in 1974 when Appalachian activists and non-Appalachian supporters founded a new organization called the Urban Appalachian Council (UAC) with offices in Over-the-Rhine, one of the predominantly Appalachian neighborhoods in the city.[47] The fledgling UAC took the position that all its activities in the areas of research, advocacy, and cultural affirmation would emphasize the distinctiveness of the Appalachian ethnic identity and the need to transform urban institutions into agencies capable of delivering culturally specific services to Appalachians. In the field of social services, for example, the council took the position that Cincinnati's social workers needed to develop an understanding of Appalachian culture in order to help their clients effectively in the inner city. The council's working paper on social welfare, which was written by Maloney, described Appalachians as "individualistic in an age that demands collective action, personalistic when others want functional relationships, [and] traditionalistic and fundamentalistic in an age of pragmatism and relativism."[48] Owing to the "differentness" of Appalachian ethnicity from the culture of the dominant class practising social work, the paper warned, traditional casework was largely ineffective among Appalachians. The paper called for social workers to develop a "cultural competence" appropriate for practising social work among particular subgroups.[49]

During the next few years, Appalachian activists began to organize to improve educational, social, and recreational services in their neighborhoods and city officials had to come to terms with an urban Appalachian constituency. In 1975, the Urban Appalachian Council opened a cultural heritage center in Over-the-Rhine, an institution combining cultural educational programs with training in community organizing.[50] In addition, Appalachian advocates lobbied for an Appalachian Cultural Heritage Alternative School in the Price Hill neighborhood and expanded community organizing efforts in other neighborhoods.[51] In 1979, Appalachians from several neighborhoods mobilized at city hall to protest the city's intention to bypass their neighborhoods in the expenditure of federal Community Block Development Grant funds.[52] Further evidence that the idea of urban Appalachian ethnicity caught on after the mid 1970s began to appear in an emerging scholarly literature that assumed the existence of urban Appalachians as an ethnic group and sought both to document its history and to influence urban social policy.[53] By the early 1980s, moreover, local writers were developing the beginnings of an indigenous literature that sought to give an Appalachian voice to the experience of Appalachians in Cincinnati.[54]

This analysis of urban Appalachian ethnic consciousness in Cincinnati suggests that the opportunity for self-definition, which had impressed Handlin and others in the 1950s as the hallmark of American civilization, had unforeseen consequences. For if the act of becoming an American endowed immigrants and their descendants with the power to chose to abandon ethnic characteristics, it could also offer the choice to retain them. By the early 1960s, social scientists were beginning to notice signs that conventional social theory, which minimized ethnic consciousness in the forging of group identity in America, could not explain the persistence of culturally specific behavior and ideas among immigrant populations. As early as 1963, Nathan Glazer and Daniel P. Moynihan observed a resurgence of ethnic identification among blacks, Italians, Jews, Puerto Ricans, and Irish in New York City.[55] "The notion that the intense and unprecedented mixture of ethnic and religious groups in American life was soon to blend into a homogeneous end product," they argued, "has outlived its usefulness. . . . One group is not as another and, notably where religious and cultural values are involved, these differences are matters of choice as well as heritage; of new creation in a new country, as well as the maintenance of old values and forms."[56] In 1963, it was the persistence of ethnic identification rather than its obsolescence that impressed Glazer and Moynihan.

By the early 1970s, what had simply begun as a single effort to make sense of the assertion of ethnic consciousness in modern America had become a flood of investigations about ethnic identification, not only in the United States, but in other countries. In 1972, Glazer and Moynihan saw sufficient evidence of the increasing assertion of ethnic consciousness in a variety of cultures to organize a conference to address what they called a noticeable transformation in the ways in which social scientists understood the concept of ethnicity. "Formerly seen as survivals from an earlier age, to be treated variously with annoyance, toleration, or mild celebration," they wrote, "we now have a growing sense that they may be forms of social life that are capable of renewing and transforming themselves."[57] Along with other writers, Glazer and Moynihan stressed particularly the growing importance of ethnicity as an ideological grounding for the assertion of group identities in American society.[58]

Glazer and Moynihan's work may be understood as an intervention in an extensive literature on the fate of ethnic characteristics in modern American society. For our purposes, however, their observations on the persistence of ethnic identification are symptomatic of a more generalized revival of ethnic consciousness in American society in the 1960s and 1970s. During these years, Cincinnati's Appalachian activists advanced their claims to urban ethnic status within the context of this larger ethnic revival. Both activists and social workers suggested that Appalachians were responding in a time-honored way to the traditional plight of migrant groups in American cities. This claim derived legitimacy in part from the social welfare planners and social workers who, in the 1950s, defined urban mountaineers as immigrants temporarily prevented by the liabilities of their traditional culture from becoming modern urban dwellers. In other words, the new definition of "Appalachian-ness" could be construed as a logical result of previous attempts to understand the behavior of Appalachians in the city.

More than this, however, the idea of Appalachian ethnicity was an invention, an exercize in self-definition in which Appalachians claimed the right to choose the extent of their ethnic identification. Their movement, built around antipoverty and neighborhood development programs, sought to establish a sense of Appalachian apartness and authenticity. The result, the particular definition of Appalachian-ness that emerged was less impor-

tant than the explicit recognition of urban Appalachian-ness as a legitimate subculture in American society. Whatever the consequences of this,
and they may still be unfolding, the effort of urban Appalachians to invent
their own existence was part of the larger ethnic revival through which
American culture reconstituted itself during the last decades of the twentieth century.

NOTES

Research for this article was supported by a grant from the National Endowment
For the Humanities to the Center For Neighborhood and Community Studies,
University of Cincinnati for a project entitled "Planning and the Persisting Past:
Cincinnati's Over-the-Rhine Since 1940." Matching grants were provided by the
Ohio Board of Regents Urban Universities Program, the Ohio Board of Regents
Linkage Grant Program, and the Murray Seasongood Foundation, Cincinnati,
Ohio. The author would like to thank Zane L. Miller and Henry D. Shapiro,
codirectors of the Center, for their comments on earlier drafts.

1. On this definition of ethnicity and its consequences, see Werner Sollors,
The Invention of Ethnicity (New York: Oxford University Press, 1989), ix–xx.

2. On the idea of urban ethnic groups as interest groups in the 1960s, see
Kenneth Fox, *Metropolitan America: Urban Life and Urban Policy in the United
States, 1940–1980* (Jackson, Miss.: University Press of Mississippi, 1986), 122–26.
On the white ethnic revival, see, for example, Michael Novack, *The Rise of the
Unmeltable Ethnics: Politics and Culture in the Seventies* (New York: Macmillan,
1971).

3. Henry D. Shapiro, *Appalachia On Our Mind: The Southern Mountains
and Mountaineers in the American Consciousness, 1870–1920* (Chapel Hill:
University of North Carolina Press, 1978), ch. 10. See also Zane L. Miller,
"Pluralizing America: Walter Prescott Webb, Chicago School Sociology, and
Cultural Regionalism," in *Essays on Sunbelt Cities and Recent America,* eds.
Robert B. Fairbanks and Kathleen Underwood (Arlington: Texas A&M University
Press, 1990), 151–76.

4. This theory suggested to social welfare planners seeking to identify the
problems of mountaineers in American cities that migrants brought with them
a constellation of ideas and habits that rendered them out of place. Because
culture was inherited and retained, moreover, it was expected that mountaineers
would always experience difficulties in adjusting top their host cities. See, for
example, Cincinnati Better Housing League, *A Tenement House Survey* (Cincinnati,
1921), 4.

5. See Oscar Handlin, *The Uprooted: The Epic Story of the Great Migrations*

That Made the American People (Boston: Little, Brown, 1952), and Will Herberg, *Protestant, Catholic, Jew* (Garden City: Doubleday, 1956). On the significance of individual choice in ethnic identification in Handlin's work, see Andrea Tuttle Kornbluh, "From Culture to Cuisine: Twentieth-Century Views of Race and Ethnicity in the City," in *American Urbanism: An Historiographical Review,* eds. Howard Gillette and Zane L. Miller (Westport, Conn., Greenwood Press, 1987), 55–58.

6. Handlin, *The Uprooted,* 305–6. For a dispute of Handlin's argument, see, for example, Rudolph J. Vecoli, "Contadini in Chicago: A Critique of *The Uprooted,*" *Journal of American History* 51 (December 1964): 407–19. For further elaborations of the argument about the new pluralism of the 1950s, see Miller, "Pluralizing America"; and Zane L. Miller and Bruce Tucker, "The Revolt Against Cultural Determinism and the Meaning of Community Action: A View From Cincinnati," *Prospects,* 15 (1990): 413–43.

7. *A Decade of Service, 1930–1940* (Cincinnati: Public Library of Cincinnati and Hamilton County, 1941), 42; Arnold B. Walker, "Will there Be a Race Riot in Cincinnati," *Bulletin of the Division of Negro Welfare* (August 1943), 2, 5, Urban League of Greater Cincinnati Papers, box 24, folder 6; *Cincinnati Times-Star,* February 21, 1944, 5:1.

8. Roscoe Giffin, *Report of A Workshop on the Southern Mountaineer in Cincinnati, April 29, 1954* (Cincinnati: Mayor's Friendly Relations Committee, 1954), 32–3.

9. Giffin, *Report,* 6, 8, 12.

10. Ibid., 12.

11. For a similar view of mountaineers as an "urban problem," see Albert N. Votaw, "The Hillbillies Invade Chicago, *Harper's Magazine* 216 (February 1958): 64–7. For a series of articles on mountaineers in Cincinnati that defined the "problems" of urban migrants, see *Cincinnati Enquirer,* July 14–20. See esp., "It's Not so Easy: Ways of the City Become Cruel Barriers to Hill Folk Trying to Get Ahead," Ibid., July 15, 1957, A:1:1.

12. See Reverend and Mrs. Michael Hamilton, "Ministry to the Southern Mountaineer: A Report on the Research Work Done by the Church of the Advent in the Neighborhood of Walnut Hills, Cincinnati, Ohio, August 1955 to August 1958" (Cincinnati: privately printed, 1958), typescript, Frank Foster Library; E. Russell Porter, "When Cultures Meet," (Cincinnati: Mayor's Friendly Relations Committee, 1962); and Father Aloys Schweitzer, "Who Is SAM? A Friendly Study of the Southern Appalachian Migrant" (Cincinnati, 1964), typescript, Frank Foster Library.

13. Giffin, *Report,* 12.

14. Porter, "When Cultures Meet," 7–9; and Schweitzer, "Who Is SAM?," 2.

15. WCKY Radio, "The Southern Mountaineer: An Audio Study of a People, a Place, and a Condition" (September 1963), transcript, Frank Foster Library, 45.

16. Ibid., 65.

17. Porter, "When Cultures Meet," 3; WCKY Radio, "The Southern Mountaineer," 7; and Schweitzer, "Who is SAM?," 8.

18. Giffin, *Report,* 32–40.

19. Roscoe Giffin, "Appalachian Newcomers in Cincinnati," in *The Appalachian Region: A Survey,* ed. Thomas R. Ford (Lexington: University Press of Kentucky, 1962), 79–84; and James S. Brown and George A. Hillery, "The Great Migration, 1940–1960," Ibid., 54–78.

20. On the discovery of poverty in the United States in the 1960s, see Michael Harrington, *The Other America* (New York: Macmillan, 1962). National interest in Appalachia had waned in the decade and a half after World War II. See Henry D. Shapiro, "John F. Day and the Disappearance of Appalachia From the American Consciousness," *Appalachian Journal* 10 (1983): 157–64. Two contemporary statements of the "rediscovery" of Appalachia in the 1960s are Ford, *The Appalachian Region;* and David S. Walls and John B. Stephenson, *Appalachia in the Sixties: A Decade of Reawakening* (Lexington: University Press of Kentucky, 1972).

21. See in particular, Harry M. Caudill, *Night Comes to the Cumberlands: A Biography of a Depressed Area* (Boston: Little, Brown, 1962), and Jack Weller, *Yesterday's People: Life in Contemporary Appalachia* (Lexington: University Press of Kentucky, 1965). For an assessment of the consequences of this new definition of the relationship between Appalachia and America, see Allen Batteau and Phillip Obermiller, "Introduction: the Transformation of Dependency," in *Appalachia and America: Autonomy and Regional Dependence,* ed. Batteau (Lexington: University Press of Kentucky, 1983), 1–13.

22. The argument that the provision of opportunities to the poor constituted the most effective means to fight poverty took shape in Cincinnati in the early 1950s. See Zane L. Miller and Bruce Tucker, "The Revolt Against Cultural Determinism and the Meaning of Community Action; and Council of Social Agencies, *The Cincinnati Report* (Cincinnati: Council of Social Agencies, 1952). Richard A. Cloward and Lloyd C. Ohlin articulated the theory of this argument in *Delinquency and Opportunity: A Theory of Delinquent Gangs* (New York: Glencoe Free Press, 1960).

23. On the history of community action, see Allen J. Matusow, *The Unravelling of America: A History of Liberalism in the 1960s* (New York: Harper and Row, 1984), 254–62; and Miller and Tucker, "The Revolt Against Cultural Determinism."

24. Michael Maloney Interview, December 20, 1985; Stuart Faber Interview, April 1, 1986.

25. Ernest N. Mynatt, "The Appalachian Experience" (Ph.D. diss., Union of Experimenting Colleges and Universities, 1987), 59ff; and Ernie Mynatt Interview, January 19, 1986.

26. In the late 1950s, with financial assistance from the Appalachian Fund, a local foundation established in 1950 by Formica Company owner Herbert Faber, Emanual Community Center on Race Street in Over-the-Rhine hired a street

worker to work with Appalachian youth. Ernie Mynatt, former school teacher and organizer from the mountains, held this position before joining the staff of the Main Street Bible Center. On the Appalachian Fund, see *Cincinnati Enquirer,* November 21, 1950, A:1:3. See also Stuart Faber Interview, April 1, 1986, and Ernie Mynatt Interview, January 10, 1986.

On the Main Street Bible Center, see "Report on the Main Street Bible Center," September 21, 1964, Archbishop Alter Papers, Saint Mary's Bible Center Folder, Archives of the Archdiocese of Cincinnati; *Catholic Telegraph,* March 19, 1965, A:3:3; Mynatt, "The Appalachian Experience," 63–4. See also, Michael Maloney Interview, December 20, 1985; and Phillip Obermiller Interview, December 18, 1986. On the relationship of volunteer work by Mt. St. Mary's seminarians to contemporary developments in the training of Roman Catholic priests, see M. Edmund Hussey, *A History of the Seminaries of the Archdiocese of Cincinnati, 1829–1979* (Norwood, Ohio: Mount St. Mary's Seminary of the West, 1979), 56–8.

27. Shirley Stenton Interview, May 19, 1986.

28. Rev. John Porter Interview, April 21, 1986; Shirley Stenton Interview, May 19, 1986; Phillip Obermiller, December 19, 1986.

29. Ernie Mynatt Interview, January 10, 1986; John Porter Interview, April 21, 1986; Minutes of the Uptown Basin Council, February to May, 1968, Urban Appalachian Council Archives (hereafter cited as UAC); *Catholic Telegraph,* August 19, A:8:3.

30. *Catholic Telegraph,* June 24, 1966, B:1:2.

31. The Community Action Commission was a federal antipoverty agency established by the Equal Opportunity Act of 1964. Hub originally referred to the hub of a wheel with spokes reaching out into the neighborhood. Later it was changed to the acronym HUB for Humans United For Better services.

32. *Cincinnati in Action,* 2, no. 11 (November 1966): 2. Virginia Coffey Interview, April 10, 1986; "The Hub: Monthly Report of Hub Activities for July, 1967," typescript, UAC Archives, Cincinnati.

33. Michael Maloney Interview, December 20, 1985; "The Hub."

34. See Minutes of United Appalachian Cincinnati, 1968–70, UAC Archives, Cincinnati.

35. United Appalachian Cincinnati Bylaws, UAC Archives, Frank Foster Library, Cincinnati; Michael Maloney Interview, December 20, 1985; Ernie Mynatt Interview, January 10, 1986. See also Kenneth Fox, *Metropolitan America: Urban Life and Urban Policy in the United States, 1940–1980* (Jackson: University Press of Mississippi, 1986), 122–6.

36. Draft Proposal, Appalachian Identity Center, Over-the-Rhine, Cincinnati, UAC Archives, folder 2, n.d.; Ernie Mynatt to Virginia Coffey, n.d. (probably 1970), UAC Archives, Cincinnati, Appalachian Identity Center Folder.

37. Ernie Mynatt, "Draft Proposal, Appalachian Youth Center, Over-the-Rhine," Cincinnati, UAC Papers, folder 2, n. d., Department of Archives and Rare Books, University of Cincinnati; Michael E. Maloney, "The Appalachian Committee

Proposal," UAC Archives, Frank Foster Library, 4; Michael Maloney Interview, December 20, 1985; *Cincinnati Enquirer,* January 1, 1973, C:5:2; Minutes of the Appalachian Community Development Association, (ACDA) December 12, 1973, ACDA Papers, Department of Archives and Rare Books, University of Cincinnati, folder 10.

38. Michael Maloney, "Cincinnati's Appalachian Community: Action Proposals For the Seventies" (paper, Frank Foster Library, Urban Appalachian Council, Cincinnati).

39. John C. Campbell, *The Southern Highlander and His Homeland* (New York: Russell Sage Foundation, 1921). On Campbell's vision of Appalachia and its consequences, see Shapiro, *Appalachia on Our Mind,* esp. ch. 8.

40. Maloney, "Cincinnati's Appalachian Community," 12, 26.

41. On the Berea workshop, see Ira Gissen, "The Mountain Migrant: The Problem-Centered Workshop at Berea," *Journal of Human Relations* 9 (1960): 26–27, 67–73; L. Richard Hudson, "Report of a Workshop on the Urban Adjustment of Southern Appalachian Migrants," typescript, Frank Foster Library; and Bertha M. Madison, "Unique Social Exploration: A Workshop on Urban Adjustment of Southern Appalachian Migrants at Berea College, Berea, Kentucky, July 8 to July 30, 1959" (Cincinnati: Division of Aid for the Aged), typescript, Public Library of Cincinnati and Hamilton County. For a similar reading of the history of social work among Appalachians in Over-the-Rhine since 1940, see Mynatt, "Draft Proposal," 2.

42. Maloney, "Cincinnati's Appalachian Community," 34–38.

43. Ibid., 5.

44. For an article summarizing the social science literature on urban Appalachian ethnicity and which itself is an intervention in the debate, see Phillip Obermiller, "Appalachians as an Urban Ethnic Group: Romanticism, Renaissance, or Revolution? and a Brief Bibliographical Essay on Urban Appalachians, *Appalachian Journal* 5 (Autumn 1977): 145–52.

45. Michael E. Maloney and Ben Huelsman, "Humanism, Scientism and Southern Mountaineers: A Review," *People's Appalachia* 2 (July 1972): 24–7, reprinted in *Perspectives on Urban Appalachians,* eds. Steven Weiland and Phillip Obermiller (Cincinnati: Ohio Urban Appalachian Awareness Project, 1978), 83–9.

46. Ibid., 92.

47. Urban Appalachian Council press release, April 9, 1974, UAC Archives, Frank Foster Library, Cincinnati. For an account of the activities of UAC, see Thomas Wagner, "Too Few Tomorrows," in *Too Few Tomorrows: Urban Appalachians in the 1980s,* eds. Phillip J. Obermiller and William W. Philliber (Boone, N.C.: Appalachian Consortium Press, 1987), 3–12.

48. Michael Maloney, "The Implications of Appalachian Culture For Social Welfare Practice," *Working Paper No. 2* (Cincinnati: UAC, September 1974), 3.

49. The Urban Appalachian Council took similar positions in working papers on education and health care, arguing that current practice required Appalachians to surrender their cultural identification as the cost of receiving effective service.

The Council argued instead that Appalachians would be more effectively served by agencies that developed empathic personalistic relationships with clients and accepted Appalachian cultural values as a basis for communication. See Phillip Obermiller, "Ethnicity and Education: the Intercultural Dimension," *Working Paper No. 5* (Cincinnati: UAC, 1974); Thomas E. Wagner, "Urban Appalachian School Children: the Least Understood of All," *Working Paper No. 6* (Cincinnati: UAC, 1974); Virginia McCoy-Watkins, "Urban Appalachian Health Behavior" (Paper delivered at the annual forum of the National Conference on Social Welfare, Cincinnati, 1974), reprinted in *Perspectives on Urban Appalachians,* 288–92.

50. Cultural Task Group of the Appalachian Committee, "Cultural Heritage Project Proposal: Washington Park School and Community," (Cincinnati, 1973), UAC Papers, folder 5, Department of Archives and Rare Books, University of Cincinnati Libraries, Cincinnati; *Appalachian Advocate,* May–June, 1975, 3:1; Mike Henson Interview, April 4, 1986.

51. *Cincinnati Enquirer,* March 14, 1978, D:1:4; and *Cincinnati Post,* February 12, 1979, 17:4. See also Kathryn M. Borman with Elaine Mueninghoff, "Lower Price Hill's Children: Family, School, and Neighborhood," Batteau, *Appalachia and America,* 211–26.

52. *Cincinnati Enquirer,* August 20, 1979, B:7:1, and December 14, 1979, B:4:2.

53. See, for example, William W. Philliber, *Appalachian Migrants in Urban America: Cultural Conflict or Ethnic Group Formation?* (New York: Praeger, 1981); Philliber and Clyde B. McCoy, eds., *The Invisible Minority: Urban Appalachians* (Lexington: University Press of Kentucky, 1981); Borman, "Lower Price Hill's Children;" John Friedl, "Health Care: The City Versus the Migrant," in Batteau, *Appalachia and America,* 189–209; and Obermiller and Philliber, *Too Few Tomorrows.*

54. Mike Henson, *Ransack* (Minneapolis, Minn.: West End Press, 1980); and Mike Henson, *A Small Room with Trouble on my Mind and Other Stories* (Minneapolis, Minn.: West End Press, 1983). See also Pauletta Hansel, "To Her Mother Lying in State," (poem), *Appalachian Journal* 10 (1982): 38–9; and Hansel, *Breathitt* (play), (Breathitt County Historical Museum, 1984).

55. Nathan Glazer and Daniel P. Moynihan, *Beyond the Melting Pot* (Cambridge: Harvard University Press, 1963). See also Milton M. Gordon, *Assimilation in American Life: The Role of Race, Religion, and National Origins* (New York: Oxford University Press, 1964); and Lewis M. Killian, *White Southerners* (Amherst: University of Massachusetts Press, 1985, orig. pub., 1970), esp. 91–119.

56. *Beyond the Melting Pot,* v–vi.

57. Nathan Glazer and Daniel P. Moynihan, eds., *Ethnicity: Theory and Experience* (Cambridge: Harvard University Press, 1975), 4.

58. See particularly Novak, *Rise of the Unmeltable Ethnics.*

ZANE L. MILLER

Planning and the Politics of
Ethnic Identity: Making Choices for
Over-the-Rhine, 1971–85

Between 1924 and 1954, metropolitan planning activities in Cincinnati were characterized by three related assumptions. First, the parts of a metropolis, including its neighborhoods and their residents, were viewed as functional systems serving the operation of the metropolis as a whole, rather than as independent units with identities and legitimate existences of their own. Second, both the metropolis as a whole and its several parts were viewed as being subject to "normal" and "organic" processes of birth, growth, maturity, and decay. From these two followed the third: It was the duty of professional planners, whether operating through a governmental agency or a private organization serving the public interest, to stave off the normal processes of decay by encouraging growth and development in the metropolis as a whole and by treating decay in local systems through rehabilitation or replacement. Thus the planners (and "reformers") of this period routinely sought to renovate or replace their city's decaying infrastructure of buildings, bridges, and roadways, most dramatically through large-scale public works programs of slum clearance and new construction; to renovate or replace their city's decaying infrastructure of political and social institutions through programs of administrative reorganization and institutional innovation, most dramatically by revising the city's charter; and to renovate or replace their city's "decaying" social structure through "social uplift" programs to improve the capacity of urban dwellers for cooperative life in the modern city, or through slum clearance and redevelopment programs that would remove "undesirable" residents (or land uses) and attract new residents (or land uses) "of the right kind" to decaying areas of the city.

By the late 1950s, the assumptions underlying the practice of metro-

248

politan planning had begun to change, along with the kinds of plans now being prepared by professional planners and the kinds of techniques proposed to implement them. In an economy of scarcity rather than of abundance, and of slow growth or no growth, it seemed more sensible to improve the operations of a city's existing systems than to attempt a program of replacement.[1] And it was in this context that "historic preservation" and "neighborhood revitalization" became central strategies in the planner's confrontation with urban decay, and local citizen participation (encouraged when necessary through "community organizing" techniques) became critical mechanisms for the achievement of preservation and revitalization programs. But because citizen participation was widely held to affect the citizen participants themselves, professional planners now began to play the role of facilitators in an effort to achieve at one time, the preservation and revitalization of existing neighborhoods and the preservation and revitalization of their existing populations.

A new interest in the history of neighborhoods and communities (as well as of bridges, public buildings, landscapes and city-scapes, and of the operations of public and private institutions) resulted from these new developments; for without a sense of the history of the neighborhood or community, people could not know what it was they were preserving and revitalizing, *who* they were preserving and revitalizing. Unlike an older tradition that treated the history of neighborhoods and communities anecdotally, as a collection of quaint and interesting facts, and which was antiquarian by intention in its discussion of the ways individuals had responded to "events" and "conditions" not of their own making, this new history sought at once to be dynamic and useful, by exploring the ways that people's choices determined the character of a place. And what was true of the past, of course, should be true of the present. Individuals possessed, or should possess, the ability and means to shape their own culture, including and especially the neighborhood in which they chose to live.

This new kind of planning through neighborhood revitalization was begun in Over-the-Rhine, a "blighted" inner-city residential area at the northern edge of Cincinnati's central business district, in 1971, and by the early 1980s had yielded four documents projecting four different futures for the neighborhood based in part on four different views of its past. All of them contained a history of Over-the-Rhine in which the ethnic characteristics of its population was discussed, but each of them construed the meaning of ethnicity differently when considering the future of Over-the-Rhine. Yet all of them treated the history of ethnic groups in a way that made control of the past crucial to the control of the future of the neighborhood.

The first of these documents consisted of a "historic renewal" plan for Findlay Market and Over-the-Rhine prepared by John C. Garner, Jr., the executive director of the Miami Purchase Association for Historic Preservation, at the request of the city's Department of Urban Development, which had placed Over-the-Rhine next on its agenda for neighborhood revitalization. Garner took care at the outset to thank residents and property owners in the neighborhood for cooperating with him in preparing the plan. He also disassociated his plan from programs for "historic restoration," i.e., the recreation of authentic interiors and building facades, or urban design patterns of the past. He defined "historic renewal" as a program of rehabilitation that would preserve the essence of past forms by permitting new construction, the adaptation of old buildings to new uses, and the renovation of old buildings in ways compatible with their surroundings. Garner made it clear, moreover, that Over-the-Rhine comprised structures of various architectural styles, but none of which could be viewed as characteristic of any of the ethnic groups associated with Over-the-Rhine.

Garner claimed that the adoption of this program would benefit the area without imposing a particular view of what the distinctive culture of the Findlay Market area or Over-the-Rhine ought to be. By defining the special architectural character of the area and by setting down rehabilitation guidelines to preserve and enhance that character, the plan would provide local residents with a new perspective on the value of "their physical environment" and encourage them to develop and protect it. Property values would increase because the renewal of buildings would extend their lives and make the area a more desirable locality in which to live.[2] But Garner did not expect the plan to displace the existing population of the area, as his history of Findlay Market and Over-the-Rhine makes clear.

The history, of course, aimed to establish the significance of the neighborhood as worthy of preservation despite the absence of any associations with "nationally significant" events or personalities—the conventional criteria tested by preservationists in their struggle against demolition programs since the 1930s. This, Garner sought to accomplish by concentrating on the ethnic history of the area rather than its industrial, commercial, architectural, or social history. The first and longest stage of that history connected the area to the migration to Cincinnati during the nineteenth century of Germans fleeing "political and social oppression and unrest," people who became known "for their great thrift and industry" and were accepted as an "integral part of the social fabric" of the city. In this period, Garner said, Cincinnati grew rapidly, in part because of its location on the Miami and Erie canals, which formed the southern and western boundary of the northern part of the basin—this was the "Rhine" of Over-the-Rhine, which by 1851 contained a population of almost twenty thousand people, two-thirds of whom listed a German state as their place of birth.[3]

Garner's history of Findlay Market, like his treatment of German immigrants, associated it not only with upward social and physical mobility but also with civic virtue. The market's name came from General James Findlay, who moved to Cincinnati in 1793, established himself as a "businessman and community leader," and served as Mayor during the early nineteenth century. He also invested in real estate, including in 1833 a plot of land immediately north of the city limits, which he and his partners subdivided in a plat showing a central rectangular space designated as Findlay Market. Findlay himself died in 1836, but in the early 1850s the executors of his will argued that the "improvement" of the area and its remoteness from other markets made it time to develop the Findlay Market. For this project, the executors gave land to the city, which in 1855 constructed a market house. Garner's history then skips to the 1970s to note that "today" the market "strongly reflects its early German heritage with second, third, and even fourth generations of the same families still setting up stands each market day," and with a Findlay Market Association, which still meets monthly "to socialize and to work towards solving the various problems facing their changing neighborhood."[4]

The next section of Garner's history backed up to consider the fate of Over-the-Rhine between 1870 and 1940. This segment noted that the "German community of the Over-the-Rhine area remained a strong and identifiable entity throughout the nineteenth century and into the first decades of the twentieth." With the beginning of World War I, however, and for reasons that Garner did not explain, "this ethnic solidity began to erode," and continued to do so at an accelerated rate through the 1930s. By 1940, as a consequence, Over-the-Rhine stood "in an advanced stage of physical and social deterioration."[5]

But that did not end Garner's history of the neighborhood, for the 1950s comprised another stage of its past. During this decade "the area began to experience an influx of southern Appalachian immigrants."

Garner characterized these immigrants—note the term—as "hard-working people" who escaped from the economically depressed southern coal country to search for better jobs in Cincinnati. In the city they found no general demand for unskilled labor, which "forced" many "onto welfare and into inexpensive housing in the Over-the-Rhine area," where they "retained their own set of values based on a strong regard for personal freedom," an attribute "that tended to isolate them from the rest of the community."[6] Then, without discussing the future of Appalachians in Over-the-Rhine, Garner turns to the final phase in his history of Over-the-Rhine.

This phase began in the 1960s when a third wave of "immigrants," blacks displaced from the city's West End by expressway construction and urban redevelopment, moved into the neighborhood. Garner attempts no characterization of these newcomers, except to note that by the mid-1960s they had begun to organize "for the purpose of achieving a stronger voice in their destiny." This effort brought "rapid results," including federal Pilot Cities program funds to build the "HUB" human services complex and community center next to Findlay Market to serve all of Over-the-Rhine, a city program of concentrated building code enforcement, and the city's designation of Over-the-Rhine as one of three target neighborhoods in the federally funded Model Cities program. Thus the area "has been in use for over 140 years; and even today reflects its ethnic development by the Germans, southern Appalachian and Black groups still living there."[7]

Garner's history, with its sanguine emphasis on the durability and vitality of Over-the-Rhine as a residential community suggested that it had a future as a lively place in which to live, shop, and do business, both for its current residents, including the poor, and for those who might be attracted to Over-the-Rhine as the result of his proposed historic renewal plan. His projection of Over-the-Rhine's continued vitality excluded no particular life-style, it should be noted, while his history, by including blacks and Appalachians as well as Germans, legitimized the presence of all of them as neighborhood residents and perhaps sought thereby to encourage remaining German-Americans to stay in the area, although their small numbers gave them the most tenuous hold on Over-the-Rhine in the latter twentieth century of the three groups. But neither this history nor the other portions of the historic renewal plan raised the issue of what might happen to the poor blacks and Appalachians if the renewal of the Findlay Market area and Over-the-Rhine through historic preservation brought in a mass of more prosperous "outsiders" whose activities might raise rents beyond the reach of the poor, displace them from the neighborhood, and frustrate the grand aim of the plan—the preservation of ethnic and social heterogeneity, as well as heterogeneity of land use and building styles, as a hall mark of the neighborhood.

This was precisely the issue that most concerned the planners working in Over-the-Rhine under the federal Model Cities Program, however, whose fear of displacing the poor through neighborhood revitalization is a constant theme of their report—the first comprehensive neighborhood plan for Over-the-Rhine—completed in 1975. Compiled by Harris Forusz, a member of the planning faculty at the University of Cincinnati and a conscientious practitioner of citizen participation planning, this plan rested in part on a history of Over-the-Rhine contained in an "existing conditions" report that emerged in 1972 from the planning process. This history, like the one prepared to accompany Garner's historic renewal plan of 1971, consisted of an ethnic history of the neighborhood but placed a greater emphasis on the degree to which the residents of the neighborhood had managed to make effective choices about their life styles.

Forusz's history told a story of the rise, decline, and imminent rejuvenation of Over-the-Rhine. It started with the arrival of thousands of German immigrants in the 1840s, who "came to the fertile Ohio Valley and may have seen it as another valley of the Rhine, complete with vineyards," although it was the Miami and Erie canal, rather than the Ohio River, which gave Over-the-Rhine its name. In the early nineteenth century the city's boundaries stopped at Liberty Street, Forusz explains, which made the area north of that street into "the Northern Liberties," so-called "because people from the city could cross Liberty to defy the Sunday blue laws against drinking, gambling, and wenching, and for the freedom given to Catholics to build churches north of Liberty Street." In 1849, Cincinnati annexed the Northern Liberties and German immigrants moved in, after which "Findlay Market soon developed and was opened in 1852 to serve the Over-the-Rhine neighborhood."[8]

In the late nineteenth century a "transplanted German community" flourished in Over-the-Rhine, where 90 percent of the population spoke the German language. Families in the neighborhood followed "the tradition of washing their homes and stoops on Saturday morning, and themselves in the evening." On Saturday nights residents flocked to such places of entertainment as Heuck's Opera House on Vine Street, to Music Hall, or to the Ahlbrandt Saloon next to Music Hall. In some of these places patrons drank beer from "high steins" and listened to "drinking music" supplied by "bands such as Brandt's up to 11:00 P.M." Despite such evidence of conviviality, "no record of criminal acts or juvenile delinquency" was to be found "among this very thrifty, gregarious, and conscientious people."[9]

Over-the-Rhine as a German community faded in the early twentieth century as the result of its residents' response to World War I, however. According to Forusz's history, German immigrants "had a belief in a German victory," and their expressions of this "sentiment" created "public distrust of the Over-the-Rhine community," and led "many Americans of German origin to abandon their beliefs and heritage for self-survival." The resulting "forced assimilation" of Over-the-Rhine's German-Americans caused the "disintegration of this proud and vital group" and their dispersal throughout the Cincinnati region, creating a vacuum only later filled by new groups. By 1940 Over-the-Rhine had entered its "dark ages," a "period of deterioration both physically and socially."[10]

During the 1950s, "the southern Appalachian migrant" established a "foothold" in the now troubled Over-the-Rhine neighborhood. This was a group with "a different set of values based on a tremendous regard for personal freedom." They had worked hard in the Southern mountain region but had fallen victim to economic exploitation on overworked land and in coal mines that "tore up the land" and led to "mass layoffs and lack of economic development." When the miners' union called a lengthy strike in 1951, many skilled workers migrated "to northern cities such as Cincinnati." By 1953, with the union and the strike "bankrupt," the unskilled workers who stuck out the strike took advantage of low bus fares to search for factory jobs in and around Cincinnati. But the men found a limited demand for unskilled labor. Unable to find work, they sought out cheap housing in Over-the-Rhine and went on welfare. Although the members of this group, said the history, "for the most part retained their values," they did so at the cost of "separating themselves from the rest of the community."[11]

In this context, according to this history, conditions in Over-the-Rhine worsened. By 1956 it had "the fastest growing crime rate in the city." Juvenile crimes rose 50 percent in fifteen years, rape, robbery, and murder occurred "frequently," and gangs appeared "with names such as 'The Hornets' [and] the 'Blue Devils'." The housing stock, moreover, remained as Over-the-Rhine's original German immigrants had found it, with 84 percent of the units lacking "baths." In Over-the-Rhine, "the

Appalachian" entered a physical environment from "another time and culture."[12]

Then in the early 1960s another "wave of immigration" hit Over-the-Rhine, "poor blacks displaced by the building of I-75 through the West End." By 1964, members of this group began "to realize some self-identity." No longer willing "to be displaced by highways, if they could avoid it," they formed organizations to "protect themselves and their homes," and by 1968 local and federal government agencies responded to their expressions of concern for the neighborhood by providing "economic and social" programs and by instituting a concentrated building code enforcement policy. In 1973, the history concluded, Model Cities programming called for the expenditure of 7.6 million dollars over five years to revitalize Over-the-Rhine and the other two target neighborhoods "through a wide spectrum of activities."[13]

These two histories of the early 1970s are nearly identical, but Forusz's account, unlike Garner's, described a pattern of ethnic group succession rather than ethnic group accumulation. As a result, it left Germans out of the neighborhood's recent past and seemed to suggest that the future belonged to either blacks or Appalachians. The comprehensive neighborhood plan for Over-the-Rhine, which Forusz and his associates completed in 1975, described neither a black nor an Appalachian neighborhood, however. Instead it proposed an ethnically neutral program of neighborhood revitalization through urban preservation, or more precisely through the recreation of a particular vision of the physical and social structure of the mid-nineteenth century "walking city," a city that had developed before the advent of either modern urban transportation systems or modern city planning. According to this vision, that city was a city of unspecialized land uses, a city with a busy street life that mixed vehicles with a variety of pedestrian activities, a city of neighborhoods unsegregated by race, ethnicity, or class, a city of two- to five-story buildings containing both dwelling units and small businesses, a city of artistically embellished building facades, a city of opportunities and choices and an intermingling of life-styles. While preserving that physical character, scale, and ambience in Over-the-Rhine, however, the plan sought to update and sanitize it, to make it clean, green, uncluttered, rich in open spaces, and safe.

Through its housing, human services, educational, economic development, and citizen participation provisions, moreover, the plan sought to provide Over-the-Rhine residents with a maximum degree of control over their destinies. The principle mechanism for achieving this goal advocated by the plan was the creation of subneighborhoods within the district—a dozen and a half "environmental areas," each focused on a small "town center" comprising a complex of commercial and human services and community organizing facilities, and located at nodes where pedestrian and vehicular traffic met. In this way, the reality of community life would create skilled citizens, no longer dependent on the ministrations of social workers or professional community organizers, and the rehabilitation of the neighborhood would also rehabilitate its residents without converting them into middle-class Americans. The plan anticipated that this process would take about fifteen years, after which, about 1990, Over-the-Rhine's own citizens could decide whether to adopt additional strategies proposed in the plan to attract more prosperous residents into the neighborhood. Until then, Over-the-Rhine would remain a territory dominated by poor individuals in pursuit of a life-style or styles defined and chosen by themselves.[14]

This plan appeared in 1975, the same year of the publication of a momento of the dedication of the renovation of the Findlay Market and the completion of the adjacent Pilot Cities human services and community center facility operated by HUB Services, Inc. Written by Father Aloysius Schweitzer, a Catholic priest long active in Over-the-Rhine, and Henry Gerbus, the vice-president of the Findlay Market Association, the momento featured pictures of the dedication ceremonies and advertisements for businesses both within and outside Over-the-Rhine. But most of it consisted of histories of Over-the-Rhine, the renovation of Findlay Market, and the development of the human services/community center. These histories stressed the role of Germans, the Catholic church, and the Findlay Market Association, added two ethnic groups to the story of Over-the-Rhine, Irish and Italians, and projected a third future for Over-the-Rhine.

The section on the history of Over-the-Rhine noted that until 1849 the territory north of Liberty Street was free of city council jurisdiction "over gamblers, bootleggers, thieves and those who wished to escape the Sunday ordinances." This disreputable period of the area's past did not persist, however, for by 1851 Over-the-Rhine north of the Miami and Erie canal contained a population of nineteen thousand people, thirteen thousand of them German, comprising "a unified ethnic community that became a bit of the Vaterland transplanted into Cincinnati, with its distinctive language, life-style, and architecture." During the next decades, Over-the-Rhine as a whole gradually divided into three sections. The southern ran from Liberty Street to the canal (later Central Parkway) and housed a predominantly German population mixed with "some" Irish and Italians. The second, almost solidly " 'High' German," surrounded the Findlay Market and stretched from Liberty Street to McMicken Street on the north. The third section, encompassing the Mohawk area along McMicken and reaching to the hills of Corryville, displayed a strong " 'Low' " German "flavor." And in all sections, until recent times, asserted the history, could be found "the same German culture," which consisted of Catholics and Lutherans speaking in "their" language or in heavily accented English, and practicing "their thrifty ways as in their many savings and loan associations" but also displaying "a lusty joy for life as in their many breweries, restaurants, biergartens and weinstubes."[15]

In dealing with the recent past, Schweitzer and Gerbus, unlike Garner and Forusz, did not talk about the migration of Appalachians and blacks into Over-the-Rhine and the consequences of that migration. Instead, they wrote an account of the renovation of Findlay Market and of the creation of the Pilot Cities human services complex, which emphasized the importance of the Catholic church and the Findlay Market Association in these innovations. This history began in 1964, when Over-the-Rhine, said Schweitzer and Gerbus, was "dying." In that year, they noted, two Franciscan Sisters of the Poor began to offer hot meals and bingo for the elderly at St. Francis Church to augment similar efforts by Sister Margaret at the Santa Maria Institute, a Catholic human services agency on Thirteenth Street. In that same year other Catholic agencies took root in Over-the-Rhine, such as the Main Street Bible Center and the "Friars Over the Rhine Mission," which conducted activities showing that "someone cared." Next, a non-Catholic community center in the neighborhood under a contract with the city's Community Action Commission opened a "modest storefront" operation at 1321 Vine Street to provide social services, employment counseling, housing information, and a "friendly ear and warm heart" to residents. That represented the "beginning of a dream" that began to materialize in 1967 when the federal government selected Cincinnati as one of fourteen cities in which to locate "pilot" projects to attack problems of poverty through the establishment of a coordinated program of social services at a single site and, in effect, through a single agency.[16]

At this point, Schweitzer and Gerbus switched the focus of their history to the Findlay Market Association by noting that in 1968 it established the Findlay Market Parking Corporation to secure more and better parking facilities near the market. The Parking Corporation soon raised money ($5,400 from the Findlay Market Association, noted the history) with which it purchased seven sites for parking lots and rented another. Then, in the spring of 1970, came the establishment of the "Findlay Market/Pilot Center Board," chaired by Father Schweitzer, to help the city and various agencies plan the renovation of Findlay Market and the development of the Pilot Cities human services/community center complex. After several meetings, the board hired an architectural/planning consultant. Then, "after endless meetings and questionnaires" to assure the participation of all parties concerned with the dual project, the "pictures and dreams" of the board began to crystallize into tentative plans and a three-dimensional model of the renewal area. Finally, in 1972, began the process of sharpening plans, releasing specifications for bids, searching for funding, and acquiring and clearing building sites. The "oldtimers" of the neighborhood found it "especially heartbreaking" to "watch Old St. John's [Catholic] Church and school go down" after 125 years of religious service, although the blow was cushioned by the renewal plan's scheme to preserve St. John's tower "as an historic landmark" and wrapping a new recreation building around it. Thus the tower could serve "as a tie with the area's historic past and a symbol of its continuing strength and vitality."[17]

This part of the story culminated in 1974 with the opening of the new community center next to Findlay Market from which HUB Services coordinated housing, financial, educational, and employment and social agency services as well as social events for neighborhood residents. The center also contained a library, meeting rooms, a post office branch, a medical clinic, and a "Free Store" facility, and provided an "in-take" staff and "outreach" personnel who went into homes and patrolled the streets in search of "needy" people.[18] But if the HUB center thus provided Over-the-Rhine as a whole, or its Findlay Market district, with just the kind of "town center" that Forusz and his associates advocated, Schweitzer and Gerbus did not project a future that would transform its residents into independent citizens. Instead, they pictured Over-the-Rhine as a continuing pocket of poverty whose residents required the assistance of local businessmen, churches, social workers, and community organizers to bolster their spirits, provide for their physical needs, and lead them in their citizen participation activities. Schweitzer and Gerbus also projected no place in Over-the-Rhine for newcomers, either as residents or as friendly helpers to the poor, and treated "German" Over-the-Rhine, except for its architecture, nostalgically and as irretrievably past while handling as normal the presence of persons of German, Irish, and Italian descent without suggesting that their ethnicity should play a role in determining the character of Over-the-Rhine. For Schweitzer and Gerbus, ethnic references functioned to establish the normality of people who ascribed to themselves an ethnic past irrelevant for their future, except as a way of reminding themselves that individuals from various backgrounds had always lived amicably in Over-the-Rhine as friendly and caring good neighbors.

A fourth version of the history and future of Over-the-Rhine appeared in connection with the development in the early 1980s of a second comprehensive plan for the neighborhood. This process began because the director of the Model Cities program declined to submit Forusz's plan to the Planning Commission for its consideration, and because the Over-the-Rhine Community Council and other neighborhood groups in the late 1970s objected vociferously to the activities of historic preservationists in the area on the grounds that they would lead to further "gentrification" in Over-the-Rhine and the displacement of the poor. In the hope of reconciling the contending parties, the city manager appointed an Over-the-Rhine Planning Task Force comprising representatives of all groups concerned with the neighborhood, including its poor residents, to prepare a plan satisfactory to all sides. Preparation of this new plan involved a five-year effort, including the writing of a new history of the neighborhood, which itself became a matter of contention. In the process of settling that argument, a coalition of antihistoric preservation residents of Over-the-Rhine submitted its version of the Over-the-Rhine story, which, with minor modifications, appeared in the new plan.[19] This version also contained an ethnic component but treated ethnicity as essentially irrelevant to the future of Over-the-Rhine and as the least significant aspect of the history of the area.

The introduction to the coalition's history identified three major themes in the history of Over-the-Rhine. It depicted the neighborhood as "a port of entry" for succeeding waves of migrants, first from Europe and then from Appalachia and the deep South, each of which left its "mark" on the neighborhood and the city. It contended that Over-the-Rhine historically comprised a concentration of the poor, the source of cheap labor for employers and of cheap housing for the poor. And it claimed that Over-the-Rhine had a historic tradition of "resistance and struggle" against "exploitation" that "continues today."[20]

The first part of the history itself dealt with the mid and late nineteenth century, when Germans in great numbers came to Over-the-Rhine after the revolutions of 1848. As the dominant group in the community they founded churches and cultural and athletic clubs, and exerted the influence that led the city's public schools to offer German language instruction in classes for a part of each day until World War I. But this part of the history emphasized that many Italians, Greeks, Spanish, and native-born Americans lived in the neighborhood during the nineteenth and early twentieth centuries, and attacked the "popular myth" that Over-the-Rhine had been built for "a *comfortable middle class community.*" Conceding that "pockets of former wealth" once existed in the area, the history argued that property owners who built most of the housing sought to "box poor people into as little space as possible" in an effort to "minimize space and maximize rents." Over-the-Rhine "workers" in the nineteenth century endured what "other urban working-class people had to endure" and what generations of their successors in the twentieth century had endured: an experience of "overcrowding, exploitation, [and] cramped lives."[21]

The next section of the residents' history covered the period between 1930 and 1960. In these years, it said, new residents migrated from the economically depressed regions of Appalachia and the deep South. In the first stage of this migration Appalachians dominated and made Over-the-Rhine "a center for Bluegrass and country music." Later, blacks moved into the neighborhood because of the destruction of much of the West End by urban renewal programs, including the construction of I-75 and "new business development." By the 1980s blacks constituted a majority of the residents, although large numbers of white Appalachians remained, giving Over-the-Rhine a population composed of two groups historically located "at the bottom of the city's economic and social ladder."[22]

The last section of the residents' history treated the period from 1960 as the story of the fight of neighborhood residents "to change this pattern of poverty and discrimination." They lost, but out of their struggle forged a "black-white coalition" that continued the fight. This coalition fought for the recognition of black and Appalachian culture in the schools, for improvements in educational programs, and against the closing of neighborhood schools. In addition, Over-the-Rhine residents joined with labor unions, churches, and "professionals" to defeat efforts of the city's business elite and "city bureaucracies" to close down the Drop Inn Center for alcoholics, a center managed by a member of the coalition but located near Music Hall, at the neighborhood's gentrifying southern edge. In addition, argued the history, "the community" fought to bring new low-income housing into the neighborhood, to secure "quality" rehabilitated housing for the poor, to effect the passage of antidemolition and antidisplacement ordinances, and to ward off in Over-the-Rhine "a national trend in which private developers, in an attempt to attract young professionals, displace low-income families and the elderly."[23]

This section of the residents' history concluded with the most recent battle conducted by the coalition, a four-year fight to prevent "the city [and] a group of preservationists, gentrifiers and real estate speculators" from listing Over-the-Rhine on the National Register of Historic Places. The Over-the-Rhine Community Council and its constituent groups had opposed this move out of a belief that it would "only fuel the current speculation occurring in the neighborhood," and although they were not successful, their fight had not been entirely futile. It had generated articles and media coverage, including a segment on the popular CBS television show "60 Minutes" and a story in the *New York Times,* through which Over-the-Rhine "gains even national attention and recognition in its struggles. WE LIVE AND GROW."[24]

Like the other three histories of Over-the-Rhine, this one did not present interethnic hostility as a feature of the past or future of the neighborhood, and like Forusz's history this one portrayed a pattern of ethnic group succession that left Over-the-Rhine in the possession of its most recent arrivals. But it differed on what these residents had done in and might do with the neighborhood. It suggested the utility of cooperating with advocates of Appalachian and black interests throughout the city to secure their commitment to the greater cause of preserving a place for the poor in Over-the-Rhine. It left no place in the future for outsiders of any sort, except poor people and those allies of the poor who agreed with the coalition's history of Over-the-Rhine and its meaning. It projected a future of continuing struggle that would not transform its residents socially, economically, or ethnically, but that would make them more militant. It suggested that residents, not religious activists, social workers, community organizers, businessmen, or other helpers of the poor had led and would continue to lead the fight of "the community" for control of the future of Over-the-Rhine, including the fight to preserve the housing stock of the neighborhood without the application of historic preservation or other design control techniques. And it presented the most recent residents of Over-the-Rhine as people who had chosen to live and remain in the neighborhood even if it meant the conduct of a relentless struggle to exclude "outsiders" hostile to the coalition and to deny such outsiders and unsympathetic city officials an effective voice in setting policy for the future of the neighborhood.

Despite their differences, these four versions of the history and future of Over-the-Rhine shared certain elements. All of them focused on the neighborhood rather than the metropolis as the fundamental unit of concern. Each contended that residents of the area had in the past and should in the future play a role of some sort in defining and shaping the neighborhood. All of them ignored evidence of intra- and inter-ethnic group conflict in the past and in the present, thereby denying such conflict as an important, much less a natural characteristic of Over-the-Rhine's history, present or future. Indeed, all of them treated ethnicity as an option and instrumental technique available to individuals as an element in their self-identification, rather than as a way of life embedded irrevocably in a particular social and physical environment, including one's member-ship in a particular social, ethnic, or racial group in a particular place. And from this position followed their assertion of the normality in the latter twentieth century of ethnic residential integration at the neighborhood level.

Together, however, they presented four different versions of the historic and continuing role of the inner city, none of which pictured it as a slum that destroyed its occupants and each of which advocated a particular brand of historic preservation and a particular vision of the future of the inner city. For Garner, the inner city seemed a lively container of heteroge-neous people (including the poor) that functioned as a staging ground for social mobility for those who chose it, a safe and interesting place to live for those who did not, and an arena for the exercise of political power for those who aspired to political leadership. For Schweitzer and Gerbus, the inner city comprised a haven for the poor, an opportunity for good-hearted Christians and other compassionate neighbors who wanted to help the poor endure their poverty, and a good place for the conduct of commerce by small businessmen. For Forusz, the inner city seemed a locality in which its least powerful residents might be strengthened through a program of urban preservation and citizen participation that would in fifteen years make them independent if relatively poor citizen activists with the capacity to decide their own social and economic status and life-styles. For the coalition of Over-the-Rhine residents, the inner city had always contained a mixture of ethnic groups and social classes. But it had been occupied largely by poor persons who, like prosperous persons, sought to shape their culture, and who, in the latter twentieth century and under the leadership of the coalition, would join together and continue the struggle against the greed and exploitation of some of their neighbors and of "outsiders" who restricted the political power of poor residents and their ability to arrange the social and physical environments of the neighborhood.

Finally, this analysis suggests the emergence by the 1970s of a new view of culture. This new view contended that individuals in the past and present did not "inherit" a culture from their race or place of origin. Instead, it contended that individuals had striven in the past and should be empowered in the present and future to define their own culture, which was thus best understood as impermanent, optional, and instrumental in nature. For city planners, this new view of culture suggested the maximum feasible participation of citizens in neighborhood conservation and rehabilitation planning as a way of helping people define their own culture, and of neutralizing the characteristics of place, including the history of the place, as the determinant of the culture of the people who lived in it or moved out of it. Citizen participation planning would thus permit the rehabilitation of a neighborhood without the fear that the revitalized neighborhood would require its residents to live in a manner or with a culture not of their own choosing.[25]

NOTES

This essay is based upon research and writing supported by a grant from the National Endowment for the Humanities for a project entitled "Planning and the Persisting Past: Cincinnati's Over-the-Rhine Since 1948," with matching grants from the Ohio Board of Regents' Urban Universities Program, the Ohio Board of Regents' Linkage Grant Program, and the Murray Seasongood Foundation of Cincinnati. The author is greatly indebted to Henry D. Shapiro for his assistance in the editing of this paper.

1. In Cincinnati, city officials noted the disappearance of undeveloped land within the city, the continued drift of population to the suburbs, and their inability to annex additional territory, Robert B. Fairbanks, *Making Better Citizens: Housing Reform and the Community Development Strategy in Cincinnati, 1890–1960* (Urbana: University of Illinois Press, 1988). They worked out citizen participation in planning and "community action" in the process of preparing a conservation

and rehabilitation plan in the context of preparing neighborhood plans for Avondale and Corryville, beginning in 1954, e.g., Cincinnati City Planning Commission and Department of Urban Renewal, *Avondale-Corryville General Neighborhood Renewal Plan* (Cincinnati: City Planning Commission and Department of Urban Renewal, Dec., 1960), esp. 1–2, 4–14. This process transformed rehabilitation into a permanent program for application to entire neighborhoods. The master planners of 1948 had defined rehabilitation as a treatment for *parts* of declining neighborhoods as a way of *postponing* the necessity for slum clearance and redevelopment up to fifteen years, Cincinnati City Planning Commission, *Residential Areas: An Analysis of Land Requirements for Residential Development 1945 to 1970* (Cincinnati: City Planning Commission, Dec. 1946), 48.

2. Miami Purchase Association, *Guidelines for Rehabilitation of The Findlay Market Historic District* (Cincinnati: Department of Urban Development, n.d. [1971]), 1–4.

3. Ibid., 6.

4. Ibid., 7, 11.

5. Ibid., 12.

6. Ibid., 11.

7. Ibid., 12.

8. Cincinnati Model Cities Physical Planning Program, *Over-the-Rhine Existing Conditions Report* (Cincinnati: Model Cities Physical Planning Program, Sept. 1972), 2.1 (1). The divisions of this report are numbered by sections and parts but not paginated. I have designated page numbers in parentheses.

9. Ibid., 2.1 (p. 2).

10. Ibid.

11. Ibid., 2.1 (2–3).

12. Ibid., 2.1 (3–4).

13. Ibid., 2.1 (5–6).

14. Cincinnati Model Cities Physical Planning Program, *Over the Rhine Clifton Heights Fairview Neighborhood Development Plan* (Cincinnati: Model Cities Physical Planning Program, Dec., 1975), esp. pp. 32–46. The vision of the mid-nineteenth century "walking city" to which I refer may be found in Sam B. Warner, Jr., *Streetcar Suburbs: The Process of Growth in Boston, 1870–1900* (New York: Atheneum, 1976, orig. publ., 1962).

15. Fr. Aloysius Schweitzer and Henry Gerbus, *The History and the Story of Findlay Market and the Over-the-Rhine Community Center: Dedication Day, June 9, 1974* (Cincinnati: VIP Offset, n.d.), pp. 4–7.

16. Ibid., 34, 41.

17. Ibid., 19, 30, 49.

18. Ibid., 35.

19. This history consists of two typed pages and an attached copy of a guest editorial in the *Cincinnati Post*, April 26, 1983, that focused on the recent history of Over-the-Rhine but also discussed its "German" period. The typed pages bear no title or authors, but the guest editorial lists its authors first and foremost as

residents of Over-the-Rhine, namely, the Rev. Randall LaFond, OFM, chairman of the Catholic Coalition for Fair Housing; Rebecca Johnson, chairwoman of the board, Contact Center, 1641 Vine Street; Ira Couch, business representative, Washing Well Laundry and Dry Cleaners, 1320 Vine Street; Michael Henson, tenant, author, 212 Orchard Street; the Rev. Allen Mitchell, Wesley Chapel United Methodist Church, 80 E. McMicken Avenue; Jack Towe, homeowner, director of Sign of the Cross [a not-for-profit housing development corporation], 1630 Republic Street; Over-the-Rhine Community Council, 1713 Vine Street, Catherine Howard, president, Nanie Hinkston, treasurer; Buddy Gray, chairman of the housing task force [of the Over-the-Rhine Community Council]. I have used only material from the typed pages, which I shall designate "Residents History of Over-the-Rhine." Copies of both documents may be found at the Cincinnati Department of City Planning in the Over-the-Rhine Planning Task Force files of Charlotte T. Birdsall, the member of the staff of the department who coordinated the planning process.

20. "Residents History of Over-the-Rhine," 1.

21. Ibid.

22. Ibid., 2.

23. Ibid.

24. Ibid.

25. For additional discussions of what I am calling "the new politics of neighborhood and culture," see Zane L. Miller, *Suburb: Neighborhood and Community in Forest Park, Ohio, 1935–1976* (Knoxville: University of Tennessee Press, 1981); "History and the Politics of Community Change in Cincinnati," *The Public Historian* 5, no. 4 (Fall 1983): 17–36; and Zane L. Miller and Bruce Tucker, "The New Urban Politics, Planning, and Development in Cincinnati, 1954–1988," in *Snowbelt Cities,* ed. Richard Bernard, (Bloomington: Indiana University Press, 1990, 91–108.

Contributors

ROBERT A. BURNHAM received his Ph.D. in history from the University of Cincinnati in 1990 and currently teaches at Macon College in Georgia. In addition to his dissertation, " 'Pulling Together' for Pluralism: Politics, Planning, and Government in Cincinnati, 1924–1959," he is the author of "The Mayor's Friendly Relations Committee: Cultural Pluralism and the Struggle for Black Advancement," in *Black Cincinnati: Journey Across Time*, ed. Henry L. Taylor.

JAMES H. CAMPBELL received his Ph.D. in history from the University of Cincinnati. He is currently an academic advisor with the Educational Development Program at the University of Cincinnati.

ANDREA TUTTLE KORNBLUH is the author of *Lighting the Way: The Woman's City Club of Cincinnati, 1915–1965* (1987) and of articles on the interaction of race, gender, ethnicity and culture in twentieth-century American urban life. She received her Ph.D. in history from the University of Cincinnati and is currently visiting assistant professor of history at the University of Cincinnati's Raymond Walters College.

BRUCE LEVINE received his Ph.D. from the University of Rochester. He is currently assistant professor of history at the University of Cincinnati. From 1981 to 1986 he was director of research for the American Social History Project sponsored by the Graduate Center of the City University of New York, and is the principal author of *Who Built America*, the first volume of its history of American working people. His study of German-American artisans in antebellum America will be published by the University of Illinois Press.

Zane L. Miller is professor of history and director of the Center for Neighborhood and Community Studies at the University of Cincinnati. He received his Ph.D. from the University of Chicago. He is the author of *Boss Cox's Cincinnati: Urban Politics in the Progressive Era* (1968); *The Urbanization of Modern America* (1973); *Clifton: Neighborhood and Community in an Urban Setting* (1976), with Henry D. Shapiro; *Suburb: Neighborhood and Community in Forest Park, Ohio* (1981); *American Urbanism, A Historiographical Review* (1987), ed. with Howard Gillette, Jr.; and of numerous essays on aspects of the American urban experience.

Jonathan D. Sarna is the Joseph H. and Belle R. Braun Professor of American Jewish History at Brandeis University. He received his Ph.D. from Yale University. Until 1990 he was on the faculty of the Hebrew Union College-Jewish Institute of Religion in Cincinnati as professor of American Jewish history and director of its Center for the Study of the American Jewish Experience. He is the author or editor of nine books, including *Jacksonian Jew: The Two Worlds of Mordecai Noah* (1981); *The American Jewish Experience* (1986); *JPS: The Americanization of Jewish Culture, 1888–1988* (1989); and *The Jews of Cincinnati* (1989), with Nancy H. Klein.

Henry D. Shapiro is professor of History (Emeritus) at the University of Cincinnati and coeditor of the Urban Life and Urban Landscape series published by the Ohio State University Press. He received his Ph.D. from Rutgers University. He is the author of *Confiscation of Confederate Property in the North* (1963); *Physician to the West: Selected Writings of Daniel Drake on Science and Society* (1970), ed. with Zane Miller; *Clifton: Neighborhood and Community in an Urban Setting* (1976), with Zane Miller; *Appalachia on Our Mind: The Southern Mountains and Mountaineers in the American Consciousness* (1978), and numerous articles on American intellectual and cultural history.

E. Bruce Tucker received his Ph.D. from Brown University. From 1983 to 1988, he held an appointment as visiting research associate at the Center for Neighborhood and Community Studies of the University of Cincinnati, and is now associate professor of history at the University of Windsor, Ontario. His current work includes a study of the development of Urban Appalachian ethnic consciousness in Cincinnati, 1850–1987.

FREDERIC TRAUTMANN received his graduate training at Purdue University. He is associate professor at Temple University, where he teaches courses in rhetoric and communication. He has translated and edited for publication the travel memoirs of numerous nineteenth-century German visitors to the United States, including Theodor Kirchhoff, *Oregon East, Oregon West* (1987) and Ernst von Hesse-Wartegg, *From St. Louis to the Gulf* (1990).